scientific study of all aspects of the phonetics and phonology

lab
phon

through scholarly exchange across disciplines

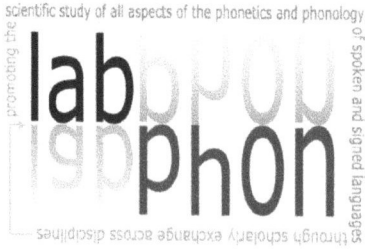

Studies in Laboratory Phonology

Chief Editor: Martine Grice

Editors: Doris Mücke, Taehong Cho

In this series:

1. Cangemi, Francesco. Prosodic detail in Neapolitan Italian.

2. Drager, Katie. Linguistic variation, identity construction, and cognition.

3. Roettger, Timo B. Tonal placement in Tashlhiyt: How an intonation system accommodates to adverse phonological environments.

4. Mücke, Doris. Dynamische Modellierung von Artikulation und prosodischer Struktur: Eine Einführung in die Artikulatorische Phonologie.

5. Bergmann, Pia. Morphologisch komplexe Wörter im Deutschen: Prosodische Struktur und phonetische Realisierung.

6. Feldhausen, Ingo & Fliessbach, Jan & Maria del Mar Vanrell (Eds.). Methods in prosody: A Romance language perspective.

ISSN: 2363-5576

Methods in prosody: A Romance language perspective

Edited by

Ingo Feldhausen

Jan Fliessbach

Maria del Mar Vanrell

language
science
press

Ingo Feldhausen, Jan Fliessbach & Maria del Mar Vanrell (ed.). 2018. *Methods in prosody: A Romance language perspective* (Studies in Laboratory Phonology 6). Berlin: Language Science Press.

This title can be downloaded at:
http://langsci-press.org/catalog/book/183
© 2018, the authors
Published under the Creative Commons Attribution 4.0 Licence (CC BY 4.0):
http://creativecommons.org/licenses/by/4.0/
ISBN: 978-3-96110-104-7 (Digital)
        978-3-96110-105-4 (Hardcover)

ISSN: 2363-5576
DOI:10.5281/zenodo.1471564
Source code available from www.github.com/langsci/183
Collaborative reading: paperhive.org/documents/remote?type=langsci&id=183

Cover and concept of design: Ulrike Harbort
Typesetting: Jan Fliessbach & Felix Kopecky
Proofreading: Adrien Barbaresi, Amir Ghorbanpour, Aysel Saricaoglu, Brett Reynolds, Conor Pyle, Daniela Kolbe-Hanna, Jeroen van de Weijer, Sebastian Nordhoff & Varun deCastro-Arrazola
Fonts: Linux Libertine, Libertinus Math, Arimo, DejaVu Sans Mono
Typesetting software: XƎLᴬTEX

Language Science Press
Unter den Linden 6
10099 Berlin, Germany
langsci-press.org

Storage and cataloguing done by FU Berlin

Freie Universität Berlin

Contents

Contents

Introduction

Ingo Feldhausen
Goethe-Universität Frankfurt am Main

Jan Fliessbach
Freie Universität Berlin

Maria del Mar Vanrell
Universitat de les Illes Balears

The field of prosody research belongs to those linguistic disciplines that have developed rapidly in recent decades. This is mainly due to the appreciation it has received in theoretical studies of grammar, but also to the technological revolution that has resulted in the widespread availability of software dedicated to conducting analyses and calculating statistics. All stages of experimental work have been affected: data collection, data processing, acoustical and statistical analysis, as well as the development of stimuli for perceptual experiments. Carefully controlled methodologies have become a standard in linguistic research for gathering empirical evidence and their development plays an increasing role in Romance linguistics. The same holds for corpus research, where large speech databases are used to investigate prosody and automatic tools are applied for analyzing the data. A number of recent publications document these developments and show how these fields of research are becoming ever more dynamic and innovative (see, e.g., Sudhoff et al. 2006; Cohn et al. 2012; Durand et al. 2014).

With the proliferation of methodological options and the emergence of research traditions defined not only by their object of interest, but also by their methodological choices (e.g. *Laboratory Phonology* or *Corpus Linguistics*), making reasoned methodological decisions is becoming an increasingly difficult task. Yet only detailed descriptions of problems encountered in the investigation of specific phenomena can provide the practical advice needed to avoid difficulties

Ingo Feldhausen, Jan Fliessbach & Maria del Mar Vanrell. 2018. Introduction. In Ingo Feldhausen, Jan Fliessbach & Maria del Mar Vanrell (eds.), *Methods in prosody: A Romance language perspective*, iii–vi. Berlin: Language Science Press. DOI:10.5281/zenodo.1441331 before they arise. Thus, the goal of this book is to encourage the reader to pause for a moment and to reflect on (some of) the methods used in our field.

While the existing volumes on methodological reflections address this issue either from a general point of view by considering different linguistic subdisciplines (e.g. Ender et al. 2012; Podesva & Sharma 2013) or by dealing with specific methodological approaches in the entire field of phonology, including prosody (e.g. Cohn et al. 2012; Nguyen & Adda-Decker 2013; Durand et al. 2014), the present book concentrates specifically on methods in prosody and intonation research. Consequently, the book has parallels with the seminal volume by Sudhoff et al. (2006). In contrast to that book, however, the present volume concentrates on Romance languages and languages in contact with Romance languages (Catalan, Italian, Portuguese, Spanish, and Quechua) – thus languages that play an important role in prosody research. Furthermore, it includes some of the latest developments in the field. Finally, the present volume embraces contributions that evaluate specific methods both with and without the presentation of new data.

Pausing and carrying out methodological reflections is an important step in scientific research and the relevance of that issue in prosody research can be seen – apart from the present volume – in the increasing number of papers (e.g. Niebuhr & Michaud 2015; Cole & Shattuck-Hufnagel 2016), conference sessions, or summer schools dedicated to that issue (e.g. Aix-en-Provence 2016[1], Vienna 2016[2]). This book is based on the session *Methods in empirical prosody research* from the 34th Romanistentag, the biannual conference of the German Association of Romance Philologists (Deutscher Romanistenverband, DRV) held between July 26th–29th, 2015 in Mannheim (Germany). The session was organized by Ingo Feldhausen, Uli Reich, and Maria del Mar Vanrell. The seven double-blind peer reviewed contributions to this volume represent a selection from the talks given at this session and bring together some of the most distinguished researchers of prosody working on Romance languages, united in the attempt to place methodological reflections at the center of their respective chapter, while also providing insight into the current state of the research projects that apply these methods.

The methodological paradigms covered in this book include the study of prosody with large corpora and spontaneous speech employing different approaches, more controlled prosodic analyses, and questions of prosodic data collection, manipulation and elicitation. The book consists of three different parts, which in

---

[1]Aix-en-Provence (France): Aix Summer School on Prosody 2016: "Methods in Prosody and Intonation Research: Data, Theories, Transcription". https://aixprosody2016.weebly.com.

[2]Vienna (Austria): Sommerschule des Deutschen Romanistenverbandes 2016: "Gesprochene Sprache in der Romania: Von der Theorie zur Empirie". https://romanistik2016.univie.ac.at/.

turn are organized into different chapters. The first part of the book is entitled *Large corpora and spontaneous speech* and consists of those papers mainly dealing with these aspects of prosody research. The second part, *Approaches to prosodic analysis*, comprises those chapters addressing different considerations relevant in analyzing prosodic data (e.g. the combination of production and perception experiments, the role of phonetic analyses or multimodal analyses). The third part is entitled *Elicitation methods* and focuses on the critical assessment of current elicitation methods. A detailed appreciation and overview of the three parts of the book and the different chapters is given in the guest foreword by Pilar Prieto.

Lastly, we, the editors, would like to thank several people who have helped and supported us in creating the present volume. First, we are highly indebted to Pilar Prieto for her comments and recommendations, and most importantly for her foreword that adds a magnificent finishing touch to this collective piece of work. We also extend our gratitude to each participant and contributor of the above-mentioned session at the congress of the German Association of Romance Philologists as well as to the authors of the individual chapters. Uli Reich deserves special mention and gratitude for his co-participation in the organization of the congress session, his relentless and fundamental logistical support, and his insightful advice on many different occasions. We also want to thank the anonymous reviewers whose critical, valuable, and insightful comments have helped to improve the present volume: Mathieu Avanzi, Stefan Baumann, Elisabeth Delais-Roussarie, Andreas Dufter, Wendy Elvira-García, Eduardo García-Fernandez, Nicholas Henriksen, José Ignacio Hualde, Conxita Lleó, Judith Meinschaefer, Trudel Meisenburg, Antje Muntendam, Oliver Niebuhr and Paul Warren. Next, we would like to thank our student assistants Julia Otto and Magalí del Valle Bertola for their different kind of help and support. Our gratitude also goes to the series editors of *Studies in Laboratory Phonology* for their interest in our volume and for providing constructive criticism and sound advice during the publication process. Furthermore, we are in debt to Sebastian Nordhoff and Felix Kopecky for their patient help with the details of producing the final manuscript and to Adrien Barbaresi, Amir Ghorbanpour, Andreas Hölzl, Daniela Kolbe-Hanna, Eleni Koutso, Audrey MacDougall, Hella Olbertz, Brett Reynolds, Aysel Saricaoglu, and Jeroen van de Weijer for proofreading.

Finally, we hope that the various contributions and the breadth of topics they deal with make the present volume a source of inspiration and insight for the linguistic research community and help to highlight the importance of profound methodological reflections.

References

Cohn, Abigail C., Cécile Fougeron & Marie K. Huffman (eds.). 2012. *The Oxford Handbook of Laboratory Phonology* (Oxford Handbooks in Linguistics). Oxford: Oxford University Press.

Cole, Jennifer & Stefanie Shattuck-Hufnagel. 2016. New Methods for Prosodic Transcription: Capturing Variability as a Source of Information. *Laboratory Phonology* 7(1). DOI:10.5334/labphon.29

Durand, Jacques, Ulrike Gut & Gjert Kristoffersen (eds.). 2014. *The Oxford Handbook of Corpus Phonology*. 1. ed. (Oxford Handbooks in Linguistics). Oxford: Oxford University Press.

Ender, Andrea, Adrian Leemann & Bernhard Wälchli (eds.). 2012. *Methods in Contemporary Linguistics*. Vol. 247 (Trends in Linguistics. Studies and Monographs /TiLSM). Berlin: De Gruyter.

Nguyen, Noël & Martine Adda-Decker. 2013. *Méthodes et outils pour l'analyse phonétique des grands corpus oraux* (Traité IC2 Cognition et traitement de l'information). Paris: Hermès Science Publications.

Niebuhr, Oliver & Alexis Michaud. 2015. Speech data acquisition: The underestimated challenge. *KALIPHO – Kieler Arbeiten zur Linguistik und Phonetik* 3. 1–42.

Podesva, Robert J. & Devyani Sharma (eds.). 2013. *Research methods in linguistics*. Cambridge: Cambridge University Press.

Prieto, Pilar. 2018. Foreword. In Ingo Feldhausen, Jan Fliessbach & Maria del Mar Vanrell (eds.), *Methods in prosody: A Romance language perspective* (Studies in Laboratory Phonology), vii–xiii. Berlin: Language Science Press.

Sudhoff, Stefan, Denisa Lenertova, Roland Meyer, Sandra Pappert, Petra Augurzky, Ina Mleinek, Nicole Richter & Johannes Schließer (eds.). 2006. *Methods in empirical prosody research*. Vol. 3 (Language, Context, and Cognition). Berlin & New York: Walter de Gruyter.

Foreword

Pilar Prieto

ICREA-Universitat Pompeu Fabra

In the last few decades, language researchers have highlighted the pivotal role of prosody in language production and language comprehension, showing the tight links between prosody and other language components such as syntax and pragmatics. First and foremost, prosody in spoken language reflects the "organizational structure of speech" (Beckman 1996). Speakers use it to separate speech into chunks of information, or prosodic constituents, thus helping listeners to parse discourse into meaningful syntactic units and sending signals about when to take turns in conversational exchanges. Secondly, prosody plays a key role in pragmatic communication. Prosodic and intonational patterns express a broad variety of communicative meanings, ranging from speech act information (assertion, question, request, etc.) and information status (given vs. new information, broad focus vs. narrow focus, contrast) to knowledge state (or epistemic position of the speaker with respect to the information exchange), affective state, and politeness (Gussenhoven 2004; Ladd 2008; Nespor & Vogel 2007; see Prieto 2015 for a review).

Speech prosody nowadays constitutes an active interdisciplinary research area which has drawn insights from different disciplines (like semantics, pragmatics, syntax, language typology, and language processing) and a variety of methodologies, including psycholinguistic and computational modeling. Given this broad spectrum, carrying out research in prosody now requires a high level of interdisciplinary awareness. It is for this reason that we welcome the initiative taken by three young but highly accomplished researchers, Ingo Feldhausen, Jan Fliessbach, and Maria del Mar Vanrell to compile a book about current research methods in prosody from a Romance perspective. The immediate aim is to offer in one volume a representative set of prosodic investigations on Romance languages which use diverse methods and data sources. However, taken as a whole, the interdisciplinary and critical perspective collectively represented here also reflects

Pilar Prieto. 2018. Foreword. In Ingo Feldhausen, Jan Fliessbach & Maria del Mar Vanrell (eds.), *Methods in prosody: A Romance language perspective*, vii–xiii. Berlin: Language Science Press. DOI:10.5281/zenodo.1441333 the methodological challenges currently facing the field of prosody. As we will see below, those challenges include the need to develop more ecologically valid research methods for data elicitation, the use of triangulation methods for analyzing and interpreting quantitative findings, the complementary phonetic and phonological analyses, and, above all, the integration of experimental and computational methods into prosodic studies.

Methods in prosody: A Romance language perspective is made up of seven chapters, which are grouped to form the three parts of the book, each one centered around a particular topic. The first part focuses on the need to devote more research to the automatic prosodic analysis of large-speech corpora, including different speech styles such as spontaneous speech and dialogues. The second part highlights the importance of taking into account the various complementary levels of prosodic analysis, such as multimodal analysis, phonetic and acoustically-based labeling systems of intonation, prosodic prominence, and prosodic phrasing, as well as perception-based analyses of prosody. The third and final part of the book deals with data elicitation methods and points to the need for more refined elicitation methods to incorporate more ecologically-valid data and triangulation methods, as well as perceptual validation methods. In the short reviews that follow, I will try to highlight the particular issue that each chapter raises but also note the special insights that respective authors offer to the field as a whole.

Under the subheading *Large corpora and spontaneous speech*, the first part of the book (Chapters 1 and 2) deals with the still undervalued application of automatic prosodic annotation tools to large oral databases, as well as the analysis of spontaneous speech for the study of prosody. As is well known, the various syntactic and semantico-pragmatic functions of prosody are manifested through the acoustic realization of prosody by means of prosodic phrasal grouping (via phrasal intonation markers), intonational prominence, and intonational modulations. Recent technological developments have greatly facilitated data collection, leading to the creation of freely accessible, large-scale audio and video corpora for various languages, such as *Glissando* for Spanish and Catalan, which constitute a potential goldmine of information on prosodic production. Similarly, acoustic/phonetic tools such as Praat (see Boersma & Weenink 2017) have had a profound impact on our ability to measure and analyze prosodic data.

In **Chapter 1**, entitled "Using large corpora and computational tools to describe prosody: An exciting challenge for the future with some (important) pending problems to solve", J. M. Garrido describes a set of tools that can take audio speech data and automatically output full orthographic and prosodic transcriptions of the audio content and then segment and align them at phoneme, syllable, word, and intonational phrase levels. The author explains a set of tools that range from automatic orthographic transcription of oral corpora, as well as tools that perform automatic transcription and word segmentation, as well as prosodic segmentation and prosodic transcription. Though many of the tools have been specifically developed for Romance languages (Catalan, French, Portuguese, and Spanish in particular), some of them have been extended to other languages. Garrido also reviews the results of pitch analysis experiments performed on large corpora.

Chapter 2 shows how spontaneous conversation can be used to uncover intonational patterns reflecting topic and focus functions. In "The intonation of pronominal subjects in Porteño Spanish: an analysis of spontaneous speech", A. Pešková examines the intonational realizations of pronominal subjects in Buenos Aires Spanish using a corpus of spontaneous conversational speech and shows that while intonational differences characterize the distinction between focused and topicalized pronominal subjects, this is not the case for the distinction between different types of topics. The analysis presented nicely combines a phonological analysis of the data using the autosegmental Sp_ToBI prosodic labeling methodology with an acoustic-phonetic analysis of the target pronouns. The author uses this twofold strategy to argue that both spontaneous speech and experimental laboratory database techniques are indispensable for the study of linguistic prosody.

Under the heading *Approaches to prosodic analysis*, the second part of the book (Chapters 3–5) covers important issues including the importance of recognizing the multimodal – that is, verbal but also gestural – nature of communication, and the desirability of looking at both perception and production in the analysis of intonation and prosodic prominence.

Research in the last few decades has highlighted the importance of visual information in linguistic communication, but more work needs to be carried out within the domain of what is now known as *visual prosody*. **Chapter 3**, entitled "Multimodal analyses of audio-visual information: Some methods and issues in prosody research", represents a good step in this direction. The author, B. Gili Fivela, nicely reviews the methods which have been used to perform multimodal analyses of audio-visual speech materials, focusing especially on linguistic distinctions conveyed by prosody (e.g., prosodic focus, sentence modality). The paper discusses a set of methods used to analyze articulatory kinematic data and speech-accompanying gestures (like head movements and facial expressions) across different sentence types, using examples from the literature mainly on Italian and other Romance languages. A good assessment of the pros and cons of articulatory and visual analysis methods of speech data is presented. The author highlights the fact that multimodal analysis of audio-visual information has helped researchers to characterize various aspects of linguistic prosody and that it is a necessary tool to provide a comprehensive analysis of prosody in communication.

An analysis of prosodic prominence can reveal important information about under-described languages. In **Chapter** 4, entitled "The Realizational Coefficient: Devising a method for empirically determining prominent positions in Conchucos Quechua", T. Buchholz and U. Reich reveal how they went about describing prosodic prominence in this Central Quechua dialect using a methodology based on acoustic measurements of duration, pitch, and intensity. From these acoustic patterns, they obtained an overall realizational value which they label the "Realizational Coefficient" by calculating the ratio of syllable duration, mean F0, pitch range, and intensity of one syllable with respect to its adjacent syllables. This calculation expresses a measure of the relative realizational strength of one syllable over others, which can be helpful in describing prominence patterns in languages that have yet to be fully analyzed.

Perceptual measures can be crucial in identifying contrastive patterns in intonational phonology. **Chapter 5**, entitled "On the role of prosody in disambiguating wh-exclamatives and wh-interrogatives in Cosenza Italian", O. Kellert, D. Panizza, and C. Petrone investigate the role of prenuclear and nuclear prosodic features in the perceptual identification of these structures in this Romance variety. A two-alternative forced-choice identification task together with reaction time measures were employed to test the listeners' ability to distinguish between the two types of sentences. While the results support the hypothesis that the most important prosodic cues for sentence-type disambiguation are located at the end of the utterance, the fact that duration patterns in initial and mid-sentence positions regions significantly predicted reaction times strongly suggests that prenuclear regions are actively exploited by listeners. The chapter also discusses why online measures like reaction times should be preferred to offline measures like gating responses. Importantly, the combination of identification tasks together with reaction times allows for an assessment of not only accuracy in prosodic disambiguating but also the time location of the processing difficulties.

The third part of the book includes two chapters (6 and 7) which deal with **elicitation methods** that can be used to collect speech data. A variety of such elicitation methods have been used in the field of prosody, with some of them like the Discourse Completion Task proving particularly useful. Although the relative advantages and disadvantages of these elicitation methods have received some attention in the literature, a systematic critical assessment of their relative efficacy and ecological validity is thus far lacking. The two articles here constitute a first step in this direction.

One of the goals of intonational phonology is to be able to identify the distinctive pitch patterns in a given language in relation to systematic pragmatic differences like speech act differences, focus categories, etc. In **Chapter 6**, entitled "The Discourse Completion Task in Romance prosody research: Status quo and outlook", M. M. Vanrell, I. Feldhausen, and L. Astruc superbly describe and critically assess the strengths and weaknesses of the Discourse Completion Task elicitation methodology, which has been extensively applied in research on Romance prosody in the last two decades. Their overall assessment of the method as a data collection instrument is positive. Among other things, they point to a set of important strengths like time-efficiency, the ease with which pragmatic and contextual factors can be controlled for, and the feasibility of using the task with illiterate or elderly participants. Among its weaknesses, they point out factors such as the dependency of the results on the initial set of discourses and also on the importance of contextual information. To address these weaknesses, the authors propose a set of modifications to the method centered around carefully crafting the context scenarios for each of the situations in order to better elicit specific speech acts and foster participant engagement. These reflections point to not only the practical need to refine this popular tool but also the need for ongoing research on data elicitation methods.

Continuing with the quest for distinctive pitch patterns, in **Chapter 7**, entitled "Describing the intonation of speech acts in Brazilian Portuguese: methodological aspects", J. Moraes and A. Rilliard assess the results of applying to a set of Portuguese data a production/perceptual methodology initially proposed by the Dutch School of prosody. The paper describes how systematic modifications of pitch contours using resynthesis techniques influence how Brazilian Portuguese listeners interpret seven speech acts. The authors also look into the well-known phenomenon of inter-speaker variability in terms of interpreting prosody and attempt to define what is universally acceptable and unacceptable across speakers in terms of various prosodic parameters. Perceptual validation of these data show on the one hand the greater importance of pitch in comparison to duration or intensity patterns in conveying prosodic distinctions in Portuguese and on the other the importance of pitch-scaling patterns, specifically the need for three pitch levels (instead of two) for the intonational phonology of speech acts in this language.

Taken as a whole, this volume will be of interest to those scholars and students of prosody and linguistics interested in broadening their knowledge about current empirical methods. It also brings us a step forward in our assessment of the variety of methods currently in use for prosodic analysis. One inescapable conclusion to be drawn from all this work is that prosodic analysis is closely intertwined with many other systems of language, including pragmatic knowledge, and that mastery of a variety of complementary methods is of vital importance for prosody researchers. Though the multidisciplinary approach reflected in this volume has already yielded a significant body of essential information regarding the use and assessment of a variety of methods in the field of prosody there is still a need for an overarching theory that can not only encompass and explain perception and production patterns — which have traditionally been studied separately — but also take into account the complex relationships between prosodic abilities and other linguistic, communicative, and cognitive skills. For example, though sometimes neglected, prosody is a robust cue for the conveyance of essential pragmatic information in communication exchanges. As we have noted above, given the range of fields involved in such an endeavor, this goal calls for a high level of interdisciplinary awareness.

There are also methodological challenges ahead, including the need to find more ecologically valid research methods that can combine experimental and computational methods in future studies (see Prieto 2012 for a review). To illustrate this, for both perception and comprehension, behavioral data should be complemented by ERP and fMRI studies for a fuller picture of how the human brain produces and processes prosodic features. Recent technological developments will greatly facilitate this kind of endeavor and will have a profound impact on our ability to measure and analyze prosodic data. This combination of high quality recorded corpora and tools that automatically code acoustic cues has proved invaluable to research and must be further exploited, for it has huge potential to yield important results. This volume can therefore be read as both a snapshot of the current state-of-the-art in prosodic analysis but also a signpost for future directions in prosodic research.

References

Beckman, Mary E. 1996. The Parsing of Prosody. *Language and Cognitive Processes* 11(1-2). 17–68. DOI:10.1080/016909696387213

Boersma, Paul & David Weenink. 2017. *Praat: Doing phonetics by computer [Computer program]*. Version 6.0.30. http://www.praat.org/.

Gussenhoven, Carlos. 2004. *The phonology of tone and intonation*. Cambridge: Cambridge University Press.

Ladd, D. Robert. 2008. *Intonational phonology*. 2nd edition. Cambridge: Cambridge University Press.

Nespor, Marina & Irene Vogel. 2007. *Prosodic phonology*. Vol. 28 (Studies in Generative Grammar). Berlin: Mouton de Gruyter.

Prieto, Pilar. 2012. Experimental methods and paradigms for prosodic analysis. In Abigail C. Cohn, Cécile Fougeron & Marie K. Huffman (eds.), *The Oxford Handbook of Laboratory Phonology* (Oxford Handbooks in Linguistics), 528–538. Oxford: Oxford University Press.

Prieto, Pilar. 2015. Intonational meaning. *Wiley Interdisciplinary Reviews: Cognitive science* 6(4). 371–381. DOI:10.1002/wcs.1352

Part I

Large corpora and spontaneous speech

Chapter 1

Using large corpora and computational tools to describe prosody: An exciting challenge for the future with some (important) pending problems to solve

Juan María Garrido Almiñana

National Distance Education University

This chapter presents and discusses the use of corpus-based methods for prosody analysis. Corpus-based methods make use of large corpora and computational tools to extract conclusions from the analysis of copious amounts of data and are being used already in many scientific disciplines. However, they are not yet frequently used in phonetic and phonological studies. Existing computational tools for the automatic processing of prosodic corpora are reviewed, and some examples of studies in which this methodology has been applied to the description of prosody are presented.

1 Introduction

The "classical" experimental approach to the analysis of prosody (questions and hypotheses, corpus design and collection, data measurement, statistical analysis, and conclusions) has until recently been carried out using mostly manual techniques. However, doing experimental research using manual procedures is a time-consuming process, mainly because of the corpus collection and measurement processes. For this reason, usually small corpora, recorded by a few number of speakers, are used, which is a problem if the results are supposed to be considered representative of a given language, for example.

Juan María Garrido Almiñana. 2018. Using large corpora and computational tools to describe prosody: An exciting challenge for the future with some (important) pending problems to solve. In Ingo Feldhausen, Jan Fliessbach & Maria del Mar Vanrell (eds.), *Methods in prosody: A Romance language perspective*, 3–43. Berlin: Language Science Press. DOI:10.5281/zenodo.1441335

Recent advances in speech processing techniques and computational power are changing the way in which experimental research in phonetics and phonology is done. These changes result in two main consequences: more storage capabilities, which allow for collecting and storing larger amounts of analysis material, and more powerful speech processing tools, which allow for the automation of some procedures. Many scientific disciplines, some of them related to speech and language, are exploiting the new challenges of processing large amounts of data in an automatic way (for example, Language and Speech Technologies, Text-to-Speech, Speech Recognition, Sentiment Analysis, Opinion Mining, Speech Analytics, and Corpus Linguistics).

The "big data" approach to analysing raw data, which consists of using huge amounts of material to be analysed by applying fully (or almost fully) automatic processes and using powerful computational tools, is currently present in many disciplines, like marketing, advertising, and medical research. Its main advantages are evident: using large datasets leads to better predictions obtained in a faster and cheaper way than traditional methods. But they also have clear disadvantages: "noise" (wrong data) is present in the data, and, if it is too high, may lead to incorrect predictions. If the "noise" is low enough, however, the sheer amount of processed material can prevent it from influencing the data.

The goal of this work is to discuss to what extent it is now possible (or it will be in the near future) to apply "big data" methods to the analysis of prosody, by designing experiments with a large quantity of speech data representing a large number of speakers, processed in a fully automatic way with no manual intervention, and to obtain reliable and relevant results for prosodic research. It is evident that in the last decades some steps in this direction have been taken in prosody research, at least to analyse larger (and more representative) corpora using more complex (and more automatic) tools: new methods and tools are being introduced for corpus collection, corpus annotation, acoustic measurement and statistical analysis.

In the next sections a review of the advances of these fields is given, with a special emphasis on some of the tools and methods developed and applied in our own research, which share as common feature the fact that they have been developed using a knowledge-based, linguistic approach for the automatic processing of speech. A brief description of how some of these tools work, and a discussion about their usefulness to automatically process large amounts of speech data, is also provided.

2 Corpus collection

Until quite recently, experimental research on prosody has involved the use of "laboratory" corpora, made up of *ad hoc* material, specially designed and recorded for the experiment, uttered by a small number of speakers, and containing a reduced number of cases of the phenomena being studied. From an experimental point of view, the advantages of this kind of material are clear, mainly the high level of control of the variables affecting the analysed phenomena. However, it also has some drawbacks, such as the need for careful corpus design, which is usually a time-consuming task, and can sometimes lead to collecting unnatural material. Recording is also a slow and sometimes expensive procedure, in which volunteer or paid speakers must be recruited.

The use of "real" corpora, not specially designed for a specific experiment, can avoid these problems if they are large enough. Ideally, the phenomena to be studied (different sentence types, stress or rhythmic patterns and syntactic or information structures, for example) would be present in a representative number, and the experimenter should simply select the desired number of examples from the corpus to obtain a "controlled" experiment from more realistic material (see Pešková, this volume). The whole corpus could even be processed and conveniently annotated with the information about the variables to be analysed without paying attention to the balance between the items representing each considered variable.

This approach is possible if the corpora are very large and contain hundreds of items that represent the variables to be analysed. This means many hours of collected speech (probably hundreds) must be annotated with the necessary information. How to obtain this kind of large and natural material arises, then, as an important methodological problem. Three possible ways to obtain larger corpora are: joint collections, corpus sharing, and the use of the Internet as a global corpus.

2.1 Joint collection

Joint collection of corpora, by several research groups or individuals, is a possible way to obtain larger speech corpora for prosodic analysis. This can be done either through funded projects, in which several groups coordinate their efforts for the design, collection, and annotation of large corpora, or cooperative initiatives, in which volunteer contributions from many people enable the creation of databases in a collective (and cheaper) way.

One existing example of the first approach is the Glissando corpus (Garrido et al. 2013). Glissando is an annotated speech corpus specially designed for the analysis of Spanish and Catalan prosody from different perspectives (Phonetics, Phonology, Discourse Analysis, Speech Technology, and comparative studies). It includes two parallel corpora, *Glissando_sp* (Spanish) and *Glissando_ca* (Catalan), designed following the same criteria and structure: two subsets of recordings, representing two different speaking styles (news reading and dialogues), which were recorded in high-quality professional conditions by 28 different speakers per language, both professional and non-professional, which represents more than 20 hours of speech available per language. Both corpora were also orthographically and phonetically transcribed and annotated with different levels of prosodic information. These features make Glissando a useful tool for experimental, corpus-based, and technological applications.

The Glissando corpus is the result of a publicly funded (Spanish Government) coordinated project of three different research groups: the Computational Linguistics Group (*Grup de Lingüística Computacional*, GLiCom) from the Pompeu Fabra University and the Prosodic Studies Group (*Grup d'Estudis de Prosòdia*, GrEP) from the Autonomous University in Barcelona, and the Group of Advanced Computational Environments – Multimodal Interaction Systems (*Grupo de Entornos Computacionales Avanzados - Sistemas de Interacción Multimodal*, ECA-SIMM), from Valladolid University. These three groups, with a common interest in prosody but coming from different research perspectives, worked together both in the design and the recording phases, taking advantage of their multidisciplinary backgrounds (both technical and linguistic). This coordinated work afforded the collection of a much larger corpus and with relevant annotation for different purposes.

The design procedure of Glissando is also an example of how to build a partially controlled corpus, in which phenomena that are potentially interesting for prosodic analyses have been included or induced in the corpus design from "natural" material, trying to keep a balance between naturalness and relevance. In the case of the news subcorpus, texts were not artificially built, but selected using automatic techniques from a larger set of real news texts, kindly provided by the *Cadena SER* radio station, to obtain the best possible coverage in terms of (theoretical) intonation groups, stress patterns, and allophonic representation. Only in some specific cases were the original texts manually modified to ensure the presence of non-frequent cases (proparoxytone words, for example) in the corpus (Escudero et al. 2009; 2010). In the case of the task-oriented dialogues subcorpus, several dialogue situations were designed to facilitate certain prosodically relevant interactions, for example, by asking a subject to obtain information which his/her dialogue partner could not provide, forcing an apology for this fact, and to change their dialogical strategies during the conversation. Finally, in the case of informal dialogues, dialogue couples that shared a common past were chosen, and they were asked to speak about these common memories in order to facilitate informal, emotional, and relaxed interactions.

Some other good examples of joint efforts to collect large, multilingual corpora for prosodic studies are the AMPER Project, which also involves many groups among the Romance space to collect a set of parallel corpora for intonation studies (Contini et al. 2002; 2003), or the C-ORAL-ROM initiative, an EU-funded project in which four different groups from four different countries collected a corpus of non-laboratory speech in French, Italian, Portuguese, and Spanish (Cresti & Moneglia 2005). In this latter case, although the corpus was not specially conceived for prosodic analyses, some work was devoted to the annotation of prosodic breaks in the four corpora and to the validation of the annotations (Danieli et al. 2004; 2005).

2.2 Corpus sharing

The use of multiple corpora is also a way to obtain larger amounts of data for experiments. There are many suitable corpora for the analysis of prosody which are available for reusing, some of them free of charge (as in the case of Glissando, distributed under a Creative Commons License). Some others are available for a fee (as with the Boston Radio News Corpus, for example; Ostendorf et al. 1995). There are also different institutions and initiatives in charge of collecting, hosting, and offering corpora for different purposes, both in America (LDC, Reciprosody) and Europe (ELRA, SLDR/ORTOLANG).

Finally, in order to make corpus reusing easier, it is important that the conventions with which corpora are annotated are as standardized as possible. Initiatives to develop standards for the annotation of prosody are still needed. An example of such effort is the proposal of an annotation scheme for prosodic events developed in the framework of the MATE project (Klein et al. 1998). There is still much work to do in this area, however.

2.3 Internet as a corpus

The Internet can be a source for data collection for prosody research, as it is already for other disciplines. There is a huge amount of speech material available on the net (radio and television broadcasts, podcasts, YouTube), although its use is usually restricted, due to legal and privacy issues (copyright, for example), and its quality may vary from media to media. There are, however, some public repositories of media data with an acceptable level of recording quality, such as the European Parliament session archives, which have already been used for several research purposes, such as the development of speech-to-speech translation systems. Most of this material provides examples of formal speech, but informal material is more difficult to obtain (and process). YouTube can be a good source for this kind of material, if copyright problems are solved, but in this case the background noise can be a problem for automatic tools, especially in F0 estimation.

3 Corpus transcription, segmentation, and annotation

Speech corpora need to include transcription and annotation to be useful for research purposes. For prosodic analysis, several types of information should ideally be available, both phonetic/phonological (phonetic or phonological transcription, prosodic phrasing) and linguistic (part-of-speech (POS), parsing, sentence type, speech acts, new/given information, focus, etc.), or paralinguistic (emotions, for example) events. The transcription and annotation of large corpora with all of this information is a task that cannot be done manually, so automatic tools are needed for the different tasks of transcription and annotation. The following subsections present a review of current tools for carrying out these tasks (orthographic and phonetic transcription and segmentation, prosodic unit segmentation, annotation of prosodic events, and annotation of linguistic information), with a special focus on two tools developed as part of our research, SegProso and MelAn.

3.1 Automatic orthographic transcription and segmentation

Orthographic transcription of oral material has traditionally been a problem for the collection of oral corpora. It is usually done by manual transcribers, who spend a large quantity of time on this task and may introduce transcription errors. Speech recognition technology (which allows for the automatic conversion of a speech signal into its corresponding orthographic transcription, by comparing the speech input to a set of acoustic models representing the phones of the input language) may be a faster alternative to face the task. However, the current performance of this technology is not accurate enough to obtain reliable transcriptions, especially with spontaneous, disfluent or noisy speech, as the acoustic models of these systems have been usually trained only with formal, clean speech, and their pronunciation dictionaries do not usually consider pronunciation variants that are atypical for standard speech (i.e. they show poor out-of-domain performance). Despite these problems, this kind of technology could provide a first automatic transcription that human reviewers could revise later, a task which would be faster than manually transcribing all of the material.

However, audio transcription tools using speech recognition technology (both public domain and commercial) do not seem to be available for this kind of task. Some existing tools do this job for other purposes, such as video caption tools (for example, the Youtube captioning tool, from Google) or speech-to-speech translation tools (such as Google Translate or Skype Translator). However, it is difficult to convert the output of these programs into a plain text transcription of input speech.

3.2 Phonetic transcription and segmentation

Manual phonetic transcription of corpora from directly listening to speech waves is an even more time-consuming task than orthographic transcription. In addition, it has to be done by human transcribers with a good background on phonetic transcription of the language, a much more specialised knowledge than the one needed to orthographically transcribe speech. Phonetic transcription of large corpora appears then to be an unaffordable task by manual means.

In this case, however, technology is already providing automatic alternatives for the phonetic transcription of speech, at least for some languages, if the orthographic transcription is provided. Phonetic aligners are tools that enable researchers to obtain a time-aligned phonetic transcription of a speech file, if an orthographic transcription of the speech wave is available. These tools are actually the result of merging two different speech technologies: automatic phonetic transcription of text, and automatic speech recognition. They usually work in two phases: first, the phonetic transcription is generated from the orthographic text, then the speech recognizer tries to align the obtained transcription with the speech wave, a task that is easier than simply trying to "guess" the phones of the speech chain using only a speech recogniser.

Several public domain phonetic aligners are available on the net, such as MAUS (Schiel 1999), WebMAUS, EasyAlign (Goldman 2011) or SPPAS (Bigi 2015). SPPAS is a tool developed at the *Laboratoire Parole et Langage* (Aix-en-Provence, France), which allows for phonetic transcription and alignment in several languages (Catalan, French, English, Spanish, Italian, Japanese, Mandarin, and Cantonese). In addition to time-aligned phonetic transcription, it also allows for obtaining other

Juan María Garrido Almiñana

automatic annotations, such as syllable segmentation, intonation group, or intonation annotation using MoMel (Hirst & Espesser 1993). Written in Python, it provides as output a Praat (Boersma & Weenink 2017) TextGrid file containing several tiers with the different levels of segmentation analysis. Figure 1 provides an example of this output for a sample Spanish sentence.

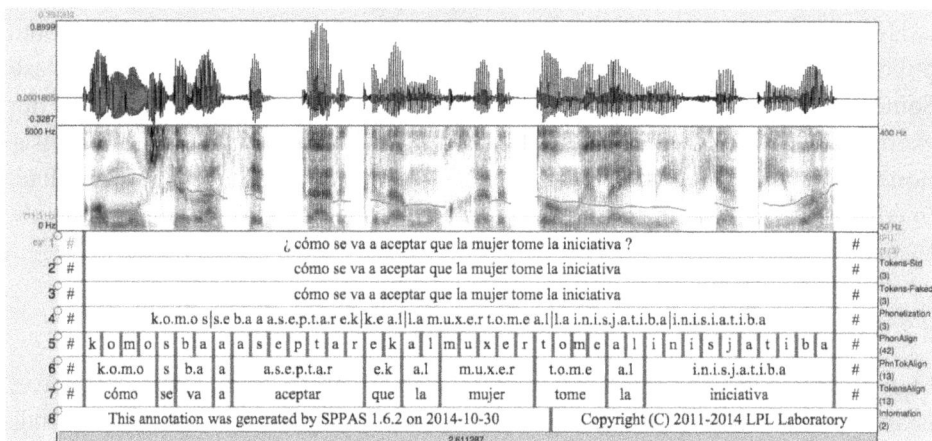

Figure 1: TextGrid file containing the phonetic transcription (in SAMPA symbols) and prosodic annotation obtained with SPPAS for the utterance *¿Cómo se va a aceptar que la mujer tome la iniciativa?* uttered by a female speaker of Spanish.

The Catalan and Spanish acoustic models necessary for the speech alignment phase have been trained using an annotated version of the Glissando corpus. For automatic phonetic transcription, SPPAS includes a phonetic dictionary for each available language, although it can be customised to use any dictionary or phonetic transcriber for this task.

The main problem of these tools is that they provide the "theoretical" transcription of the input speech, not the actual pronunciation of the speaker, as they are based on the automatic transcription of the text, not on the acoustic analysis of the phones which make up the speech chain. The reliability of these tools is far from being perfect, but it seems good enough to process large amounts of data. In the case of SPPAS, for example, Bigi (2012) presents the results of an evaluation of the French aligner using three different corpora, AixOx, Grenelle, and CID, and the error rate of phonetisation errors moves between 8.8% and 14.5%. Apart from phonetisation errors, misplacements of phone boundaries can also appear. This gives poorer results than desired, which makes a later phase of manual review of the output necessary, a task which is much faster than a fully manual transcription from scratch.

10

3.3 Automatic segmentation of prosodic units

Prosodic phrasing annotation (marking prosodic unit boundaries, such as syllables or intonation units) has also been a traditional bottleneck in prosody studies. One reason for this is the lack of a common list of prosodic units across models and approaches in prosodic phonology: some units, such as syllables or intonation groups, are generally accepted, but there is less consensus about the definition or name of others (intermediate phrase, phonological word, stress group, or foot, for example). But it can also be due to the difficulty of the annotation task itself: it is known, for example, that human annotators show only reasonably high agreement levels in the task of intermediate phrase boundary detection (see Syrdal & Mc Gory 2000, among others), in addition to the fact that it is a very time-consuming task when done by humans, as in the case of the previously reviewed transcription tasks.

Previously mentioned tools (EasyAlign, SPPAS) allow, in addition to automatic phonetic transcription, the automatic annotation of some prosodic boundaries, such as syllables or intonation groups. However, some other public domain tools specifically oriented to this task are also available, such as APA (for the automatic identification of syllable and tone unit boundaries; see Cutugno et al. 2002 or Petrillo 2004), Analor (which provides tone unit segmentation; Avanzi et al. 2008) or SegProso (for the annotation of syllables, stress groups, intonation groups, and breath groups; Garrido 2013b). SegProso is actually a set of Praat scripts which add to an input TextGrid file which contains the orthographic and phonetic transcription of the utterance and four new tiers with the prosodic unit segmentation. Originally designed for the annotation of speech in Spanish and Catalan, Seg-Proso was later extended to Brazilian Portuguese and Mandarin Chinese, and more recently, to French. Figure 2 presents an example of this tool's output, in Praat TextGrid format. SegProso needs, as input, a wav file and its corresponding orthographic and phonetic transcription in a TextGrid file.

Automatic tools for the identification of prosodic boundaries are built either using data-driven (automatic creation of models from the analysis of large sets of annotated data) or knowledge-based techniques (using linguistic and phonetic rules manually developed by experts). Knowledge-based tools may approach this task from two different perspectives:

- In the first, acoustical approach, prosodic boundaries are detected from the acoustic analysis of the signal. For the detection of intonation unit boundaries, for example, APA and Analor try to identify acoustic cues such as pauses and boundary tones; APA tries to detect syllables by searching

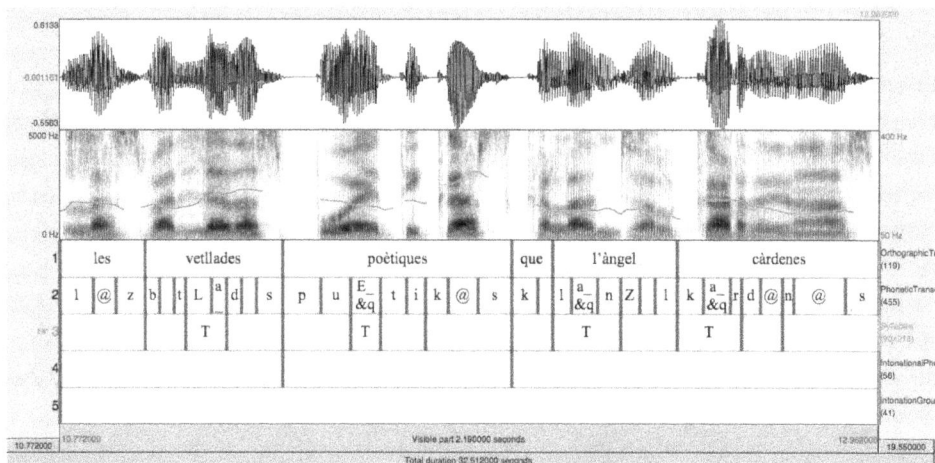

Figure 2: TextGrid and waveform corresponding to the utterance "les vetllades poètiques que l'Ángel Cárdenas", spoken by a female professional speaker.

acoustic indices of syllabic nuclei; and finally, SegProso looks for relevant F0 movements for the identification of intermediate phrases and F0 resets, an acoustic cue that has also been claimed to be an indicator of the presence of prosodic boundaries (Garrido 1996; 2001, among others).

- In the second approach, the prosodic annotation is carried out by taking advantage of previously obtained annotations, mainly phonetic transcription. For syllable annotation, for example, SegProso uses the phonetic transcription provided as input, which must contain information about the location of the (theoretically) stressed syllables to determine syllable boundaries by means of a set of "phonological" rules which predict how phonetic symbols must be grouped; a similar approach is used for the annotation of stress groups (their boundaries are established using both the syllable limits previously derived from the phonetic transcription and the information about stressed vowels available in the phonetic transcription tier) and intonation groups (boundaries are derived from the pause information present in the phonetic transcription).

The approach based on the use of previously derived annotations seems to be, in general, more reliable than the first one, as it can be inferred from the results of the evaluation of SegProso with Spanish and Catalan data presented in Table 1 and 2 (Garrido 2013b). The goal of the evaluation was to check to what extent the tool is able to correctly place prosodic unit boundaries in a small automatic annotation task. A set of 100 utterances for each language was selected as an evaluation corpus. The results of the evaluation showed an excellent performance of the syllable and breath group scripts for both languages (whose rules make annotations from previously obtained annotation tiers), a slightly lower performance rate in the case of stress group annotation (derived also from the phonetic transcription), and a lower performance of the intonation group script (whose rules detect potential boundaries from the acoustic analysis of the F0 curves). The lower performance of the stress group detector illustrates the risks of the first approach, as almost all the errors were due to errors in the annotation of the stressed vowels in the phonetic transcription tier, which had been also generated by automatic means. The lower performance of the intonation group detector shows that work still needs to be done to improve the acoustic detection of prosodic boundaries, although, in this case, the results are good enough to consider that they can be used as a starting point for a second phase of manual revision.

3.4 Prosodic annotation

The annotation of prosodic phenomena (intonation, stress, and tone) presents similar problems to prosodic units, such as the lack of a common inventory of annotation symbols, or the existence of several prosodic and metrical theories. In the case of intonation, ToBI (Silverman et al. 1992) is largely used by people working in the framework of the autosegmental model for phonological prosodic analysis, but there are other conventions which have been used outside this framework, such as MoMel/INTSINT (Hirst et al. 2000), the IPO model ('t Hart et al. 1990; Garrido 1996), or Speech Melodic Analysis (*Análisis Melódico del Habla*, Cantero Serena & Font-Rotchés 2009).

Until very recently, the annotation of intonation events has been carried out manually, and consequently, has been very time consuming. Probably the first automatic tool for the annotation of intonation curves was MoMel, developed by Daniel Hirst and Robert Espesser at the *Laboratoire Parole et Langage* of Aix-en-Provence, France (Hirst & Espesser 1993). In the case of ToBI, some automatic annotation tools have recently appeared, such as AuToBI (Rosenberg 2010) or Eti-ToBI (Elvira García et al. 2015), or are still in development (Escudero et al. 2014a; 2014b; 2014c; González et al. 2014). Outside the ToBI framework, there are also some tools which implement other models of prosodic representation, such as the one developed by Mateo to implement the Speech Melodic Analysis annotation system (Mateo Ruiz 2010a,b), or MelAn (Garrido 2010).

Table 1: Results for the evaluation of the Spanish corpus (Garrido 2013b)

Unit	N of boundaries (automatic version)	N of boundaries (revised version)	Correct boundaries	Moved boundaries	Deleted boundaries	Added boundaries	Pct. of correct boundaries (automatic version)	Pct. of actual boundaries correctly predicted
Syllables	1821	1824	1824	0	0	0	100	100
Stress groups	568	568	496	72	0	0	87.32	87.32
Intonation groups	308	297	254	21	33	22	82.46	85.52
Phonic groups	122	122	122	0	0	0	100	100

Table 2: Results for the evaluation of the Catalan corpus (Garrido 2013b)

Unit	N of boundaries (automatic version)	N of boundaries (revised version)	Correct boundaries	Moved boundaries	Deleted boudaries	Added boundaries	Pct. of correct boundaries (automatic version)	Pct. of actual boundaries correctly predicted
Syllables	1574	1574	1574	0	0	0	100	100
Stress groups	628	628	543	85	0	0	86.46	86.46
Intonation groups	354	323	274	31	49	18	77.40	84.82
Phonic groups	168	168	168	0	0	0	100	100

MelAn is an automatic tool for stylisation, annotation, and modelling of intonation contours, which is an automatic implementation of the intonation modelling framework presented in (Garrido 1996; 2001), inspired by the IPO model. According to this model, F0 contours are made up of a set of relevant inflection points that can be assigned to a high (Peak, P) or low (Valley, V) tonal level, as can be observed in Figure 3. Two more symbols for extra high (P+) and extra low (V–) levels are also used. It is then a phonetic annotation tool, in the sense that it does not try to capture the phonological tones behind the F0 curves, rather the pitch movements which are relevant from an acoustic-perceptual point of view, a much more feasible goal for an automatic tool at the current state of the art.

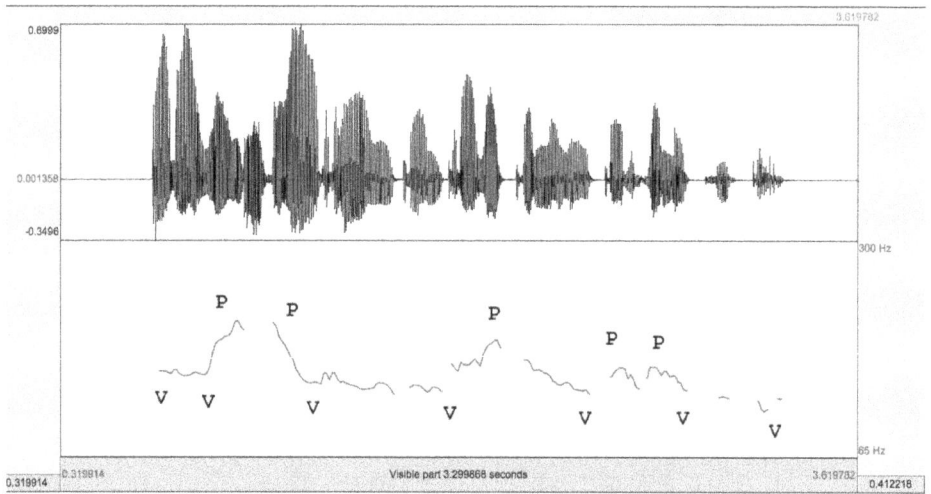

Figure 3: Waveform and annotated F0 contour for the utterance *Aragón se ha reencontrado como motor del equipo*, uttered by a female speaker of Peninsular Spanish. Relevant inflection points are marked with P and V labels, following the intonational annotation conventions described in Garrido (1996; 2001).

MelAn performs the annotation procedure in two stages: stylisation, in which the original F0 trace is reduced to a set of relevant inflection points using the Praat stylisation functionality; and annotation, in which the obtained inflection points are annotated with a label indicating the relative height of the F0 value within the tonal range of a breath group. At the end of this process, both F0 values at the inflection points and intonation labels are stored in a TextGrid as the one presented in Figure 4.

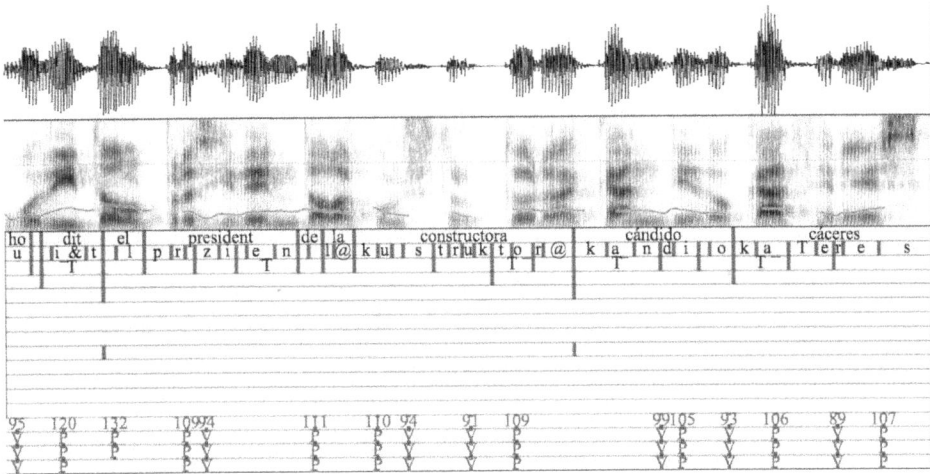

Figure 4: Waveform, F0 contour, spectrogram and annotation of the utterance *ho ha dit el president de la constructora, Cándido Cáceres*, uttered by a speaker of central Catalan. The last four tiers in the TextGrid present the output obtained with MelAn.

As stated before, the ideal goal of this kind of phonetic annotation tool is that the obtained labels are able to capture the relevant movements for the transmission of intonational information from the original F0 contour, rather than to capture phonological, linguistically relevant tonal events. In order to analyse to what extent MelAn meets this requirement, several perceptual evaluations were carried out to determine to what extent the annotated representation of F0 contours can be used to recover the original F0 trace, or at least to obtain a similar one, perceived close enough to the original one by native listeners of the analysed language. The procedure was the same in all cases: listeners had to listen to pairs of synthesized stimuli, both obtained from the same utterance, the first one generated with the original F0 contour and the second one generated with a simplified F0 contour derived from a symbolic MelAn representation, and rate the degree of similarity between them. This process of resynthesis was done using ModProso, another Praat-based tool developed for this purpose (Garrido 2013a). Figures 5 and 6 present an example of one of these pairs for a Spanish utterance.

As shown in Table 3, the final global score was around 4 on a 1–5 scale, that is, a quite acceptable similarity between both contours, both for Spanish and Catalan. Similar results were obtained for other languages such as Mandarin Chinese (Yao & Garrido 2010), as shown in Table 4, or Brazilian Portuguese (Silva & Garrido 2016). These results seem to indicate that MelAn generates symbolic representations of F0 contours that are very similar in perceptual terms to the original ones in all of the analysed languages, some of them quite far away from a typological point of view.

Additionally, it can also be useful to automatically annotate prosodic corpora with tonal events if the goal is to capture perceptually relevant movements. Of course, as the results of the evaluation also show, the symbolic annotation obtained may contain errors in some cases, which lead to a poorer rate in the perceptual evaluation task. These errors may come from different sources (errors in the estimation of the F0 curve, errors in the stylisation process, or errors in the assignment of the P/V label to a specific inflection point), but they do not seem to be frequent enough to provide an annotation that can be considered unacceptable. And again, if a more accurate annotation is needed, it can be manually corrected by a human expert.

Table 3: Results of the perceptual evaluation for Spanish (left) and Catalan (right) (Garrido 2010)

Spanish		Catalan	
Utterance number	Average rating	Utterance number	Average rating
1	4.8	1	4.2
2	3.9	2	4.1
3	3.1	3	1.6
4	2.8	4	4.5
5	2.4	5	4.8
6	4.6	6	4.7
7	3.9	7	4.7
8	4.2	8	4.1
9	4.5	9	3.7
10	4.4	10	3.0
11	4.5	11	2.4
12	4.0	12	3.3
13	4.5	13	4.2
14	4.9	14	4.2
15	4.2	15	4.5
16	4.7	16	4.8
17	4.0	17	2.8
18	3.5	18	4.4
19	3.8	19	4.4
20	4.3	20	4.3
Total	4.05	Total	3.935

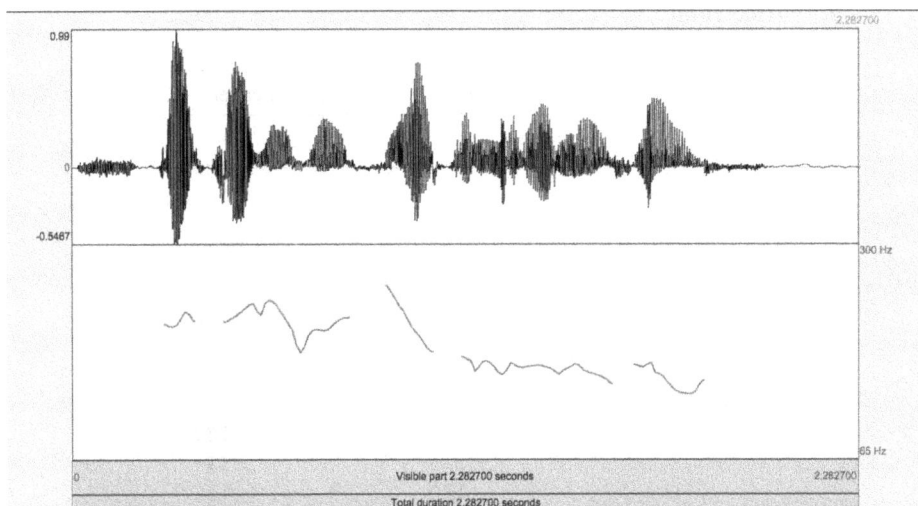

Figure 5: Waveform and F0 contour of the synthesised version of the utterance *Y cada vez la tendremos más*, uttered by a Spanish female speaker. The F0 contour used to generate this version is the original one.

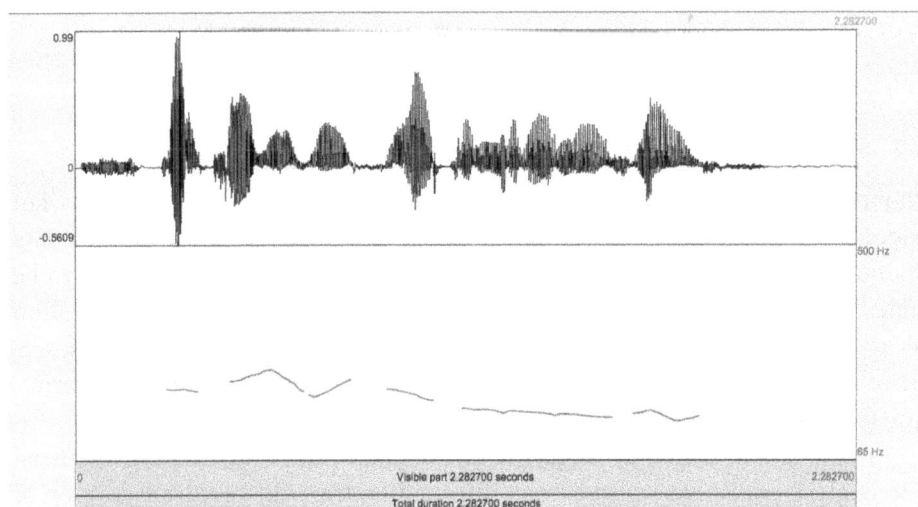

Figure 6: Waveform and F0 contour of the synthesised version of the utterance *Y cada vez la tendremos más*, uttered by a Spanish female speaker. The F0 contour used to generate this version is the modelled one.

Juan María Garrido Almiñana

Table 4: Results of the perceptual evaluation for Mandarin Chinese (Yao & Garrido 2010)

Stimulus	Mean score speaker 1	Mean score speaker 2
1	4.85	4.70
2	4.60	2.85
3	3.60	4.50
4	3.75	3.40
5	4.40	2.40
6	4.80	3.80
7	4.50	3.45
8	4.05	3.35
9	4.95	4.75
10	4.55	2.80
11	3.55	2.80
12	3.15	3.75
13	4.60	4.55
14	4.80	3.65
15	4.25	2.25
16		4.90
17	4.90	3.75
18	4.45	3.45
19	4.65	4.30
20	4.55	4.65
Total	4.36	3.70

3.5 Annotation of other linguistic information

Phonetic annotation of corpora at segmental and suprasegmental levels is not enough if the intended use of these corpora is to perform analyses to relate phonetic and higher level linguistic variables. Linguistic information has to be added then, a huge task if attempted by manual means. Relevant information for prosodic analysis may include POS, morphological and syntactic labels, sentence type, speech acts, information structure, focus, or paralinguistic information (such as intended emotions).

Automatic annotation of linguistic information can be carried out by using text analysis tools that try to extract information from the text transcription of the speech and align it with the purely prosodic annotation. In the case of morphosyntactic analysis, for example, there are many tools for many languages, but not many of them are available as public domain software. FreeLing (Carreras et al. 2004) is one example among many of a free tool for multilingual morphosyntactic analysis of texts. Pragmatic or paralinguistic annotation is currently more difficult to carry out by automatic means, but research is being done in those areas. TexAFon (Garrido et al. 2014) is an example of a text analysis tool that includes some (still rudimentary) modules to automatically extract paralinguistic and pragmatic information from text. Fully developed in Python, it was conceived initially as a set of text processing tools for automatic normalization, phonetic transcription, syllabification, prosodic segmentation, and stress prediction from text, but it has recently been improved to also include some text analysis procedures for automatic detection of sentence type, speech acts, and emotions. The evaluation results, described in Garrido et al. (2014) and Kolz et al. (2014), indicate that these modules do not yet produce a reliable enough output to be used for fully automatic annotation of large corpora, but in any case, they are similar to other state-of-the art tools.

3.6 An example of automatic annotation: The Glissando corpus

According to this quick review, it seems that the current state of the art in the development of automatic tools for speech annotation considers complete annotation of large corpora by these means as a feasible task. Although the result won't be as accurate as if obtained by manual means, it will likely be good enough to consider for later uses and analyses, maybe after a manual review, which is always faster than if done completely by hand. That was the case, for example, for the Glissando corpus: all the speech material, both in Spanish and Catalan, which had previously been manually transcribed, was automatically processed to obtain several levels of segmental and suprasegmental annotation: phonetic transcription (SAMPA), segmentation into prosodic units (syllables, stress groups, intonation groups, and breath groups), and annotation of tonal events at intonation contours. Some linguistic annotation was also added, but not using automatic tools. Figure 7 shows an example of the resulting annotation, in Praat TextGrid format.

The annotation procedure involved two phases:

- An automatic phase, in which several tools were used to obtain the different levels of representation (phonetic transcription and alignment, by means of the Cereproc transcription, segmentation and alignment tool provided by Barcelona Media; prosodic unit segmentation, by means of Seg-Proso; and intonation annotation, by means of MelAn).

- A manual phase, in which a manual revision of the automatic output (phonetic transcription and prosodic units) and a manual annotation of linguistic information was carried out. This second phase allowed for manual revision of an important part of the corpus (the news subset in both languages), and some minor parts to be annotated with speech act information.

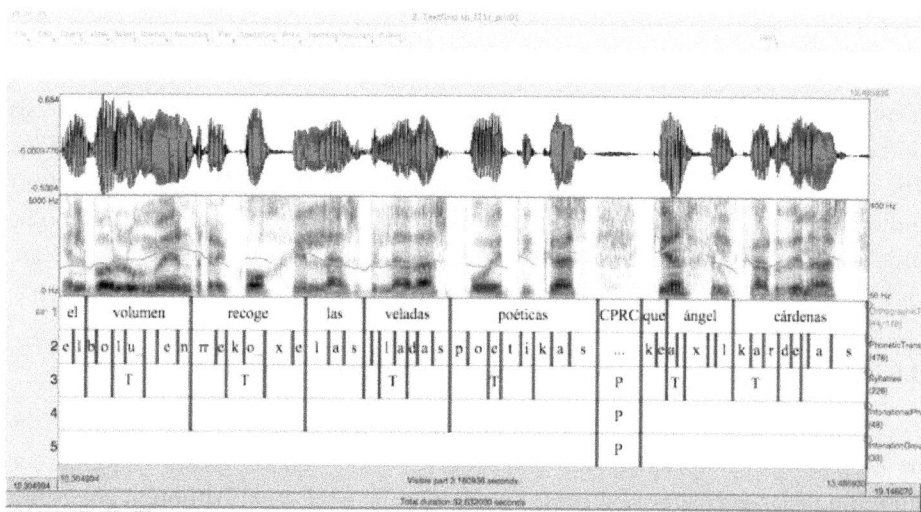

Figure 7: Sample TextGrid containing the annotation of the Glissando corpus.

4 Measurement and analysis

The measurement and statistical analysis of the acoustic data from large corpora cannot be done manually either. Some current tools, such as Praat (for acoustic analysis) or R (for statistical processing), allow automation of these procedures by means of scripts. These tools allow the development of more complex tools for specific purposes, such as MelAn, which includes, in addition to the stylisation and annotation scripts, a set of Praat and R scripts for contour modelling (the extraction of intonation patterns from the input corpus, the calculation of their frequency, and the analysis of their relation to any higher level linguistic variable annotated in the corpus).

The modelling phase in MelAn allows the researcher to obtain two kinds of patterns: global, defined at Intonation Group (IG) level, which model the global evolution of P and V inflection points along the IG; and local, defined at Stress

Group (SG) level, which represent the local shape of F0 patterns. Figure 8 illustrates this modelling scheme, with the P and V reference lines representing global patterns drawn on the F0 curve, and Figure 9 and Figure 10 present two examples of local final patterns and their corresponding inflection point labels.

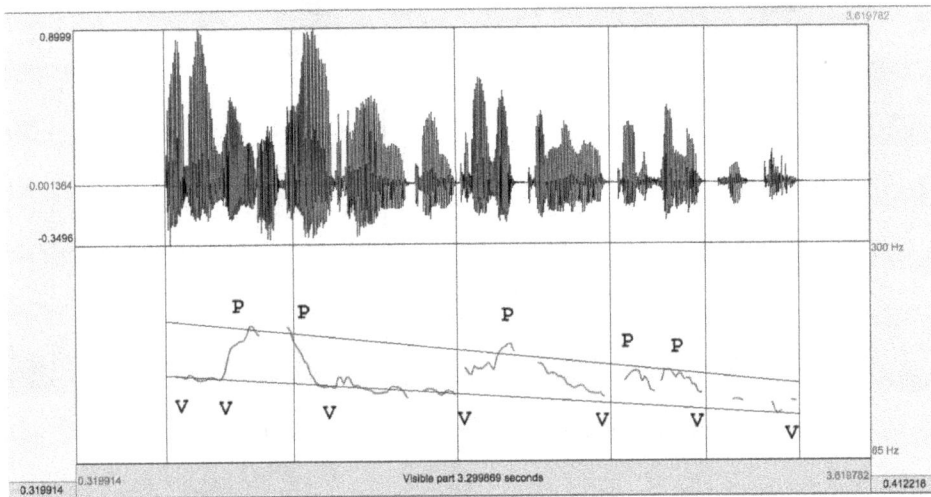

Figure 8: Waveform and annotated F0 contour for the utterance "Aragón se ha reencontrado como motor del equipo", uttered by a female speaker of Peninsular Spanish. Vertical lines indicate SG boundaries.

The output of this modelling procedure is twofold: first, a full inventory of local patterns in the input corpus for the different types of SG considered, with indication of their frequency in the analysed corpus (illustrated in Table 5); and second, mean global patterns for the different considered IG types (Table 6).

Local pattern labels presented in Table 5 are the result of concatenating the labels representing all the inflection points that make up the pattern. In addition, each inflection point label also includes two extra symbols to represent the position of the point with respect to the nucleus of its container syllable ("I", for "initial", close to the beginning of the syllable nucleus; "M", for "middle", close to the centre of the nucleus; and "F", for "final", close to the end of the nucleus) and the syllable of the SG where the inflection point is located ("0" if the syllable is the stressed one; "1" if the syllable is the one after the stressed one; and so on). For example, the label "VI0_PM0_VF0" used to describe the pattern illustrated in Figure 9, indicates that this pattern is made up of three inflection points, all three located in the stressed syllable of the SG: the first one has V ("valley") level, and is located close to the beginning of the syllabic nucleus; the second one has

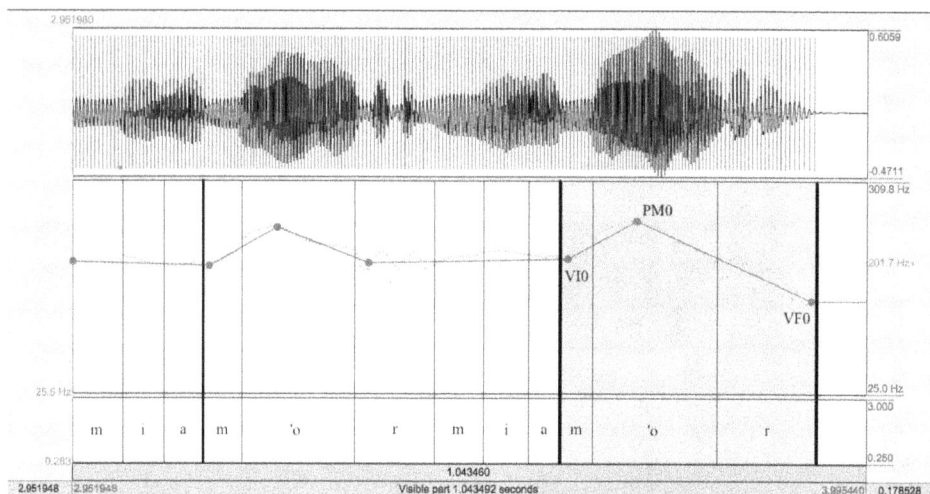

Figure 9: Example of rise-fall pattern: VI0_PM0_VF0 (Garrido 2012b)

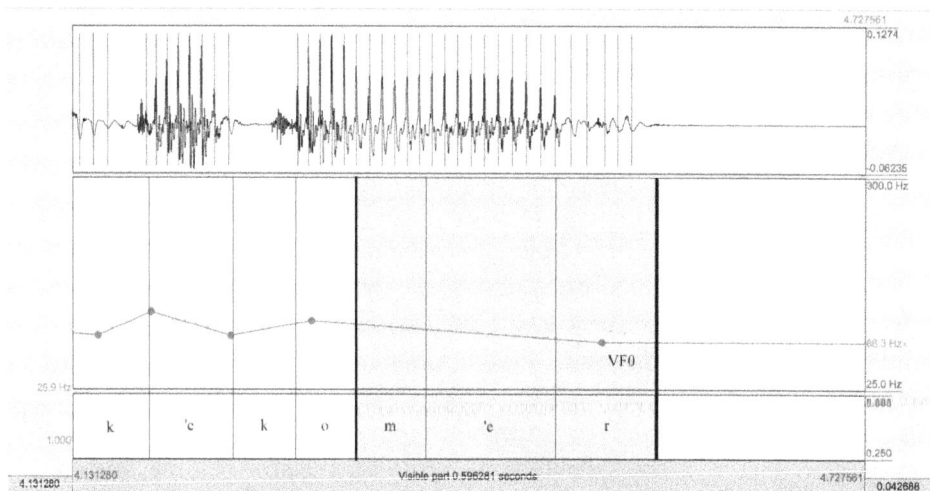

Figure 10: Example of falling pattern: VF0 (Garrido 2012b)

P ("peak") level, and is close to the centre of the syllable nucleus; and finally, the third one also has V level, and is located in the vicinity of the end of the syllabic nucleus. In other terms, it is an example of a "rise-fall" F0 pattern.

Table 5: Simplified sample of an output file containing the list of extracted internal patterns obtained from the analysis of a part of the Glissando Catalan news subcorpus (Garrido et al. 2013). The "INTERIOR" label indicates that patterns appear in internal position within SG.

Pattern	N of Syllables	Stressed Syllable	SG Position	N of Cases
0	1	1	INTERIOR	382
VI0_PM0	1	1	INTERIOR	172
PM0	1	1	INTERIOR	140
PI0	1	1	INTERIOR	134
VF0	1	1	INTERIOR	123
0	2	1	INTERIOR	205
PI0	2	1	INTERIOR	100
PI1	2	1	INTERIOR	90
VI0_PM0	2	1	INTERIOR	82
PM0	2	1	INTERIOR	69

Global patterns presented in Table 6 represent the two mean reference lines calculated for each considered IG type ("INICIAL", for initial IG within the sentence; "FINAL", for sentence final IG; "INTERIOR", for IG which are not initial nor final within the sentence; and "INICIAL_FINAL", for IG which contain a whole sentence). Each reference line is defined by two values: the F0 value at the beginning of the reference line (which coincides with the beginning of the IG) and the mean slope of line. These lines can be calculated using Hertz or semitones as units and define the tonal range and register for each type of IG. This output can be used for different types of analyses, as illustrated by the studies described in the next sections.

Table 6: Simplified sample of an output file containing the list of global F0 patterns obtained from the analysis of a part of the Glissando Catalan news subcorpus (Garrido et al. 2013). The "INICIAL", "INTERIOR", "FINAL" and "INICIAL_FINAL" labels indicate the position of the IG within the sentence (initial, internal, final or initial and final at the same time, respectively).

Sentence Mood	IG Position	Number of Cases	Mean Initial Value P	Mean Final Value P	Mean Slope P	Mean Initial Value V	Mean Final Value V	Mean Slope V
ENUNCIATIVA	FINAL	404	141.82	91.15	-37.55	109.07	69.21	-29.32
ENUNCIATIVA	INICIAL	1946	149.52	109.80	-22.92	112.97	85.06	-12.05
ENUNCIATIVA	INICIAL_FINAL	363	158.91	90.57	-45.30	120.27	69.18	-33.74
ENUNCIATIVA	INTERIOR	1823	137.50	106.15	-18.17	108.13	80.72	-14.78
EXCLAMATIVA	FINAL	2	238.59	62.06	-157.77	129.81	84.67	-44.31
EXCLAMATIVA	INICIAL	84	181.17	124.05	-49.21	134.53	86.06	-43.55
EXCLAMATIVA	INICIAL_FINAL	52	204.94	118.99	-93.99	141.13	86.45	-49.36
EXCLAMATIVA	INTERIOR	5	186.84	99.35	-81.39	139.53	80.26	-55.74

5 Using automatic techniques for the study of prosody: Some examples

The next subsections present some examples of how this methodology has been applied to the study of prosody in different languages and conditions. All of these studies were carried out using the tools and methods described in the sections above.

5.1 Analysis of pitch patterns in Spanish neutral speech

The goal of the studies presented in (Garrido 2012b; 2012a) was the description of the pitch patterns used in Spanish read neutral speech by different professional speakers, using a large corpus and a fully automatic procedure. The idea was to determine to what extent the use of automatic techniques could provide a reliable description of the intonation patterns which appear in a large corpus (actually, three different corpora of read speech collected for text-to-speech purposes, read by three different speakers, two women and a man, containing 33,730 internal and 11,460 final SG). The analysed material was automatically annotated using SegProso and MelAn, and a complete list of the patterns which appeared in non-final (Garrido 2012a) and final (Garrido 2012b) IG position was obtained. No manual revision of the resulting annotation was carried out.

Tables 7, 8 and 9 present an excerpt of three of the obtained frequency lists, the ones corresponding to declarative, interrogative, and exclamative sentences, respectively.

These lists were used to define a reduced set of the most frequent IG final intonation patterns, both at sentence-final and non-sentence-final position. Three main groups of patterns were defined: falling (Figure 11), rising (Figure 12), and rise-fall (Figure 13). The most frequent patterns obtained are similar to the ones defined in previous studies using manual methodologies: in the case of falling patterns, for example, PI0_VM0_VF0 pattern (high F0 level at the beginning of the last stressed syllable of the intonation group, and F0 fall during the stressed syllable, which may finish at the end of the stressed syllable or in one of the post-stressed syllables, if there are any), the most frequent one in declarative sentences in the analysed corpus, is equivalent to the H+L* L% tone in the ToBI framework, and VF0 (low F0 level along all the stressed syllable, and even beyond if there are post-stressed syllables), the second pattern in the frequency list for this sentence type, is equivalent to the L* L% tone, reported to be one of the prototypical boundary tones for this sentence type in Spanish; for rising patterns, VI0_PM0_P+F0 pattern (low F0 level at the beginning of the final stressed syllable, followed by an F0 rise until the middle of the same syllable, to arrive at an even higher F0 level at the end of the stressed syllable), the most frequent one in interrogative sentences, would be equivalent to the L* HH% boundary tone, considered prototypical of Spanish interrogative sentences (Estebas-Vilaplana & Prieto 2008). These patterns are also equivalent to the ones defined in Navarro's classical study on Spanish intonation (Navarro Tomás 1944).

Table 7: Most frequent sentence-final patterns in declarative sentences (Garrido 2012b)

Pattern	Number of Syllables SG	Sentence Mood	Number of Cases
PI0_VM0_VF0	1	AFIRM	173
VF0	1	AFIRM	171
PI0_VF0	1	AFIRM	130
VI0_PM0_VF0	1	AFIRM	91
VI0_VF0	1	AFIRM	89
PI0_VI1_VF1	2	AFIRM	198
PI0_VF0_VF1	2	AFIRM	114
VI1_VF1	2	AFIRM	112
PI0_VI1_VM1	2	AFIRM	80
PI0_VF0_VM1	2	AFIRM	65
PI0_VI1_VF2	3	AFIRM	13
PI0_VI1_VM2	3	AFIRM	11
PM0_VI1_VF2	3	AFIRM	9
PI0_VF0_VM2	3	AFIRM	8
PI0_VF0_VF2	3	AFIRM	7
VI1_VF2	3	AFIRM	7

Table 8: Most frequent sentence-final patterns in interrogative sentences (Garrido 2012b)

Pattern	Number of Syllables SG	Sentence Mood	Number of Cases
VI0_PM0_P+F0	1	INT	29
VI0_PF0	1	INT	19
VM0_PF0	1	INT	17
PI0_VF0	1	INT	16
VI0_PM0_VF0	1	INT	16
VI1_PF1	2	INT	23
VI1_PM1	2	INT	21
VI1_PM1_P+F1	2	INT	17
VI1_PM1_PF1	2	INT	15
PI0_VI1_VF1	2	INT	11
VI0_VI1_PM1_P+F1	2	INT	11
VM1_PM2	3	INT	2

Table 9: Most frequent sentence-final patterns in exclamative sentences (Garrido 2012b)

Pattern	Number of Syllables SG	Sentence Mood	Number of Cases
VI0_VF0	1	ADM	11
VI0_PM0_VF0	1	ADM	9
0	1	ADM	8
PI0_VF0	1	ADM	6
PI0_VM0_VF0	1	ADM	6
VI0_VM1	2	ADM	4
PI0_VI1_VF1	2	ADM	3
PI0_VI1_VM1	2	ADM	3
PM0_VM1	2	ADM	3
PM0_VM1_VF1	2	ADM	3
VI0_PM0_PI1_VM1	2	ADM	3
VI0_PM0_PI1_VM1_VF1	2	ADM	3
VI1_VM1	2	ADM	3
VM0_VF1	2	ADM	3

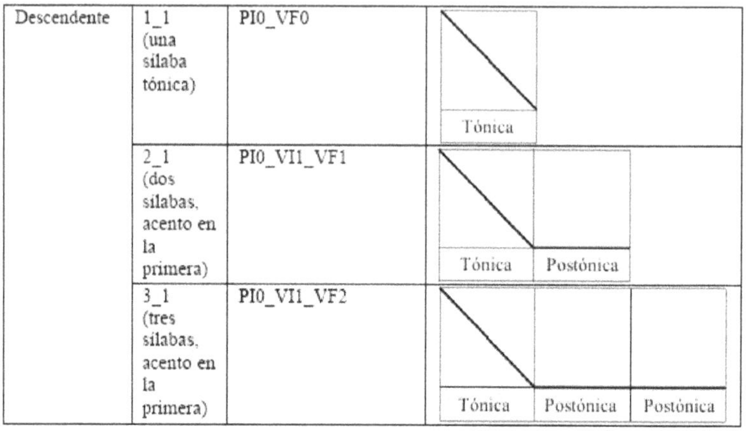

Descendente	1_1 (una sílaba tónica)	PI0_VF0	Tónica
	2_1 (dos sílabas, acento en la primera)	PI0_VI1_VF1	Tónica / Postónica
	3_1 (tres sílabas, acento en la primera)	PI0_VI1_VF2	Tónica / Postónica / Postónica

Figure 11: MelAn labels and schematic representation of the most frequent sentence-final falling ("descendente") patterns (Garrido 2012b).

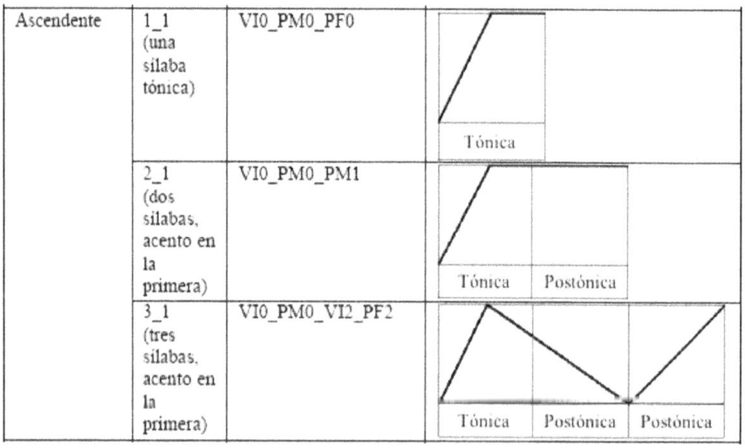

Ascendente	1_1 (una sílaba tónica)	VI0_PM0_PF0	Tónica
	2_1 (dos sílabas, acento en la primera)	VI0_PM0_PM1	Tónica / Postónica
	3_1 (tres sílabas, acento en la primera)	VI0_PM0_VI2_PF2	Tónica / Postónica / Postónica

Figure 12: MelAn labels and schematic representation of the most frequent sentence-final rising ("ascendente") patterns (Garrido 2012b).

Circunflejo		VI0_PM0_VF0	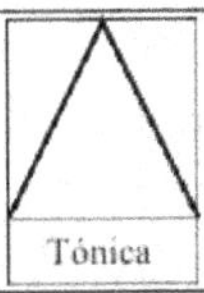
	2_1 (dos sílabas. acento en la primera)	VI0_PM0_VI1_VF1	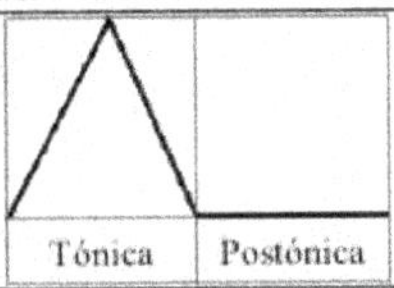
	3_1 (tres sílabas, acento en la primera)	VI0_PM0_PI1_VF2	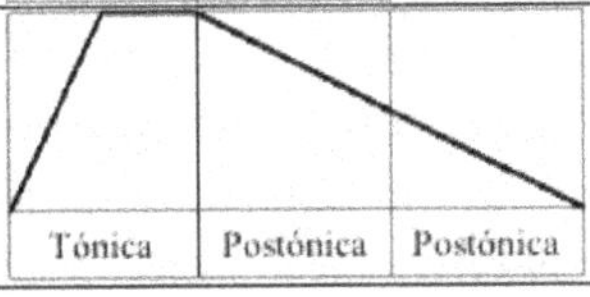

Figure 13: MelAn labels and schematic representation of the most frequent sentence-final rise-fall ("circunflejo") patterns (Garrido 2012b).

The results show that the employed methodology was useful to obtain reliable results in intonation analysis from large collection of data. In addition, MelAn labels allow for the description of intonation patterns in more detail than other annotation conventions, as they provide information about the number of inflection points in the pattern, its relative height (peak or valley), and its location within SG. This level of detail enables the researcher to distinguish, for example, between the VI0_PM0_P+F0 pattern, which is the prototypical final pattern for interrogative sentences, as stated before, and VI0_PM0_PF0 ("continuation rise" pattern), in which the final F0 reaches a lower F0 height than in the previous one (P instead of P+), and which is the rising pattern that is typical of non-final intonation groups. Both patterns are labelled in the ToBI framework with the same L* HH% label. Finally, the lists of patterns obtained with MelAn provide much more information about the variety of intonation patterns used in a large corpus, something very difficult to achieve when analyzing small corpora by manual means.

The results presented in Table 9 also illustrate one of this methodology's drawbacks: when the analyzed data is scarce, as in this case with the number of exclamative sentences in the corpus, the distribution of the observed patterns shows some dispersion and no clear tendencies are observed in their frequency of use.

5.2 Analysis of pitch patterns in Mandarin Chinese

The study described in Yao & Garrido (2015) is an example of the application of this methodology to a language different from Spanish, and to a prosodic phenomenon different from intonation. The goal of this work was the description of the phonetic realisation of tones in Mandarin Chinese, using a corpus of isolated utterances and paragraphs, recorded by nine different native speakers of Mandarin Chinese, three men and six women (651 sentences, 15,873 syllables in total). Adapted versions of SegProso and MelAn were used to annotate all syllables in the corpus (the natural domain for tones), and to obtain a list of the most frequent pitch patterns associated to the tones defined in classical studies of Mandarin Chinese. In this case, as no automatic phonetic aligner for Mandarin Chinese was available, phonetic transcription in Praat was done manually.

Table 10 summarizes the results of the analysis of these lists, showing which of the five F0 patterns were most frequently observed for tones 1, 2, 3 and 4, the number of times that they appeared in the corpus, and their relative frequency within the total number of analysed syllables showing that tone. In this case, as the patterns cover one single syllable, the pattern labels are made up only by the concatenation of the labels of each detected inflection point, with no label to indicate the syllable number. The "0" label indicates that no inflection point was detected within the syllable. The results seem to indicate that canonical pitch shapes of Chinese tones may present some "alotonic" variants, with different possible shapes for each theoretical realisation. So, for example, tone 1, which is described in classical studies of Mandarin Chinese as a "high" tone (Chao 1922) presents most frequently in patterns containing one or two "P" inflection points, but also as a variant with an initial low inflection point, followed by a high inflection point in the middle of the syllabic nucleus (VI_PM).

Table 10: Most frequent pitch patterns in the four analysed tones (Yao & Garrido 2015)

Tone	Pattern	Frequency	Tone	Pattern	Frequency
1 (2799)	PI	28.76 (805)	3 (2602)	VM	15.37 (400)
	0	24.90 (697)		0	12.07 (314)
	VI_PM	8.75 (245)		PI_VM	11.80 (307)
	PF	7.15 (200)		VI	10.11 (263)
	PI_PF	6.07 (170)		VF	5.38 (140)
2 (3347)	VM	21.84 (731)	4 (5805)	PI	27.46 (1594)
	0	18.29 (612)		0	12.16 (706)
	VI	11.41 (382)		PI_VF	10.30 (598)
	VF	6.66 (223)		PM	7.44 (432)
	PI_VM	6.54 (219)		PI_VM	6.74 (391)

The use of MelAn to process this large sample of acoustic data (thousands of syllables for each analysed tone) allowed for the description of the phonetic variation of the linguistic speech patterns, a fact which is much more difficult to detect and describe using manual methodologies.

5.3 Analysis of pitch patterns in Spanish emotional speech

MelAn and SegProso tools were used in Garrido (2011) to automatically annotate the INTERFACE corpus (Hozjan et al. 2002), a corpus of Spanish emotional
speech read by two professional actors, a woman and a man, imitating different
emotional states (joy, disgust, anger, fear, surprise, sadness, and neutral). The
corpus was not fully analysed for this study, only a subset of 5,859 utterances,
representing the six considered emotions (4,201) and the neutral state (1,658). The
inventory of pitch patterns provided by MelAn allowed for the analysis of the
most frequent patterns associated to each emotion (Table 11 and Table 12). As
illustrated in these tables, the number of items for the most frequent patterns is
rather small, and some variation is observed in the data.

A similar study, also aimed at describing the pitch patterns associated with
the expression of emotions in Spanish, is described in Laplaza & Garrido (2014),
but in this case, the corpus was much smaller (only 525 utterances, read by a
professional actor imitating the different intended emotions, 21 in this case, so
there were only 25 utterances representing each emotion). The results, if analysed separately by emotion, showed a large dispersion of the patterns, which
was interpreted as an indication that much larger corpora were needed to obtain
significant data about most patterns when using this methodology. For this reason, pitch patterns were not described separately for each emotion, but only for
comparing emotional and non-emotional utterances (Table 13).

These two studies illustrate once more that the results may show some dispersion when the size of the corpus is not large enough. This was even clearer in
the case of the second corpus, with only 25 utterances for each of the 21 analysed
emotions, so the obtained patterns had to be reanalysed not considering emotion
as a discriminating variable to get more significant results.

Despite this fact, the patterns observed in both studies were consistent with
previous descriptions of Spanish emotional speech, such as the one by Navarro
Tomás (1944), in which the use of a "rise-fall" final pattern was considered to be
a typical mark of emotional speech, but coexisting with other falling and rising
patterns. This "rise-fall" pattern described by Navarro coincides with the VI0_-
PM0_VF0 pattern (low F0 level at the beginning of the stressed syllable, F0 peak
in the middle of the same syllable, and low F0 level again at the end of the same
syllable) observed among the most frequent patterns in both studies, but coexisting with other falling (VF0) and rising patterns (VI0_PM0_PF0). The results
presented in Table 11 show also that this "rise-fall" pattern is used to express
only some emotions, such as joy, disgust, surprise, or fear. Anger and sadness
did not illustrate this pattern.

Table 11: Most frequent pitch patterns in the 1-syllable final (sentence final) SG, both for neutral and emotional speech (Garrido 2011).

Emotion	Male Speaker	N	Female Speaker	N
Joy	VI0_PM0_VF0 (C)	11	VF0 (D)	7
	0	5	VI0_PM0_VF0 (C)	5
	VF0 (D)	5	0	4
			VI0_PM0_PF0 (A)	4
			VI0_V-M0 (D)	4
Disgust	0	7	VF0 (D)	9
	VI0_PM0_VF0 (C)	5	VI0_PM0_VF0 (C)	5
	VM0 (D)	5	PI0_VM0_PF0 (A)	4
			PI0_VM0_VF0 (D)	4
			VI0_PI0_VM0_PF0 (A)	4
Anger	0	5	VF0 (D)	11
	VM0 (D)	4	0	7
	VF0 (D)	3	PI0_VM0_VF0 (D)	5
			VI0_V-F0 (D)	5
Fear	VI0_PM0_VF0 (C)	18	VF0 (D)	14
	PM0_VF0 (D)	8	VI0_PM0_VF0 (C)	9
	0	5	0	8
Surprise	VI0_PM0_VF0 (C)	19	VI0_PM0_VF0 (C)	27
	VI0_PM0_PF0 (A)	6	VI0_PF0 (A)	5
	PM0_VF0 (D)	5	VI0_PM0_PF0 (A)	4
Sadness	0	9	0	6
	PI0_VM0_PF0 (A)	5	PF0 (A)	6
	VM0 (D)	5	PI0_VM0_VF0 (D)	6
			VI0_PM0_PF0 (A)	6
Neutral	VM0 (D)	17	VF0 (D)	44
	VI0_VM0 (D)	13	VI0_VF0 (D)	15
	VF0 (D)	12	VM0 (D)	13

Table 12: Most frequent pitch patterns in the 2-syllable final (sentence final) SG, both for neutral and emotional speech (Garrido 2011).

Emotion	Male Speaker	N	Female Speaker	N
Joy	0	8	VI0_VM1 (D)	8
	VI0_PF0_PI1_VM1 (C)	7	VM1 (D)	7
	VI0_PM0_PI1_VM1 (C)	6	VI0_PM0_VM1 (C)	6
			VI0_VF1 (D)	6
Disgust	0	12	VI0_VM1 (D)	9
	VI0_PM0_VF0 (C)	9	0	8
	VI1 (D)	9	VM1 (D)	7
Anger	VF0 (D)	5	VM1 (D)	16
	VI0_PM0_VM1 (C)	4	VF1 (D)	11
	VI0_PM0_VI1 (C)	3	VI0_VM1 (D)	9
	VI0_VF0 (D)	3		
	VI1 (D)	3		
Fear	VI0_PM0_PI1_VF1 (C)	11	0	13
	VI0_PM0_VI1_VF1 (C)	9	VI0_PM0_VM1 (C)	11
	0	7	VM1 (D)	11
	VI0_PM0_PI1_VM1 (C)	7		
Surprise	VI0_PM0_PI1_VM1 (C)	7	VI0_PM0_PI1_VM1 (C)	13
	VI0_PM0_PI1 (A)	6	VI0_PF0_PI1_VM1 (C)	10
	VI0_PM0_PI1_P+M1 (A)	5	VI0_PF0_VM1 (C)	7
			VI0_PM0_VM1_VF1 (C)	7
Sadness	PI0_VM0_PI1 (A)	9	PI0_VM0_VI1_PM1_PF1 (A)	6
	0	8	PI1_VM1 (D)	6
	PF0 (A)	6	PM1 (A)	6
	PM0_VF0 (D)	6		
Neutral	PI0_VI1_VM1 (D)	32	VM1 (D)	30
	VI1 (D)	24	VF1 (D)	25
	0	15	VI0_VM1 (D)	25

Table 13: Most frequent pitch patterns in the 1-syllable and 2-syllable final (non-sentence final and sentence final) SG, both for neutral and emotional speech (Laplaza & Garrido 2014).

Condition	Non-sentence final		Sentence final	
	1 syllable	2 syllable	1 syllable	2 syllable
Neutral	VI0_PM0_PF0	PI0_VI1_VM1	VF0	PI0_VI1_VM1
	VI0_PM0_VF0	0	VI0_VF0	VM1
	VI0_PF0	PM0_VI1_VM1	PI0_VM0	VI1_VM1
	PI0_VF0	PI0_VI1_VF1	VM0	PI0_VF0_VM1
	PF0	VI1_PM1	VI0_VM0	PI0_VM1
Emotional	0	PI0_VM1	VF0	VM1
	VF0	VI0_PI1_VF1	VI0_PF0	VI0_VM1
	VI0_PM0_VF0	PM0_VM1_PF1	VI0_PM0_VF0	PI0_VM1
	PF0	PM1_VF1	VI0_VF0	VF1
	PI0_VF0	VI0_PF0_VM1_VF1	VI0_PM0_PF0	PI1_VM1

Table 14: Most frequent patterns appearing in sentence-final position (Garrido & Rustullet 2011). The "ENUNCIATIVA" label indicates that patterns appear in declarative sentences.

Pattern	Number of Syllables SG	Stressed Syllable	Speech mood	Number of cases
PF0	1	1	ENUNCIATIVA	6
VI0_PF0	1	1	ENUNCIATIVA	6
PI0	1	1	ENUNCIATIVA	3
VF0	1	1	ENUNCIATIVA	3
VI1	2	1	ENUNCIATIVA	5
VI0_PM0_PM1	2	1	ENUNCIATIVA	4
PI0_VF1	2	1	ENUNCIATIVA	3
PI0_VI1_PM1	2	1	ENUNCIATIVA	3

5.4 Analysis of pitch patterns in Spanish dialogues

Finally, the analysis described in Garrido & Rustullet (2011) provides an example of the application of this methodology to the analysis of pitch patterns in Spanish dialogue speech. The analysed material consisted of four dialogues between two radio professional speakers and extracted from the Glissando corpus: three task oriented dialogues (one about travel information, one about university information, and the last about tourist information), and one informal dialogue, with a total duration of 22 minutes and 53 seconds (2,964 analysed SG).

In this case as well, the analysed material was not very large, and again, the dispersion of the data was noticeable, as shown in Table 14, which presents the observed sentence-final pitch patterns for declarative sentences: although some patterns appeared more frequently than others, the number of items for each detected pattern was quite small, and the differences were not clear enough to extract general conclusions.

6 Conclusions

The experiments outlined in the previous sections seem to indicate that the use of fully automatic tools (such as MelAn) to process intonation can provide results that are comparable with the ones obtained by manual techniques, and offer new possibilities for the study of prosodic variation, as they enable researchers to obtain the full inventory of intonation patterns present in a corpus with detailed information about the frequency of each one.

However, input data has to be large enough to obtain a significant number of examples of each observed pattern and to get reliable results about the relative frequency of each pattern. The challenge, then, is to collect the necessary amount of speech to obtain reliable results, something that is difficult to do with classical corpus recording approaches, as was the case with the analyses of emotional speech, in which the number of utterances which represented each emotion was rather small.

At any rate, corpus-based techniques are a clear challenge for prosody research in the future, and even now, they can be used to carry out relevant research if a significant amount of speech material is available for analysis. There is a large number of automatic tools to complete the different tasks associated to the experimental analysis of prosody (corpus collection, corpus annotation, measurement and analysis), although in some specific steps, such as orthographic transcription, manual work seems still unavoidable. The accuracy of these tools, although it is not perfect, seems to be high enough to consider their use even without manual post-processing of the data, if the amount of speech data available for analysis is sufficient, and the noise introduced by the automatic tools can be balanced with the quantity of processed data. Or at least, these tools can drastically reduce the time devoted to manual annotation.

Such a corpus-based, "big data" approach to the analysis of prosody offers new methodological ways, as already mentioned, for the study of prosodic invariance, a classical problem in phonetic and phonological description of prosody: prosodic invariance can be established by analysing the speech of many different speakers, not only two or three, offering a much higher description power. But it is also a challenge for the study of prosodic variation at all levels (geographical, situational, intra, and interspeaker).

It is evident, however, that this approach presents still some important problems: for example, in many cases it is still difficult to obtain such a large amount of speech for analysis, especially in the case of endangered or minority languages, and with an acoustic quality that makes it suitable for automatic processing; and more complex and accurate tools are necessary, in order to improve the reliability of the annotated data used for analysis. But it seems clear that current research on speech technology and phonetics will provide such tools in the near future, and these corpus-based methodologies will become the norm in prosody analysis, as well as in other disciplines dealing with speech processing.

Acknowledgements

I would like to show my gratitude to Kimber Fodge for her help with the review of this chapter.

References

't Hart, Johan, René Collier & Antonie Cohen. 1990. *A Perceptual Study of Intonation: An experimental-phonetic approach to speech melody*. Cambridge: Cambridge University Press.

Avanzi, Mathieu, Anne Lacheret-Dujour & Bernard Victorri. 2008. Analor. A tool for semi-automatic annotation of French prosodic structure. In *Proceedings of Speech Prosody 2008*, 119–122.

Bigi, Brigitte. 2012. SPPAS: A tool for the phonetic segmentation of speech. In Nicoletta Calzolari, Khalid Choukri, Thierry Declerck, Mehmet Uğur Doğan, Bente Maegaard, Joseph Mariani, Asuncion Moreno, Jan Odijk & Stelios Piperidis (eds.), *Proceedings of the 8th International Conference on Language Resources and Evaluation (LREC'12)*, 1748–1755. Istanbul, Turkey.

Bigi, Brigitte. 2015. SPPAS - Multilingual Approaches to the Automatic Annotation of Speech. *"The Phonetician" - International Society of Phonetic Sciences* 111-112. 54–69.

Boersma, Paul & David Weenink. 2017. *Praat: Doing phonetics by computer [Computer program]*. Version 6.0.30. http://www.praat.org/.

Cantero Serena, Francisco José & Dolors Font-Rotchés. 2009. Protocolo para el análisis melódico del habla. *Estudios de Fonética Experimental* (18). 17–32.

Carreras, Xavier, Isaac Chao, Lluís Padró & Muntsa Padró. 2004. Freeling: An open-source suite of language analyzers. In Maria Teresa Lino, Maria Francisca Xavier, Fátima Ferreira, Rute Costa & Raquel Silva (eds.), *Proceedings of the 4th International Conference on Language Resources and Evaluation (LREC'04)*. Lisbon, Portugal.

Chao, Yuen. 1922. Experimental methodology on Chinese tone values. *Science* 7(9). 871–882.

Contini, Michel, Jean Pierre Lai, Antonio Romano & Stefania Roullet. 2003. Vers un Atlas prosodique des variétés romanes. In Jean-Claude Bouvier (ed.), *Sempre los camps auràn segadas resurgantas, Mélanges offerts a Xavier Ravier* (Collection Méridiennes), 73–84. Toulouse: CNRS Univ. de Toulouse-Le Mirail.

Contini, Michel, Jean Pierre Lai, Antonio Romano, Stefania Roullet, Lourdes de Castro Moutinho, Rosa Lídia Coimbra, Urbana Pereira Bendiha & Suzana Secca Ruivo. 2002. Un Projet d'Atlas Multimédia Prosodique de l'Espace Roman. In Bernard Bel & Isabelle Marlien (eds.), *Proceedings of the 1st International Conference on Speech Prosody*, 227–230. Aix-en-Provence: Laboratoire Parole et Langage.

Cresti, Emanuela & Massimo Moneglia. 2005. *C-ORAL-ROM: Integrated reference corpora for spoken Romance languages*. Emanuela Cresti & Massimo Moneglia (eds.). Vol. 15 (Studies in Corpus Linguistics). Amsterdam: John Benjamins.

Cutugno, Francesco, Leandro D'Anna, Massimo Petrillo & Enrico Zovato. 2002. APA: Towards an automatic tool for prosodic analysis. In Bernard Bel & Isabelle Marlien (eds.), *Proceedings of the 1st International Conference on Speech Prosody*. Aix-en-Provence: Laboratoire Parole et Langage.

Danieli, Morena, Juan María Garrido, Massimo Moneglia, Andrea Panizza, Silvia Quazza & Marc Swerts. 2004. Evaluation of Consensus on the Annotation of Prosodic Breaks in the Romance Corpus of Spontaneous Speech 'C-ORAL-ROM'. In Maria Teresa Lino, Maria Francisca Xavier, Fátima Ferreira, Rute Costa & Raquel Silva (eds.), *Proceedings of the 4th International Conference on Language Resources and Evaluation (LREC'04)*. Lisbon, Portugal.

Danieli, Morena, Juan María Garrido, Massimo Moneglia, Andrea Panizza, Silvia Quazza & Marc Swerts. 2005. Evaluation of Consensus on the Annotation of Prosodic Breaks in the Romance Corpus of Spontaneous Speech 'C-ORAL-ROM'. In Emanuela Cresti & Massimo Moneglia (eds.), *C-ORAL-ROM: Integrated reference corpora for spoken Romance languages*, 257–276. Amsterdam: Benjamins.

Elvira García, Wendy, Paolo Roseano & Ana María Fernández Planas. 2015. Una herramienta para la transcripción prosódica automática con etiquetas Sp_-ToBI en Praat. In Adrián Cabedo Nebot (ed.), *Perspectivas actuales en el análisis fónico del habla: Tradición y avances en la fonética experimental*, 455–464. València: Universitat de València.

Escudero, David, Lourdes Aguilar, Antonio Bonafonte & Juan María Garrido. 2009. On the definition of a prosodically balanced corpus: Combining greedy algorithms with expert guide manipulation. *Procesamiento del lenguaje natural* (43). 93–101.

Escudero, David, Lourdes Aguilar, César González, Valentín Cardeñoso & Yurena Gutiérrez. 2014a. Preliminary results on Sp_ToBI prosodic labeling assisted by an automatic fuzzy classifier. In *Proceedings of the 7th International Conference on Speech Prosody*, 457–461.

Escudero, David, Lourdes Aguilar, César González, Yurena Gutiérrez & Valentín Cardeñoso. 2014b. On the use of a fuzzy classifier to speed up the Sp_ToBI labeling of the Glissando Spanish corpus. In Nicoletta Calzolari, Khalid Choukri, Thierry Declerck, Hrafn Loftsson, Bente Maegaard, Joseph Mariani, Asuncion Moreno, Jan Odijk & Stelios Piperidis (eds.), *Proceedings of the 9th International Conference on Language Resources and Evaluation (LREC'14)*, 1962–1969. Reykjavik, Iceland.

Escudero, David, César González, Juan María Garrido, Emma Rodero, Lourdes Aguilar & Antonio Bonafonte. 2010. Combining greedy algorithms with expert guided manipulation for the definition of a balanced prosodic Spanish-Catalan radio news corpus. In Mark Hasegawa-Johnson (ed.), *Proceedings of the 5th International Conference on Speech Prosody*. Chicago.

Escudero, David, César González, Carlos Vivaracho & Valentín Cardeñoso. 2014c. A fuzzy classifier to deal with similarity between labels on automatic prosodic labeling. *Computer Speech & Language* 28(1). 326–341.

Estebas-Vilaplana, Eva & Pilar Prieto. 2008. La notación prosódica del español: una revisión del Sp_ToBI. *Estudios de fonética experimental* 17. 263–283.

Garrido, Juan María. 1996. *Modelling Spanish intonation for text-to-speech applications*. Bellaterra: Universitat Autònoma de Barcelona dissertation.

Garrido, Juan María. 2001. La estructura de las curvas melódicas del español: Propuesta de modelización. *Lingüística Española Actual* 23(2). 173–209.

Garrido, Juan María. 2010. A tool for automatic F0 stylisation, annotation and modelling of large corpora. In Mark Hasegawa-Johnson et al. (ed.), *Proceedings of the 5th International Conference on Speech Prosody*. Chicago, IL.

Garrido, Juan María. 2011. Análisis de las curvas melódicas del español en habla emotiva simulada. *Estudios de Fonética Experimental* 20. 205–255.

Garrido, Juan María. 2012a. Análisis fonético de los patrones melódicos locales en español: Patrones acentuales. *Revista Española de Lingüística* 42(1). 79–107.

Garrido, Juan María. 2012b. Análisis fonético de los patrones melódicos locales en español: Patrones entonativos. *Revista Española de Lingüística* 42(2). 95–125.

Garrido, Juan María. 2013a. ModProso: A Praat-Based tool for F0 Prediction and Modification. In *Proceedings of TRASP 2013*, 38–41.

Garrido, Juan María. 2013b. SegProso: A Praat-Based tool for the Automatic Detection and Annotation of Prosodic Boundaries. In *Proceedings of TRASP 2013*, 74–77.

Garrido, Juan María, David Escudero, Lourdes Aguilar, Valentín Cardeñoso, Emma Rodero, Carme de-la-Mota, César González, Carlos Vivaracho, Sílvia Rustullet, Olatz Larrea, Yesika Laplaza, Francisco Vizcaíno, Eva Estebas Mercedes Cabrera & Antonio Bonafonte. 2013. Glissando: A corpus for multidisciplinary prosodic studies in Spanish and Catalan. *Language Resources and Evaluation* 47(4). 945–971.

Garrido, Juan María, Yesika Laplaza, Benjamin Kolz & Miquel Cornudella. 2014. TexAFon 2.0: A text processing tool for the generation of expressive speech in TTS applications. In Nicoletta Calzolari, Khalid Choukri, Thierry Declerck, Hrafn Loftsson, Bente Maegaard, Joseph Mariani, Asuncion Moreno, Jan Odijk & Stelios Piperidis (eds.), *Proceedings of the 9th International Conference on Language Resources and Evaluation (LREC'14)*, 3494–3500. Reykjavik, Iceland.

Garrido, Juan María & Sílvia Rustullet. 2011. Patrones melódicos en el habla de diálogo en español: Un primer análisis del corpus Glissando. *Oralia: Análisis del discurso oral* (14). 129–160.

Goldman, Jean-Philippe. 2011. EasyAlign: an automatic phonetic alignment tool under Praat. In *Proceedings of the 12th Annual Conference of the International*

Speech Communication Association 2011 (INTERSPEECH 2011), 3240–3243. Florence, Italy: Curran Associates, Inc.

González, César, Carlos Vivaracho, David Escudero & Valentín Cardeñoso. 2014. Combination of variations of pairwise classifiers applied to multiclass tobi pitch accent recognition. In *Proceedings of the 7th International Conference on Speech Prosody*, 418–422. Dublin, Ireland.

Hirst, Daniel, Albert Di Cristo & Robert Espesser. 2000. Levels of representation and levels of analysis for the description of intonation systems. In Merle Horne (ed.), *Prosody: Theory and Experiment*, vol. 14 (Text, Speech and Language Technology), 51–87. Dordrecht: Springer Netherlands.

Hirst, Daniel & Robert Espesser. 1993. Automatic modelling of fundamental frequency using a quadratic spline function. *Travaux de l'Institut de Phonétique d'Aix* (15). 71–85.

Hozjan, Vladimir, Zdravko Kacic, Asunción Moreno, Antonio Bonafonte & Albino Nogueiras. 2002. Interface databases: Design and collection of a multilingual emotional speech database. In Manuel González Rodríguez & Carmen Paz Suarez Araujo (eds.), *Proceedings of the 3rd International Conference on Language Resources and Evaluation (LREC'02)*, 2024–2028. Las Palmas de Gran Canaria, Spain.

Klein, Marion, Niels Ole Bernsen, Sarah Davies, Laila Dybkaer, Juan María Garrido, Henrik Kasch, Andreas Mengel, Vito Pirrelli, Massimo Poesio, Silvia Quazza & Claudia Soria. 1998. *Supported Coding Schemes.* Deliverable D1.1., LE Telematics Project LE4-8370 (MATE).

Kolz, Benjamin, Juan María Garrido & Yesika Laplaza. 2014. Automatic prediction of emotions from text in Spanish for expressive speech synthesis in the chat domain. *Procesamiento del Lenguaje Natural* 52. 61–68.

Laplaza, Yesika & Juan María Garrido. 2014. Analysis and Synthesis of Emotional Speech in Spanish for the Chat Domain. A Parametric Approach. In J. L. Navarro-Mesa (ed.), *Advances in Speech and Language Technologies for Iberian Languages (Proceedings of the Second International Conference, IberSPEECH 2014*, vol. 8854, 1–10. Las Palmas de Gran Canaria, Spain: Springer.

Mateo Ruiz, Miguel. 2010a. Análisis melódico del habla: protocolo para la automatización de la obtención de los datos de la curva estándar. *Phonica* 6. 49–90.

Mateo Ruiz, Miguel. 2010b. Scripts en Praat para la extracción de datos tonales y curva estándar. *Phonica* 6. 91–111.

Navarro Tomás, Tomás. 1944. *Manual de entonación española.* New York: Hispanic Institute.

Ostendorf, Mari, Patti Price & Stefanie Shattuck-Hufnagel. 1995. *The Boston University radio news corpus*. Tech. rep. Boston University.

Pešková, Andrea. 2018. Intonation of pronominal subjects in Porteño Spanish: Analysis of spontaneous speech. In Ingo Feldhausen, Jan Fliessbach & Maria del Mar Vanrell (eds.), *Methods in prosody: A Romance language perspective* (Studies in Laboratory Phonology), 45–79. Berlin: Language Science Press.

Petrillo, Massimo. 2004. *APA: An object oriented system for automatic prosodic analysis*. Università degli Studi di Napoli Federico II dissertation.

Rosenberg, Andrew. 2010. AuToBI: A tool for automatic ToBI annotation. In *Proceedings of the 11th Annual Conference of the International Speech Communication Association 2010 (INTERSPEECH 2010)*, 146–149. Makuhari, Chiba, Japan: Curran Associates, Inc.

Schiel, Florian. 1999. Automatic Phonetic Transcription of Non-Prompted Speech. In *Proceedings of the ICPhS*, 607–610. San Francisco.

Silva, Cristiane Conceição & Juan María Garrido. 2016. Validación perceptiva de dos procedimientos de representación de la melodía aplicados al español, al portugués brasileño y al español como lengua extranjera. *Onomázein Revista de lingüística, filología y traducción* (34). 242–260.

Silverman, Kim, Mary E. Beckman, John F. Pitrelli, Mari Ostendorf, C. Wightman, Patti Price, Janet B. Pierrehumbert & Julia Hirschberg. 1992. TOBI: A standard for labeling English prosody. In Bruce L. Berwing, Terrance M. Nearey & John J. Ohala (eds.), *Proceedings of the 1992 International Conference on Spoken Language Processing*, 867–870.

Syrdal, Ann K. & Julia Mc Gory. 2000. Inter-Transcriber Reliability of ToBI prosodic labelling. In *Proceedings of the 6th Int. Conf. on Spoken Language Processing (ICSLP 2000)*, vol. 3, 235–238. Beijing, China.

Yao, Junming & Juan María Garrido. 2010. Validación perceptiva de un sistema de anotación automática de contornos de F0 aplicado al Chino Mandarín. In *Actas del IX Congreso Internacional de Lingüística General*, 2422–2437. Universidad de Valladolid.

Yao, Junming & Juan María Garrido. 2015. Variación fonética de los tonos estándar del Chino Mandarín. Un estudio de corpus. In Adrián Cabedo Nebot (ed.), *Perspectivas actuales en el análisis fónico del habla. Tradición y avances en la fonética experimental*, 187–196. Anejo 7 de Normas, Revista de Estudios Lingüísticos Hispánicos, Departamento de Filología Española, Universitat de València.

Chapter 2

Intonation of pronominal subjects in Porteño Spanish: Analysis of spontaneous speech

Andrea Pešková

Universität Osnabrück

Based on spontaneous data obtained in face-to-face free conversations, the present paper discusses the impact different information-structural functions have on intonational realizations of pronominal subjects (PS) in Buenos Aires Spanish (Porteño). The study applies the Spanish ToBI labeling system and examines its applicability to spontaneous speech. One of the questions addressed is whether PS with different functions have clear phonological correlates. It will be shown that intonation plays an important role in distinguishing topics from focus, but not in the interpretation of different types of topics. By means of an acoustic-phonetic analysis, the research also demonstrates that overt PS are not always emphatic or contrastive, as commonly asserted in previous, mostly theoretical, studies. Despite a high degree of variability found in the data, the paper argues for the need to use spontaneous material as well as further laboratory phonology techniques in the study of grammatical variation.

1 Introduction

Numerous recent studies in prosody research have investigated what effects information structure (IS) has on intonation and word order (see for Spanish, e.g., Face 2001; Gabriel 2010; Vanrell & Fernández-Soriano Forthcoming; Uth 2014 and many others). The first aim of the present paper is to contribute to the exploration of this interface, presenting and discussing intonational patterns of overt pronominal subjects (PS) with different pragmatic-discourse functions in Spanish, a typically null-subject language. The variety under study is the so-called

Andrea Pešková. 2018. Intonation of pronominal subjects in Porteño Spanish: Analysis of spontaneous speech. In Ingo Feldhausen, Jan Fliessbach & Maria del Mar Vanrell (eds.), *Methods in prosody: A Romance language perspective*, 45–79. Berlin: Language Science Press. DOI:10.5281/zenodo.1441337

Andrea Pešková

Porteño Spanish, a variety characteristic of Buenos Aires, and the recordings were carried out in Argentina in 2008 and 2009. The second aim of this paper is to discuss the applicability of the Spanish Tones and Break Indices (ToBI) labeling system to spontaneous speech data.

To the best of my knowledge, the prosodic characteristics of pronominal subjects (PS) have not thus far been systematically studied for any spoken Spanish dialect, despite the huge interest in the expression or omission of PS in Spanish. The phenomenon has been studied from different perspectives, such as the Generative theory of language (see, e.g., Chomsky 1981; 1995; Rizzi 1986; Biberauer et al. 2010; for Spanish see, e.g., Luján 1999), variationist sociolinguistics (see, e.g., Silva-Corvalán & Enrique Arias 2001; Otheguy et al. 2007; Carvalho et al. 2015), or typological works (see, e.g., Dryer 2013). It is well known that Spanish is a language where null subjects are common and represent the unmarked variants of PS. This raises the question as to why prosodic or intonational aspects of PS should be studied in a typically null-subject language. Here a brief review of this issue is warranted (see also §2 for more details). Although traditional as well as generative grammarians usually assume that the PS must be realized in Spanish only if it signals focus, emphasis, or contrast, or if the verb form exhibits ambiguities, results from extensive variationist and corpus-based research demonstrate that Spanish-speakers very often express a PS in non-focal, non-contrastive, or non-ambiguous contexts. By means of an acoustic analysis, the findings of this paper will support the previous and extensive variationist research. As we will see, PS can have different functions in a discourse and their use is thus strongly linked to the IS, with some further intervening factors possible (see, e.g., Carvalho et al. 2015; Pešková 2015; for an overview). As Posio (2012: 14) points out, one theoretical as well as methodological complication arises from the fact that the (non)connection of *contrastivity* and *emphasis* to subject pronoun expression has been accounted for without considering any prosodic analysis. How exactly can *contrastivity* and *emphasis* be defined in terms of prosodic criteria? It seems that whereas *emphasis* is usually connected with focus in general, *contrastivity* refers either to contrastive topics or contrastive focus. So what is the role of prosody in distinguishing the various IS categories of the PS? Whereas experimental and empirical data are available on intonational aspects of focus in different languages, including several varieties of Spanish (for *Porteño* see, e.g., Colantoni & Gurlekian 2004; Gabriel et al. 2010; Feldhausen et al. 2011; Le Gac 2014), we know very little about the prosodic features of different kinds of topics in the various spoken dialects of Spanish and in spontaneous speech in general. Féry (2007) assumes that IS categories might have no invariant grammatical (phonological, syntactical or morphological) correlates and that grammatical cues only "help speaker and hearer to sort out which element carries which information structural role" (Féry 2007: 161). Interestingly, Frascarelli (2007) shows that different IS categories (including PS) have clear intonational correlates in Italian. A one-to-one correspondence between intonation pattern and IS category would be very helpful in reconstructing IS in natural speech. Nevertheless, such a correspondence is not self-evident, given that natural languages are full of ambiguities and intonation is no exception. A phonological correlation in one language need not be present in another. As shown, for instance, in Frota & Prieto (2015), Romance languages and their dialects can differ considerably from each other with respect to their tonal inventories.

Since this volume deals with methodological issues, an essential question is which data and methods are suitable for studying the phenomenon under discussion, namely expression of PS and their connection to IS. So far, the IS and especially marking of (nominal) focus have been predominantly studied by means of sentences either formulated by an author or obtained by different experimental techniques such as picture-based elicitation in which speakers are asked to produce sentences in pre-constructed *question-answer* contexts (for *Porteño* see, e.g., Gabriel 2010). However, intonational realizations of IS categories can depend on the exact design of such experiments; in other words, different methods may yield rather different results (see Niebuhr & Michaud 2015, who underline that besides the tasks the selection of speakers can likewise play a very important role in speech data acquisition). One way to avoid the possibility of infelicitous intonation in laboratory data is to use spontaneous speech, which can provide important evidence for how speakers use the language in a natural context. The present study will use spontaneous speech data which stem from recorded undirected natural conversations, a method applied traditionally in sociolinguistic and variationist research (see, e.g., Labov 1984; Silva-Corvalán & Enrique Arias 2001). The main advantage of this empirical method is that it yields speech that is casual, informal, and as natural as possible (Silva-Corvalán & Enrique Arias 2001: 52). Not only do such data present an interesting source for the intonational patterns and different IS categories, but they are also crucial for studying the use of PS in a pro-drop language, because whether a PS is expressed or omitted is very much related to the discourse. However, since spontaneous conversations cannot be controlled for IS or the expression of PS in advance, one of the greatest challenges for a researcher using this "natural" data is to establish well-defined IS categories in order to be able to reconstruct the IS and to explain the expression of PS in it. A further question is whether and in what way intonation plays a role in reconstructing the IS in discourse.

Regarding the intonational analysis, the present paper applies the Spanish ToBI prosodic annotation system (Aguilar et al. 2009), which is based on the Autosegmental-Metrical model of intonation (Pierrehumbert 1980). Lately, ToBI has become popular not only among phonologists and intonationists but also among researchers from other fields of linguistics. ToBI is designed to be language-specific yet "universal" in the sense that a community of users apply the same set of conventions related to intonational research across languages (for a cross-linguistic ToBI proposal see Hualde & Prieto 2016). Despite its versatility, how-ever, the application of ToBI labels has proved to be in some ways problematic because of concerns about subjective variations in the interpretation of intona-tion. Why can such discrepancies among ToBI labelers arise? One reason may be that interpreting the phonetic-phonology interface is especially complicated since it presents a notorious degree of variability across speakers and contexts, and this is likely to be even more the case in spontaneous speech. The present study thus suggests that separating the two tonal levels, phonetic and phonolog-ical (see Hualde & Prieto 2016 for a proposal in the same direction), can be very helpful for reducing ambiguity in spontaneous speech data, allowing us to better understand the phenomenon under study.

Another important issue involved in examining the intonation of spontaneous speech is the relationship between models of intonation derived from speech pro-duced under controlled laboratory conditions and the very variable patterns we see in spontaneous speech. According to Bruce & Touati (1990: 37), it is essential to have "a fairly detailed model based on experience from studies of artificial, lab-oratory speech, in order to be able to extract interesting features of prosody from spontaneous speech" (Bruce & Touati 1990: 37; cf. Face 2003). Hence, the present study will test how closely the intonational patterns of IS categories based on laboratory-derived data match what we find in spontaneous speech data. For example, Face (2003) compared Spanish declaratives in laboratory-elicited and spontaneous speech and detected some phonetic differences in F0 rises through stressed syllables, F0 peak alignment, downstepping, and final lowering. But he concludes that considerable work remains to be done on the phonological anal-ysis of intonation patterns found in spontaneous data and their relationship to pragmatic meaning (Face 2003: 129). The present research hopes to take a step closer toward determining such relationships for the phenomenon under study.

The outline of the paper is as follows. §2 reviews the research on PS in Spanish, necessary for understanding the complexity of the phenomenon under study, and shows why prosodic analysis can be important in any research on PS in a pro-drop language. §3 describes the methodology applied in this study and discusses issues related to the application of the ToBI system. §4 presents the results of the study and makes a proposal for how the tonal variation found in the data could be explained. Finally, the paper ends with some concluding remarks in §5.

2 Importance of prosodic analysis

Let us begin this section with a very short example (1) from the data of the present study, by way of illustration.

(1) (¿La conoces?) Sí, la   conozco   un montón.
                     yes her know-1SG.PRES a   lot

Yo con Ale fui   al   colegio desde que tengo   cinco
I   with Ale go-1SG.PAST to.the school since that have-1SG.PRES five
años.
years
'(Do you know her?) Yes, I know her very well. I went to school with Ale starting at age five.'

Note that the female speaker starts her response with a null subject (*Sí, Ø la conozco*), as we would expect, whereas the second sentence begins with an overt PS *yo* (in bold). A traditional explanation that the pronoun is overtly realized here for the purpose of ambiguity cannot be supported, as the PS appears with a non-ambiguous verbal form *fui* ('I went' / preterit). Interestingly, only 32% of all ambiguous verbal forms (*N*=514) appear with overt PS in the data examined in the present research, and their occurrence is connected mostly with other factors such as information structure.

Moreover, the context in (1) neither establishes any contrastive relationships to any other reference nor represents a switch-reference. By means of intonational analysis of the elements under discussion, the study will test (1) whether the PS found in the data are "emphatic", or "strongly stressed", as is generally assumed, and (2) whether the different informational-structural functions of overt PS exhibit prosodic correlates. The following two sections present the concept of the strongly stressed, emphatic PS, as well as other functions of the PS in discourse.

2.1 "Strongly stressed" PS

Spanish has lexical stress, which is phonologically contrastive and in most cases located on the penultimate syllable. The Spanish pronominal system includes *pronombres tónicos* (stressed pronouns) and *pronombres átonos* (unstressed pronouns), sometimes described with the dichotomy strong vs. weak pronouns (e.g. *él* 'he-NOM' vs. *le* 'him-DAT'). The Spanish subject pronouns are strong pronouns (e.g. [no.'so.tɾos], 'we') and thus bear a stressed syllable exactly like lexical words (e.g. ['so.pa], 'soup').

Some studies assume that Spanish subject pronouns "are always strongly stressed" (Zagona 2002: 25). However, it is not clear if the notion *strongly stressed* refers here to lexical stress or pitch accent. The example offered by the author, however, seems to point indirectly to the latter (2).

(2) Estudiantes, no creo   que falten.
     students   not think-1SG.PRES that lack-3PL.PRES

'Students, (I) don't think are lacking.' (Zagona 2002: 22, her example 46)

Zagona (2002: 22) explains that the word *estudiantes* ('students') here is a dislocated topic and is thus "not strongly stressed". Here we must specify that the word *estudiantes* is de-accented, but it must bear a lexically stressed syllable, because Spanish word stress is phonemic. Thus, Zagona's definition and example indirectly imply that PS can never be de-accented in Spanish.

Besides duration and intensity (not considered in the present study), the fundamental frequency (F0) is one of the most important acoustic correlates of stress in Spanish and an important element of intonation (Hualde 2005: 239–246). Metrically strong syllables (σ^*) generally serve as "anchoring points for intonational pitch accents" in Spanish (Hualde & Prieto 2015: 358). As already formulated above, one of the questions that need to be addressed is whether we can rely on intonational properties to reconstruct the IS of overtly realized PS. In work on another Romance null-subject language, Cardinaletti & Starke (1999: 58) provide evidence that subject pronouns in Italian "can be prosodically unaccented". Another study on Italian by Frascarelli (2007: 695) connects *intonationally* strong pronouns with a rising tone, while weak pronouns are linked to a low ("destressed") tone. The former are interpreted as referring to aboutness-shift topics, while the latter refer to familiar topics. Furthermore, Frascarelli assumes that contrastive topics as well as focus are produced by a high tone.[1] The present paper on Spanish thus tends to be interested in verifying the relationship between

---

[1]Since methodological issues are one of the concerns of this paper, it might be pointed out that Frascarelli's generalizations are based on only 100 minutes of conversations, from which a total of 173 sentences have been extracted, and the distribution of different pitch accents and potential variation (due to the spontaneous nature of the data) in the corpus remains unclear.

different informational-structural functions of PS and their prosodic as well as syntactic (here: word order) correlates (see §3).

2.2 "Emphatic" and other PS

As already mentioned, many scholars assume that overt PS are always emphatic or contrastive in (consistent) null-subject languages (see, e.g., Luján 1999: 1311-1312 for Spanish; Fehrmann & Junghanns 2008: 199 for Czech, a West-Slavic null-subject language). For example, the study by Biberauer et al. (2010: 7) within the Minimalist approach claims that overt PS "tend to have (...) an emphatic interpretation" (3).

(3) Él habla   español.
    he speak-3SG.PRES Spanish
    'HE speaks Spanish.' (from Biberauer et al. 2010: 7, their example 6b)

In my understanding of (3), the use of the capitalized pronoun HE in the English translation signals an emphatic reading in the sense that it is 'he' (and not another person) who speaks Spanish. However, this kind of *focal* (*emphatic*) reading would fail in an example like (1).

In the literature, many assumptions and misleading or absent definitions on "contrastiveness", "strongly stressed PS", and "emphatic pronouns" are based on constructed sentences but rarely supported by empirical data (the exceptions being sociolinguistic or variationist studies). Generally, *contrastivity* seems to refer to either contrastive topics or contrastive focus (sometimes no distinction is made), whereas *emphasis* is commonly connected with focus and the prosodic highlighting of one part of a sentence.[2]

We know from previous empirical research on focus marking in *Porteño* Spanish that focal (nominal) subjects in preverbal position are realized typically with a rising-falling pitch accent and usually have much longer duration than other realizations of pitch accents (Pešková et al. 2012: 383). However, example (1) clearly does not indicate a focalization of the overt PS, first, because the pronoun *yo* is not pronounced with a tonal target typical of focus (see §3), and, second, because it is dislocated and thus cannot be a focus in Spanish. Let us assume that the pronoun *yo* is a familiar topic since it maintains the same-reference in the conversation. If that is the case, the question is whether such familiar topics are produced systematically as a "phonologically weak (...) low tone" (Frascarelli 2007: 712). Though

---

[2]Emphasis is very often also equated with expressivity, affectivity, or emotionality (see, e.g., Pustka 2015).

Frascarelli's findings come from Italian, we could assume similar tendencies in typologically close Spanish.[3]

This paper assumes in total five IS functions of PS (Table 1), which have emerged from an extensive review of the use of PS and the need to carefully distinguish between the different possible roles of PS in discourse (see Pešková 2014; 2015, and studies cited there). These categories were proposed in order to explain the expression/omission of PS in Spanish.

Table 1: IS functions of PS

Category	Form of the PS
PS as a Focus (F)	overt
PS as a Contrastive topic (Tc)	overt
PS as a Disambiguating topic (Td)	overt
PS as an Aboutness-shift (new) topic (Ta)	overt or null
PS as a Familiar (given) topic (Tf)	overt or null

Focus, according to Krifka (2007: 18) "indicates the presence of alternatives that are relevant for the interpretation of linguistic expressions". Note that syntactic marking of a focal subject, that is, its placement in the rightmost position, is its important characteristic in Spanish (4).

(4) Focus (F)
Esto no lo digo   **yo,** lo dice   Transparency.
this not it say-1SG.PRES I   it say-3SG.PRES Transparency

'It is not me who says this, it's Transparency.'

As for a contrastive topic, it is defined as an "aboutness topic that contains a focus" (Krifka 2007: 44). It mostly indicates a switch-reference and creates "oppositional pairs" (Chocano 2012: 143) (5).

(5) Contrastive topic (Tc)
En España la gente usa   el pretérito perfecto mucho más.
in Spain the people use-3SG.PRES the pretétito perfecto much more

---

[3] Additionally, *Porteño* Spanish is known for its "Italian intonation" due to migration-induced contact. Similar intonational and rhythmic patterns have been demonstrated between this Spanish variety and different Italian dialects (see, e.g., Vidal de Battini 1964; Colantoni & Gurlekian 2004; Benet et al. 2012). This issue will not be explored here, however.

Nosotros usamos   más el indefinido.
we   use-1PL.PRES more the indefinido

'In Spain people use the pretérito perfecto much more. We use the indefinido more.'

The aboutness-shift topic introduces or reintroduces a new reference that does not contrast with any preceding element in the context. In example (6), the speaker is talking about cultural activities in Buenos Aires. Then she changes the topic and addresses the listeners directly. The overt pronoun *ustedes* signals here a switch-reference.

(6) Aboutness-shift topic (Ta)
     ¿Y **ustedes** qué conocen   de   acá?
     and you   what know-3PL.PRES from here

     'And you, what do you know here?'

A familiar topic refers to given or previously mentioned information in a discourse (7). PS as familiar topics commonly have a null form; in the data of the present study only 11% of them had an overt form.[4]

(7) Familiar topic (Tf)
     Mi hermano es   un intelectual teórico-académico.
     my brother be-3SG.PRES an intellectual theoretical-academic
     Hizo   un máster en politología   y   filosofía.
     do-3SG.PAST a   master in political.science and philosophy

     'My brother is an academic intellectual. He did a master's in political science and philosophy.'

And finally, there is also a so-called disambiguating topic (8), i.e. an "aboutness-shift or familiar topic which is overtly realized in order to disambiguate referential and/or morphological ambiguities in contexts that lack semantic predictability" (Pešková 2014: 62).

---

[4]Some instances where it was not immediately clear whether a PS represented a contrastive topic (Tc) or non-contrastive topic (Ta or Tf) were resolved by means of a simple test whereby a different type of discourse marker or connector was added. Whereas phrases containing contrastive topic PS can be introduced by some contrastive (or contra-argumentative) connectors such as *en cambio* or *a diferencia* 'in contrast', phrases containing non-contrastive topics can only be introduced with a kind of explanatory connector which simply announces the subject in advance, such as *en cuanto a* 'regarding'.

(8)   Disambiguating topic (Td)
     [La ingeniería   ambiental] tenía   otro   perfil que
     the environmental engineering have-3SG.PAST another profile that
     iba   más con el perfil que **yo** me identificaba.
     go.3SG.PAST more with the profile that I   me identify.1SG.PAST
     'Environmental engineering used to have a different profile that was
     more consistent with the profile I identified with.'

In this example, the verbal form *identificaba* is in imperfect, which presents
syncretism between the first and third person singular in Spanish. The pronoun
is used here to ensure a correct interpretation of the reference; without it, the
hearer could interpret the sentence as 'the profile identified me' instead of 'I
identified with the profile'. If the context provides semantic predictability and
information is accessible to a listener, the expression of the PS in such cases is
not necessary.

The following section presents the data examined in the present study and the
methodology used in the transcription of the intonational properties of PS.

3 Data and methodology

3.1 Corpus

The data analyzed were obtained in the course of approximately 10 hours of free
interviews recorded (for the most part) with a Marantz HD Recorder (PMD671)
and Sennheiser Microphone (ME64) in Buenos Aires in 2008 and 2009. The interviewees were 18 males and 18 females (19–45 years old) with tertiary-level
education, and all of them were monolingual speakers of *Porteño* Spanish. As for
the length of the interviews, four interviews were one hour long each and the
other interviews lasted 10–30 minutes.

The data were transcribed in a word processor document by two native Spanish speakers and checked by three different researchers. The resulting corpus
comprised 118,514 words in total, of which interviewees produced 90,087, the
remainder being produced by the interviewers. The material contained in total
10,748 finite (personal) sentences with PS, of which 967 sentences had overtly
realized subject pronouns and were therefore used for the analysis on which this
study is based.[5] It should be pointed out that 72 instances of overt PS in the corpus

---

[5]Typical Argentinean fillers or tags, where the PS is always present (e.g. *Mirá **vos**,* lit. look you,
'Wow', 'I'll be darned!'), as well as cases where the subject appears without a predicate (e.g.
¿Fueron a Europa? 'Did youPL go to Europe?' *Yo, a Italia, nada más.* 'Me, to Italy, nothing
more.') were not considered.

had to be excluded because distracting elements such as laughter, creaky voices, overlapping turns, hesitations, or noises made acoustic analysis difficult or impossible. This illustrates one of the main disadvantages of using spontaneous spoken corpora for research. Moreover, spontaneous speech cannot be controlled in advance for the length and complexity of words or whole utterances, or for the use of PS and IS. Nonetheless, the selected method offers certainly a valuable source of (almost) natural speech and important data for the understanding of phenomenon under study: the use of PS in a discourse.

3.2 ToBI labeling

The present study was limited to two aspects of intonation. First, it described the tonal realization of pitch accents associated with a metrically strong syllable of the target word (the PS), and, second, it observed the existence of a boundary tone after the PS. In other words, it was examined whether the subject was produced by a low or a high tone (or combination of both) and whether it was separated or not from the rest of the sentence by a prosodic boundary. Other prosodic phenomena such as intensity, duration, rhythm and speech rate, or fluency were not considered.

The acoustic analysis was carried out using Praat (Boersma & Weenink 2017) and applying the Sp_ToBI labeling system for the tonal annotation (Aguilar et al. 2009; Estebas-Vilaplana & Prieto 2008; Prieto & Roseano 2010). As many studies have shown (most recently Hualde & Prieto 2015), there is considerable intonational variation among the different European and American varieties of Spanish. I thus followed the intonational inventory of *Porteño* Spanish as proposed by Gabriel et al. (2010; 2013) (see also earlier works by Toledo 2000; Kaisse 2001; Colantoni & Gurlekian 2004). This inventory is based on semi-spontaneous speech obtained by means of the so-called Discourse Completion Task, which has become standard in many intonational studies (see, e.g., Prieto & Roseano 2010; Frota & Prieto 2015; the (dis)advantages of this method are discussed by Vanrell et al. 2018, this volume).

Gabriel et al. (2010: 288–290) assume seven pitch accents for *Porteño* Spanish: a low tone (L*), a high tone (H*), three rising bitonal pitch accents (L+H*, L+¡H*, L+<H*), a falling tone (H+L*), and a rising-falling pitch accent (L+H*+L) (Figure 1):[6]

---

[6] A rising pitch accent with a shifted peak L+>H* has been replaced by an L+<H* in the latest proposals on Spanish ToBI (see Hualde & Prieto 2015). Similarly, the M% boundary tone used in former works has been changed to !H%. This study follows these new modifications. Moreover, the Spanish ToBI includes an L*+H (realized as a low tone on the tonic syllable followed by a rising movement on the posttonic syllable), which is very seldom encountered in *Porteño*.

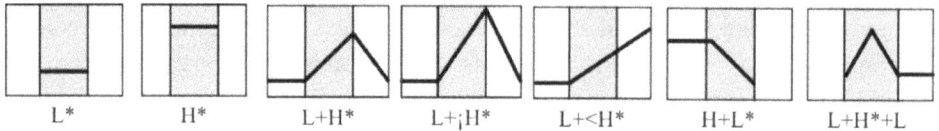

Figure 1: Inventory of pitch accents in Porteño Spanish (according to Gabriel et al. 2010).

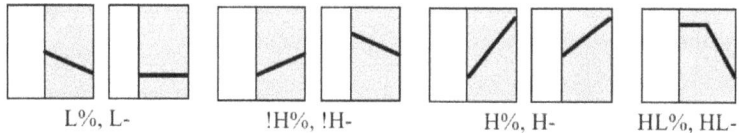

Figure 2: Inventory of boundary tones in Porteño Spanish (according to Gabriel et al. 2010).

The corpus subset containing PS was analyzed and all instances of pitch accents were duly noted. Next, each instance was examined to see if the subject was separated from the rest of the material by a boundary tone. Gabriel et al. (2010) assume three monotonal (L, H, downstepped-high !H) boundary tones and one bitonal (HL) boundary tone. All of them are attested at the end of intonational phrases (IPs) as well as at the end of intermediate phrases (ips) (Figure 2).[7]

As can be surmised, *Porteño* pitch accents as well as boundary tones have different distributional properties. For instance, the tritonal pitch accent L+H*+L is commonly found in the nuclear position, where it expresses emphasis or marks a focus (see Gabriel et al. 2010; Feldhausen et al. 2011). The realization of L+H* (formerly called "early peak") is typical of prenuclear accents in this variety, whereas the L+<H* (formerly called "late peak") is found sporadically in the *Porteño* data (see Pešková et al. 2012). Since pronominal subjects occur mainly in the prenuclear (sentence-initial) position (92% of the PS in the data of the present study), their tonal realization is expected to have an L+H* (with the peak located at the end of the accented syllable) or occasionally L+<H* (with the peak aligned with the postaccentual syllable).[8] Another possible prenuclear accent is a H*, found in different sentence types especially at the very beginning of utterances. Ad-

---

[7]Additionally, Gabriel et al. (2011) observe three boundary realizations H-, HL-, and LH- at the intermediate phrasal boundaries (break index 3) after subject (besides some other boundary cues such as pitch reset and pre-boundary upstep). These phonetic differences were not relevant for the present study.

[8]The pitch accent L+H*—associated with the PS in sentence-initial or preverbal position—was also found in the nuclear position when it was followed by an intermediate boundary tone (e.g. Yo [L+H* H-] *nunca hacía los deberes*, Figure 3).

ditionally, there are certain "intermediate" cases, where, for instance, the pitch movement is falling in the posttonic syllable but the peak is located in the onset of the nucleus of the same syllable. Is this still an L+H* or is it an L+<H*? According to the definition given by the Spanish ToBI system, it should be L+<H* (as the peak is located outside the accented syllable), yet the realization is perceived very differently from a typical L+<H* as described by Sp_ToBI. The rising pitch movement can also be either very brusque or very moderate. Nevertheless, all such pitch realizations were labeled L+H* in the present study. As a rich variation in pitch accents was attested in the data, the present study applied the Spanish ToBI labels using broad phonetic transcription (see Hualde & Prieto 2016) and in accordance with the following criteria. If a pitch accent associated with the PS was rising, it was labeled L+H* or L+<H* (depending on the pitch movement in the posttonic syllable). If the pitch accent had a high or a low plateau, it was labeled H* or L*, respectively. If the pitch accent was falling within the accented syllable, it was labeled H+L*. And finally, if the pitch accent had a rising-falling pitch contour within the stressed syllable, the label L+H*+L was used.[9]

The advantage of ToBI labels is that in principle they provide simplified representations of tonal events and are easy to read. However, several difficulties were encountered in applying the ToBI labels to spontaneous speech. By way of contrast, we first show in Figures 3 and 4 examples of the F0 contour for a rising pitch accent (L+H*) associated with the monosyllabic PS *yo* ('I') that conforms to the archetypical pattern: the rise starts at the onset of the syllable and ends at the end of that syllable; the difference between the minimal and maximal pitch is 80 Hz (6 ST) (Figure 3), and 100 Hz (7.5 ST) (Figure 4).

On the other hand, prosodic annotation proved more difficult for utterances from the corpus like *yo tomo mucho mate*, illustrated in Figure 5. Here the pitch reaches a high plateau (H) (166–162 Hz), but no preceding initial dip is observed or perceived clearly either, since the voiceless palato-alveolar fricative [ʃ] in the word *yo* ([ʃo]) causes gaps in the acoustic report and has no definite pitch.

---

[9] A reviewer has rightfully objected to the fact that prosodic annotation was carried out by only one person (the author) and therefore a subjective element may well have been present in the labeling. While this is true, the author is an experienced labeler of Argentinean intonation, and in this instance whenever ambiguous data were encountered they were discussed with other trained ToBI labelers (who were also experts in the Argentinean variety). Moreover, the results from previous research showed generally a high agreement between the trained labelers and give evidence to regard the ToBI systems as a standard reference for prosodic annotation (see Escudero et al. 2012 for Catalan ToBI; Feldhausen 2016 for Spanish ToBI). However, I do not rule out the possibility that such tests will be carried out on this data prior to any future research, not only for the ToBI labeling, but also for the IS categories proposed here.

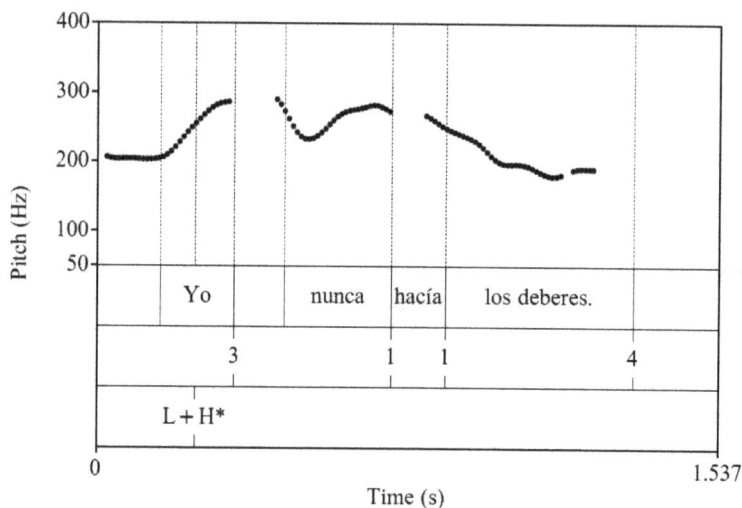

Figure 3: F0 contour of the utterance *Yo nunca hacía los deberes* ('I never did my homework'), with a rising pitch accent on the pronoun *yo*.

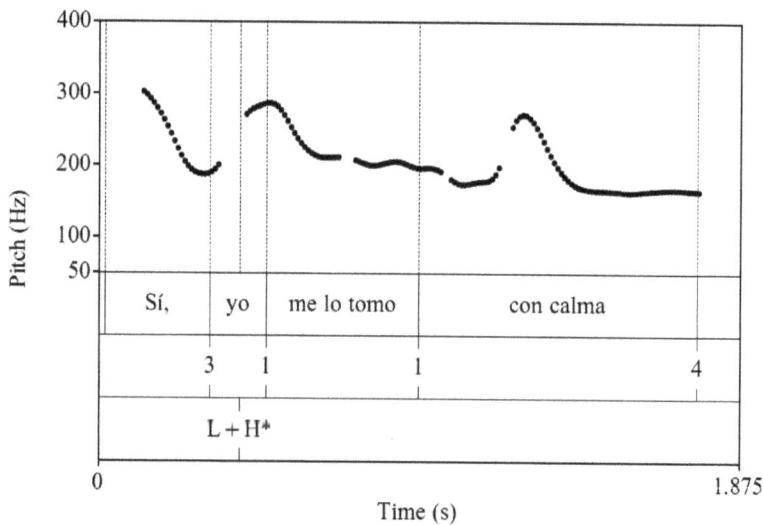

Figure 4: F0 contour of the utterance *Yo me lo tomo con calma* ('I take it easy'), with a rising pitch accent on the pronoun *yo*.

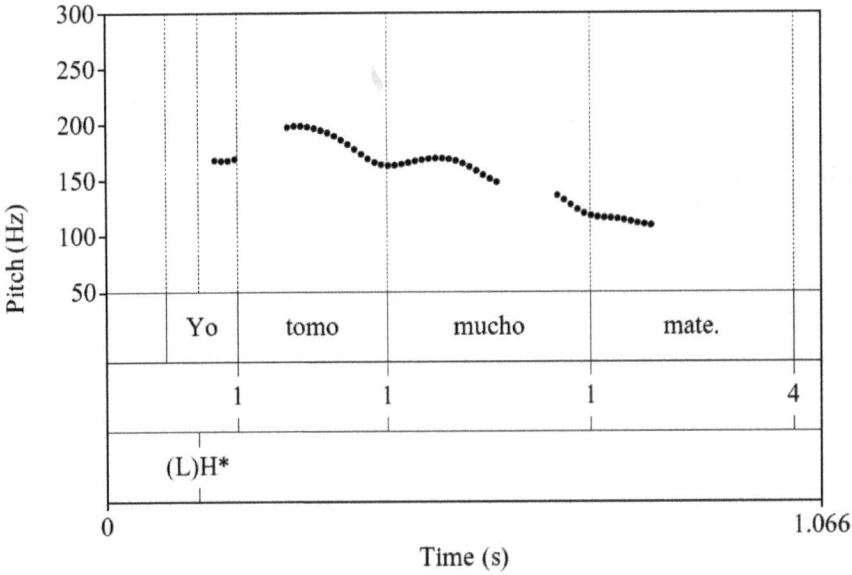

Figure 5: F0 contour of the utterance *Yo tomo mucho mate* ('I drink a lot of mate'), with a high pitch accent on the pronoun *yo*.

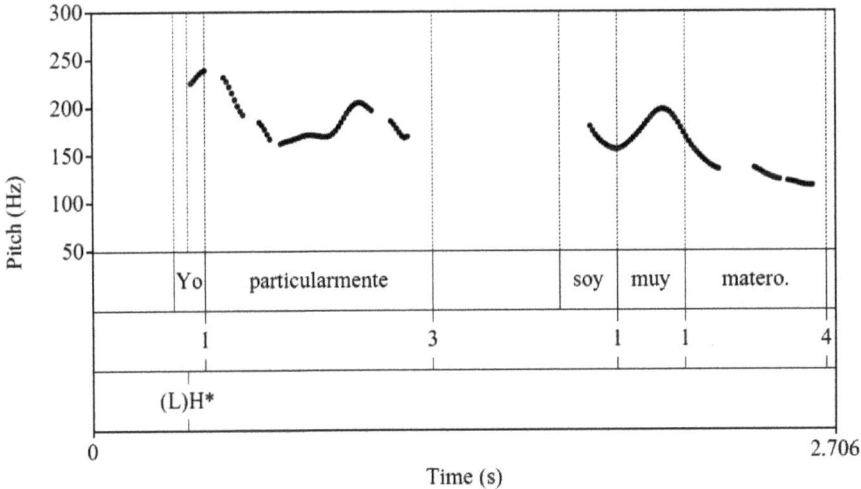

Figure 6: F0 contour of the utterance *Yo particularmente soy muy matero* ('I am particularly fond of mate'), with a very slightly rising pitch accent on the pronoun *yo*.

Besides voiceless segments, monosyllabic pronouns such as *yo* ('I'), *él* ('he'), or *vos* ('you') followed by another stressed syllable (such as ['ʃo.'to.mo]) represented another difficulty in the analysis of the spontaneous data. Such (tonal) clash contexts can trigger a timing reorganization and earlier peak placement of the accents involved, or reduction of the two underlying gestures, resulting in a single one (Prieto et al. 1995). This means that in such contexts the speaker does not implement both pitch accents phonetically or that the low target from the default L+H* is not realized overtly because it lacks phonetic material.

Figure 6 shows another example of the pronoun *yo* produced by the same speaker. In comparison to the previous example, we observe here that the first pitch accent on the monosyllabic pronoun *yo* displays a high pitch movement that is slightly rising (222–241 Hz; 1.4 ST). Again, there is no pitch movement in the voiceless consonant, but the short rising movement is clearly perceived. In music, for example, such a difference corresponds approximately to a difference between the notes A and B in the third octave. Is it a rising (L+H*) or just a high target (H*)? All the intermediate cases found in the data were somewhat tricky, but very similar to the variation one sees, for instance, in vowels, which can be observed by measuring their formants (frequency components). Vowels very often display a large dispersion and variability (which depend on the context, speech rate, etc.), and they may even overlap each other, making it impossible to draw clear boundaries between them. Considering all the difficulties, the present paper will argue that though the tonal event (Figure 5; Figure 6) is a H* from the phonetic perspective, it is an L+H* from the phonological perspective.

4 Results

This section presents results of the analysis of tonal realizations of the expressed subject with different discourse-pragmatic functions (*N*=976). It should be emphasized that the IS functions of overt PS were defined according to the pre-established categories, after the intonational properties of the overt PS were described. This step was necessary especially for identifying "emphatic" (here: focal) subjects. We will see that there are clear intonational differences between focus and topic: whereas preverbal focal PS as well as one third of the right-shifted focal PS in the present data set had a F0 rising-falling contour with its peak located within the accented syllable, the prevailing tonal realization of all types of topics was a rising tone. However, we also observed a high degree of variation regarding the type of pitch accents associated with topics.

The distribution of all overt PS in the corpus was as follows: Aboutness-shift topic (45%) > Familiar topic (31%) > contrastive topic (11%), Focus (8%) > Disambiguating topic (5%). These percentages clearly show that instances of the obligatory expression of PS (F, Tc, Td) were much less common than instances of the variable (i.e. omissible) PS (Ta, Tf).

4.1 Pronominal subjects as focus

Seventy-six subject pronouns expressing focus appeared in postverbal (clause-final) (*N*=43) or preverbal position (*N*=33) (Figure 7).[10] In both of these positions, the PS bear the nuclear accent. As all focal PS must be overtly realized in Spanish, different types of focus were not distinguished. However, the PS as a contrastive focus prevailed; in both preverbal and postverbal position.

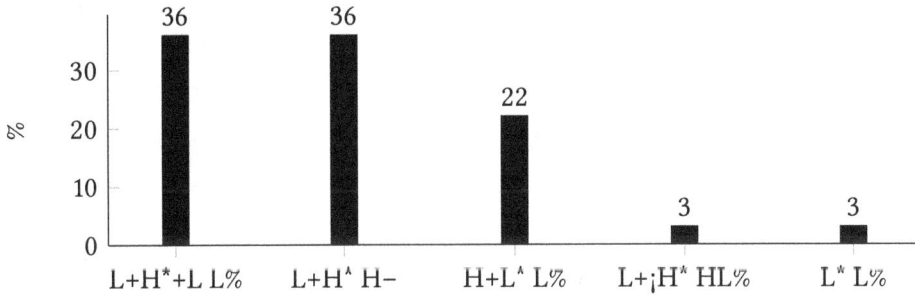

Figure 7: Percentages for different pitch accents of PS as focus (in postverbal position).

Figure 8 offers an example of the pronoun subject *nosotras* ('we-F') in postverbal and clause-final position.[11] The pronoun shows a typical tritonal pitch accent, which displays an arc pattern within the metrically strong syllable *-so-* and is characterized by and perceived as a rising-falling tonal movement.

Focal subjects in the data were realized as a tritonal (L+H*+L), a falling (H+L*), or a low (L*) pitch contour if they appeared at break index 4 (L%). If the subject

---

[10]Seven cases of preverbal focus and four cases of postverbal focus were excluded from the analysis.

[11]The context of this example was as follows:

   (i)   *No terminábamos de entender cuál era la línea, no solamente del colegio, sino la que teníamos que seguir **nosotras**.*
       ('We could not understand what the line was, not only in the school, but also the one WE had to follow.')

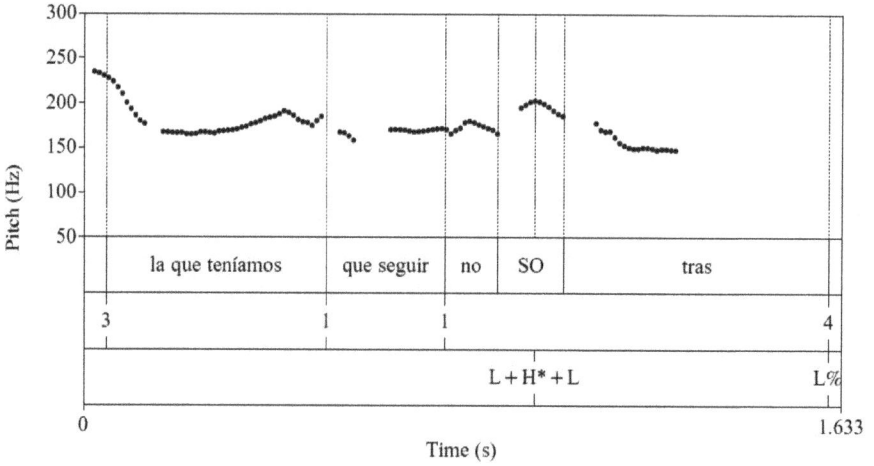

Figure 8: F0 contour of the utterance *la que teníamos que seguir **noso-tras*** ('the one we had to follow') with a postverbal subject as focus (break index 4), realized with an L+H*+L (L%).

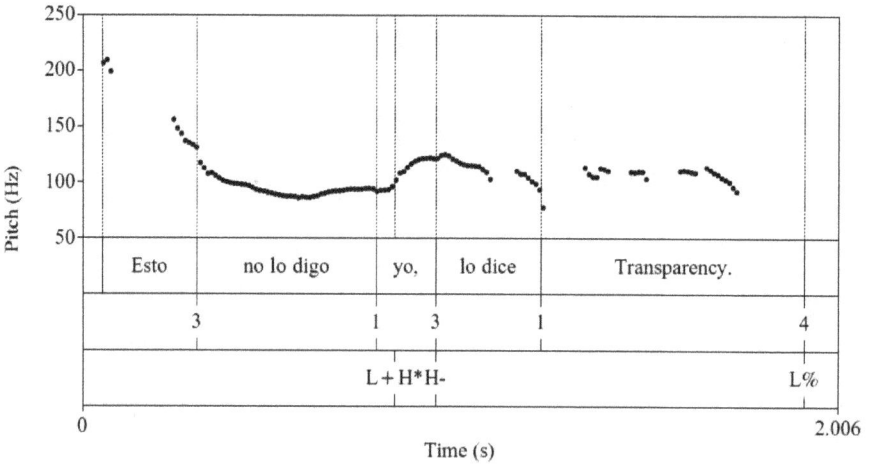

Figure 9: F0 contour of the utterance *Esto no lo digo **yo**, lo dice Trans-parency* ('It's not me who says this, it's Transparency') with a postver-bal subject as focus (BI 3), realized with an L+H* (H–).

appeared at the end of an intermediate phrase (H–), it was realized as an L+H* (Figure 9).

As for the tonal configuration L+¡H* HL%, this pattern appeared in only one instance in the data set, the interrogative sentence *¿Te dijo **ella**?* (in the context *Who told you that?* '*Did SHE tell you that?*'). The boundary tone HL% is typical for yes-no questions in the variety under study (see Gabriel et al. 2010).

Since Spanish exhibits a greater flexibility in word order and the focus is usually shifted to the rightmost position of the sentence, it shows less "flexibility in the placement of the nuclear accent (or main phrasal stress)" (Hualde & Prieto 2015: 358). Nevertheless, the PS is realized with an L+H*+L (Figure 10) in cases of preverbal focus subject placement.[12] Only five such instances of focal preverbal subjects were found in the data.

Besides prosodic or syntactic marking of focus in Spanish, other strategies may be used to express focus, namely cleft constructions (e.g. *Yo soy quien te llamó*, 'It was me who called you') or focusing adverbs associated with the PS such as *también* ('also') or *por lo menos* ('at least'). In these cases, the subject is realized predominantly with a rising L+H* tone, which can but does not have to be separated by a high boundary tone from the rest of the material (H–) (Figure 11; Figure 12).

4.2 Pronominal subjects as Topics

Most overtly realized PS in the data were topics, with the following distribution: Ta (*N*=442), Tf (*N*=304), Tc (*N*=110), Td (*N*=44) (see Figure 13).[13]

All the types of topics clearly preferred the rising tone L+H*, which could occur

---

[12]The context of this example is as follows:

  (ii) *Yo sí vivo en Buenos Aires y actúo en Buenos Aires y juego en Buenos Aires, no puedo hablar como entrerriano no por no estar orgulloso de mi pueblo sino para entrar en sintonía con la gente con la que yo estoy trabajando.*
  ('If I live and act in Buenos Aires and play in Buenos Aires, I cannot speak as a person from Entre Ríos, not because I'm not proud of my home town but rather so that I can get along with the people I am working with.')

  At first glance, the second pronoun *yo* is omissible. However, the speaker wants to highlight the subject and this is made clear in the intonation, since the pitch movement shows a tritonal pattern on *yo* and subsequent postfocal deaccentuation (on *estoy trabajando*). For this reason, the pronoun *yo* is assumed to be a focus.

[13]Sixty-one PS expressing a topic were excluded from analysis due to poor sound quality.

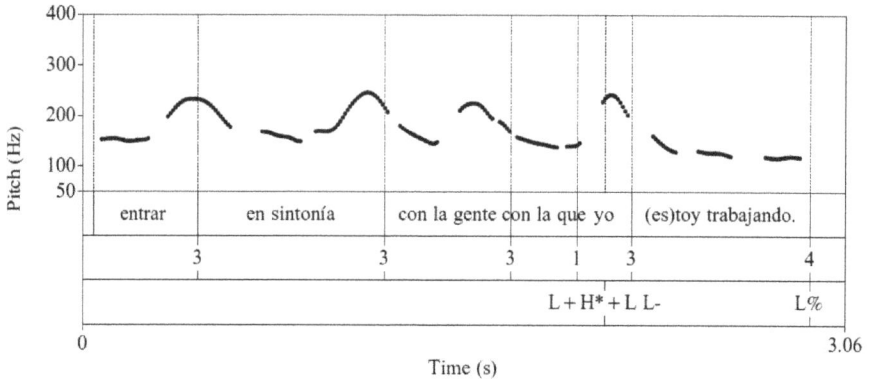

Figure 10: F0 contour of the utterance *para entrar en sintonía con la gente con la que yo estoy trabajando* ('to get along with the people who I am working with') with a preverbal PS as focus, realized with an L+H*+L (L–).

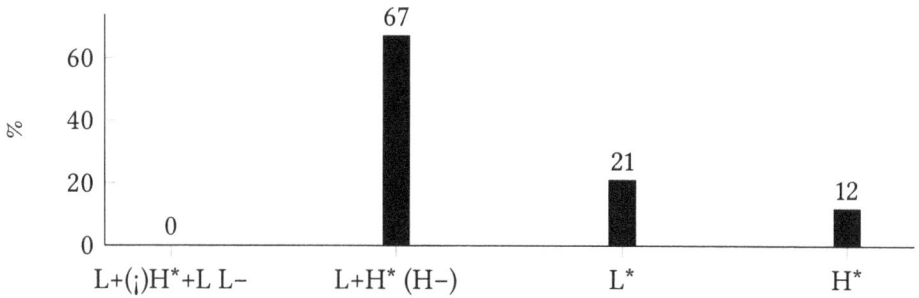

Figure 11: Percentages for different pitch accents of PS as a focus (in preverbal position).

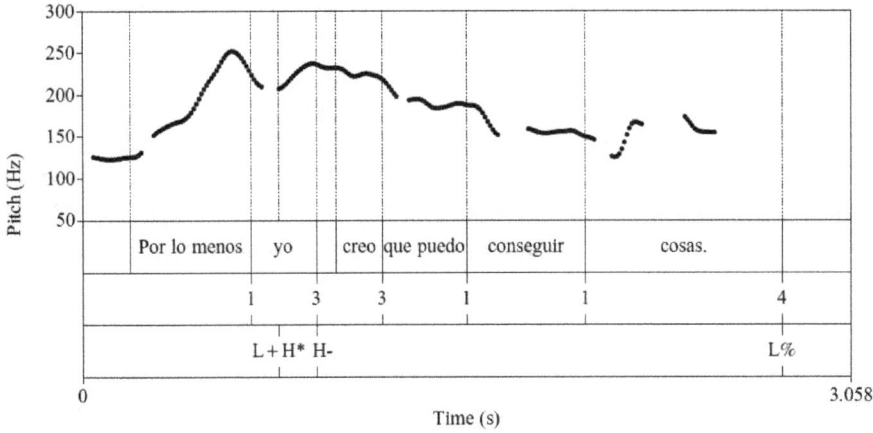

Figure 12: F0 contour of the utterance *Por lo menos **yo** creo que puedo conseguir cosas* ('At least I believe that I can achieve things') with a focusing adverb and a preverbal PS realized with an L+H* (H–).

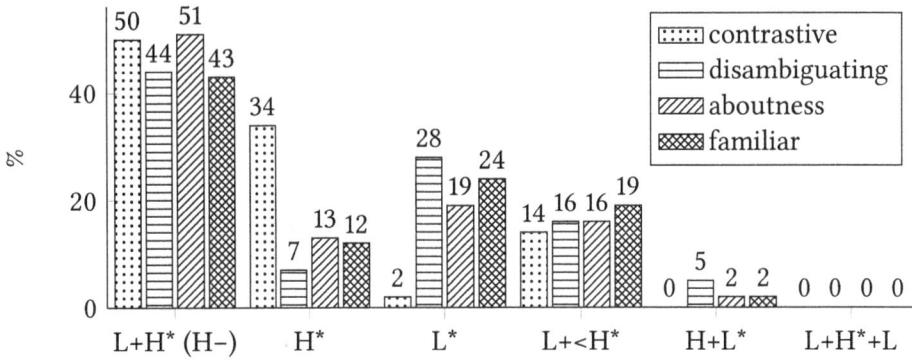

Figure 13: Tonal realizations of different types of topics.

optionally with a high boundary tone (H–) (Figure 14).[14] There were no significant differences between the topic types in terms of this pitch accent ($\chi^2(3)=4.324$,
p=0.229). The findings that Spanish can also sometimes accent (i.e. realize a rising pitch accent on) old information (e.g. familiar topics) and that the words can
lack a pitch accent in a prenuclear position are consistent with some previous
studies (see, e.g., Cruttenden 1993; Face 2003).

We should specify that the boundary tone or pause after a subject-topic is
not obligatory and thus does not represent any cue for distinguishing among
different kinds of topics. It was attested in only 29% of the instances found in
the present data set. However, the monosyllabic pronouns (*yo, vos, él*; 'I, you
(informal), he') exhibited fewer boundary tones (14%) in comparison to "longer"
pronouns (*nosotros, ustedes, ella, ellos*; 'we, you (formal), she, they') (49%).[15]

Another example of a topic with a typically rising pitch accent, associated with
the metrically strong syllable of the PS, is illustrated in Figure 15.

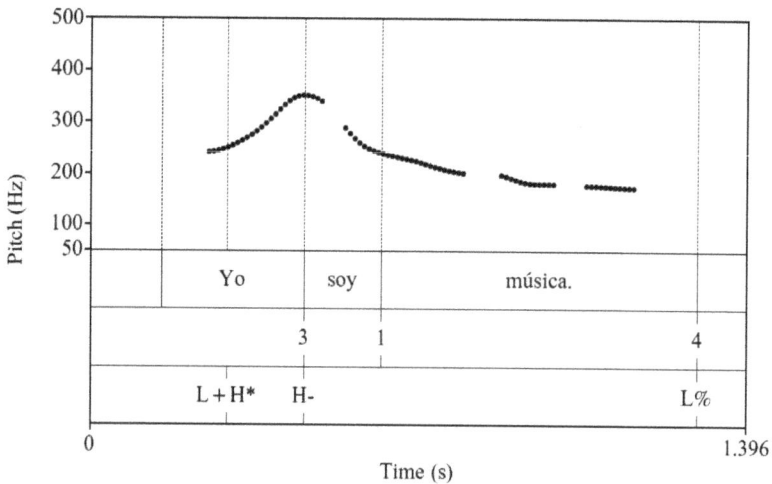

Figure 14: F0 contour of the utterance *Yo soy música* ('I am a musician')
with a preverbal PS as a familiar topic, realized with an L+H* (H–).

[14]In this example, the speaker was answering the simple question *¿Qué hacés?* ('What do you
do?'). Notice that the pronoun *yo* is very long and sharply rising; its function seems to correspond to an introductory discourse marker along the lines of "as for me".

[15]Feldhausen & Patin (2010) found that, similarly to pronominal subjects, left-dislocated objects
are also not always marked with a boundary tone in *Porteño* Spanish. Other varieties of Spanish, however, may show a different picture. For example, Feldhausen (2016) shows that left
dislocations (objects) in Peninsular Spanish require an obligatory boundary, independently of
the length of the dislocated element. For prosodic marking in different Romance varieties see
D'Imperio et al. (2005); Frota et al. (2007); and Feldhausen et al. (2010).

Further tonal realizations of PS as a topic were a high tone (H*), a low tone (L*), or a rising tone with a displaced peak (L+<H*). The falling tone (H+L*) was atypical and occurred only after a high boundary tone (Figure 16).[16]

Moreover, one difference between contrastive topics and other types of topics was observed. Whereas the second predominant pitch accent of contrastive topics was a high tone (Figure 17),[17] disambiguating, aboutness, and familiar topics preferred a low tone (Figure 18).[18] An L* almost never appeared with contrastive topics (2%). These two attested differences were statistically significant (H*: $\chi^2(3)=28.575$, p=0.000 and L*: $\chi^2(3)=16.260$, p<0.001).

Further results indicated that right-dislocated (familiar) topics were always realized as a low tone (L*) and separated by a low boundary tone (L–) from the preceding prosodic unit (Figure 19).

It should be noted that a boundary tone can be crucial for distinguishing focal PS from subject-topics, which are both realized as an L* in the rightmost position. This shows a complex relationship between the tonal events of a whole sentence. While the focus-domain is separated by a high tone (H–), the topic-domain is separated by a low tone (L–) from the preceding prosodic material.

And finally, there was another interesting tendency with regard to the peak position of PS when it was compared with pitch accents associated with other words within one prosodic unit. Pitch in the less accessible IS categories (F, Tc, Ta) reached the maximal point in one prosodic phrase more frequently than in the more accessible IS categories (Tf, Td). For instance, while the focal PS exhibited the highest pitch in 93% of cases, contrastive topic PS in 68%, and aboutness-shift topic PS in 43%, the pitch of PS as a familiar topic did so in only 33% of cases, and disambiguating topic in 37% (Figure 20). The fact that disambiguating topic was prosodically less "prominent" than focal subjects or contrastive topics supports the assumption that it represents a kind of familiar or aboutness-shift topic whose function is simply to undo referential ambiguities in (semantically unpredictable) contexts.

---

[16]In this example, as in other similar cases, we observe no pitch excursion (due to the falling interpolation). The label H+L* serves here a purely practical purpose, i.e., it helps to distinguish and systematize the contours encountered in the data.

[17]The context of this example is as follows:

    (iii)   *Sí, aparte a los extranjeros no les gusta amargo. A mí, yo lo tomo amargo.*
           ('Generally, foreigners do not like it [*mate*] bitter. As for me, *I* drink it bitter.')

[18]Here we can assume that the word *yo* (in a prenuclear position) is simply unaccented. Again, the label L* serves here a largely practical purpose.

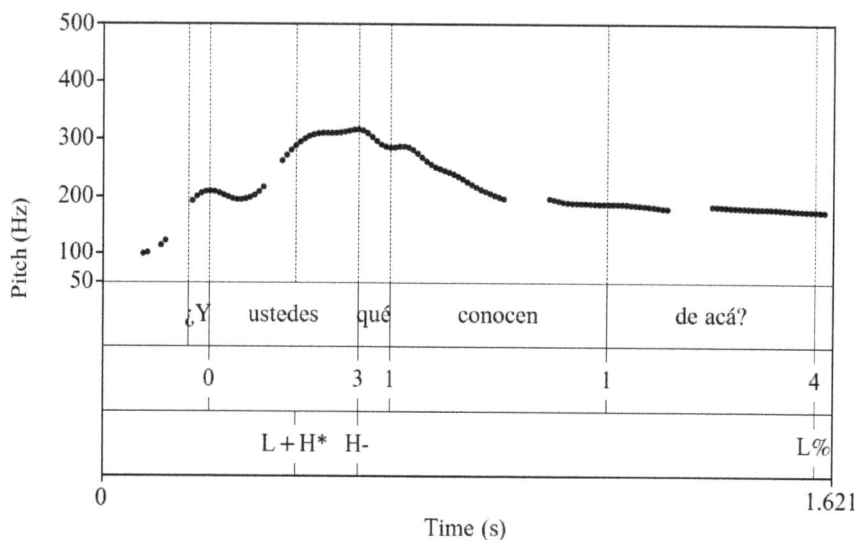

Figure 15: F0 contour of the utterance *¿Y **ustedes** qué conocen de acá?* ('And you, what do you know here?') with a preverbal PS as an aboutness-shift topic, realized with an L+H* (H–).

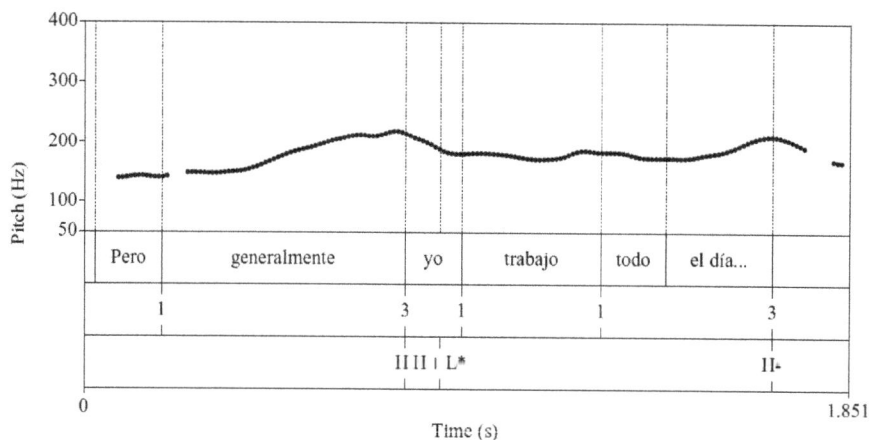

Figure 16: F0 contour of the utterance *Pero generalmente **yo** trabajo todo el día* ('But in general, I work all day long') with a preverbal PS as a familiar topic, realized with a H+L*.

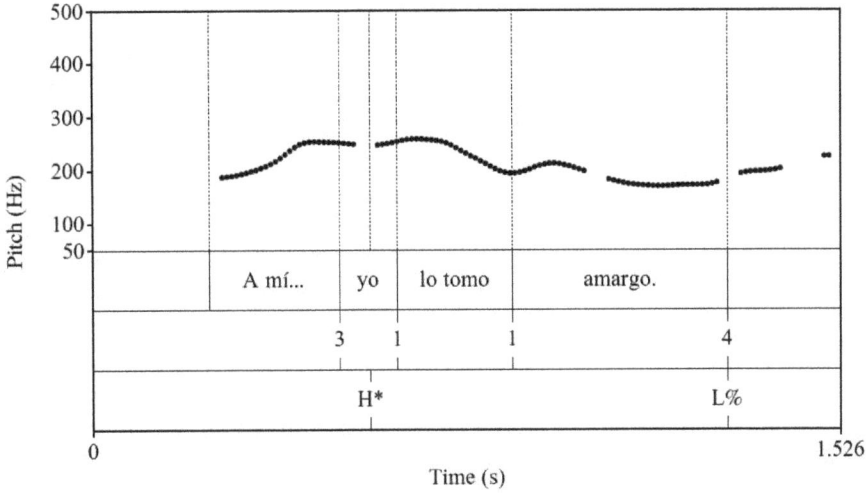

Figure 17: F0 contour of the utterance *Yo lo tomo amargo* ('I drink it bitter') with a preverbal PS as a contrastive topic, realized with a H*.

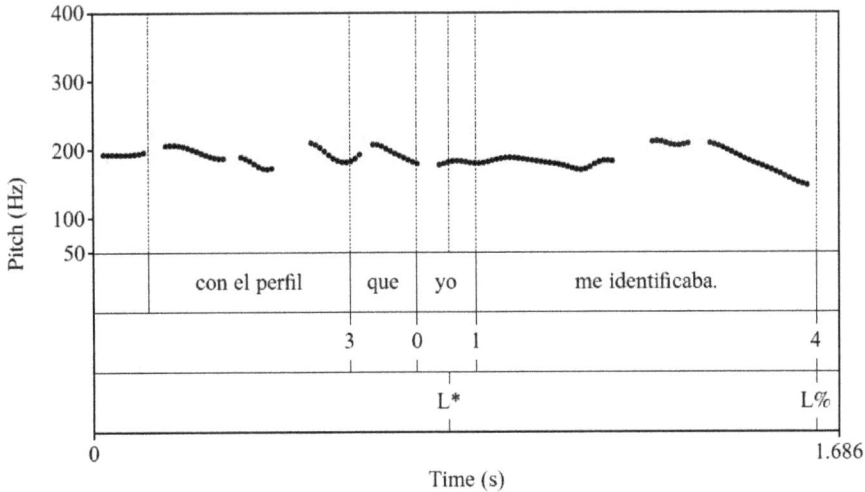

Figure 18: F0 contour of the utterance *con el perfil que yo me identificaba* ('with the profile that I identified with') with a preverbal PS as a disambiguating topic, realized with an L*.

69

Andrea Pešková

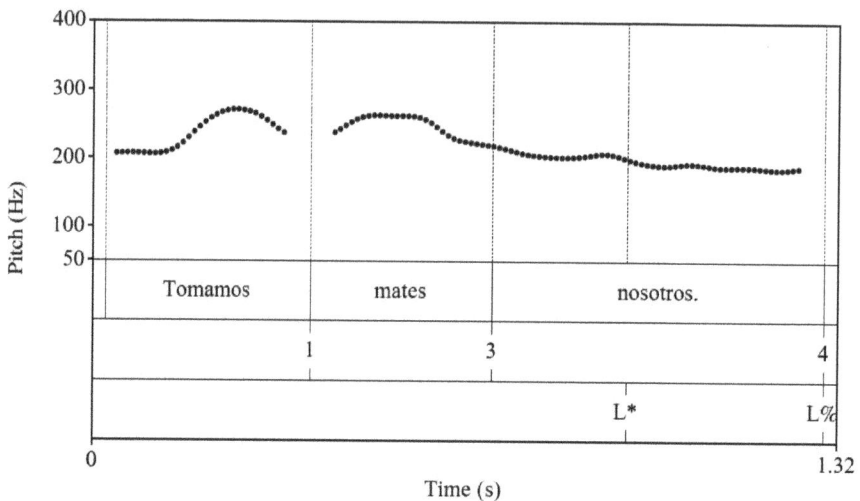

Figure 19: F0 contour of the utterance *Tomamos mates **nosotros*** ('We drink *mates*'; lit. 'Drink *mates* we') with a postverbal PS as a (familiar) topic, realized with an L*.

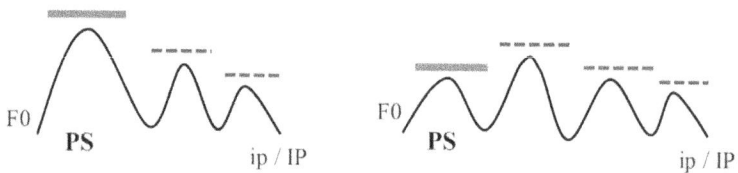

Figure 20: Schematic representation of a prosodic ip/IP unit with a preverbal PS with maximal pitch (left) and non-maximal pitch (right).

At this juncture, it is worth mentioning the study by Rello & Llisterri (2012), who measured different acoustic correlates of pronominal anaphora in ambiguous contexts in Spanish. They proposed that a prosodically prominent element should be more accessible for anaphoric reference than a non-prominent one. They found some important differences regarding the duration of pause (which is longer with more distant antecedents than with closer antecedents), as well as the duration of anaphoric pronouns (which are shorter with more distant antecedents). Additionally, the mean F0 range of the anaphoric pronoun is greater when there is a more distant (less accessible) than a closer (more accessible) antecedent. This patterns with the tendencies observed in the present study as well. Hence, further research is needed that examines not only F0 contours but also

70

other prosodic parameters such as duration, scaling, tonal level and span, and so on. But even with more in-depth phonetic analysis, the question would remain as to what the underlying phonological category is. How can tonal variation be explained and integrated into theories of the grammar of intonation?

As we observed, the present data, not surprisingly, exhibited abundant tonal (inter-speaker as well as intra-speaker) variation, especially in the preverbal non-focal position. I suggest that all the attested tonal realizations of the (preverbal) topics are phonetic realizations of the underlying tone /L+H*/, which represents a typical prenuclear and/or sentence-initial accent in this variety. The tonal variation can have various explanations: the pitch accent [L+<H*] was observed mostly in contexts where the subject was followed by a clitic pronoun; in the case of [H*], the leading tone was often unexpressed in contexts of tonal clashes or with voiceless consonants; and, finally, the [H+L*] was found systematically after a high boundary (H–) (seen in Figure 16). This example shows how phonetic realizations can undergo certain phonological processes such as assimilation, by which the pitch accent acquires certain features from another tonal event: here we see that as the metrically strong syllable occurs directly after a H–, the pitch accent associated with this syllable has a falling pattern affected by the preceding high F0. An abstract (tonal) analysis, taking into account the observed variation in linguistic data, is summarized in (9)[19] and (10)[20] (V = Verb).

(9) PS as a focus

$$
\text{/L+H*+L/} \rightarrow
\begin{array}{ll}
\text{[L+H*+L]} & \text{/ \_\_ L– V (postfocal deaccentuation)} \\
\text{[L+H*+L], [H+L*], [L*]} & \text{/ V\_\_ L\%} \\
\text{[L+H*], [L+¡H*]} & \text{/ V\_\_ H– or HL\%}
\end{array}
$$

(10) PS as a topic

$$
\text{/L+H*/} \rightarrow
\begin{array}{ll}
\text{[L+H*], [L+<H*], [H*], [L*]} & \text{/ \_\_ V} \\
\text{[H+L*], [H*]} & \text{/ H–\_\_ V}
\end{array}
$$

Let us add that the different pitch accents may represent contrastive units in other contexts, but such contrasts can be neutralized, as can be commonly observed in segmental phonology (e.g. the difference between /r/ and /ɾ/ is neutralized in Spanish at the beginning of the word, where only [r] is possible). According to Hualde & Prieto (2016: 13), the occurrence of neutralization is "even

---

[19] Additionally, focal PS realized as L+H*, L*, or H* were found in cleft constructions or with focusing adverbs.

[20] The topics in postverbal position were predominantly realized with L* in declarative sentences.

greater in the intonational component. The proper understanding of neutralization phenomena is helped by the recognition of two levels of analysis in addition
to surface phonetics."

At the end of this section, we will come back to the utterance *Yo tomo mucho
mate* (Figure 5), a case where the speaker has insufficient phonetic material to
implement two pitch accents. We saw that such tonal clashes make an analysis
and generalization quite difficult. One methodological possibility for proving the
association between a tonal category and a given IS-category would be (1) to
change the material (e.g. use the three-syllable paroxytonic noun *Rodrigo* instead
of the monosyllabic pronoun *yo*), (2) to place the new material in the exactly same
context, and (3) to let the same speaker produce the sentence. After effecting
these changes, the contour in Figure 21 is obtained.

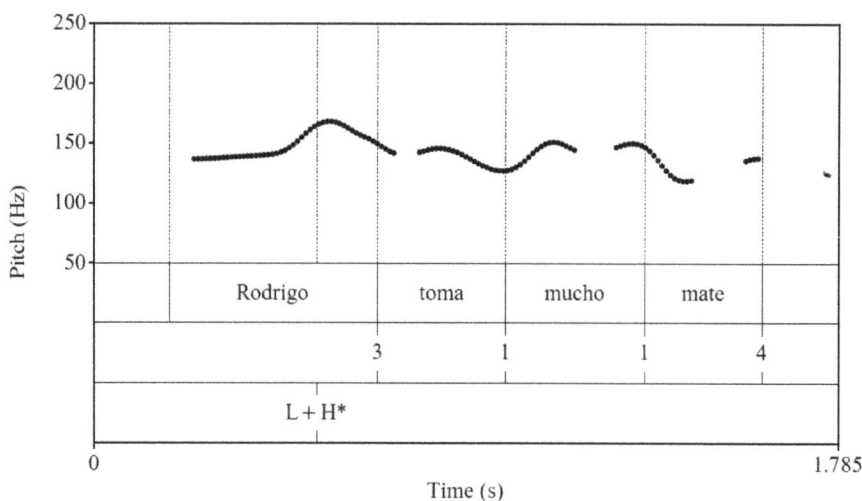

Figure 21: F0 contour of the utterance *Rodrigo toma mucho mate* ('Rodrigo drinks a lot mate'), with an L+H* rising pitch accent.

In this fashion, we could obtain evidence that the same speaker realizes the
topic with a rising F0 movement during the σ^* with the F0 peak located at its
end (thus, L+H*). Nevertheless, this procedure would involve some sort of artificially prompted elicitation, with all that that implies for the authenticity of the
intonational output. Another possibility would be to test by means of different
perception experiments whether the two tonal events (set in appropriate contexts) represent contrast or not (see, e.g., Vanrell 2006; Feldhausen et al. 2011;
Borràs-Comes et al. 2014). Hence, further empirical work is still needed, which

ideally would combine a corpus-based (i.e. quantity-based) approach with different experimental laboratory techniques to achieve a better understanding of the tonal categories in natural discourse.

5 Conclusion

The objective of the present paper was (1) to show how intonational analysis can enhance the study of PS with different IS functions in *Porteño* Spanish (a typically null-subject language), and (2) to discuss the applicability of the ToBI labeling system to the intonation of speech obtained from face-to-face free conversations, a traditional sociolinguistic method for studying spontaneous and informal speech.

The study proved by means of intonational analysis that overt PS are not perforce "emphatic" or "contrastive" categories, as is usually assumed in theoretical studies. Moreover, it was demonstrated that intonation together with syntax (here: word order) is relevant in distinguishing topics from focus (L+H* vs. L+H*+L), while contextual conditions play an important role in determining different types of topics. Both of the intonational patterns (L+H*, L+H*+L) found in spontaneous data fit the patterns that have been encountered in semi-spontaneous data on Argentinean Spanish in previous research. Besides the typical tritonal realization, focus can also have other tonal realizations in cases where it is expressed in cleft constructions or with a focal adverb. As for different kinds of topics, the results showed that the prevailing pitch accent is a rising L+H*, which may have various phonetic realizations, and that there seem to be no strictly consistent (in phonological terms) correlates for such topics in *Porteño* Spanish.

A second question explored in this paper was the suitability of the (Spanish) ToBI labeling system for describing the intonational properties of PS. We have seen and outlined some problems and limitations of the system, regarding especially the treatment of the phonetics-phonology interface in spontaneous data (see, e.g., Breen et al. 2012). Nonetheless, in spite of the difficulties presented (e.g. tonal clashes, voiceless segments, disfluencies, articulation rate etc.), ToBI can be considered an appropriate and useful tool for intonation modeling in spontaneous speech, as it allows the user to systematize tonal characteristics and detect patterns of categories in the data. The apparent limitation of the system may serve only as an opportunity for further innovative reanalysis and perhaps a refining of the labels with greater phonetic detail.

The observed (inter- as well as intra-speaker) variation, not only in the intonational properties of PS seen here but in the use of PS in general, has sometimes been regarded as either problematic or of little concern for some linguistic theories. But it is important to remember that we can still determine certain patterns across speakers despite such variation. This supports the idea "that structured linguistic variation is an intrinsic part of speakers' grammatical knowledge" (Carvalho et al. 2015: xiii).

Of course, the present study has left many issues unaddressed. Besides leaving out more phonetic details, it has not studied emotions, different degrees of expressive force, types of sentences, and other additional factors (such as evidentiality and epistemicity), which might also have an impact on intonational patterns. But I hope that the study has taken—if not an important, at least an interesting—step forward not only in the study of overtly realized PS in Spanish, but also in the study of spontaneous speech in general.

Acknowledgments

I would like to thank Ingo Feldhausen, Jan Fliessbach, and Maria del Mar Vanrell, as well as two anonymous reviewers for their thoughtful observations and very helpful comments. My thanks also go to Uli Reich for his comments on an earlier version of this paper, and Michael Kennedy-Scanlon for checking the English. It goes without saying that all errors remain my own.

References

Aguilar, Lourdes, Carme de-la Mota & Pilar Prieto. 2009. *Sp_ToBI. Training Materials.* http://prosodia.upf.edu/sp_tobi/en/, accessed 2016-4-13.

Benet, Ariadna, Christoph Gabriel, Elena Kireva & Andrea Pešková. 2012. Prosodic transfer from Italian to Spanish: Rhythmic properties of L2 speech and Argentinean Porteño. In Qi-uwu Ma, Hongwei Ding & Daniel Hirst (eds.), *Proceedings of the 6th International Conference on Speech Prosody*, 438–441. Shanghai, China: Tongji University Press.

Biberauer, Theresa, Anders Holmberg, Ian Roberts & Michelle Sheenan. 2010. *Parametric variation: Null subjects in Minimalist theory.* Cambridge: Cambridge University Press.

Boersma, Paul & David Weenink. 2017. *Praat: Doing phonetics by computer [Computer program].* Version 6.0.30. http://www.praat.org/.

Borràs-Comes, Joan, Maria del Mar Vanrell & Pilar Prieto. 2014. The role of pitch range in establishing intonational contrasts. *Journal of the International Phonetic Association* 44(1). 1–20. DOI:10.1017/S0025100313000303

Breen, Mara, Laura C. Dilley, John Kraemer & Edward Gibson. 2012. Inter-transcriber reliability for two systems of prosodic annotation: ToBI (Tones and Break Indices) and RaP (Rhythm and Pitch). *Corpus Linguistics and Linguistic Theory* 8(2). 277–312.

Bruce, Gösta & Paul Touati. 1990. On the analysis of prosody in spontaneous dialogues. *Working Papers (Lund University, Dept. of Linguistics)* 36. 37–55.

Cardinaletti, Anna & Michal Starke. 1999. The typology of structural deficiency: On the three grammatical classes. In Henk van Riemsdijk (ed.), *Clitics in the languages of Europe* (Empirical Approaches to Language Typology, Eurotyp 20-5), 145–233. Berlin: De Gruyter Mouton.

Carvalho, Ana M., Rafael Orozco & Naomi Lapidus Shin. 2015. *Subject pronoun expression in Spanish*. Washington: Georgetown University Press.

Chocano, Gema. 2012. On the fronting of non-contrastive topics in Germanic. In Esther Torrego (ed.), *Of grammar, words, and verses. In honor of Carlos Piera* (Language Faculty and Beyond 8), 143–169. Amsterdam: John Benjamins.

Chomsky, Noam. 1981. *Lectures on Government and Binding*. Dordrecht: Foris.

Chomsky, Noam. 1995. *The Minimalist Program*. Cambridge, MA: MIT Press.

Colantoni, Laura & Jorge Gurlekian. 2004. Convergence and intonation. Historical evidence from Buenos Aires Spanish. *Bilingualism: Language and Cognition* 7. 107–119.

Cruttenden, Alan. 1993. The deaccenting and reaccenting of repeated lexical items. In David House & Paul Touati (eds.), *Proceedings of ESCA workshop on prosody*, 16–19. Lund.

D'Imperio, Mariapaola, Gorka Elordieta, Sónia Frota, Pilar Prieto & Marina Vigário. 2005. Intonational phrasing in Romance: The role of syntactic and prosodic structure. In Sónia Frota, Marina Vigário & Maria J. Freitas (eds.), *Prosodies*, 59–97. De Gruyter.

Dryer, Matthew S. 2013. Expression of pronominal subjects. In Matthew S. Dryer & Martin Haspelmath (eds.), *The World Atlas of Language Structures Online*. Leipzig: Max Planck Institute for Evolutionary Anthropology.

Escudero, David, Lourdes Aguilar, Maria del Mar Vanrell & Pilar Prieto. 2012. Analysis of intertranscriber consistency in the Cat_ToBI prosodic labelling system. *Speech Communication* 54(4). 566–582.

Estebas-Vilaplana, Eva & Pilar Prieto. 2008. La notación prosódica del español: una revisión del Sp_ToBI. *Estudios de fonética experimental* 17. 263–283.

Face, Timothy L. 2001. Focus and early peak alignment in Spanish intonation. *Probus. International Journal of Latin and Romance Linguistics* 13. 223–246.

Face, Timothy L. 2003. Intonation in Spanish declaratives: Differences between lab speech and spontaneous speech. *Catalan Journal of Linguistics* 2. 115–131.

Fehrmann, Dorothee & Uwe Junghanns. 2008. Subjects and scales. In Marc Richards & Andrej L. Malchukov (eds.), *Scales* (Linguistische Arbeitsberichte 86), 189–220. Leipzig: Universität Leipzig.

Feldhausen, Ingo. 2016. Inter-speaker variation, Optimality Theory and the prosody of clitic left-dislocations in Spanish. *Probus. International Journal of Latin and Romance Linguistics* 28(2). 293–333.

Feldhausen, Ingo, Christoph Gabriel & Andrea Pešková. 2010. Prosodic phrasing in Argentinean Spanish: Buenos Aires and Neuquén. In Mark Hasegawa-Johnson et al. (ed.), *Proceedings of the 5th International Conference on Speech Prosody.* Chicago, IL.

Feldhausen, Ingo & Cédric Patin. 2010. *Left-dislocations in Romance and Bantu: Accounting for their phrasing pattern.* Paper presented at the conference Tone and Intonation 4 conference, Stockholm.

Feldhausen, Ingo, Andrea Pešková, Elena Kireva & Christoph Gabriel. 2011. Categorical perception of Porteño nuclear accents. In *Proceedings of the 17th International Congress of Phonetic Sciences*, 17–21. Hong Kong.

Féry, Caroline. 2007. Information structural notions and the fallacy of invariant correlates. In Caroline Féry, Gisbert Fanselow & Manfred Krifka (eds.), *The notions of information structure* (Working Papers of the SFB 632 Interdisciplinary Studies on Information Structure 6), 161–184. Potsdam: Potsdam: Universitäts-Verlag.

Frascarelli, Mara. 2007. Subjects, topics and the interpretation of referential Pro: An interface approach to the linking of (null) pronouns. *Natural Language and Linguistic Theory* 25(4). 691–734.

Frota, Sónia, Mariapaola D'Imperio, Gorka Elordieta, Pilar Prieto & Marina Vigário. 2007. The phonetics and phonology of intonational phrasing in Romance. In Pilar Prieto, Joan Mascaró & Maria-Josep Solé (eds.), *Segmental and prosodic issues in Romance phonology*, 131–153. Amsterdam: John Benjamins.

Frota, Sónia & Pilar Prieto. 2015. Intonation in Romance: Systemic similarities and differences. In Sónia Frota & Pilar Prieto (eds.), *Intonation in Romance*, 392–418. Oxford: Oxford University Press.

Gabriel, Christoph. 2010. On focus, prosody, and word order in Argentinean Spanish. A Minimalist OT Account. *Revista Virtual de Estudos da Linguagem* 4. 183–222.

Gabriel, Christoph, Ingo Feldhausen & Andrea Pešková. 2011. Prosodic phrasing in Porteño Spanish. In Christoph Gabriel & Conxita Lleó (eds.), *Intonational Phrasing in Romance and Germanic: Cross-Linguistic and Bilingual Studies*, 153–182. Amsterdam: John Benjamins.

Gabriel, Christoph, Ingo Feldhausen, Andrea Pešková, Laura Colantoni, Su Ar Lee, Valeria Arana & Leopoldo Labastía. 2010. Argentinian Spanish intonation. In Pilar Prieto & Paolo Roseano (eds.), *Transcription of intonation of the Spanish language*, 285–317. München: Lincom.

Gabriel, Christoph, Andrea Pešková, Leopoldo Labastía & Bettiana Blázquez. 2013. La entonación en el español de Buenos Aires. In Laura Colantoni & Celeste Rodríguez Louro (eds.), *Perspectivas teóricas y experimentales sobre el español de la Argentina*, 99–115. Frankfurt am Main: Vervuert.

Hualde, José Ignacio. 2005. *The Sounds of Spanish*. Cambridge: Cambridge University Press.

Hualde, José Ignacio & Pilar Prieto. 2015. Intonational variation in Spanish. European and American varieties. In Sónia Frota & Pilar Prieto (eds.), *Intonation in Romance*, 350–391. Oxford: Oxford University Press.

Hualde, José Ignacio & Pilar Prieto. 2016. Towards an International Prosodic Alphabet (IPrA). *Laboratory Phonology: Journal of the Association for Laboratory Phonology* 7(1). 1–25.

Kaisse, Ellen M. 2001. The Long Fall: An intonational melody of Argentinean Spanish. In Julia Herschensohn, Enrique Mallén & Karen Zagona (eds.), *Features and interfaces in Romance*, 148–160. Amsterdam: John Benjamins.

Krifka, Manfred. 2007. Basic Notions of Information Structure. In Caroline Féry, Gisbert Fanselow & Manfred Krifka (eds.), *Interdisciplinary Studies on Information Structure: The notions of information structure* (Working Papers of the SFB 632 Interdisciplinary Studies on Information Structure 6), 13–56. Potsdam: Potsdam: Universitäts-Verlag.

Labov, William. 1984. Field methods of the project of linguistic change and variation. In John J. Baugh & Joel Scherzer (eds.), *Language in use: Readings in sociolinguistics*, 51–72. Englewood Cliffs: Prentice Hall.

Le Gac, David. 2014. Topic and focus intonation in Argentinean Porteño. In Nick Campbell, Dafydd Gibbon & Daniel Hirst (eds.), *Proceedings of the 7th International Conference on Speech Prosody*, 819–823. Dublin, Ireland.

Luján, Marta. 1999. Expresión y omisión del pronombre personal. In Ignacio Bosque & Violeta Demonte (eds.), *Gramática descriptiva de la lengua española*, 1275–1315. Madrid: Espasa Calpe.

Niebuhr, Oliver & Alexis Michaud. 2015. Speech data acquisition: The underestimated challenge. *KALIPHO – Kieler Arbeiten zur Linguistik und Phonetik* 3. 1–42.

Otheguy, Ricardo, Ana Celia Zentella & David Livert. 2007. Language contact in Spanish in New York: Toward the formation of a speech community. *Language* 83(4). 770–802.

Pešková, Andrea. 2014. Information structure and the use of pronominal subjects in Spanish. In Dina El Zarka & Steffen Heidinger (eds.), *Methodological issues in the study of information structure*, 43–67. Graz: John Benjamins.

Pešková, Andrea. 2015. *Sujetos pronominales en el español porteño: Implicaciones pragmáticas en la interfaz sintáctico-fonológica*. Vol. 394 (Beihefte zur Zeitschrift für romanische Philologie). Berlin: De Gruyter.

Pešková, Andrea, Ingo Feldhausen, Elena Kireva & Christoph Gabriel. 2012. Diachronic prosody of a contact variety: Analyzing Porteño Spanish spontaneous speech. In Kurt Braunmüller & Christoph Gabriel (eds.), *Multilingual individuals and multilingual societies*, 365–389. Amsterdam: John Benjamins.

Pierrehumbert, Janet B. 1980. *The phonology and phonetics of English intonation*. Bloomington: MIT dissertation.

Posio, Pekka. 2012. *Pronominal subjects in Peninsular Spanish and European Portuguese. Semantics, pragmatics, and formulaic sequences*. Pekka Posio (ed.). Helsinki: University of Helsinki Press.

Prieto, Pilar & Paolo Roseano (eds.). 2010. *Transcription of Intonation of the Spanish language*. Munich: Lincom.

Prieto, Pilar, Jan van Santen & Julia Hirschberg. 1995. Tonal alignment patterns in Spanish. *Journal of Phonetics* 23. 429–451.

Pustka, Elissa. 2015. *Expressivität. Eine kognitive Theorie angewandt auf romanische Quantitätsausdrücke*. Berlin: Erich Schmidt Verlag.

Rello, Luz & Joaquim Llisterri. 2012. Prosodic correlates of pronoun disambiguation in Spanish. *Estudios de Fonética Experimental* 21. 195–214.

Rizzi, Luigi. 1986. Null object in Italian and the theory of pro. *Linguistic Inquiry* 17. 501–557.

Silva-Corvalán, Carmen & Andrés Enrique Arias. 2001. *Sociolingüística y pragmática del español* (Georgetown studies in Spanish linguistics). Washington, DC: Georgetown University Press.

Toledo, Guillermo Andrés. 2000. H en el español de Buenos Aires. *Langues et Linguistique* 26. 107–127.

Uth, Melanie. 2014. Spanish preverbal subjects in contexts of narrow information focus: Non-contrastive focalization or epistemic-evidential marking? *Grazer Linguistische Studien* 81. 87–104.

Vanrell, Maria del Mar. 2006. A scaling contrast in Majorcan Catalan interrogatives. In Rüdiger Hoffmann & Hansjörg Mixdorff (eds.), *Proceedings of the 3rd International Conference on Speech Prosody*, 807–810. Dresden.

Vanrell, Maria del Mar, Ingo Feldhausen & Lluïsa Astruc. 2018. The Discourse Completion Task in Romance prosody research: status quo and outlook. In Ingo Feldhausen, Jan Fliessbach & Maria del Mar Vanrell (eds.), *Methods in prosody: A Romance language perspective* (Studies in Laboratory Phonology), 191–228. Berlin: Language Science Press.

Vanrell, Maria del Mar & Olga Fernández-Soriano. Forthcoming. Language variation at the prosody-syntax interface: Focus in European Spanish. In Marco García García & Melanie Uth (eds.), *Focus Realization and Interpretation in Romance and Beyond* (Studies in language companion series). Amsterdam/Philadelphia: John Benjamins.

Vidal de Battini, Beatriz E. 1964. *El español de la Argentina.* Buenos Aires: Consejo Nacional de Educación.

Zagona, Karen. 2002. *The syntax of Spanish* (Cambridge Syntax Guides). Cambridge: Cambridge University Press.

Part II

Approaches to prosodic analysis

Chapter 3

Multimodal analyses of audio-visual information: Some methods and issues in prosody research

Barbara Gili Fivela

University of Salento

The chapter aims to discuss some methods which have been adopted to perform multimodal analyses of audio-visual speech materials, focusing on linguistic distinctions conveyed by prosody. Attention is paid firstly to the production and, secondly, to the perception of speech prosody in its audio and visual dimensions. As for visual information, the paper discusses both articulatory gestures directly involved in the production of speech (e.g., lip gestures) and information that may be more traditionally considered, and referred to, as speech accompanying gestures (head movements and facial expressions). In any case, the main characteristics of the various methods are described thanks to specific examples found in the scientific literature, focusing mainly on Italian and some other Romance languages. The final goal is to highlight the advantages and disadvantages related to the specific methodological choices, clarifying the key aspects in order to make the reader able to choose among the various methods and offering the relevant references for a deeper understanding.

1 Introduction

In his 1995 work, David Crystal defines prosody as

> a term used in SUPRASEGMENTAL PHONETICS and PHONOLOGY to refer collectively to variations in PITCH, LOUDNESS, TEMPO and RHYTHM (Crystal 1995; capitals in the original).

Barbara Gili Fivela. 2018. Multimodal analyses of audio-visual information: Some methods and issues in prosody research. In Ingo Feldhausen, Jan Fliessbach & Maria del Mar Vanrell (eds.), *Methods in prosody: A Romance language perspective*, 83–122. Berlin: Language Science Press. DOI:10.5281/zenodo.1441339

The term "prosody" is indeed used to refer to the modulation of the aforementioned parameters with reference to units higher than phonemes in the prosodic hierarchy, e.g. syllables and phrases. In this respect, intonation, stress, tone, and, for some linguists, rhythm as well, may be regarded as prosodic features (Beccaria 1994). As the above-mentioned definition highlights, prosody is usually seen as a matter of phonetics and phonology, that is a matter of sounds, related to spoken communication. In this perspective, prosody has often been investigated as if it was unimodal, involving sound only (to give a few examples, see the contributions related both to acoustics and perception of speech since the sixties, e.g., Lehiste 1975; Lehiste & Wang 1977). However, prosody may be clearly expressed by means of the visual channel. In sign language; for instance, prosody does not pertain to the sound domain as it is expressed by facial expressions, head and body movements as well as gesture duration and tension (e.g. Nespor & Sandler 1999; Wilbur 2000; Sandler 2005). In similar cases, therefore, prosody pertains to the visual rather than the audio domain.

Even though the tendency may be to treat prosody as if it was unimodal, some investigations more easily and naturally acknowledge the multimodal character of prosody; the fact that, in spoken communication, it usually relates to both audio and visual information. For instance, Cavé et al. (1996) recorded ten subjects while answering to yes/no questions and found out that a rising-falling eyebrow movement was associated with a fundamental frequency (henceforth, F0) rise in 71% of cases, suggesting a linguistically-driven relation between eyebrow movement and intonation. Other studies have shown that linguistic information is expressed by both visual and audio information. In fact, visual information has been reported to be used to highlight prominent words in an utterance (Krahmer & Swerts 2007; Swerts & Krahmer 2008) or to give positive or negative feedback (Barkhuysen et al. 2005), and visual expressions were found to signal the end of a sentence or a speaker turn (Barkhuysen et al. 2008). Noteworthy, in various of the studies which take into account the multimodal nature of prosody, a debated issue relates to the relevance of visual vs. audio information in conveying prosody. Indeed, according to some works, audio information appears to play a crucial and major role in comparison to visual information (e.g., House 2002; Dijkstra et al. 2006; Dohen & Loevenbruck 2009, Srinivasan & Massaro 2003), while in other works the relevance of audio and visual cues seems to be more balanced, and one cue appears to be somehow related to the other one (e.g. Crespo-Sendra et al. 2013) – for details, see §3.1.

In line with a traditional view of what may be of strict interest to linguistic research, investigating prosody as if it were unimodal may be sufficient enough to shed light on the linguistic message conveyed. Indeed, felicitous communication may be just unimodal in those contexts in which either the audio or the visual signal is the only source of information (e.g., in conversations on the phone or via sign language). In general, the information in one channel is sufficient to interpret the message (e.g., it is fully included in the verbal signal with no clear added value of multimodal analyses). Nevertheless, multimodality is often exploited and it is also very powerful in communication. Actually in some cases, both unimodal and multimodal communication may take place simultaneously, as two different communication channels may be differently used at the same time, with a relevant impact on the message conveyed. For instance, Gili Fivela & Bazzanella (2014: 118–119) discuss an example in which two local contexts[1] are created, with the message (and prosody too) being conveyed in a unimodal way in one context and in a multimodal way in the other, with the result of inducing two completely different interpretations. In particular, the authors show that, in the case of a person who speaks with someone on the phone (someone who has access only to the verbal signal in a non-face-to-face conversation) and has someone else standing in front of him/her (someone who has access to both audio and visual information in a face-to-face conversation), the speaker may actually convey verbally a message to the interlocutor on the phone while, at the same time, denying the content of the message to the person standing in front, by means of visual information available only to him/her. In a similar situation, depending on the source of information available to the interlocutor (audio only, or audio-visual), then, the interpretation of the utterance changes as its "truth value" is modified. In the example given by the authors, a woman is talking on the phone with an interlocutor to whom she wants to express politeness and a positive message, while showing to another interlocutor standing in front of her, by means of mimicry and gestures, that the politeness and the content of the message expressed through the phone is false. Thus, a speaker conveys two completely different meanings, being aware of the different information available in the uni- and in the multimodal communication.

Indeed, in

> the process of understanding we do not only refer to what is said, but we
> also resort to a network of paralinguistic and extralinguistic means, as those
> expressed by changes in prosody (which intervenes with a crucial role [...]),
> gesture, gaze, smiles, laughter, and kinetic devices, such as nodding. These

---

[1]Akman & Bazzanella (2003) propose the existence of both a global and a local context, the former corresponding to an a priori component (including, e.g., the participants' sociolinguistic data, their respective (and mutual) knowledge/beliefs), the latter being constructed during the interaction and concerning linguistic (that is, knowledge of the preceding and following discourse), gestural, and action levels.

verbal and nonverbal means can function in an integrative or opposing way, both in assuming or negating the truth of the propositional content, and in upgrading or mitigating the related illocutionary force (Gili Fivela & Bazzanella 2014: 100).

Therefore, the multimodality of communication (which moreover is often available even in computer mediated communication, e.g., via Skype) cannot be denied. As a matter of fact the integration of both audio and visual information is considered here to be crucial in order to obtain a complete overview of what plays a role in both message production and interpretation. For this reason, in the following sections of this chapter the attention is focused on some methods which have been adopted in the literature on prosody to perform multimodal investigations of speech material and are related to linguistic distinctions.

However, before focusing on the core of the paper, several issues should be clarified. Firstly, when referring to multimodal communication, the intent is, quite straightforwardly, to refer to the integration of verbal and visual communication, that is a communication that takes place thanks to both the verbal signal and what we do to produce it, and the visual signal, that is what we do while producing it, which does not correspond (only) to sounds.[2] In this respect, the speech sounds and their acoustic characteristics (as well as the articulatory gestures to produce them) are clearly considered as part of the verbal channel. However, articulatory gestures necessary to produce at least some sounds, that is those for which external articulators offer information (e.g. bilabials vs. non-bilabials, rounded vowels and consonants produced or affected by lip protrusion), are visible through the visual channel, although they offer information that is tightly related to the production of the verbal signal. Finally, facial expressions, head movements and body gestures in general surely constitute a part of the visual signal that is less directly related to the mechanics of speech production and, in a sense, for this reason represent a specific added value to multimodal communication (adding on to the message interpretation as in the above-mentioned example). This differentiation within the visual information available will be considered in the following sections, where, though, the attention will be restricted to gestures involving the face and head (thus not all body gestures will be considered, e.g., no hand gestures).[3]

---

[2]In principle, this includes the information related to the visual context as a whole, including, but not being limited to, the speaker expressions and gestures.

[3]Given this wide view on what is relevant in the visual channel (from lip gestures needed to articulate speech to head gestures accompanying linguistic meanings), there is not one single definition of gesture that fits the discussion. Rather, the reader is referred to the definition(s) of gesture relevant within the various frameworks referred to in the parts of the paper.

Secondly, a distinction between analyses and information has to be made. Indeed, in this paper the attention is also oriented towards different types of multimodal analyses, those being the methods we use to investigate speech and prosody (e.g., intonation) as conveyed by more than one modality. In this respect "multimodal" simply indicates that more than one channel is taken into account in the analysis. However, multimodal information (differently from analysis) corresponds to the integration of information stemming from different channels or the way the coding/decoding of information is affected as it happens through/ is conveyed by different channels. Consistently, multimodal analyses and multimodal information do not always match, as it is possible to perform, for instance, multimodal analyses of sound and speech gestures that convey either unimodal or multimodal information. As for the former, it brings to mind investigations on prosody and inner articulator gestures, such as that of the tongue, in which the analysis is multimodal (it relates to sound, e.g., intonation, and visual information, e.g., eyebrow movements or even lip gestures), but the information offered to the interlocutor is unimodal as conveyed/included in one channel only (sound); as for the latter, examples are those concerning, say, prosody and facial expressions or prosody and even outer articulatory gestures, in which both the analysis and the information is multimodal (it relates to both audio and visual information).

Given these premises, in the following sections attention is concentrated on methods used for performing multimodal analyses on prosody in speech material conveying multimodal, audio-visual information, and in particular referring to linguistic distinctions. Methods will be described thanks to examples found in literature mainly on Italian and some other Romance languages. The main goal is to highlight and discuss advantages and disadvantages related to the adopted methodologies, clarifying the key aspects to allow the reader to choose from the various methods and suggesting the relevant references for their deeper understanding. The studies described also exemplify research questions which have been addressed by means of the various methods while, at the same time, offering material for discussion on advantages and disadvantages. Such discussion centers on both practical issues and on the impact of methodological choices on theoretical considerations and models that can be referred to. Attention is devoted firstly to the production of speech prosody together with articulatory gestures, head movements and facial expressions (§2) and, secondly, to the interplay of speech prosody and visual cues in perception (§3). Finally, concluding remarks complete the paper (§4).

2 Production

2.1 Introduction

Multimodal analyses of speech prosody may mainly regard the analysis of verbal speech signal including an examination of either articulatory gestures directly involved in the production of the verbal signal or gestures which accompany the production of speech. These, while not being directly physiologically related to the production of speech sounds, are, however, linked to the message conveyed. As for articulatory gestures directly involved in the production of the verbal signal, think of gestures involving the lips, as external articulators, or even tongue movements (in the latter, though, gestures may be part of a multimodal analysis but are not considered as part of a message which is interpreted multimodally). Regarding gestures that accompany the production of speech, consider eyebrow movements, as well as head position, which are not physiologically necessary for speech production, but may be related to it and therefore may offer information to the interlocutor. The way materials are collected and analyzed varies and depends on the type of data investigators want to focus on.

One of the most important choices in studying multimodal communication regards/relates to the way to elicit material to be investigated, exactly as it happens in unimodal investigations. In fact, the elicitation method influences the speech style that will be focused on and, at least to a certain extent, the data that will be collected both in quantitative and qualitative terms.[4] In investigating linguistic prosody in speech production within a multimodal perspective, the choice often regards very controlled speech styles, obtained by eliciting isolated sentences or sentences in context (e.g., short dialogues inducing the intended pragmatic interpretation on the target utterance/word), including target words or pseudowords. In fact, methods to elicit more spontaneous-like speech styles are not significantly considered in the literature on multimodal analyses of multimodal communication, even though the scientific community has been quite recently taking them into account at least for investigating unimodal communication (e.g., recordings of semi-spontaneous speech, such as Map Task (Brown et al. 1983; Anderson et al. 1991), spot-the-difference dialogues (Savy & Cutugno 2009; Pean et al. 1993) or even possibly more spontaneous speech, such as that obtained by means of the Discourse Completion Task (Blum-Kulka et al. 1989, Vanrell et al., this volume) or dialogues (e.g., Geng et al. 2013).

---

[4]To get an idea of the amount of change in prosodic characteristics that depend on the speech style, think, for instance, about results of comparisons of read and spontaneous speech: the latter shows more syllables produced per second and, on average, a wider F0 range (Blaauw 1995) as well as a high number of rising boundaries (Ayers 1994; Blaauw 1995).

In any case, the choice of speech style is heavily influenced by the type of data to be collected, as will be discussed in the following section with particular reference to tracking and imaging data.

2.2 Methods for data collection and analysis: some examples

In works which adopt a multimodal perspective, data collection usually involves the recording of verbal signals simultaneously with tracking or imaging data.

Tracking data are those collected by recording the position in time of specific markers. They are usually collected by means of either optotracking systems, exploiting cameras that record the infrared 3D signal reflected by markers glued on the speaker face (e.g., eyebrows, lips), or systems recording the position in time of electrodes that are placed within an appropriate electromagnetic field. In the latter, recording takes place by means of systems such as magnetometers or electromagnetic articulographs that work thanks to electrodes that may be glued both on the speaker's face and in the speaker's mouth (e.g., eyebrows, lips, tongue). Independently of the system adopted, the procedure consists of gluing markers/electrodes on the articulators to track, using three stable positions (usually behind the ears and either on the nose or, if possible, on the upper incisors) for head position normalization. In all cases, the corpus recorded is usually highly controlled, the number of repetitions recorded for each item and speaker is quite high (e.g., 7 to 10), while the number of subjects is limited (it was even one in earlier studies, but is increasing and now may reach even 10, at least in the case quite recent recording systems are adopted). Various research questions on prosody have been answered by collecting such kind of data.

For instance, Avesani et al. (2007; 2009) investigate the accent-induced articulatory strengthening, focusing on the kinematics of lip movements in the production of syllables which are variably prominent, being unstressed, stressed and nuclearly accented. They collect articulatory data by means of ELITE, an automatic optotracking movement analyzer, which allows 3D kinematic data acquisition and synchronous recording of the acoustic signal. Markers considered for the analysis are those glued on the lower and upper lip, and on both the tip of the nose and the earlobes for head position normalization. Eight repetitions are recorded of nonce-words (CVCV(C)CV, where C = [b, m]; V=[a, i]) produced by two female speakers (of two varieties of Italian). The target words are inserted in declarative sentences in short dialogues to elicit the intended interpretation, so that the penultimate syllable of the nonce-words can be unstressed, stressed or nuclearly accented in a contrastively focused constituent.

To make a slightly different example that relates to intonation, in Stella et al. (2014) articulatory differences in the alignment of the L+H* pitch accent with the lip gestures are investigated, focusing on the syllable [ma] in three different languages, that is Italian, Spanish and Catalan. In such languages, in fact, the L+H* pitch accent conveys different pragmatic functions, as it expresses a narrow-contrastive focus in the latter two languages while it is non-focal in the former; the goal is then to check if there are differences in the phasing of the acoustic rise (L+H*, produced by a rising laryngeal gesture) with the lip gestures to produce [ma]. In this work, an AG500 articulograph is used to track speech gestures (simultaneously with the acoustic signal registration), by gluing 4 sensors on the tongue, 2 on upper and lower lips (see Figure 1), 2 on upper and lower incisors and 2 behind the ears, for head movement normalization. The authors record 8 speakers in total, and ask them to produce 10 repetitions of a corpus composed by pseudowords such as [mi.'ma.mi] and [mi.'ma.mi.ma]. Target words are inserted in dialogues consisting of two question-answer exchanges, built in such a way that the answers including declarative sentences with non-focal or contrastive correction focus in a prenuclear position.

Under imaging data, a set of quite different techniques may be included, ranging from the video recording of speakers (e.g., her/his head, half of her/his body; Ekman & Friesen 1978) to the collection of, say, tongue imaging data during speech production (by means of ultrasound systems; Stone 2005). Of course, investigating what happens inside the mouth, as already mentioned, may be more

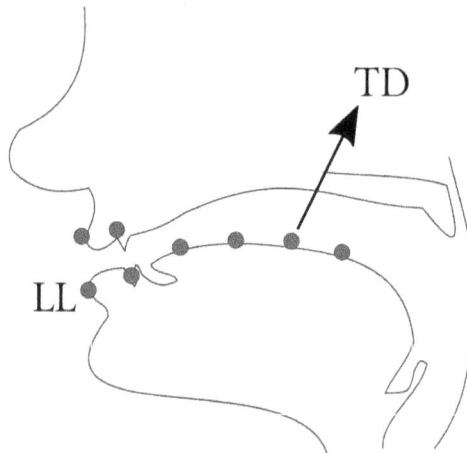

Figure 1: Sensors glued on the articulators; LL and TD stand for Lower Lip and Tongue Dorsum, respectively.

useful for a multimodal analysis of speech production rather than for an analysis of multimodal information in speech communication and, therefore, will not be further discussed in this paper. However, when considering the collection of speech data together with the video of, say, the speaker's head, the method for data collection is quite straightforward and consists of recording audio and video simultaneously, obtaining time aligned audio and video materials. Digital cameras are used for audio-video recordings, with the highest frame rate per second possible. In the case of these methods too, various research questions may be addressed.

For instance, Crespo-Sendra et al. (2013) collect audio-video material in order to investigate (also perceptually) the interaction between intonation and facial gestures in the expression of information-seeking and incredulity yes/no questions in Catalan and Dutch. They perform audio-video recordings of 5 subjects for each language thanks to a digital camera that records (25 frames per second) the upper body and face of subjects. Participants are asked to read (for ten times) "in an expressive fashion" the target sentences inserted in dialogues inducing the two intended interpretations of yes/no questions.

To offer another example, Gili Fivela (2015) also exploits the use of a digital camera to acquire both audio and video signals (the upper body and face – see Figure 2) while 5 subjects read aloud, for at least five times, short discourses aimed to simulate a Discourse Completion Task (Blum-Kulka et al. 1989, Vanrell et al., this volume).[5] In this work, facial expressions and head movements are investigated across sentence modalities, considering statements, wh-questions and exclamations with the aim to check if visual information could be more important for the message interpretation when it represented non-neutral, thus marked, information (e.g., in wh-questions conveying surprise or in exclamations vs. neutral statements).

Let's now turn to discussing methods adopted for analysis. Data analysis, as expected, changes depending on data collection, though, when the goal is to perform multimodal analysis of multimodal information related to prosody, the analysis usually concerns both the verbal and the visual modalities.

Methods used for analysing speech sounds are assessed, due to the long tradition of studies focused on both qualitative and quantitative aspects. In fact,

---

[5]The simulation consisted in having the subjects memorize the target sentence that was proposed within various contexts used to induce the different interpretations. This procedure was needed to create a communication context that was as natural as possible, though the sentence structure and composition could not be left to the speaker's choice. Such high control on the productions was necessary as, at a later stage of investigation, various combinations of audio and video signals had to be matched (see below).

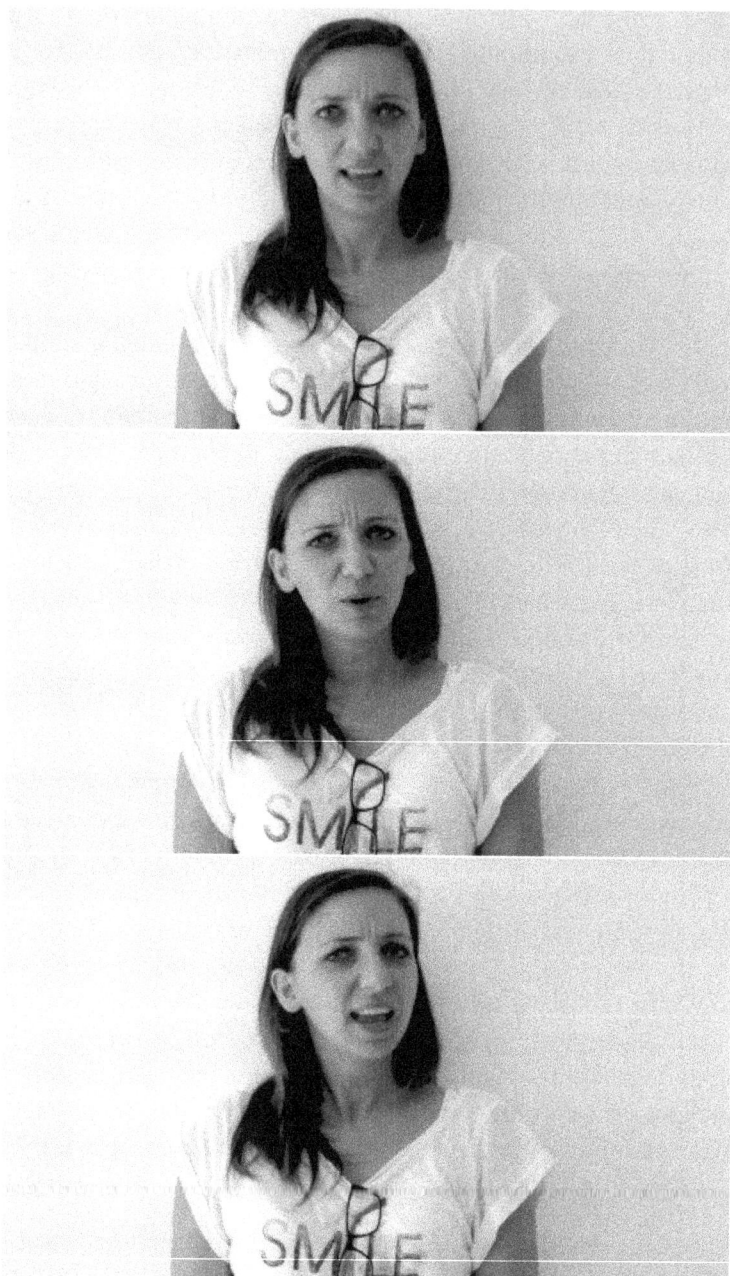

Figure 2: Examples of snapshots taken from the recording of a surprised wh-question (from the corpus used in Gili Fivela 2015); changes in visual information is clearly detectable.

since the 60s, speech prosody has been studied by performing acoustic measurements of various parameters, such as duration, F0, intensity. However, especially when linguistic information is at issue, the analysis usually involves qualitative evaluations too, that stem from examination aiming to highlight the existence of linguistic categories out of the variation of phonetic parameters. In the case of prosody, and particularly in the case of intonation, this is true, for instance, for all the works whose goal is the identification of phonological categories within the Autosegmental-Metrical theory (Pierrehumbert 1980; Ladd 1996; Beckman 1997). Methods adopted for these purposes are not particularly new to the field of Romance linguistics or even general linguistics and therefore will not be discussed in detail here.

As for visual information in the production of clearly linguistic information (e.g., prosodic focus, sentence modality) the situation is more heterogeneous. On the one hand, a relatively long tradition of studies has systematically investigated speech production and the synchronization of acoustic signal and articulatory movements/gestures. These works have focused on speech articulatory gestures as a whole, rather than on visual information, and were inspired for instance by Browman and Goldstein's proposal within the task dynamics (Browman et al. 1984; Browman & Goldstein 1985; for prosody, e.g. Edwards et al. 1991; Beckman et al. 1992 and following works on jaw movements related to prosodic structure Byrd & Saltzman 1998; 2003; see also Gili Fivela 2008 and Avesani et al. 2007, as mentioned above; for intonation, D'Imperio et al. 2007; Prieto et al. 2007; Mücke et al. 2009). Though the focus of such works is not on visual information, lip movement is quite often focused on, which may also be seen as a relevant part of visual information related to speech and speech prosody. The analysis usually regards the vertical or the horizontal movement of markers/electrodes whose position was previously recorded. In some cases, analyses relate to the position of specific electrodes (e.g. the one glued on the lower lip), while in other cases it may already be related to derived measures (e.g., a track corresponding to the lip aperture signal — i.e. to the distance between the positions recorded for the two lips — is directly taken into account). In any case, relevant landmarks are identified in the labelling phase (e.g., onset and offset of gestures on the position track, at the zero-crossings in the corresponding velocity signals; the velocity peak of gestures on the velocity track) and measures are taken of their temporal (ms) and spatial (mm) characteristics. These measures allow then to calculate other, derived, measures, such as gesture duration and displacement or gesture stiffness (as the ratio between peak velocity and displacement). Statistical analysis is then performed on these measures and usually also related to more traditional acoustic measures performed on the very same recordings (as audio was simultaneously recorded).

The usual method adopted in similar investigations may be exemplified by taking into account one of the foundational works concerning prosody. Byrd & Saltzman (1998) analyze kinematic data by three subjects to check, among other things,

> whether multiple levels of prosodic boundaries can be distinguished in the spatio-temporal patterning of articulation (Byrd & Saltzman 1998: 173).

They basically look at the articulatory correlates of final lengthening, a phenomenon which had already been found acoustically by the end of prosodic constituents (Oller 1973; Wightman et al. 1992). In order to achieve their goal, the authors record a CV sequence within which five different prosodic boundaries were realized. By means of a magnetometer system (EMMA, by Perkell et al. 1992), the authors record the horizontal and vertical position of two electrodes glued on the upper lip and the lower lip, and, after the recordings, calculate the Lip Aperture signal as corresponding to the Euclidean distance between the two lips. By means of a software dedicated to signal processing (HADES, Rubin 1995) they automatically mark (at the zero-crossings in the corresponding velocity signals) the onset/offset of the lip closing/opening movement for each of the consonants in the target sequence. On the basis of the movement onset, peak, offset, and movement peak velocity the authors calculate a number of dependent variables, such as the duration of the pre-boundary opening and post-boundary closing movement and of the transboundary interval (that is, the duration of pre-boundary opening and post-boundary closing; Byrd & Saltzman 1998: 179). Articulatory data, together with data concerning the acoustic characteristics of the sequences under investigation allow the authors to show, for instance, that three levels of prosodic boundaries may be statistically distinguished by the temporal and spatial characteristics of lip gestures which are adjacent to the boundaries (e.g., by the lengthening of the pre-boundary opening movements and mainly by the lengthening of post-boundary closing movements).

Along similar lines, though the kinematic data were acquired by means of an optotrack system, Avesani et al. (2007; 2009) analyze data on accent-induced articulatory strengthening, as already mentioned. They label and measure acoustic data by means of Praat (Boersma & Weenink 2017) while articulatory data are analyzed by means of *Interface* (Tisato et al. 2005). To offer more details on the analysis phase, it is worth to recall that, firstly, the authors check each utterance for the realization of pitch accents on the target syllables; secondly, they center their attention on the lip aperture and take spatial (mm) and temporal (ms) measures of the onset, the target and the peak velocity of both the opening and the closing gestures. They then calculate various dependent measures, such as gesture duration, its displacement, peak velocity, time-to-peak velocity (which is the duration of the acceleration phase) and gesture stiffness (as the ratio between peak velocity and displacement). By statistically analyzing acoustic and articulatory data the authors show, among other things, that in the production of one speaker:

> compared to stressed, unstressed syllables show shorter acoustic and articulatory duration, smaller displacement, equal peak velocity, shorter TTP and higher stiffness for both opening and closing gestures (Avesani et al. 2007: 983).

The authors observe that, for the same speaker, a dynamic mechanism of linear rescaling seems to take place when accented syllables rather than stressed syllables were taken into account. However, for the other speaker different dynamics seem to characterize gestures when considering different levels of prominence, that is linear rescaling does not seem to necessarily take place.

Other studies adopt very similar methods to investigate intonation, and in particular the intergestural coordination between laryngeal and supralaryngeal gestures. In fact, tonal alignment may be investigated as a matter of coordination between gestures to produce F0 modulation and gestures to produce segments, syllables or other units, that is as a coupling of tonal and oral gestures (D'Imperio 2002; Ladd 2008; Prieto & Torreira 2007). For instance, the investigation on Italian, Catalan and Spanish by Stella et al. (2014) mentioned above may help in exemplifying the methods exploited in the analysis. To perform their analysis the authors label tonal targets and segmental boundaries by means of a Praat script and label the articulatory data by means of a MatLab graphical user interface-based software for multimodal articulatory data inspection and analysis, MAYDAY (Sigona et al. 2015). The Praat TextGrids, containing segmental and tonal labels, are imported in MAYDAY, where the articulatory data are then semi-automatically labelled, marking the onset, offset and peak velocity of each opening and closing gesture realized to produce the CV target sequence in the target words. Latencies between tonal targets and articulatory landmarks are then computed by means of a MatLab script. The method described so far may be considered to be quite traditional (apart from the choice in the software and scripts to label and measure the articulatory data, which pretty much varies depending on the laboratory and research group). What is worth mentioning as for the methodological choices is that, rather than just analyzing measures by means of statistics to identify significant differences, in this work a MatLab script is also implemented and used to obtain graphical plots of the alignment patterns in order to visually inspect the timing relations between tonal and oral gestures. The graphical plot of the alignment patterns is based on the mean temporal values for the 10 repetitions analyzed for each item (that is for each speaker, each syllable and word stress type). As shown in Figure 3, the alignment plot is formed by 4 tiers (Segments, Tones, Lower Lip and Tongue Dorsum), showing the temporal values of articulatory, segmental and tonal landmarks normalized at the onset of the target word. Visual inspection of the alignment patterns and two-way ANOVA allow the authors to highlight the quite stable alignment of tonal targets with articulatory landmarks.

To conclude, methods used in the analysis of the interplay between gestures for producing speech and acoustic features of speech are quite well known, though there are not many works adopting such methods to deal with prosody in Romance languages.

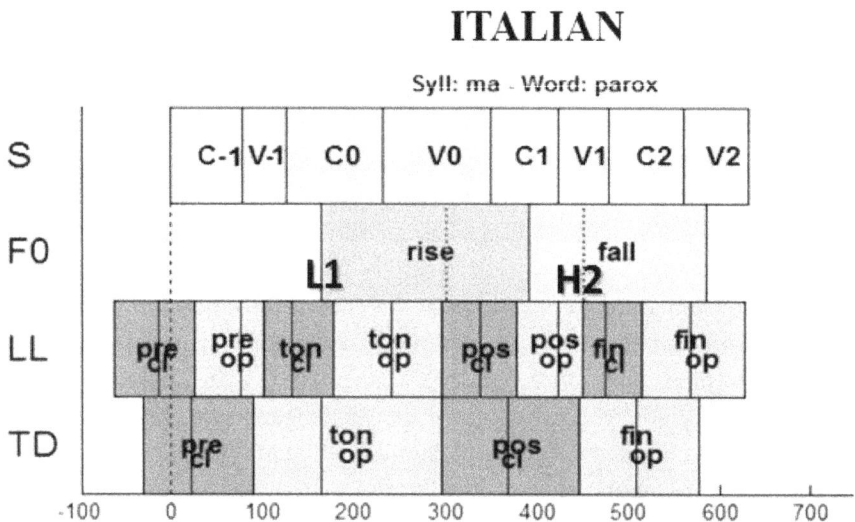

Figure 3: Patterns of alignment of L+H* productions in Italian (see also Stella et al. 2014); the 4 tiers in the alignment plot (from top to bottom, Segments, Tonal events, Lower Lip and Tongue Dorsum) show the temporal values of articulatory, segmental and tonal landmarks normalized at the onset of the target word.

On the other hand, interest in the production of visual information which is not directly related to the articulation of speech units (that is, it is not physiologically related to the production of speech sounds, but rather to the message conveyed) is even more rare in investigations related to the linguistic message. In fact, methods for investigating visual information in communication are assessed, but intensive studies on the role of such information in the coding and decoding of linguistic prosody and message have definitely not been a top priority (see §1).

In the early 80s a system to code facial expressions and head movements was proposed by Ekman (Ekman & Friesen 1978; Ekman et al. 2002) and it is still used nowadays. The system is called the *Facial Action Coding System* (FACS) and it identifies *Action Units* (AUs), corresponding to the activation of one or more muscles producing a change in the facial appearance. AUs are identified by numbers (letters+numbers in some cases) and names (e.g., AU 4 – *Brow Lowerer*): the former are basically arbitrary and their association to names helps in learning the coding system, even though the actual coding by experienced coders refer to numbers rather than names. The coding is basically performed by observing movements of the skin, specific parts of the face (to start with the coder's own face in the learning phase) and the head. Indeed, these movements allow to identify the appropriate AU that took place and to code it appropriately together with a score of its intensity. Indeed, AUs and their combinations can be described also in terms of intensity levels (from A, that is "trace", to E, that corresponds to "maximum"). For instance, the images reported in Figure 4, starting from top to bottom may be labelled as AU4 *Brow Lowerer*, AU4+7 *Brow Lowerer + Lid Tightener* and AU2 - *Outer Brow Raiser*; their intensity level may be labelled as *C- Marked or Pronounced.*

The coding system has been used even quite recently to label visual information related to prosodic information that clearly plays a linguistic role. For instance, in both the previously mentioned works by Crespo-Sendra et al. (2013) and Gili Fivela (2015), after the recording of audio-video material (to be then used in perception experiments) a coding of the main patterns of facial expressions observed during the target utterances (usually on the nuclear accented word) was given. For instance, Crespo-Sendra et al. (2013: 6) report that

> for information-seeking interpretations the most common facial expression consisted of a combination of action units AU1 + 2 (Inner and Outer Brow Raisers) and head movement M59 (Head Down and Head Up). For incredulity question interpretations, the most common pattern was a combination of AU4 (Brow Lowered), M59 + 58 (Head Down and Head Back) and squinting of the eyes. (Crespo-Sendra et al. 2013: 6)

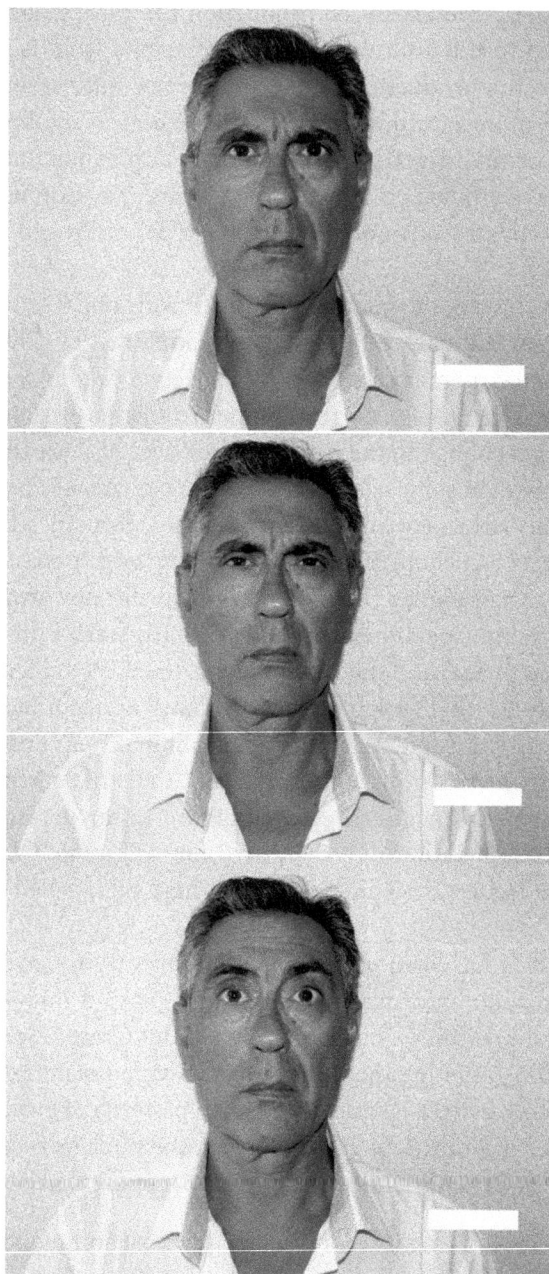

Figure 4: Examples of coding of Action Units involving Brows: AU4 Brow Lowerer (first picture) or AU4+7 Brow Lowerer + Lid Tightener (second picture) and AU2 - Outer Brow Raiser (third picture).

On the contrary, in her work on statements, wh-questions conveying surprise and exclamations, Gili Fivela (2015) analyzes all the recorded audio-video sequences and labels the following main patterns in terms of FACS :

- for statements, AU0 - *Neutral face* and AU M69 – *Head and/or Eyes Look at Other* or M59 - *Head Shake Up and Down*

- for wh-questions (surprise and positive attitude), AU4+7 - *Brow Lowerer + Lid Tightener* or AU2 - *Outer Brow Raiser* and M60 - *Head Shake Side to Side*

- in exclamations (positive attitude), AU2 - *Outer Brow Raiser* or AU4 - *Brow Lowerer* and M59 - *Head Shake Up and Down.*

Results show a clear difference in eyebrow and lid gestures when comparing neutral statements and other sentence modalities, while wh-questions expressing surprise and exclamations (both underlying positive attitude) show eyebrow and lid gestures which are not always easily distinguishable (e.g., eyebrows rising or lowering usually take place in both questions and exclamations produced with a positive attitude, possibly with *Lid tightening* in questions). On the other hand, results show that head movements seem to be similar in statements and exclamations *(with head shaking up or down)*, while wh-questions differ more clearly (because usually accompanied by *head shaking side to side*).

Therefore, the analysis of visual information is performed with reference to a well-known coding system, with the aim of finding a correlation between prosodic sound features and visual prosody in expressing linguistic information. However, take note that the FACS coding system would require more than one coder/ transcriber to analyze the data and, moreover, more than one coder/transcriber which was officially trained in using the FACS coding system (for which inter-transcriber agreement thresholds are known too). To the author's knowledge, this methodological procedure, in particular as for the official training, has not been really followed in works on linguistic prosody, probably due to practical reasons. However, as for the number of transcribers, the situation brings to mind what is required for the coding of intonation patterns within the ToBI system or with the coding of Map-Task dialogues, for which having more than one transcriber would be methodologically correct and for which, not surprisingly, inter-transcriber agreement thresholds have also been proposed in the literature (Silverman et al. 1992; Beckman 1997; Isard & Carletta 1995).

Barbara Gili Fivela

2.3 Advantages and disadvantages of the methods presented

As for the use of optotracking systems, magnetometers or electromagnetic articulographs, the advantages, of course, relate to the chance of observing the articulatory correlates of prosody (e.g., lengthening or strengthening phenomena) together with the timing of other articulatory and acoustic events (e.g. the timing of F0 peaks). This allows investigators to propose and refine models of gestural dynamics related to linguistically relevant prosodic events and, the other way around, to consider linguistically relevant prosodic events as related to gestural dynamics too.

For instance, thanks to the articulatory investigation Byrd & Saltzman (1998) showed that various levels of prosodic boundaries are distinguished by the temporal and spatial characteristics of articulatory gestures adjacent to the boundaries. In such a model, which is further developed in a following paper (Byrd & Saltzman 2003), they propose that this lengthening is related to a specific prosodic gesture that regulates the duration of gestures at prosodic boundaries. Mentioning another work described above, it is the sum of acoustic and articulatory data that allows Avesani et al. (2007) to illustrate that syllable and vowel prominence are somehow directly proportional to the length, the velocity and the displacement of lip closing gestures. Furthermore, these data allow the authors to relate their results to a mass-spring gestural model (Browman & Goldstein 1995; Fowler 1995; Saltzman 1995; Saltzman & Munhall 1989), arguing that, at least for one out of the two speakers considered, results can be accounted for by a single mechanism of linear rescaling. Thanks to both articulatory and acoustic data, Stella et al. (2014) show that in the three languages they considered the investigated acoustic tonal targets have a quite stable alignment with articulatory gestures. Moreover, they argue that results may be related to the *Coupled Oscillator Model* of speech production (Goldstein et al. 2009), and that the rising tonal gesture would be in anti-phase relation with both the consonantal and the vocalic gesture.

Disadvantages relate to the heaviness of data collection, which has an impact on both the number of speakers who are usually recorded and the complexity of data analysis; these aspects, of course, affect the whole experimental design, as they orient the choice of speech style and corpus to be recorded. These first observations especially apply to data collection by means of articulographs, though the number of speakers considered in the studies has been gradually increasing over years. Moreover, the time required on average for the set-up, needed for gluing the sensors onto the subjects, both outside and inside the mouth, and the quite frequent event of a detachment of the glued sensor during data collection, make the whole recording phase time-consuming and challenging for both subjects and experimenter. In this respect, recording by means of diverse systems has various consequences as big differences may regard different versions of the same system (e.g., AG500 is far more instable than the new AG501 – Stella et al. 2012; 2013 – and therefore it is obviously more difficult to record bigger corpora by means of the former than the latter). Whatever the system is, it is obviously true that recording articulatory data is more challenging than acquiring acoustic data only (sometimes even because of the difficulties in recruiting subjects willing to have electrodes glued, say, in their mouth).

Moreover, data collected in articulatory studies usually correspond to very controlled speech material. Though, especially now that more stable machines are available, dialogical speech involving two speakers is collected by means of two systems at the same time (e.g., Geng et al. 2013), in most cases, data acquisition consists in exploiting one system and collecting very controlled, read speech data (e.g., see experiments described in the previous section). In fact, a single coil/articulator trajectory is extremely sensitive to the segmental environment not only in the sense that it may be modified by co-articulation, as expected and as observed for segments in acoustic data. The relevant point here is that it is the single coil/articulator to be investigated (e.g. lower lip, tongue dorsum) and in order to be able to observe its trajectories it is necessary to ensure the presence of significant (detectable) gestures from and to not adjacent segments. In this respect, segmental contexts that would not be problematic in acoustic investigations (where reaching of the set of expected articulatory targets in the sequence may ensure the necessary acoustic information) are in fact very problematic in articulatory investigations. For instance, given a pseudoword such as [mimi], thus including bilabial consonants produced by means of lip and jaw gestures, the tongue dorsum position for [i] will only slightly vary, and the risk is to be unable to unambiguously detect a significant tongue gesture in the [i]-to-[i] cycle; thus, an [a]-to-[i] cycle would be preferable such as in [mami] or [mima]. Of course, these constraints do not have an impact only on investigations of segments. As exemplified in the experiments described in the previous sections, they are relevant in prosodic investigations too, where reference to segments is usually needed and target words are usually chosen in order to satisfy the above-mentioned basic requirements.

Finally, labelling, measurements and data analysis relate to various sensors (e.g., tongue dorsum for vowel articulation and lower lip for bilabial consonant) and axes (e.g. the z-axis for vertical movement and the x-axis for front-back horizontal movement). This means that a specific software is needed for labelling and measurements (e.g., HADES mentioned in relation to Byrd & Saltzman's 1998 paper, *Interface* mentioned in relation to Avesani et al. 2007; 2009 works, or MAYDAY, which was developed at CRIL for dealing with both kinematic data and ultrasound images, Sigona et al. 2015); moreover, it means that the amount of data is not easy to manage, especially when it also has to be related to data on acoustic prosody, e.g. to F0 changes.

Turning to the imaging techniques, they also imply advantages and disadvantages. Gaining a wider view of the interaction between audio and visual information may shed light on relevant factors that affect linguistic meaning and that are usually not taken into account in linguistic investigations. For instance, Gili Fivela (2015) reports a clear difference in eyebrow and lid gestures when comparing neutral statements and the other sentence modalities considered, while underlining a similarity in the head movements observed during statements and exclamations. These observations may actually be of help when considering the phonological coding of intonational events. For instance, wh-questions are quite often found to be phonologically identical to statements (e.g., various contributions in Frota & Prieto 2015, starting from the paper on Italian, i.e. Gili Fivela et al. 2015). Multimodal investigations may show that the adoption of the same intonational pattern in statements and wh-questions could be problematic because of a number of other cues that speakers may use to distinguish statements from questions, among which visual cues could be considered besides, say, lexical and syntactic ones. That is, in the long run, a wider perspective in investigating speech may offer hints on the impact of visual information on the variation observed in speech in general, as for both pattern choice and phonetic implementation.

As for the disadvantages, the use of cameras for acquiring both audio and video may imply a loss in the acoustic signal quality. The choice is then taken to be more appropriate when no accurate and extensive acoustic measurements or manipulations are performed. Another possible disadvantage may relate to criteria for subject selection, as some of the subjects, especially those who may already have troubles in immerging themselves in the given context during audio-recordings, may be even more clumsy if they know that video-recording is going on.

3 Perception

3.1 Introduction

Investigations regarding the integration of audio-visual information in the perception of prosody have been strongly influenced by works on the McGurk effect, that is, on the integration of visual and auditory information which are not always consistent.

In their 1976 work, McGurk & MacDonald asked their subjects to judge stimuli corresponding to the production of syllables [ba], [da], [ga], playing through a talking head both stimuli in which either audio or video was available and stimuli in which both audio and video were available, though they were not always congruent (that is, for instance, both the audio and the visual information corresponded to the production of [ba] or the audio corresponded to [ba] while the video showed the lip movement for [ga]). Of course, attention was paid to the realization of stimuli that seemed as natural as possible, and indeed, as the authors stated,

> Dubbing was carried out so as to ensure, within the temporal constraints of telerecording equipment, that there was auditory-visual coincidence of the release of the consonant in the first syllable of each utterance (McGurk & MacDonald 1976: 746.)

In particular, results of perception of stimuli in which the audio corresponded to [ba] while the lip movement was that corresponding to [ga], showed that listeners reported hearing [da]; moreover, when subjects were presented the audio for [ga] on to the lip movement for [ba], apart from [da], they mainly reported hearing [gabga], [bagba], [baga] or [gaba]. The authors argued that in the [ba]-audio/[ga]-video condition the acoustics for [ba] had features shared with [da] but not with [ga], that the visual information was consistent with both [ga] and [da] and that, therefore, subjects were sensitive to the common information in both modalities.

The influence of visual information on the perception of audio information reported by McGurk & MacDonald represented a milestone in the investigation of multimodal perception, with clear methodological and theoretical impacts. Such impacts are considered in the following sections as for their influence on the investigation of prosody in more recent studies, that basically started from the end of the 90s (see Lansing & McConkie 1999 on the identification of statements vs. questions on the basis of visual cues in the upper facial regions and the observation that the recognition of prosodic information from visual cues alone was more difficult than that of auditory cues).

Before addressing the specific methods adopted in the case of multimodal analyses, it is worth recalling that the focus here is the perception of linguistic information conveyed by prosody: methods to unimodally investigate this issue are quite well-known and are also used for multimodal investigations. For instance, identification and discrimination tests are used in checking for the existence of categorical perception which, on the basis of the perception of segments, and consonants in particular (Liberman et al. 1957; see the contradicting results for vowels by Fry et al. 1962), has been often taken to be a property of phonological (linguistic) units. In particular, specific characteristics are often expected in the identification of linguistically relevant sounds in that, in a traditional categorical perception paradigm such as the one proposed for consonants by Liberman and colleagues in 1957, given a continuum of stimuli, when subjects are asked to identify the linguistic category they belong to, results are expected to be S-shaped, with a sharp switch from the perception of a category to the perception of another one; when subjects are asked to discriminate the same stimuli, that is they are given pairs or triplets of those stimuli and asked to judge whether some of them are equal or not, they are expected to be more sensitive to differences across categories, that is difference between intermediate stimuli in an S-shaped plot.[6] The existence of categorical perception has been investigated with respect to intonation categories too, adopting the same methods and formulating the same hypothesis, but reaching quite contradicting results which are more in line with those obtained for the perception of vowels (e.g., see the contradictory results reported by Vanrell 2006; Schneider et al. 2006 and Niebuhr & Kohler 2004, and the discussion in the latter). A discussion of methods to unimodally investigate prosody and intonation, and for instance to design identification and discrimination tests is out of the scope of the present paper (but see, for instance, Gussenhoven 1999; 2004; Gili Fivela 2008; Prieto 2012) However, it is worth remembering that at least identification tests are often used in investigating multimodal perception too (see the next section) and that a possible distinction drawn among the various methods used to investigate the perception of prosody may be useful to understand the criteria of selection of methods considered here. In particular, as proposed by Gili Fivela (2008), it is possible to distinguish methods for collecting subject's metalinguistic judgements and procedures for directly recording speaker's response and action taking. Among the former, methods are included requiring judgements on perceptual equivalence of stimuli, on successful imita-

---

[6]Of course these expectations are in line with a quantal theory of speech (Stevens 1972; 1989; see also Stevens & Keyser 2010), according to which categories correspond to quantal regions, clearly different from each other and whose members show acoustic and auditory characteristics which are quite stable, despite changes in articulatory settings. However, it is worth recalling that, following works on natural categories and their corresponding semantic categories (Rosch 1975: 193; see also e.g. Berlin & Paul 1969) showing that members of a category do not necessarily share an equal degree of membership, some works on segmental phonological categories (Kuhl 1991) and on intonation categories too (Schneider et al. 2006; 2009; Gili Fivela 2012) addressed issues concerning the presence of prototypes or best examples, assuming the existence of non-homogenous categories - including prototypes - and the possibility to perceive differences in meaning or shades of meaning within a category (Gili Fivela 2012).

tion, asking for prominence judgements, for semantic differences, semantic scaling, goodness rating, matching, as well as in identification and discrimination in categorical perception paradigms; among the latter, methods are included asking for imitating stimuli, collecting eye tracking data, asking to perform games using audio stimuli and, in general, methods including reaction time measurements (for discussion, Gili Fivela 2008).

For space limits, in what follows only some methods relying on subjects' metalinguistic judgements are basically referred to (e.g., investigations on neurophysiological correlates of multimodal perception are not discussed).

3.2 Methods for data collection and analysis: some examples

Data collection usually involves base stimuli including both audio and video, though this information may either be natural (audio and video taken from recording of speaker's production) or synthetic (audio corresponding to synthetic speech and video relating to computer-animated heads, that is talking heads). Synthetic stimuli are necessarily used when continua are investigated and need to be judged by speakers. In these cases, both audio and video continua (typically representing the shift between two categories) may be created and synchronized with each other or one continuum may be created, e.g., the audio one, and synchronized with a sort of neutral condition on the other channel, e.g., regarding visual information. In other cases, audio-video natural recordings are used, and the manipulation usually aims at crossing audio and visual conditions, rather than at realizing continua of changes. In these cases, the audio and video signals in the original recordings are separated via software, offering audio files and video clips that can be used as stimuli in audio-only and video-only tasks and that can also be crossed to obtain incongruent audio-visual stimuli, usually by creating all the possible combinations of audio and video cues.

A check on the relevance of audio and visual information is often carried out in investigations, with audio-only and video-only stimuli included in perception tests. However, in line with the traditional testing of the McGurk effect, the experimental procedure often also includes an explicit check for the audio-visual integration, by means of audio-visual stimuli obtained by matching congruent and non-congruent audio and video information.

In all cases, audio-visual stimuli are created by paying specific attention to the audio-visual information synchronization, to create stimuli that are as natural as possible and that are free of artefacts. Short pre-tests may indeed be used to check for the quality of stimuli. Stimuli are presented to subjects in random order, and usually in different blocks, and subjects are typically asked to perform an identification test and to judge whether stimuli are instances of one or another category. Reaction times in answering are measured in some investigations, and subjects may also be asked to score by means of Likert scales how confident they were when answering or how much they liked the specific item with respect to the category it was judged to belong to. Answers to (not manipulated) original recordings can be taken as control for every single subject or a control task may be included in the design, to check for subject comprehension of the task and stimuli.

For instance, House (2002) investigates intonational cues and visual facial cues to the interrogative and statement mode in Swedish. In a first experiment, he manipulates the acoustic information only, creating two sets of six stimuli in which the focal accent peak is shifted and two F0 ranges for the focal accent are considered. As for the visual information, no head, eye or eyebrow movement is visible in the talking head presented to 11 subjects. On the basis of audio-visual stimuli, created by paying specific attention to the audio-visual synchronization, subjects are asked to judge whether the speaker intended to produce a statement or ask a question, and to mark on a 1-to-5 scale how much confident they are in their choice. However, in a second experiment, involving 27 subjects, the author uses the same audio stimuli, pairing them, in two different sets, with the movement configurations conveying either an interrogative (slow up-down head nod and eyebrow lowering) or a declarative mode (a smile throughout the whole utterance, a short up and down head nod and eye narrowing). The author can then demonstrate that the addition of the facial cues reinforces the information given by declarative intonation and inhibits that by the interrogative intonation: basically, the interrogative face introduces more confusion to the perception of the stimuli and, subjects are less confident than when judging audio with no changing visual information.

Srinivasan & Massaro (2003) analyze the perception of echoic questions and statements in English, presenting subjects with an auditory continuum that was crossed with a visual continuum, using synthetic speech and a talking head. In a first experiment, the authors present subjects with statement/question pairs in order to identify the pair which was best discriminated and used the acoustic and visual parameters of that pair as prototypical in order to synthesize the stimuli to be used for investigating audio-visual integration. They used *Wavesurfer* (Sjolander & Beskow 1999) for investigating the acoustic parameters and a speech software tool called *MarkupGUI* (Wouters et al. 1999) to modify the acoustic (pitch contour, amplitude, duration) and visual (eyebrow, head tilt) parameters. In the second experiment, sixteen subjects evaluate stimuli (4 sentence pairs, auditorily, visually and bimodaly), judging each of the conditions 16 times in two sessions (8 times per session). Finally, in a third experiment, the visual and prosodic cues previously exploited are considered as useful to create synthetic versions of an ideal statement and an ideal question and are then varied independently of one another. This way a five step series is created so that it

> becomes more question-like with changing pitch contour (of the entire sentence), and increasing amplitude and duration (of the final syllable). The visual continuum becomes more question-like with increasing eyebrow raise and head tilt (Srinivasan & Massaro 2003: 9).

Forty-three subjects judged the stimuli (8 repetitions) realized by means of the 'Baldi' synthetic talking head and the Festival synthetic speech. The authors report strong individual differences in the perception of auditory or visual cues and in general a stronger relevance of auditory cues (results were replicated in a follow-up experiment in which either the visual cues were doubled in magnitude or the auditory cues were more ambiguous, narrowing the range of variation in the statement-question continuum)

Turning to Romance languages, more recently, Borràs-Comes et al. (2011) describe two perception experiments in which stimuli, represented by manipulated speech and/or video signal, are used to test the integration of audio and visual information and, in particular, the interaction of intonational and gestural information in the distinction between counter-expectational questions and narrow focus statements; a second goal is to identify the facial gestures conveying the counter-expectation interpretation. To reach the first goal, the authors use an acoustic continuum representing the shift, in Catalan, from a typical narrow focus statement to a typical counter-expectational question (which are both realized with a rising pitch accent followed by a low boundary tone); as for visual information, a continuum of facial gestures is created by means of a 3D animated character, tuning its movements in order to represent different levels of activation of an incredulity expression. In a second experiment, subjects judge stimuli composed by video information only, corresponding to animated sequences in which the same 3D character conveys incredulity in 4 different levels of activation by means of the three main gestures involved, that is brow furrowing, eyelid closure and backward head movement, in all possible combinations. In both experiments stimuli are presented in random order by means of the software E-prime to eighteen Catalan listeners, who judge 5 blocks of stimuli. The subjects have to express their preference as for the interpretation of the utterances and the software also collects their response times apart from the response frequencies. As for the interaction of audio and visual information, results described by Borràs-Comes et al. (2011) show that the impact of intonation decreases as the visual counter-expectation interpretation information is clearer. The relevance of both audio and visual information is shown by reaction time measurements, as intonation has a great impact on them but it also interacts with gestures. However, as the second experiment shows, brow furrowing is crucial in distinguishing counter-expectation questions from narrow focus statements when dependent on facial gesture information, but subjects also rely on the other visual features (that appear to be given a specific degree of importance: brow furrowing > backward head movement > eyelid closure).

In terms of methods adopted to collected perception data, audio-video recordings are also used in the literature, rather than talking heads, together with a manipulation solely aimed at crossing audio and visual conditions rather than at realizing continua of changes.

To propose some examples, Crespo-Sendra et al. (2013), as already mentioned, record audio-visual material in order to create stimuli for a perception experiment. The final aim is to compare the interaction between intonation and facial gestures in the expression of information-seeking and incredulity yes/no questions in Catalan and Dutch. The authors check for the audio-visual integration by means of audio-video stimuli, and for the contribution of both audio and video by means of audio-only and video-only stimuli. The audio and video signals in the original recordings are separated (by means of the software Adobe Premiere), the audio files and the video clips are then used as stimuli in the audio-only and video-only tasks respectively. As for the audio-video task, original recordings are used as congruent stimuli, while non-congruent stimuli are obtained by manipulating the audio-video signals (with the above-mentioned software). Manipulation consists in matching, for each speaker, all the possible combinations of audio and video cues for the various interpretations (e.g., neutral face-incredulous intonation and incredulous face-neutral intonation). Once a pre-test of the material ensures their naturalness and lack of artefacts, the tests can take place (each preceded by a training phase). Crespo-Sendra et al. (2013) ask their subjects to perform the video-only and audio-only test in a different order, and both before the audio-visual task, which is also preceded by a short documentary projection to avoid possible learning effects. In addition, they have a short final control task to confirm that the 10 audio-only and video-only stimuli (by a new speaker) are unambiguously interpreted by participants. All tasks are run by means of E-Prime. Thus, given a stimulus, subjects have to choose between a neutral and an incredulous information seeking question. The authors find that, in both languages, visual cues have a stronger impact than auditory cues to induce correct identification of incredulity in questions. However, languages differ as for the weight given to the cues. Indeed, as audio-video stimuli show, Catalan listeners give more weight to facial cues than Dutch listeners.

As a final example, Gili Fivela (2015), as mentioned in §2.2, investigates facial expressions across sentence modalities, considering wh-questions, statements and exclamations in Italian. Similarly to Crespo-Sendra et al. (2013), the author checks for the audio-visual integration by means of audio-only, video-only and audio-visual stimuli, including both congruent and incongruent stimuli. The procedure followed is very similar, apart from the fact that the separation of audio and video channel is performed by means of a public domain software, Virtual-Dub, a simple break is taken before the audio-visual task and the answers to (not manipulated) original recordings are taken as control for every single subject (no final control task is included in the design). The entire experiment is run by means of the software Presentation and subjects are asked both to choose between three options, which is a statement, a question and an exclamation, and to rate on a 7-point Likert scale the negative-positive attitude of the speaker. The analysis of subject answers in favour of the three given options shows a fairly articulated picture and the lack of a systematic positive influence of video over audio or vice versa. In particular, video information related to neutral statements does not interfere with audio information; on the contrary, video information regarding questions, and, though to a lesser extent, that related to exclamations affect the interpretation of the audio information on neutral statements.

3.3 Advantages and disadvantages of the methods presented

The main advantage of the methods used to investigate the perception of multimodal information is considered here to be, of course, the chance of observing both the audio and the visual correlates of prosody, and the possibility of understanding how they are integrated. Moreover, some methodological choices allow to do so even in the case of artificial continua of variation. All in all, these methods allow to investigate the communication of prosody as the multimodal phenomenon it usually is. However, results reported in the literature so far are quite composite and much work still needs to be done to really understand the issue.

For instance, it was the investigation of audio-visual integration that allowed House (2002) to show that the addition of facial cues reinforced the information offered by declarative intonation only, while it inhibited the information related to interrogative intonation (as the interrogative face introduced confusion to the perception of the stimuli). Along quite similar lines, by investigating both audio and visual information Borràs-Comes et al. (2011) could show that the impact of intonation decreased as the visual (counter-expectation interpretation) information was clearer, while Srinivasan & Massaro (2003) could report a stronger relevance of auditory cues, apart from strong individual differences in the perception of auditory or visual cues.

Additionally, similar investigations can specifically emphasize the relationship between the quantity and quality of information in audio (in terms of phonetic and phonological information available) and in video and their role in audio-visual integration. For instance, Crespo-Sendra et al. (2013) found that, in both Catalan and Dutch, visual cues have a stronger impact than auditory cues to induce correct identification of incredulity in questions, though Catalan listeners give more importance to visual cues than Dutch listeners, probably because of the more subtle distinction due to acoustic information in Catalan (pitch range difference) with respect to the information available in Dutch (where a different sequence of tonal events, that is a different set of phonological categories, characterize the contours of the utterances under investigation). Nevertheless, as Gili Fivela (2015) argues, the picture on the audio-visual integration of information is quite articulated, and this may explain the lack of consistent results on a systematic positive influence of video over audio or vice versa. In particular, results on Italian show that visual information on surprised questions and exclamations affect the interpretation of audio information on neutral statements, but not the other way around, independently of the information available on the audio channel (i.e. on the phonological pattern which was implemented). Thus, marked facial expressions and head movements (in her work associated to questions and exclamations) seem to affect the interpretation of utterances which are not associated to marked information on the same channel (in her work, neutral statements), rather than to affect information which is ambiguous in the other channel, that is sound.

Not surprisingly, then, these investigations possibly support different theories of speech perception, such as the single channel model (SCM), the weighted averaging model (WTAV) and the fuzzy logical model of perception (FLMP) (for a discussion, see Massaro 1989; Massaro & Cohen 1993; Srinivasan & Massaro 2003).[7] A discussion of the models is out of the scope of the present paper. How-

---

[7]Briefly, according to the SCM only one of the auditory and visual channels of information is functional on any given bimodal input, that is, SCM is a non-integration model according to which a single channel of information can be processed at any one time. However, according

ever, it is worth mentioning here that Srinivasan & Massaro (2003: 20) found that the FLMP was not significantly better than the WTAV/SCM models, while Borràs-Comes et al. (2011) do not assume a clear position as for the model (WTAV or FLMP) that is better supported by their data, though they suggest that their results could be consistent with FLMP (especially for the relevance of both audio and visual information shown by reaction time results). Along similar lines, Crespo-Sendra et al. (2013) argue that their results agree with the FLMP, as an ambiguous or weaker cue in one modality seems to enhance the role of the other modality. However, Gili Fivela (2015) observes that her results seem to support the idea that it is not only the relation of information available in the channels that plays a role (e.g. the visual information and the phonological pattern implemented and conveyed by means of the audio channel), but also the balancing of information within the same channel. Indeed, the visual information in questions (and partly in exclamations) affects the audio interpretation of statements, but not the other way around (visual in statements does not equally affect audio in questions). Thus, investigating the perception of multimodal prosodic information is still needed to really answer the question concerning the role of audio and visual information and the way they are integrated. Luckily, this can be done also by resorting to quite a high number of subjects for each perception experiment, which makes results more solid and generalizable.

As for disadvantages related to the methods described here, it is important to underline that they correspond to difficulties rather than to real disadvantages. As a matter of fact, one main difficulty is detected in data collection, mainly because of the need to ensure naturalness in the stimuli used for perception experiments. This aspect brings us back to difficulties in collecting the speech material to be used to create stimuli, that is in eliciting as spontaneous and as natural sounding speech as possible (see §2.3). However, the naturalness of stimuli to be used in perception experiments also strongly depends on the manipulation procedures applied to cross the audio and visual information. In this respect, the details given by McGurk & MacDonald (1976: 746)[8], already put the issue in the correct light, emphasizing the importance of the temporal alignment of auditory and visual information. Even if the concern is not directly the segmental information, as in the original McGurk & MacDonald investigation, this is an important matter any time a manipulation is necessary to match information conveyed by

---

to the other two models, different sources of information may be processed. According to the WTAV, they "are averaged according to the weight assigned to each modality" (Srinivasan & Massaro 2003: 10), while according to the FLMP the influence of one modality is going to be greater when the other is weaker and more ambiguous.

[8] See citation reported above.

different channels, for instance, any time incongruous stimuli are created. In fact, the naturalness of stimuli represents one of the most important factors to warrant the reliability of collected perceptual data. It may be important to keep the issue in mind even before the creation of incongruous stimuli, that is when the originals are segmented. Indeed, as Gili Fivela (2015: 211) observes, generating files of very similar duration (and, in particular, audio-video composed by the same number of frames) and in which the utterance starts after a given time-interval from the starting point of the file may be of great help in facilitating the best match when modifying the pairing of the two channels in order to generate the various audio-video combinations. Of course, the utterance duration itself within the file may be another issue as, even warranting the same starting point in the production of speech and visual information, a problem may relate to the matching of the utterance length and this may require some extra manipulation. Moreover, particularly when considering visual information and prosody or, more specifically, intonation, explicit attention has to be devoted to the alignment of visual and audio information when pitch accents are realized, as the peaking of visual information aligned with pitch accents is reported in the literature (e.g., Cassell et al. 1994; Loehr 2004; Swerts & Krahmer 2008). So the manipulation phase is very delicate and a final check on the naturalness of stimuli is needed to warrant the results of perception data collection.

4 Conclusions

The paper offers an overview of the methods used in the literature on prosody and intonation to perform multimodal analyses of audio-visual material conveying linguistic information in speech. Importantly, as for visual information, the paper discusses both articulatory gestures directly involved in the production of speech (e.g., lip gestures) and information that may be more traditionally considered and referred to as speech accompanying gestures (focusing on head movements and visual expressions).

Methods adopted to investigate speech production and perception are considered, by mainly describing experimental designs of works focusing mainly on Italian and some other Romance languages. The quite detailed description of methods offered in sections 2.2 and 3.2 aims at emphasizing the key aspects allowing the reader to choose among the various methods and aims at offering the relevant references for their deeper understanding. Additionally, it represents a necessary, preliminary step to discuss advantages and disadvantages related to the different methodological choices, both by highlighting very practical issues or drawbacks related to them and by stressing their impact in terms of theoretical issues and models they are used to refer to.

In very general terms, visual information as a whole may be taken to belong to the extralinguistic context the speakers resort to in order to understand messages and optimize them in production. However, some specific visual information clearly participates in conveying strictly linguistic information, such as sentence modality (see §2.2). The relevance of such visual cues with respect to the audio ones is still to be understood (e.g., see §3.3). However, the importance of resorting to both audio and visual cues is quite clear when thinking of most communication going on in everyday life. Moreover, it is clear also in specific situations. For instance, it is possible to create different local contexts in which the "truth value" of an utterance changes, by exploiting the flow of information in the channels or modalities available to the speakers (that is audio-only or audio-video, as discussed by Gili Fivela & Bazzanella 2014 and recalled at the beginning of the paper – see §1).

The examples discussed and the possible specific suggestions given in the paper are in line with the idea that multimodal analyses of multimodal, audio-visual information may be useful in order not only to understand the relation between the various sources of information we usually exploit in communication per se, but also to shed a possible new light on the variability otherwise observed in acoustic and articulatory investigation of speech material. The visual information may indeed represent an extra factor to be considered, besides those usually focused on in linguistic investigations, such as the lexical and syntactic make-up of utterances. Indeed, it may shed light on the variation observed in speech as for both pattern choice and phonetic implementation. Along this line of reasoning, it is plausible that the relevance of visual information could also play a role in relation to the differences observed in the perception of members of the same categories. In this respect, the existence of prototypes and non-prototypes, also mentioned in relation to the perception of intonation categories (e.g., Schneider & Möbius 2005; Schneider et al. 2006; 2009; Gili Fivela 2012; see Footnote 2 in §3.1), could also turn out to be relevant to the issue. Indeed, a non-prototypical member of a category, judged because of its acoustic characteristics, may actually be judged differently once that visual information is also considered. This would be in line with the possibility to resort to intra-category variability to express shades of meanings by means of the modulation of acoustic and, possibly, visual information too.

Barbara Gili Fivela

References

Akman, Varol & Carla Bazzanella. 2003. The complexity of context. *Journal of Pragmatics* 35(3). 321–329.

Anderson, Anne H., Miles Bader, Ellen Gurman Bard, Elizabeth Boyle, Gwyneth M. Doherty, Simon Garrod, Stephen Isard, Jacqueline Kowtko, Jan McAllister, Jim Miller, Catherine Sotillo, Henry S. Thompson & Regina Weinert. 1991. The HCRC Map Task Corpus. *Language and Speech* 34. 351–366.

Avesani, Cinzia, Mario Vayra & Claudio Zmarich. 2007. On the articulatory bases of prominence in Italian. In *Proceedings of ICPhS*, 981–984. Saarbrücken, Germany.

Avesani, Cinzia, Mario Vayra & Claudio Zmarich. 2009. Coordinazione vocale-consonante e prominenza accentuale in italiano. La sfida della Articulatory Phonology. In G. Ferrari, R. Benatti & M. Mosca (eds.), *Linguistica e modelli tecnologici di ricerca* (Pubblicazioni della Società di Linguistica Italiana), 353–386. Roma: Bulzoni.

Ayers, Gayle. 1994. Discourse functions of pitch range in spontaneous and read speech. *OSU Working Papers in Linguistics* (44). 1–49.

Barkhuysen, Pashiera, Emiel Krahmer & Marc Swerts. 2005. Problem detection in human-machine interactions based on facial expressions of users. *Speech Communication* 45. 343–359.

Barkhuysen, Pashiera, Emiel Krahmer & Marc Swerts. 2008. The interplay between the auditory and visual modality for end-of-utterance detection. *Journal of the Acoustical Society of America* 123(1). 354–65.

Beccaria, Gian Luigi. 1994. *Dizionario di linguistica e di filologia, metrica, retorica.* Torino: Einaudi.

Beckman, Mary E. 1997. A Typology of Spontaneous Speech. In Yoshinori Sagisaka, Nick Campbell & Norio Higuchi (eds.), *Computing Prosody. Computational Models for Processing Spontaneous Speech*, 7–26. New York: Springer.

Beckman, Mary E., Jan Edwards & Janet Fletcher. 1992. Prosodic structure and tempo in a sonority model of articulatory dynamics. In G.J. Docherty & D.R. Ladd (eds.), *Papers in Laboratory Phonology II: Gesture, Segment, Prosody*, 68–86. Cambridge: Cambridge University Press.

Berlin, Brent & Kay Paul. 1969. *Basic Color Terms: Their Universality and Evolution.* Berkeley: University of California Press.

Blaauw, Eleonora. 1995. *On the perceptual classification of spontaneous and read speech.* Utrecht, Netherlands: OTS (Institute for Language & Speech) dissertation.

Blum-Kulka, Shoshana, Juliane House & Gabriele Kasper. 1989. Investigating crosscultural pragmatics: An introductory overview. In Shoshana Blum-Kulka, Juliane House & Gabriele Kasper (eds.), *Cross-cultural Pragmatics. Requests and Apologies*, 1–34. Norwood (NJ): Ablex.

Boersma, Paul & David Weenink. 2017. *Praat: Doing phonetics by computer [Computer program]*. Version 6.0.30. http://www.praat.org/.

Borràs-Comes, Joan, Cecilia Pugliesi & Pilar Prieto. 2011. Audiovisual competition in the perception of counter-expectational questions. In Giampiero Salvi, Jonas Beskow, Olov Engwall & Samer Al Moubayed (eds.), *Proceedings of the 11th International Conference on Auditory-Visual Speech Processing*, 43–46. Stockholm: Volterra.

Browman, Catherine & Louis Goldstein. 1985. Dynamic modeling of phonetic structure. In V. Fromkin (ed.), *Phonetic Linguistics*, 35–53. New York: Academic Press.

Browman, Catherine & Louis Goldstein. 1995. Dynamics and Articulatory Phonology. In R. Port & T. Van Gelder (eds.), *Mind in Motion: Explorations in the Dynamics of Cognition*, 175–193. Cambridge, MA: The MIT Press.

Browman, Catherine, Louis Goldstein, J. A. Scott Kelso, Philip Rubin & Elliot Saltzman. 1984. Articulatory synthesis from underlying dynamics. *Journal of the Acoustical Society of America* 75. 22.

Brown, Gillian, Anne Anderson, George Yule & Richard Shillcock. 1983. *Teaching talk*. Cambridge: Cambridge University Press.

Byrd, Dany & Elliot Saltzman. 1998. Intragestural dynamics of multiple phrasal boundaries. *Journal of Phonetics* 26. 173–199.

Byrd, Dany & Elliot Saltzman. 2003. The elastic phrase: Modeling the dynamics of boundary-adjacent lengthening. *Journal of Phonetics* 31. 149–180.

Cassell, Justine, Catherine Pelachaud, Norm Badler, Mark Steedman, Brett Achorn, Tripp Becket, Brett Douville, Scott Prevost & Matthew Stone. 1994. Modeling the interaction between speech and gesture. In *Proceedings of the 16th Annual Conference of the Cognitive Science Society*.

Cavé, Christian, Isabelle Guaïtella, Roxane Bertrand, Serge Santi, Françoise Harlay & Robert Espesser. 1996. About the relationship between eyebrow movements and F0 variations. In *Proceeding of Fourth International Conference on Spoken Language Processing. ICSLP '96*, 2175–2178. Philadelphia, PA: IEEE.

Crespo-Sendra, Verònica, Costantijn Kaland, Marc Swerts & Pilar Prieto. 2013. Perceiving incredulity. The role of intonation and facial gestures. *Journal of Pragmatics* 47. 1–13.

Crystal, David. 1995. *A Dictionary of Linguistics and Phonetics*. Oxford (UK): Blackwell Publishing.

D'Imperio, Mariapaola. 2002. Language-specific and universal constraints on tonal alignment: The nature of targets and "anchors". In Bernard Bel & Isabelle Marlien (eds.), *Proceedings of the 1st International Conference on Speech Prosody*, 101–106. Aix-en-Provence: Laboratoire Parole et Langage.

D'Imperio, Mariapaola, Robert Espesser, Hélène Loevenbruck, Caroline Menezes, Noël Nguyen & Pauline Welby. 2007. Are tones aligned with articulatory events? Evidence from Italian and French. In Jennifer Cole & José Ignacio Hualde (eds.), *Laboratory phonology 9*, vol. 4-3 (Phonology and phonetics), 577–608. Berlin: Mouton de Gruyter.

Dijkstra, Christel, Emiel Krahmer & Marc Swerts. 2006. Manipulating Uncertainty. The contribution of different audiovisual prosodic cues to the perception of confidence. In Rüdiger Hoffmann & Hansjörg Mixdorff (eds.), *Proceedings of the 3rd International Conference on Speech Prosody*, 1–4. Dresden.

Dohen, Marion & Hélène Loevenbruck. 2009. Interaction of audition and vision for the perception of prosodic contrastive focus. *Language and Speech* 52. 177–206.

Edwards, J., Mary E. Beckman & Janet Fletcher. 1991. The articulatory kinematics of final lengthening. *Journal of the Acoustical Society of America* 89(1). 369–382.

Ekman, Paul & Wallace Friesen. 1978. *Facial Action Coding System: A Technique for the Measurement of Facial Movement*. Palo Alto: Consulting Psychologists Press.

Ekman, Paul, Wallace Friesen & Joseph C. Hager. 2002. *Facial Action Coding System: The Manual on CD ROM. A Human Face*. Salt Lake City.

Fowler, Carol. 1995. Acoustic and kinematic correlates of contrastive stress accent in spoken English. In Fredericka Bell-Berti & Raphael J. Lawrence (eds.), *Producing Speech: Contemporary Issues*, 355–373. New York: AIP Press.

Frota, Sónia & Pilar Prieto. 2015. Intonation in Romance: Systemic similarities and differences. In Sónia Frota & Pilar Prieto (eds.), *Intonation in Romance*, 392–418. Oxford: Oxford University Press.

Fry, Dennis B., Arthur S. Abramson, Peter D. Eimas & Alvin M. Liberman. 1962. The identification and discrimination of synthetic vowels. *Language and Speech* 5. 171–189.

Geng, Christian, Alice Turk, James M. Scobbie, Cedric Macmartin, Philip Hoole, Philip Richmond, Alan Wrench, Marianne Pouplier, Ellen G. Bard, Ziggy Campbell, Catherine Dickie, Eddie Dubourg, William Hardcastle, Evia

Kainada, Simon King, Robin Lickley, Satsuki Nakai, Steve Renals, Kevin White & Ronny Wiegand. 2013. Recording speech articulation in dialogue: Evaluating a synchronized double electromagnetic articulography setup. *Journal of Phonetics* 41(6). 421–431.

Gili Fivela, Barbara. 2008. *Intonation in Production and Perception: The Case of Pisa Italian*. Alessandria: Edizioni dell'Orso. Memorie del Laboratorio di Linguistica della Scuola Normale Superiore di Pisa.

Gili Fivela, Barbara. 2012. Meanings, shades of meanings and prototypes of intonational categories. In Gorka Elordieta & Pilar Prieto i Vives (eds.), *Prosody and meaning* (Interface explorations), 197–237. Berlin & Boston: De Gruyter Mouton.

Gili Fivela, Barbara. 2015. L'integrazione di informazioni multimodali: prosodia ed espressioni del volto nella percezione del parlato. In Elena Pistolesi, Rosa Pugliese & Barbara Gili Fivela (eds.), *Parole, gesti, interpretazioni: Studi linguistici per Carla Bazzanella*, 107–127. Roma: Aracne.

Gili Fivela, Barbara, Cinzia Avesani, Marco Barone, Giuliano Bocci, Claudia Crocco, Mariapaola D'Imperio, Rosella Giordano, Giovanna Marotta, Michelina Savino & Patrizia Sorianello. 2015. Varieties of Italian and their intonational phonology. In Sónia Frota & Pilar Prieto (eds.), *Intonation in Romance*, 140–197. Oxford University Press.

Gili Fivela, Barbara & Carla Bazzanella. 2014. The relevance of prosody and context to the interplay between intensity and politeness: An exploratory study on Italian. *Journal of Politeness Research* 10(1). 97–126.

Goldstein, Louis, Hosung Nam, Elliot Saltzman & Ioana Chitoran. 2009. Coupled Oscillator Planning Model of Speech Timing and Syllable Structure. In H. Fujisaki, J. Shen & G. Fant (eds.), *Frontiers in Phonetics and Speech Science*, 239–250. Beijing: The Commercial Press.

Gussenhoven, Carlos. 1999. Discreteness and gradience in intonational contrasts. *Language and Speech* 42. 281–305.

Gussenhoven, Carlos. 2004. *The phonology of tone and intonation*. Cambridge: Cambridge University Press.

House, David. 2002. Intonation and visual cues in the perception of interrogative mode in Swedish. In *Proceedings of ICSLP 2002*, 1957–1960.

Isard, Amy & Jean Carletta. 1995. Replicability of transaction and action coding in the Map Task corpus. In *Proceedings of AAAI Spring Symposium on Empirical Methods in Discourse Interpretation*. Palo Alto, CA.

Krahmer, Emiel & Marc Swerts. 2007. The effect of visual beats on prosodic promi-nence: acoustic analyses, auditory perception, and visual perception. *Journal of Memory and Language* 57. 396–414.

Kuhl, Patricia. 1991. Human adults and human infants show a 'perceptual magnet effect' for the prototypes of speech categories, monkeys do not. *Perception and Psychophysics* 50. 93–107.

Ladd, D. Robert. 1996. *Intonational phonology*. Vol. 79 (Cambridge studies in lin-guistics). Cambridge: Macmillan.

Ladd, D. Robert. 2008. *Intonational phonology*. 2nd edition. Cambridge: Cam-bridge University Press.

Lansing, C. R. & George W. McConkie. 1999. Attention to facial regions in the segmental and prosodic visual speech percept ion tasks. *Journal of Speech, Lan-guage, and Hearing Research.* 526–539.

Lehiste, Ilse. 1975. The phonetic structure of paragraphs. In Antonie Cohen & Sieb Nooteboom (eds.), *Structure and Process in Speech Perception*, 195–206. Springer-Verlag.

Lehiste, Ilse & William Wang. 1977. Perception of sentence and paragraph bound-aries with and without semantic information. In Wolfgang Dressler & Oskar Pfeiffer (eds.), *Phonologica*, 277–283.

Liberman, Alvin M., Katherine S. Harris, Howard S. Hoffman & Belver C. Grif-fith. 1957. The discrimination of speech sounds within and across phoneme boundaries. *Journal of Experimental Psychology* 54(5). 358–368.

Loehr, Dan. 2004. *Gesture and Intonation*. Washington, DC: Georgetown Univer-sity dissertation.

Massaro, Dominic W. 1989. Testing between the TRACE model and the fuzzy logical model of speech perception. *Cognitive Psychology* 21(3). 398–421.

Massaro, Dominic W. & Michael Cohen. 1993. The paradigm and the fuzzy logical model of perception are alive and well. *Journal of Experimental Psychology* 122(1). 115–124.

McGurk, Harry & John MacDonald. 1976. Hearing lips and seeing voices: A new illusion. *Nature* 264. 746–748.

Mücke, Doris, Martine Grice, Johannes Becker & Anne Hermes. 2009. Sources of variation in tonal alignment: Evidence from acoustic and kinematic data. *Journal of Phonetics* 37. 321–338.

Nespor, Marina & Wendy Sandler. 1999. Prosody in Israeli sign language. *Lan-guage and Speech* 42. 143–176.

Niebuhr, Oliver & Klaus Kohler. 2004. Perception and cognitive processing of tonal alignment in German. In *Proceedings of the International Symposium on Tonal Aspects of Languages: Emphasis on Tone Languages*, 155–158. Beijing.

Oller, D. K. 1973. The effect of the position in utterance on speech segment duration in English. *Journal of the Acoustical Society of America* 54. 1235–1247.

Pean, Vincent, Sheila M. Williams & Maxine Eskenazy. 1993. The design and recording of ICY, a corpus for the study of intraspeaker variability and the characterisation of speaking styles. In *Proceedings of Eurospeech 1993*, 627–630. Berlin, Germany.

Perkell, Joseph S., Marc H. Cohen, Mario A. Svirsky, Melanie L. Matthies, Iñaki Garabieta & Michel T. T. Jackson. 1992. Electromagnetic midsagittal articulometer systems for transducing speech articulatory movements. *Journal of the Acoustical Society of America* 92. 3078–3096.

Pierrehumbert, Janet B. 1980. *The phonology and phonetics of English intonation.* Bloomington: MIT dissertation.

Prieto, Pilar. 2012. Experimental methods and paradigms for prosodic analysis. In Abigail C. Cohn, Cécile Fougeron & Marie K. Huffman (eds.), *The Oxford Handbook of Laboratory Phonology* (Oxford Handbooks in Linguistics), 528–538. Oxford: Oxford University Press.

Prieto, Pilar, Doris Mücke, J. Becker & Martine Grice. 2007. Coordination patterns between pitch movements and oral gestures in Catalan. In *Proceedings of ICPhS*, 989–992. Saarbrücken, Germany.

Prieto, Pilar & Francisco Torreira. 2007. The segmental anchoring hypothesis revisited: Syllable structure and speech rate effects on peak timing in Spanish. *Journal of Phonetics* 35. 473–500.

Rosch, Eleanor H. 1975. Cognitive representations of semantic categories. *Journal of Experimental Psychology: General* 104(3). 192–233.

Rubin, Philip E. 1995. HADES: A case study of the development of a signal analysis system. *Applied speech technology.* 501–520. Boca Raton, FL, CRC Press.

Saltzman, Elliot. 1995. Dynamics and Coordinate Systems in skilled sensorimotor activity. In T. van Gelder & R. Port (eds.), *Mind as Motion: Explorations in the Dynamics of Cognition*, 150–173. Cambridge, MA: MIT Press.

Saltzman, Elliot & Kevin G. Munhall. 1989. A dynamical approach to gestural patterning in speech production. *Ecological Psychology* 1. 333–382.

Sandler, Wendy. 2005. Prosodic constituency and intonation in a sign language. In *Linguistische Berichte*, vol. 13, 59–86.

Savy, Renata & Francesco Cutugno. 2009. CLIPS: Diatopic, diamesic and diaphasic variations in spoken Italian. In Michaela Mahlberg, Victorina González-

Díaz & Catherine Smith (eds.), *On-line Proceedings of 5th Corpus Linguistics Conference* (paper 213). http://ucrel.lancs.ac.uk/publications/cl2009/213_FullPaper.doc.

Schneider, Katrin, Grzegorz Dogil & Bernd Möbius. 2009. German boundary tones show Categorical Perception and perceptual magnet effect when presented in different contexts. In *Proceedings of the 10th Annual Conference of the International Speech Communication Association 2009 (INTERSPEECH 2009)*, 2519–2522. Brighton, UK: Curran Associates, Inc.

Schneider, Katrin, Britta Lintfert, Grzegorz Dogil & Bernd Möbius. 2006. Phonetic grounding of prosodic categories. In Stefan Sudhoff, Denisa Lenertové, RolandMeyer, Sandra Pappert, Petra Augurzky, Ina Mleinek, Nicole Richter & Johannes Schliesser (eds.), *Methods in Empirical Prosody Research*, 335–362. Berlin: De Gruyter.

Schneider, Katrin & Bernd Möbius. 2005. Perceptual magnet effect in German boundary tones. In *Proceedings of the 6th Annual Conference of the International Speech Communication Association 2005 (INTERSPEECH 2005)*, 41–44. Lisbon, Portugal: Curran Associates, Inc.

Sigona, Francesco, Antonio Stella, Mirko Grimaldi & Barbara Gili Fivela. 2015. MAYDAY: A software for multimodal articulatory data analysis. In Antonio Romano & I. Meandri Rivoira (eds.), *Aspetti prosodici e testuali del raccontare: dalla letteratura orale al parlato dei media, Atti del 10° convegno AISV*, 173–184. Torino: Edizioni dell'Orso.

Silverman, Kim, Mary E. Beckman, John F. Pitrelli, Mari Ostendorf, C. Wightman, Patti Price, Janet B. Pierrehumbert & Julia Hirschberg. 1992. TOBI: A standard for labeling English prosody. In Bruce L. Berwing, Terrance M. Nearey & John J. Ohala (eds.), *Proceedings of the 1992 International Conference on Spoken Language Processing*, 867–870.

Sjolander, K. & J. Beskow. 1999. *WaveSurfer: An open source speech tool*. Stockholm, Sweden: Center for Speech Technology (CTT) at KTH. https://www.speech.kth.se/wavesurfer/wsurf_icslp00.pdf.

Srinivasan, Ravindra. J. & Dominic W. Massaro. 2003. Perceiving prosody from the face and voice: Distinguishing statements from echoic questions in English. *Language and Speech* 46(1) 1–22.

Stella, Antonio, Maria del Mar Vanrell, Massimiliano Iraci, Pilar Prieto & Barbara Gili Fivela. 2014. Intergestural coordination between tonal and oral gestures in Catalan, Italian. In Susanne Fuchs, Martine Grice, Anne Hermes, Leonardo Lancia & Doris Mücke (eds.), *Proceedings of the 10th International Seminar on Speech Production*, 421–424. Cologne, Germany.

Stella, Massimo, Paolo Bernardini, Francesco Sigona, Antonio Stella, Mirko Grimaldi & Barbara Gili Fivela. 2012. Numerical instabilities and three-dimensional electromagnetic articulography. *Journal of Acoustic. Soc. of Am.* 132(6). 3941–3949.

Stella, Massimo, Antonio Stella, Francesco Sigona, Paolo Bernardini, Mirko Grimaldi & Barbara Gili Fivela. 2013. Electromagnetic Articulography with AG500 and AG501. In *Proceedings of the 14th Annual Conference of the International Speech Communication Association 2013 (INTERSPEECH 2013)*, 1316–1320. Lyon, France.

Stevens, Kenneth N. 1972. The Quantal Nature of Speech: Evidence from Articulatory-acoustic Data. In David Jr. Edward & Peter B. Denes (eds.), *Human Communication: A Unified View*, 51–66. New York: McGraw-Hill.

Stevens, Kenneth N. 1989. On the quantal nature of speech. *On the quantal nature of speech* 17. 3–45.

Stevens, Kenneth N. & Samuel J. Keyser. 2010. Quantal theory, enhancement andoverlap. *Journal of Phonetics* 38(1). 10–19.

Stone, Maureen. 2005. A Guide to Analyzing Tongue Motion from Ultrasound Images. *Clinical Linguistics and Phonetics* 19(6-7). 455–502.

Swerts, Marc & Emiel Krahmer. 2008. Facial expressions and prosodic prominence: comparing modalities and facial areas. *Journal of Phonetics* 36(2). 219–238.

Tisato, Graziano, Piero Cosi, Carlo Drioli & Fabio Tesser. 2005. Interface. Strumenti interattivi per l'animazione delle teste parlanti. In Piero Cosi (ed.), *Misura dei parametri, Etti del I convegno nazionale dell'AISV, Padova*, 817–846. Brescia: EDK Editore.

Vanrell, Maria del Mar. 2006. A scaling contrast in Majorcan Catalan interrogatives. In Rüdiger Hoffmann & Hansjörg Mixdorff (eds.), *Proceedings of the 3rd International Conference on Speech Prosody*, 807–810. Dresden.

Vanrell, Maria del Mar, Ingo Feldhausen & Lluïsa Astruc. 2018. The Discourse Completion Task in Romance prosody research: status quo and outlook. In Ingo Feldhausen, Jan Fliessbach & Maria del Mar Vanrell (eds.), *Methods in prosody: A Romance language perspective* (Studies in Laboratory Phonology), 191–228. Berlin: Language Science Press.

Wightman, Colin, Stefanie Shattuck-Hufnagel, Mari Ostendorf & Patti Price. 1992. Segmental durations in the vicinity of prosodic phrase boundaries. *Journal of the Acoustical Society of America* 91(3). 1707–1717.

Wilbur, Ronnie B. 2000. Phonological and prosodic layering of non-manuals in American sign language. In Karen Emmorey & Harlan Lane (eds.), *The Signs of Language Revisited*, 215–247. Mahwah, NJ: Lawrence Erlbaum Associates.

Wouters, Johan, Brian Rundle & Michael Macon. 1999. Authoring tools for speech synthesis using the sable markup standard. In *Proceedings of Eurospeech*, 963–966.

Chapter 4

The realizational coefficient: Devising a method for empirically determining prominent positions in Conchucos Quechua

Timo Buchholz
Freie Universität Berlin

Uli Reich
Freie Universität Berlin

We initially sketch a phonological theory in which the culminativity of word accents acts as only one out of four main functional goals for the configuration of prosodic devices and claim that languages exhibit many differences therein. Thus, in the study of many languages whose prosody is not extensively studied, as is the case for most languages spoken in situations of plurilingualism together with Romance Languages, we need reliable methodologies to determine their particular organization of time, tone, segmental strength and intensity. Using data from a Central Quechua dialect, we propose such a method consisting of a complex pragmatic and metrical annotation in Praat and its statistical exploration in R. We conclude with a discussion of preliminary results and shortcomings to be resolved.

1 The phonological perspective: Competing motivations of prosodic devices

In the study of the phenomena involved in what has been called "accent", "stress" and/or "prominence" in different and partially incompatible terminologies,[1] we

---

[1] See Beckman (1986) for an impressively well-informed historical overview that sheds some light on the genesis of the terminological confusion and suggests ways out of it. Note that her

Timo Buchholz & Uli Reich. 2018. The realizational coefficient: Devising a method for empirically determining prominent positions in Conchucos Quechua. In Ingo Feldhausen, Jan Fliessbach & Maria del Mar Vanrell (eds.), *Methods in prosody: A Romance language perspective*, 123–164. Berlin: Language Science Press.
DOI:10.5281/zenodo.1441341

can draw a line of progress in typological research that puts the universality of the assumption that every phonological word has a single primary accent into question. Early structuralist theory (Trubeckoj 1939) used "main tone" (germ. *Hauptton*) to illustrate the *culminative* (germ. *gipfelbildend*) function in phonological systems as opposed to the *delimitative* and the *distinctive* functions. An accent was conceived of as being "culminative" in the sense that it is the most prominent position in a syntagmatic sequence of hierarchically organized accents. Later, culminativity was developed as a core concept of Metrical Phonology in order to derive "stress" by the hierarchical build-up of prominence in metrical grids (Liberman & Prince 1977: 262; Hayes 1995: 24–25).

In many languages, sometimes called "stress-accent languages", accents are also "accumulative" in the sense that they attract all out of four possible prosodic parameters, namely intensity, duration, pitch and segmental strength. Thus, an accented syllable is believed to show salient pitch events, to be longer, to not reduce vowels, or even diphthongize them (traditionally, the preference for accented syllables for being bimoraic has been coined in Prokosch's Law), to show more complex onsets and codas and to be louder.

A glance at the phonological configuration of tone languages, however, shows that a conception of word accents that accumulate all phonetic instances of strength does not hold cross-linguistically. In tone languages, tones can be associated with many syllables in one word, as Yip (2002) shows in her seminal work. See her example from Chilungu, a language from the Bantu family, in which one tone is associated with many vowels (Yip 2002: 68):

(1)   kú-sóóbólól-à ku-soobolol-a

      to sort out   H

---

own typological proposal is privative: non-stress languages are languages that are defective with regard to the set of properties that define stress languages. In the following, we will use the term WORD ACCENT to designate the abstract phonological knowledge of one and only one syllable in a prosodic word that is perceived as stronger than all other syllables in that word. In principle, it does imply neither the phonetic cues that may realize it in a given stretch of speech, nor the phonological domain that projects it. Accents can be specified in the lexicon or projected by metrical algorithms that construct alternating *prominence* in a hierarchically ordered metrical grid. In the latter case, word accents are the topmost prominent position in such a grid. The term "stress", as it is used in the literature, is widely synonymous with our notion of "word accent", but implies also aspects of its realization, as in the typological dichotomy of stress-accent and pitch-accent languages. Since we want to keep these notions strictly apart in order to describe their relation precisely, we will avoid the term "stress" wherever it is possible, in spite of its widespread usage in the literature we rely on.

As Yip (2002), among many other scholars working on tone languages, shows convincingly, this one-to-many relation is not the end of the story; many languages also show the inverted relation, associating many tones with the nucleus of one syllable, a situation that is familiar from boundary tones found in many intonational languages.

Duration can also show up without strict association with a word accent. Thus, in Wolof, a Western Atlantic language spoken in Senegal without distinctive tones at the word level, both vowels and consonants show distinctive duration, both for lexical contrasts (2a, b) and the expression of focus (2c, d).[2] Long syllables (bimoraic, hence heavy) are possible in basically every position (3) and in more than one position in the word (4) (examples from Ka 1989; 1994 and Voisin-Nouguier 2002).

(2) a. fat   : faat
       clean.up   kill

    b. gën : gënn
       better   milk

    c. ma dem : maa dem
       I   go   [I]$_{Foc}$ go

    d. mu dem : moo   dem
       he goes   [he]$_{Foc}$ goes

(3) a. 'boole
      mix

    b. te'raanga
      hospitality

    c. 'dajaloò
      gather

(4) a. 'woowandòo
      call.together

    b. 'feesalukàay
      instrument.used.to.fill

    c. ji'géénubìir
      pregnant.woman

---

[2]Note that the contrasts in (2c) and (2d) appear as focus morphology in the literature. In other cases of the focus system, the morphological contrasts are expressed by segmental modification and addition. See Voisin-Nouguier (2002) and Rialland & Robert (2001) for the full system.

(5)   a. ˈtabax
          build

       b. ˈndaje
          meeting

Ka (1989; 1994) claims that in instances of words with light syllables only and in words with one or more heavy (=long) syllable, the first (3c, 5) or the first heavy syllable (3b, 4c), respectively, receives stress. If the heavy syllable occurs after two light ones (3c), it is perceived as having secondary prominence, while primary prominence falls on the initial syllable. In this language, then, duration appears as being as independent from a culminative word accent as tone is in so-called tone languages. As we shall see, the Central Quechua dialects show a distribution of length that comes close to this phonological constellation. Finnish and Latin are European Languages that show distinctive duration independent from word accent, but Latin shows some restrictions that Finnish does not have. German is a quantity language that comes quite close to a "prototypical stress accent language": it has vocalic duration only in "stressed" syllables (Becker 1996). Thus, the independence of duration from word accent shows varying degrees and it is far from clear where we should set the threshold to tell types apart.

Another feature of word accents is that the nuclei of the syllables that bear it, unlike its neighbors, are never reduced, rather often diphthongized and that they show more segmental contrasts than the nuclei of other syllables. Interestingly, exactly this feature has been shown repeatedly as being dependent on what has been called the rhythm type of a given language (Dauer 1983; Auer 1993; 2001; Dufter 2003). In Romance languages, e.g., it holds for European Portuguese, which shows exactly the vocalic reductions and consequently strong restrictions on segmental inventory claimed as general properties of syllables less prominent than the one with the word accent in word rhythmic languages (formerly "stress-timing"). It does not hold as clearly for most varieties of Spanish, Standard Italian or even Brazilian Portuguese, that are taken as instances of syllable rhythmic languages (formerly "syllable-timing", Abaurre & Galves 1998; Reich 2002), but in Brazilian Portuguese, vocalic reduction still occurs more than in Spanish and Italian.

In Spanish, the only property of lexical phonology related to the preference of word accents to be bimoraic is the distribution of diphthongs (cf. /beneˈswela/ vs. /benesoˈlano/), while the nuclei of all syllables are fully pronounced in most cases. However, there can be no doubt at all that Spanish does have a word accent that invariably is the locus of major tonal events if they are realized. It is simply less dominant than its European Portuguese counterpart is. Again, we find different constellations of features that are held to define types. Where should we draw the line?

The last feature we want to mention in this complicated introduction is intensity. Intensity does not seem to play any phonological role at all but as a feature of word accents. Beckman (1986: 160), however, it shows that this property cannot be generalized across languages, since in Japanese intensity is independent from the position of the accented syllable. Intensity, then, also fails to form a universal feature of the strongest syllable in the word.

Given these facts, culminativity rather seems to describe an optional than a universal concept of accents. We hypothesize that culminativity is a functional principle that is counterbalanced by others. Distinctivity is directly antagonistic, as it dissociates time, tone, segmental quality and intensity to enhance the possibilities of paradigmatic contrast for phonological word forms. Thus, the culminativity of word accents grows at the expense of the distinctive potential of prosodic devices. Vice versa, the use of prosodic devices for distinctive functions levels the dominance of word accents, since time, tone, sonority and intensity can be distributed over different positions in the word or phrase. Delimitation may conspire with culminativity towards the overall target of identifying words or phrases in a given chain of speech, but in all systems with non-peripheral word accent, boundary tones, final lengthening and segmental processes like consonantal strengthening and epenthesis of glottal stops are also likely to diminish the phonetic saliency of the syllable bearing word accent. Another core function of accents, absent in structuralist phonology, is rhythmicity, as recognized since the early days of Metrical Phonology (Liberman & Prince 1977; Hayes 1995), but put into a theoretical framework that takes culminativity as universal and thus misses the functional particularities between different aspects of prosodic form. In many languages, the assignment of primary accents does not depend on foot construction (van der Hulst 1999: 72). Rather, the assignment of alternating strengths of acoustic events in time appears to be an independent functional domain of prosody with which lexical accents may, but need not, coincide. The functional target of rhythmicity surely is neither distinctivity, nor culminativity, nor delimitation. To the contrary, it enhances the isochronous distribution of alternating prominence at the expense of all the three functions recognized by the Prague school.

In our view, particular phonologies are organized as instances of decisions between (at least) these major functional goals. Ideal types can be set as abstract possibilities that no language ever reaches because of the competing drives towards the other ends of this space of prosodic possibilities. In the ideal type of a culminative prosodic system, tonal events, duration, segmental strength and intensity would occur but in the one and only prominent syllable of every word. In the ideal type of a distinctive prosodic system, tones, duration, segmental contrasts and intensity are scattered all over and boundaries between words or phrases are blurred. In the ideal type of a delimitative prosodic system, tones, duration and intensity occur at the boundaries of wordless phrasal chains without prominence. Finally, in the ideal type of a rhythmic prosodic system, we would find isochronally recurring contours of prominence, just as in music (Reich & Rohrmeier 2014). Natural phonologies balance the competing drives towards these ideal types as they fulfil their communicative goals in the variational space of human languages, constrained by universal cognitive principles and the historical traditions of social networks.

In the end, the view we are defending aims at the abolition of dichotomic typologies and pleads for their passage to particular phonological configurations within a polydimensional space defined by competing functional principles. This is very much in line with, while a step more radical than, views on prosodic typologies defended by Hyman (2009; 2014), in his impressive command of facts from the phonologies of many languages in the world.[3] He comes to a conclusion that is not only wise for theory building, but also mandatory for the great empirical endeavor of the study of language: it is better to look at what languages do than to brood upon fictitious universals.

Research into the prosodic phonologies of languages that are not very well known, as is the case for most contact languages of the Romance languages outside Europe, must bear in mind that any constellation of the main prosodic devices may be the case in the language under study. Thus, they must be controlled for independently, but in relation to each other. And we can take nothing for granted.

2 The project and a short overview over the method of data elicitation

The methodological considerations we will expose in the following pages are part of our research project *Zweisprachige Prosodie: Metrik, Rhythmus und Intonation zwischen Spanisch und Quechua* ('Bilingual prosody: metrics, rhythm and

---

[3]The main difference is probably that Hyman still recognizes the typological validity of concepts such as "stress accent language" and "tone language", while the relevant configurations are only possibilities among others in our prosodic universe.

intonation between Spanish and Quechua'), funded by the Deutsche Forschungs-gemeinschaft. The overall goal of the project is the development of a prosodic theory of bilingualism on empirical grounds.

Our data was gathered through fieldwork in Huari, Conchucos, Ancash, Peru during the months of September-October 2015. The elicitation methodology aims at producing semi-spontaneous data, that is, speech produced naturally in dialogues under pragmatic and lexical constraints, in turn influencing prosody. Informants were asked (always in pairs) to play the following dialogical games in which any interaction could only be done orally, gestures were not permitted:

1. Picture-naming. Participants had to name objects shown to them on picture cards.

2. A version of memory. Participants took turns guessing where a certain picture on a card was. The cards had been shown to them for a short time and then flipped over.

3. Map-task (Anderson et al. 1991). Participants were provided with two maps, one with a path drawn between the objects shown on it, the other without the path. They were not allowed to see each other's maps. The participant with the map had to explain the path to the other one, who had to follow it by drawing it on their own map. The maps differed in some of the objects shown. Resulting communicative conflicts had to be resolved orally.

4. Story re-telling. Participant A would listen to a recording of a story (invented by the investigators and spoken for the recording by their local collaborator and advisor, Quechua teacher and native speaker Gabriel Barreta (GB)[4]). They would then tell the story to the other participant B, who had been waiting outside while the recording was playing. After being told the story, participant B would tell the story to one of the interviewers, with the possibility of correction by participant A.

5. A version of "Who am I?". Participant A would be told the name of a person known to both participants, and participant B had to guess the person's identity.

---

[4]Our deep gratitude and friendship goes to Gabriel Barreta and his family in Huari as well as to Leonel Menacho López and his wife Ana in Huaraz, who have provided invaluable help with local logistic and linguistic questions and without whom our fieldwork could not have been successful.

6. Guessing the contents of boxes. Both participants were provided with closed cardboard boxes and would take turns guessing their contents from just moving the boxes, shaking or weighing them by hand.

The content items of games 1–4 were restricted by means of the props provided, i.e. the cards, the maps and the recordings, to consist mostly of a set of lexical items varying through the possibilities of Quechua syllabic and moraic structure. Hence, the pictures on the cards displayed objects aimed at eliciting words ranging from two light (L) syllables to two heavy (H) and one light syllable, e.g. *tsu.ku* (L-L) 'hut', or *qi.llay.yuq* (L-H-H) 'rich man'. The subsequent games utilized the same lexical items (elicited by means of the same pictures, also on the maps, or the recording) wherever possible. Adjustments to these items were made after a first trial session with our principal local collaborator GB, who gave us local words for several of the metrical constellations that were to be elicited.

Care was taken to have the experiments take place in rooms that were as quiet as local conditions allowed. Participants would play the games in both Quechua and Spanish, going through all the games first in one language, and then the other. Audio recordings of the games were made using a Marantz PMD 670 audio recorder in connection with a Røde NT-1A condenser microphone in 44.1 KHz PCM. In total, excluding the trial with GB, 40 participants (22 females, 18 males, all bilinguals, mean age=22 years) were recorded in 20 sessions, yielding about 7 hours of Spanish and 6 hours of Quechua experimental data. All informants participated voluntarily, gave us their written consent to be recorded and for the resulting data to be published maintaining their anonymity, and were remunerated for their participation.

3 Methodology

3.1 The challenge: determining prosodic constellations on empirical grounds

As far as we know, the determination of positions of prominence in a language where they are unknown has not been studied extensively. In grammatical treatments of understudied (i.e., almost all non-European) languages, accent placement usually is dealt with cursorily: the author describes the positioning of strongest prominence, sometimes differentiating between several acoustic realizations, in a seemingly intuitive manner. Matters such as accent domain, acoustic correlates, function of prominence and interaction with other prosodic phenomena are rarely dealt with in systematically ordered empirical procedures, but attributed by intuition. Effectively, this means that the describing linguist "hears" accent positions in the language of their informants and generalizes from this audio perception. While we recognize that this was the only methodology available in many cases, we submit that it is not a methodology appropriate for scientific research since it allows for a number of non-trivial descriptive distortions due to perceptual biases on behalf of the describing linguist.[5] If the linguist's first language is one where the lexical accent is culminative and accumulative, as for example in English or German, then we cannot discard the possibility that this phonological background will influence them to a certain degree in their perception of the language they are studying. This will be even more the case if the linguist in question is not a specialized phonologist who might be aware of their own biases in this regard. With the concept of a universal culminative word accent, one is already excluding a large subset of the possible shapes accent systems assume (see, e.g., Hyman 2014 for an overview, and Kügler & Genzel 2012 for a particularly diverging case).

Moreover, in the case of the so-called central dialects of Quechua, we are faced with distinctive length, whose interference with accent placement and realization has never been discussed, and a considerable disagreement even in the existing (impressionistic) literature on accent position, domain and its acoustic correlates. Some of these dialects are described as having primary accent on the penult (Trager 1945 for Huaraz Quechua, Parker 1976 for Ancash-Huaylas Quechua, Adelaar 1977 for Tarma Quechua), others (and sometimes the same by another author) as having it on the initial syllable of the word (Parker 1976 for Huaraz Quechua, Hintz 2000 for Corongo Quechua, Hintz 2006 for South Conchucos Quechua). In most cases, a secondary accent is said to exist on the "other" position, i.e. penult or initial syllable (all of them agreeing at least that no other position is a strong contender), and that their prominence ranking can be reversed under certain morphological, pragmatic or conversational conditions (none of which are agreed upon by any two authors); some recognize a kind

---

[5]To clarify: our goal is by no means to insult or belittle the efforts of linguists that have done extensive research on otherwise little studied languages. We applaud their endeavors and think that both we and the linguistic community in general are highly indebted to them. However, many of these studies took place several decades ago, when prosodic theory was even more in its infancy than it is today and when, even more crucially, large-scale audio recordings of small languages that could be analyzed appropriately and shared with the academic community were not feasible, due to technical and logistic problems. Many of these researchers had to make do with what they had, and it is no doubt better that they gave an impressionistic description of accent systems in their languages than none at all. Nonetheless we think it is time that with the technical means at our disposal, the methodology to describe prominence systems in these languages should be reevaluated.

of division of labor between acoustic correlates in the realization of prominent positions. Our own visual and acoustic inspection of our own data does nothing to let us decide tentatively in favor of any of the hypotheses suggested in the literature. In fact, it complicates matters, since we often encounter utterances almost entirely devoid of any phrase-internal intonational movement that could reasonably be correlated with lexical pitch accent positions. Intonational movement, if it occurs, seems to respond to a domain above the word and to be severely restricted in its inventory: Utterance-initial rises and utterance- or possibly phrase-final falls and rises are almost exclusively observed. From this inspection, the hypothesis that our Quechua variety does not assign an accent position at the lexical level seems to be at least as probable as any of the suggestions cited above. Another problem is that speakers generally do not receive any education on Quechua and a very traditional one on Spanish, and a bias that accords Spanish greater prestige in academic matters definitely persists. Hence, speaker perceptions on where an "accent" might lie in a given Quechua word and what it might consist of are, if they exist at all, heavily influenced by these social conditions. We therefore thought it necessary to devise a methodology that would help us determine positions of realizational strength from the speech signal, in order to determine without such biases (inherent also in our own perceptions) the nature and domain of regular prominences in the Conchucos variety of Quechua our data is from. In the present study, semi-spontaneous data is used. Hence, phenomena of speech style and individual style are also included in the data. Further research could however easily apply the same method to more controlled data. In the remainder of the text, whenever we say something about "Quechua" without further variational qualification, we mean it to be about the variety of Quechua spoken in Huari, Conchucos, studied by us.

3.2 Goals of the present contribution

While the goal of our overall research project is the development of a prosodic theory of bilingualism on empirical grounds, the present contribution does not yet aim so high. Faced with the conflicting descriptions in the literature and our own data regarding accent placement described above, we think it is important to devise a methodology which arrives at a less biased description of the acoustical data we base our phonological theories on. Given that the question of the domain of accent placement is absolutely vital for any hypotheses regarding the behavior of prosodic domains in a plurilingual context, we take this to be an inevitable first step. Hence, the goal of this contribution is not to say anything about Quechua-Spanish bilingualism, but to provide evidence for the feasibility and usefulness of its methodology in helping us derive hypotheses about accent placement in a language where this is not known; more specifically, to investigate the possibility by means of acoustic measurements that our variety of Quechua does not assign accent at the lexical level.[6] While all analytical tools and statistic procedures are not new in particular, their complex application to metrical and pragmatic variables has not been endeavored in any empirical prosodic project we know of.

3.3 Methodology – annotation

All the usable Quechua data elicited through the means of the communicative games outlined in section 2 were transcribed and translated by bilingual students of the Universidad Nacional Santiago Antunez de Mayolo (UNASAM) in Huaraz, Ancash, Peru, and morphologically glossed by students of the Pontificia Universidad Católica del Perú (PUCP) in Lima, Peru using ELAN (Wittenburg et al. 2006). All further annotations were done by one of the authors as diligently as possible. In a follow-up investigation on a larger corpus we will also have a part of the corpus annotated by two independent annotators in order to arrive at a measure of inter-annotator agreement.

---

[6]There is a substantial body of literature on Spanish-Quechua bilingualism with regard to all levels of linguistic description, including prosody, such as O'Rourke (2005; 2007; 2008; 2009); Muntendam (2010); O'Rourke (2010; 2012); Muntendam (2012a; 2012b); van Rijswijk & Muntendam (2014); Muntendam & Torreira (2016); Muysken & Muntendam (2016). All of it is concerned with Southern or Ecuadorian varieties of Quechua (that are more closely related to each other than to Central Quechuan varieties), where accent placement seems not to be problematic. Due to the fact that in other systematic domains of the language, such as morphology and segmental phonology, the Southern and Ecuadorian varieties are different enough from the Central ones as a whole (not considering their considerable internal variation) to be judged mutually unintelligible, we are hesitant to just assume that the findings in the literature on the interaction between Southern Quechua and Spanish intonation, e.g., can easily be applied to our variety. Mountainous regions notoriously harbor enormous variation in a relatively small geographic area, that this applies also to the realm of prosody is by now well-known at least from the case of the varieties of Basque, where more or less every prosodic parameter regarding accent placement can be found (cf. e.g. Hualde et al. 2008; van der Hulst 2010; Aurrekoetxea et al. 2012). That the varieties of Quechua vary with regards to their accent placement to a considerable degree has also been recognized, see Wetzels & Meira (2010). Our goal here is only to provide a better basis for a description of the accent placement in the variety of Quechua we are studying. Only in subsequent studies will we hopefully have to say something about bilingualism.

Timo Buchholz & Uli Reich

3.3.1 Syllables

Using a corrected version of the transcription as basis, we built on it by adding a syllabic annotation on a map-task by two male speakers (FB03 and WB04) in Praat (Boersma & Weenink 2017). An example of what the syllable annotation looks like can be found in Figure 1. Tiers 4 and 5 in the Praat textgrid are reserved for syllable annotation (one tier for each speaker). Annotation boundaries were aligned as closely as possible with corresponding beginnings and endings of segmental material. A transcription system was used that aims at grouping together segments belonging to the same relevant class in Quechua.

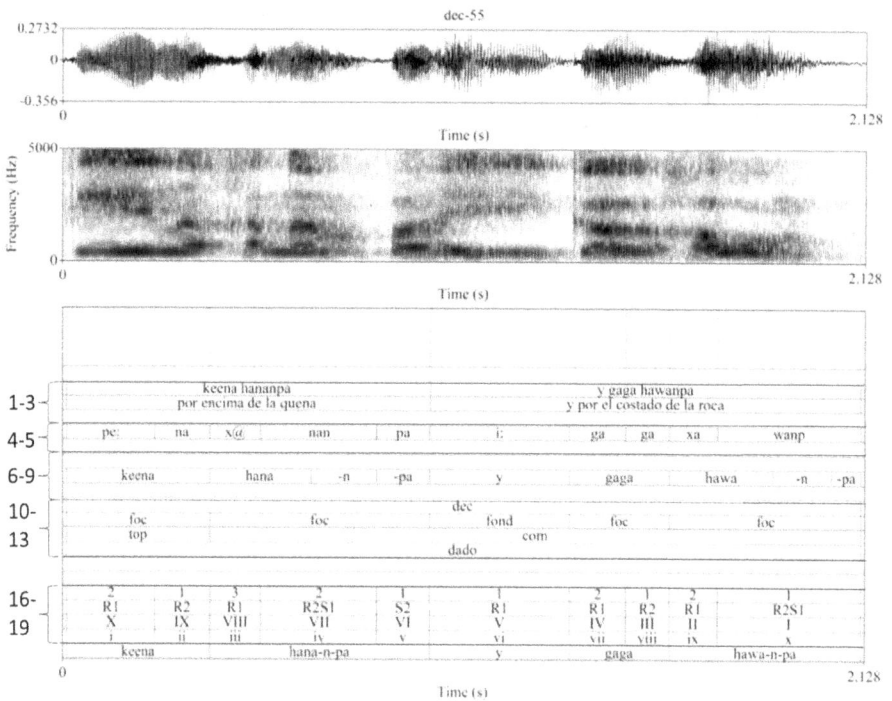

Figure 1: Waveform, spectrogram and text grid of the utterance *keena hananpa y gaga hawanpa*.

This was done to avoid illusions of perfect phonetic transcribability of spontaneous data on the one hand and to facilitate categorizations using these classes in the analysis on the other. Thus, in the example in Figure 1, what is morphophonologically written in (6)

134

(6)   keːna hana-n-pa   i   gaga hawa-n-pa
     flute above-3S.POSS-GEN and rock below-3S.POSS-GEN

     above the flute and below the rock

is transcribed as in (7).

(7) <peː|na|x@|nan|pa|iː|ga|ga|xa|wanp>

Voiceless plosives are transcribed with <p>, back fricatives [x ɣ h] with <x>, all nasals with <n>, reduced vowels with <@>, etc. Note that a phonetically somewhat more accurate rendering of the part transcribed as <x@nanpa> would be [xənampa]. Another remark needs to be made regarding syllable structure. Note that in the transcription of /hawa-n-pa/, as opposed to /hana-n-pa/, <wanp> has been grouped as one syllable, with a syllable structure of CVCC, something which has not been described in the existing phonologies of Quechua varieties (cf. Parker 1976 where a maximal syllable is either CVC or CVː). This is because of the complete elision of the vowel /a/ of the genitive marker -pa in this case, as can also be seen on the spectrogram in Figure 1, where there is no visible release of the plosive in the part corresponding to <wanp> as opposed to the plosive in the part corresponding to <nanpa>. This elision of vowels (as well as their sometime reduction) is a very frequent phenomenon in our variety of Quechua, occurs both utterance-finally and medially and is not restricted to this particular morpheme (which can also be realized fully). Note that we transcribed what was spoken and not any assumed underlying forms.

Tiers 6–9 in the textgrid are used for a morphological annotation and glosses (two tiers for each speaker). Whereas the syllabic transcription is a reduced transcription of the actual realization, the morphological annotation represents morphemes in a form close to standard descriptions. Interval boundaries in the morphological tiers were made to coincide as closely as possible with the corresponding sound changes in the speech signal, however this was not always possible: a frequent example involves the copula *ka-* together with the progressive *-yka-*, as in

(8) ka-yka-n
     COP-PROG-3S

     'S/he is in the process of being/having.'

Here the usual (but not the only) realization is [keːkan], arising from a regular process of monophtongization in many central Quechua varieties, thus making it impossible to determine where in the speech signal the boundary between the root and the progressive suffix lies. In such cases, labels on the morphological tier received a <?> after or before the connecting hyphen in the annotation.

3.3.2 Information structural annotation

As can be seen from Figure 1, the next four tiers in the annotation textgrid are used for information structural pragmatic categories. Tier 10 annotates the speech act, with the categories DEC for declaratives, PREGQ for queries, PREGCH for checks and IMP for imperatives. Tier 11 is used for the annotation of focus-background structure, with FOC for focus and FOND for background. Tier 12 annotates topic-comment structure, with TOP, topic, and COM, comment; tier 13 annotates givenness in the discourse with the categories of *dado* 'given', and *nuevo* 'new'. These annotations were made based on judgments about what role the parts of the utterance in question played in the discourse, not based on the presence or absence of morphological markers that have been described as encoding information structural meaning in Quechua (cf. e.g. Wölck 1972; Weber 1986; Muysken 1995; Gómez Rendón 2006). Building on standard approaches to pragmatics and information structure (Austin 1962; Searle 1969; Chafe 1976; Bolinger 1989; Rooth 1992; Grice & Savino 1997; Baumann 2006; Krifka 2007, among many others) we elaborated the following set of key notions:

- A DECLARATIVE is adding a proposition to the common ground, regardless of whether this proposition is claimed by the speaker to be true (asserted) or not.

- A QUERY asks for information needed to complete a proposition, whether regarding its components (constituent question) or its truth value (polar question).

- A CHECK asks for confirmation that a proposition in the common ground should be considered to be true in the relevant world of discourse.

- An IMPERATIVE represents a command by the speaker (to the hearer) that a certain state of affairs in the world should be changed so as to conform to a proposition.

- In FOCUS are those parts of an utterance to which alternatives are saliently evoked and discarded; those which make a difference to propositions about states of affairs already in the common ground.

- Correspondingly, in the BACKGROUND are those parts of an utterance to which alternatives are not evoked, that are not in focus; background is complementary to focus.

- TOPIC is that part of a discourse that is currently being talked about or advanced by one of the participants in the discourse to be talked about henceforth, it is the frame of reference under which comments are to be understood.

- COMMENTARY is that which is talked about the topic; it is information that is added to the common ground regarding the topic.

- GIVEN are referents that are active in the discourse, whether they have been activated by linguistic or extralinguistic means.

- NEW are referents newly introduced into the discourse, they become active through their first (linguistic or extralinguistic) mention.

These definitions are not without their problems: in particular, there exist certainly many more types of speech act than just the four defined above; new and given are categorical impositions on a multitude of states of discourse activation that probably should be thought of as forming a graded scale; different types of focus such as information focus and contrastive focus can and have been argued for (for a proposed hierarchy of them see Féry 2013), and it is probably useful to further divide background into tail and link, as proposed by Vallduví (1992). However, this part of the annotation is complex enough as it is, and we therefore decided to restrict ourselves to the above-mentioned categories, believing that they should suffice for the time being for the purposes of determining the relevance of information structural categories for the realization of prosody in our data.

These categories encode related but clearly distinct notions. Interactions may arise, e.g. when a new topic is introduced into the discourse it will often be in focus because it is then that it is contrasted with other alternatives. However, once it is introduced and well known, it is frequently not mentioned anymore, but the comments made about it are still divided between focus and background. This is only to make the point that the two are neither complementary nor the same, nor are any of the other categories defined above and annotated in separate tiers the same. We hold that it is not possible to further reduce these categories, such as they are defined above, without severely limiting one's descriptive power and hence the scope of phenomena one would like to explain.

It has only been possible to annotate these information structural categories in such comparative detail and on the basis of only discourse pragmatic considerations because the annotators both also designed the experiments that produced the semi-spontaneous data (controlling a large percentage of the content words metrically) and were present during the course of the experiments as silent participants. Thus both the states of affairs that are talked about as well as the (linguistic and extralinguistic) discursive progression of events are well known to us, and our annotations (of course remaining interpretations to a certain degree, but this is valid for all annotations) are anchored in and informed by these facts.

3.3.3 Positional annotation

Tiers 16–19 in Figure 1 demonstrate what we call positional annotation. In order to create the intervals, a Praat script first cut the entire map task recording with its textgrid into chunks at the speech act grid that correspond roughly to conversational moves and are surrounded by (small) silences. Another script then detected in which of the two syllable tiers, annotating the two speakers respectively, there were more intervals and made four empty copies of its intervals in tiers 16–19, thus selecting only the more dominant speaker for each such chunk to be analyzed. In most cases, this yielded sound-textgrid pairs without any speaker overlap. In those cases where there was speaker overlap, the parts where the less dominant speaker was speaking were excluded from the analysis. The intervals in tiers 16–19 were then labelled as follows, creating the positional annotation:

Tier 16 annotates syllable position in the word counting from its right edge, using Arabic numerals (1, 2, 3, 4, etc.). Thus, in the example given and starting from the right, the syllable <wanp> receives in its corresponding interval on tier 16 a <1>, <ha> a <2>; the right <ga> from *gaga*, because it is a separate word, again receives a <1>, and to its left the other <ga> a <2>. "Word" here refers to the morphological word in Quechua whose structure all grammars agree upon, i.e. consisting of a root plus several suffixes. Theoretically, due to the agglutinative nature of Quechua, any number of suffixes could be attached to a root; in practice, the furthest a syllable was annotated as being removed from the right word boundary in this corpus was 6, and 3 was not often exceeded. The implicit assumption here is that the domain of the morphological word is largely isomorphic with a relevant prosodic domain, e.g. the prosodic word in Quechua, if it exists, although this is in fact unknown. Note that what is annotated here are syllables as defined in the part on syllable transcription and transcribed in tiers 4 and 5, not morphemes.

Tier 17 annotates syllable position in the word counting from its left edge as well as morphological category (root or suffix). The labeling consists of either "R", for root, or "S", for suffix, plus an Arabic numeral indicating position and whose counting is reset at the border between root and suffix. To clarify using the example from figure 1: Starting from the left, <peː> and <na> are labelled <R1> and <R2> respectively, because they are both part of the root of the verb. Proceeding, <x@>, as the first syllable of the next word, gets labelled <R1> again, but <nan>, because it consists both of the second part of the root *hana-* 'above' and the first suffix *-n* "3rd singular possessive", is labelled <R2S1>. With this twofold annotation, it is possible to examine both position from left-edge word boundary and whether a syllable is part of the root or the suffixes of a word as influencing factors on prosody in the later analysis.

Tier 18 annotates syllable position in the whole utterance counting from its right edge using large Roman numerals (I, II, III, IV, etc.). The utterance is here defined as consisting of what is labelled as one conversational move between (short) pauses, hence everything one speaker says "in one go". This may correspond in many cases to a prosodic phrase, if only to postulate a prosodic domain distinct from the word in Quechua. Whether this phrase is in itself composed of further smaller phrases that are not isomorphic with the (postulated) prosodic word in Quechua is not known (see Grice et al. 2000 for discussion of the concept). To look at the example, the interval on tier 18 corresponding to the rightmost syllable <wanp> is labelled with a <I>, from there the numbering increases rightward until the interval corresponding to the leftmost syllable, <peː>, which gets labelled <X> for being the tenth syllable in the entire phrase counting from the right.

Tier 19 works exactly as tier 18, only counting from the left edge of the utterance/phrase and with the numbering being done in small Roman numerals (i, ii, iii, iv, etc.). Thus, the leftmost syllable <peː> here gets labelled <i>, and <wanp> at the right edge <x>, for being the tenth syllable in the phrase if counting from the left.

Proceeding in this way has several advantages: Only by using four tiers for positional measurements can we exactly observe and quantify prosodic behavior at both the left and the right edge of two domains, that of the word and that of the phrase. Note that none of the tiers annotates information already given in another tier; since both word length and phrase length are highly variable, the left-counting tiers can only give precise positional information at the left edge of the domain, and vice versa for the right-counting ones. This procedure incorporates standard assumptions in every theory of metrical phonology (e.g. Liberman

& Prince 1977; Hayes 1995; van der Hulst 1999).[7] Since it is so far unknown which prosodic domains play a role in prominence assignment in Quechua, it would be inadvisable to neglect one of these domains by not annotating for syllabic position in it. On the other hand, if the later analysis shows consistent results e.g. in the prosodic behavior of syllables counted from the right edge of the phrase but not the word, it will be possible to conclude that this domain definitely does play a role. We think that the domains annotated as they are here are the best possible candidates so far for playing a role in influencing prosodic phenomena and only after the final analysis will it be possible to see where they need to be further refined.

To complete the description of the annotation process, there is also a derivative tier of the morphological tier, tier 20, that annotates word-length elements by copying the tier of the morphological annotation and leaving only those boundaries that are to the left of the beginning of the root of a word (using information from tier 17). A script in Praat was written for that and the results checked. This helps to take important measurements in relation to word length, an information that wasn't contained in the textgrid up to that point, as will be seen in the next section.

3.4 Measurements

A Praat script was written that used the information encoded in the annotation textgrids detailed above. Per annotated syllable, it was used to extract the relevant annotational information from the tiers in the textgrid described above, i.e. what word the syllable belongs to, which one of the two speakers is uttering it, what information structural categories it is annotated for, what position according to the positional annotations it has, etc. Acoustic measurements per syllable were also taken by it from the sound files in the corpus. The measurements taken can be divided into two kinds: absolute and relative.

3.4.1 Absolute measurements

We extracted measurements of F0, intensity and duration, all of which have been shown to variously play a role in the encoding of prominence. In particular, the absolute measurements taken were:

---

[7]If our method were to show that no kind of prominence is computable from the edges we would have to assume prominence as a diacritic in the phonological word in Quechua. This is hard to believe. Rather, we expect some aspects to be derived metrically and others to be lexically fixed.

1. Syllable duration in ms

2. Mean F0 per syllable in Hz

3. Minimum F0 per syllable in Hz

4. Maximum F0 per syllable in Hz

5. Position of minimum and maximum F0 within the syllable

6. Pitch range within the syllable in Hz

7. Mean intensity per syllable

From the measurements for F0 minimum and maximum, the script further created a categorical measurement of F0 movement for each syllable: if minimum and maximum were at least 30 Hz and 100 ms (about one standard deviation of the syllable duration in the sample) apart from each other, the syllable would be assigned one of the labels "rising" or "falling", depending on whether the movement was from minimum to maximum or the other way round; if these criteria were not met, the syllable was assigned the label "level".

3.4.2 Relative measurements

The relative measurements are based on the deliberation that prominence by definition is a relative concept. It is impossible to make a statement about the prominence of a syllable just from knowing that e.g. it has a certain mean F0 value or even that it has a large pitch range, without a comparison with the corresponding values of other units, i.e. that of adjacent syllables or the mean value of the word the syllable is a part of. That is exactly what the relative measurements do (for a similar approach, see Pamies Bertrán 1996). For most of the absolute measurements, the script also produces relative values that serve as a comparison with the corresponding acoustic parameter on three levels: that of the adjacent syllable (left and right if they exist, i.e. if the syllable isn't itself at a domain edge), that of the word, and that of the phrase (each as defined within the annotation method described above). These are the relative measurements obtained per syllable:

1. Syllable duration divided by average syllable duration within the phrase

2. Syllable duration divided by average syllable duration within the word

3. Syllable duration divided by duration of the left-adjacent syllable (if it exists)

4. Syllable duration divided by duration of the right-adjacent syllable (if it exists)

5. Mean F0 of the syllable divided by mean F0 of the phrase

6. Mean F0 of the syllable divided by mean F0 of the word

7. Mean F0 of the syllable divided by mean F0 of the left-adjacent syllable (if it exists)

8. Mean F0 of the syllable divided by mean F0 of the right-adjacent syllable (if it exists)

9. Pitch range of the syllable divided by pitch range of the left-adjacent syllable (if it exists)

10. Pitch range of the syllable divided by pitch range of the right-adjacent syllable (if it exists)

11. Mean intensity of the syllable divided by mean intensity of the phrase

12. Mean intensity of the syllable divided by mean intensity of the word

13. Mean intensity of the syllable divided by mean intensity of the left-adjacent syllable (if it exists)

14. Mean intensity of the syllable divided by mean intensity of the right-adjacent syllable (if it exists)

A few remarks need to be made regarding these measurements. In general, the script was written so as to recognize when a syllable had no left- or right-adjacent syllable, so it wouldn't take the corresponding relative measurement. Then, because they are obtained by dividing the value of a parameter for the syllable that is being investigated by the corresponding value of another unit, all of these relative measurements are naturally grouped around the value 1 in the sense that if they are larger than 1, it means that the value of the syllable in question is higher than that of the unit it is compared with; if it is below 1 it is lower than that of the other unit in comparison; if it is exactly 1 the two values compared are the same. These values increase exponentially, therefore their log-10s were taken so that they are now grouped around 0, increase linearly and statistical measurements such as means can be applied to them.

Note that we originally intended to also compare formant measurements between syllables in order to look at vowel reduction as a correlate of non-prominence. However, implementing this would not be straightforward, as only phonologically same vowels that are adjacent could be reasonably compared, and then only via a derived measure comparing e.g. distance between F1 and F2, as an indicator of centralization of the vowel. However, centralization is not the only way of reducing vowels,[8] so this would still be an insufficient procedure. We decided to exclude vowel quality from the scope of this preliminary study and to perform a detailed analysis of it later.

3.5 Putting things into interaction

A total of 1019 syllables of the pilot corpus were annotated and measured in the way described above. 26 of these had to be excluded because of overlap between speakers, reducing the number of syllables that can be used in the analysis to 993. After applying the steps described above, there are now per syllable up to 43 numerical (ratio and interval) variables obtained through the acoustic measurements and 12 categorical (nominal and ordinal) variables obtained by extraction of the relevant annotation information from the textgrid. A further categorical variable, syllable type (C, CV, V:, CVC etc.), was derived from the syllable annotation by using regular expressions in R (R Core Team 2016). Now, the purpose of this approach is to bring to light the effect each of the linguistic categories encoded in the annotation has on realizational strength, which is supposed to encode phonological prominence. For this purpose, the data was imported into R, so that the measurements could be plotted in dependence on the categorical variables, either in isolation or in conjunction. There are two important points to consider. The first is that in our pilot corpus, we do not have a balanced sample with regards to frequency of occurrence of the variants the categorical variables

---

[8]Note that in two studies on (unstressed) vowel reduction in Cusco Spanish (Delforge 2008) and Cusco Quechua (Delforge 2011), the phenomenon is described as existent and wide-ranging but consisting phonetically of instances of vowel devoicing with no apparent centralization. While this might well be the case, the fact that Cusco Quechua and the Central Quechua varieties are so different in many other respects means that we are unwilling to simply transfer these conclusions to our case. Besides, Delforge (2011) never connects vowel reduction in Cusco Quechua with any prosodic properties of the language, so that the relation between vowel reduction and stress or accent in Quechua remains entirely unexplored so far.

may assume. That is, if we were to compare the mean values of the rightmost syllable in the word with that of the fifth rightmost syllable in the word just like that, the results would be skewed, because there are just 15 syllables in the corpus that are annotated as being in the fifth rightmost position of the word, whereas there are 410 syllables in rightmost position within the word. The same would happen when comparing declaratives with imperatives; while there are more than 600 syllables annotated as belonging to the former category, there are only 15 for the latter. Differences in variance between the two groups to be compared would result more from the differences in sample size than from any inherent properties of the underlying populations. Ideally we would need a much larger sample, so even rarer variants and conditions would still have enough oc-currences to allow for a meaningful comparison. Since this is not feasible with the sample size we have, a preliminary solution must be to exclude rare variants and to only work with those that have a reasonable number of occurrences in the dataset. The second point is related, but of a more linguistic nature. When comparing measurements, again, between the rightmost, the second rightmost and the third rightmost syllable of a word, the results will be of little value if care isn't taken to make sure that the second and third rightmost syllables aren't sometimes initial syllables, a fact that might influence prosodic realization. In other words, it makes more sense to compare syllables belonging to words of the same length.

3.6 The realizational coefficient

One approach that is interesting to pursue exploits the nature of the relative mea-surements taken. Since they are all (log-10s of) ratios of a parameter measured for one syllable to that of an adjacent (left or right) syllable or larger unit, they are all at the same scale and therefore comparable. They can also be used in combina-tion. Adding together relative values for one measurement with those of another and dividing by their number, we get average ratios per syllable of several param-eters at once. For example, we can get an overall realizational value for the ratio of one syllable to its adjacent syllables by taking the relative values of syllable duration divided by that of its left- and right-adjacent syllables, as well as those for mean F0, pitch range and intensity, adding them together and dividing them by the number of values added (eight in this case). Since these values express relative realizational strength of one syllable over others, we may name the re-sult (somewhat tongue-in-cheek) the overall realizational coefficient(s). With the help of these coefficients we can determine the relative realizational strength of any syllable position in our data, as well as (by comparison with the singular relative measurements) its contributing factors. Thus it is possible to show not only why a certain syllable position is strong when viewed e.g. at the word level, and what parameter is responsible for this, but also why it might not be very salient at another level (e.g. the phrase level), for example because the effect one parameter has at one level is overruled by that of another at another level. It needs to be pointed out that the same coefficients cannot always be used equally. Syllables at phrase edges have empty pauses to one of their sides, and the Praat script did not take relative measurements for them towards that side, see §3.4.2. For that reason, when looking at phrase-level measurements, the values comparing syllables with average syllable values in their phrase were used. In theoretical terms, using these realizational coefficients will help us to disentangle the interaction of the different means of creating prominence at different levels.

4 Preliminary results

In the following, some of the findings resulting from looking at the measurements at the different syllable positions under some of the information structural conditions will be presented and discussed. The purpose is here to explore the capabilities and limitations of the method described for creating profiles of realizational prominence in the data. In order to gain a comprehensive overview of the multidimensional dataset, hundreds of combinations of conditions were examined in different ways. We can only report on a few of the ones that seem to be most promising for future exploration. Since the sample is not balanced, we decided not to use any inferential statistics in order not to create false impressions of the general validity of our results unsuitable to the exploratory nature of this study.

4.1 Prominent syllables: Penultima

One important overall finding that derives from several ways of looking at the data is that the penultimate syllable is indeed prominent in the sense that something is happening there, but that it isn't at all certain that the prosodic domain of which this is the penultimate syllable is really isomorphic with the word as defined here. To explore this finding in more detail, let us proceed from looking at overall values to more individual ones:

Figure 2 shows barplots of the median values obtained for the first four syllable positions in the word (we left out the fifth and sixth due to small token size and better visibility) counted from the right word boundary, for the whole dataset used. The ends of the bars indicate the (medians of the) ratio of the parameter measured for the respective syllable position, divided by its immediate neighbours to the left and right (where applicable). The parameters used are mean F0 per syllable (red), pitch range (orange), duration (blue), intensity (green) and all four combined and divided by their number (black, from here on called "the left-right overall coefficient", see above). Considering the left-right overall coefficient, the penultimate syllable of the word obtains median (0.0081) and mean (0.0072, sd=0.1197) values only slightly above zero (meaning that at least half of its values are better than those of its adjacent syllables). Almost all other syllable positions also have median values slightly above zero, and their quartiles (see Table 1) range very far both below and above zero. Hence the penult is not particularly *more* prominent in this regard than other positions. The values for the left-right overall coefficient are very small here, even compared to the already small scale used in this figure.[9] This reflects the fact that the parameters it is composed of do not show a uniform pattern, i.e. do not unequivocally indicate a prominence for the penult at all. For example, the penult actually has a median slightly below zero for the parameter of duration, and at zero for the parameter of pitch range. Duration seems to instead favour the anteantepenult and pitch range the ultima, and also for mean F0, the median values for the penult do not stand out particularly from those of the antepenult. Hence, the picture we get from this very first approach to the data is less than unified, and does not seem to indicate a state of

---

[9] It has to be borne in mind how these graphs are to be read: the values on the y-axis are logarithms of base-10 (log-10) of the ratio of a value obtained in a parameter for a syllable in the indicated position divided by the values obtained for the same parameter by either its adjacent syllables or the larger unit (word/phrase), thus representing relative realizational strength of the syllable in that parameter (see §3). A value of zero on the y-axis therefore means that the syllable is equally strong in the parameter as the unit it is compared with, positive values mean that it is realizationally stronger relative to the compared unit, negative values mean that it is weaker. A log-10 value of 0.1 corresponds to a ratio of about 1.259:1 (meaning that the value for the syllable is about 25 % higher than that of the unit it is compared with), a log-10 value of 0.04 to a ratio of 1.096:1 (a little less than 10 % higher), a log-10 value of 0.02 to a ratio of 1.047:1 (a little less than 5 % higher), a log-10 value of 0 to a ratio of 1:1, a log-10 value of -0.02 to a ratio of 0.955:1 (a little less than 5 % below the value for the compared unit), a log-10 value of -0.04 to a ratio of 0.912:1 (a little less than 10 % below), and a log-10 value of -0.1 to a ratio of 0.794:1 (a little more than 20 % below), and so on, to give an example. The barplots indicate the median value for each syllable position. Each individual measurement obtained above zero means that this *individual* syllable is more realizationally strong in the parameter measured than its *specific and individual* neighbors. A median above zero thus means that this is the case for at least half of all syllables in this position. Because of the lower quartiles reaching below zero (see Table 1) and the differing token sizes per syllable position, there is no contradiction with several positions having their medians above zero: this only means that there is a smaller percentage of syllables that are less realizationally strong than their individual neighbors.

affairs in which all acoustic parameters unite in order to make a single syllable in the domain of the prosodic word stand out from all others. Taking a look at specific conditions, word lengths and the individual realizational parameters will hopefully provide more detailed insight.

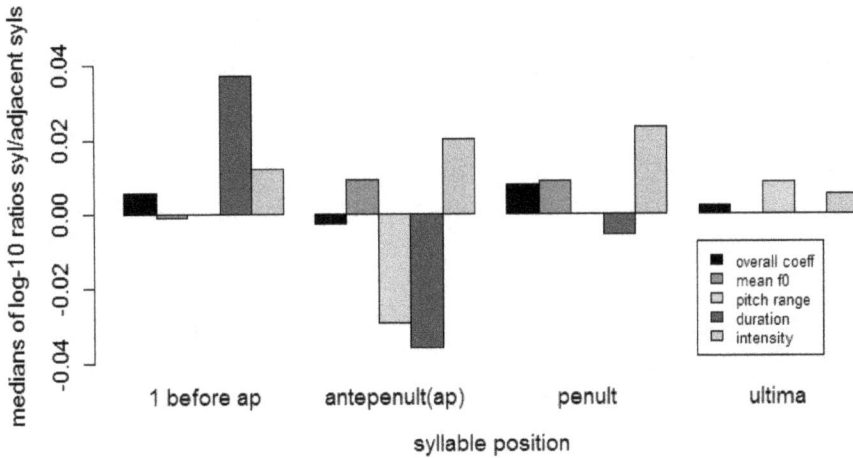

Figure 2: Barplots comparing the medians of 5 log-10 ratios obtained by dividing the value for the syllable by that of its adjacent syllables in the word, ordered according to syllable position in the word from the right word boundary: the overall (black), mean F0 (red), pitch range (orange), duration (blue) and intensity (green) left-right coefficients for the entire sample. N (1 before antepenult) = 49; N (antepenult) = 136; N (penult) = 281; N (ultima) = 255

4.2 Word length

As explained above, by controlling for word length we eliminate possible effects of left-edge phenomena. If only words of the same length are compared, we can observe not only the right, but also the left edge of the word. The syllable position that is leftmost in the graph is now also the leftmost syllable in the word. Additionally, token sizes for each syllable position are now equal (almost, because of elimination of syllables for reasons such as speaker overlap or being at the edge of the phrase). We can thus create more reliable prominence profiles for each word length. Unfortunately, in this sample, this kind of reduction also means that we can only effectively observe words from lengths 2–4 (see token sizes given in the descriptions for the figures).

Table 1: Values for relative parameters in words of all lengths, counting from the right word boundary (see Figure 2)

type of co-efficient	syllable position in word	lower quartile	median	mean	upper quartile	sd	N tokens (syllables)
overall	3 before antepenult	−0.09176	−0.06776	−0.06776	−0.04375	0.06790292	2
	2 before antepenult	−0.05519	0.02811	0.01336	0.05518	0.08698023	11
	1 before antepenult	−0.04438	0.00570	0.01235	0.07184	0.10113552	49
	antepenult	−0.061365	−0.002598	−0.007605	0.048850	0.10058366	136
	penult	−0.059410	0.008110	0.007206	0.078412	0.11970251	281
	ultima	−0.061826	0.002242	0.003760	0.083105	0.12473560	255
mean f0	3 before antepenult	−0.032162	−0.021081	−0.021081	−0.010000	0.03134178	2
	2 before antepenult	−0.003155	0.007354	0.007931	0.027405	0.04696297	11
	1 before antepenult	−0.0319673	−0.0009873	−0.0057637	0.0106195	0.04610146	49
	antepenult	−0.009671	0.009344	0.006082	0.026019	0.05388791	136
	penult	−0.007283	0.008938	0.006025	0.031923	0.05610093	281
	ultima	−0.025128	−0.000083	0.002712	0.024209	0.08117007	255
pitch range	3 before antepenult	−0.37810	−0.17418	−0.17418	0.02975	0.5767830	2
	2 before antepenult	0.0000	0.1431	0.1552	0.2426	0.3651206	11
	1 before antepenult	−0.19496	0.00000	0.07306	0.28384	0.4362566	49
	antepenult	−0.35170	−0.02925	−0.06869	0.15508	0.4262779	136
	penult	−0.22749	0.00000	0.02314	0.28935	0.4921704	281
	ultima	−0.231225	0.008477	0.005969	0.316592	0.5207739	255

Table 2: Values for relative parameters in words of all lengths, counting from the right word boundary (see Figure 2)

type of co-efficient	syllable position in word	lower quartile	median	mean	upper quartile	sd	N tokens (syllables)
duration	3 before antepenult	-0.1461	-0.1414	-0.1414	-0.1368	0.01308885	2
	2 before antepenult	-0.19105	-0.05224	-0.07615	0.06760	0.17805208	11
	1 before antepenult	-0.120304	0.037103	0.002385	0.151268	0.20698473	49
	antepenult	-0.16943	-0.03586	-0.01976	0.11743	0.20664683	136
	penult	-0.169099	-0.005398	-0.016198	0.149812	0.24136864	281
	ultima	-0.158923	0.000000	-0.003881	0.154910	0.23593383	255
intensity	3 before antepenult	0.010245	0.012472	0.012472	0.014700	0.006300656	2
	2 before antepenult	-0.007806	0.016768	0.006260	0.022976	0.025963067	11
	1 before antepenult	-0.004430	0.012249	0.009791	0.023763	0.023103567	49
	antepenult	0.004583	0.020092	0.018961	0.035845	0.027377440	136
	penult	0.009766	0.023370	0.022498	0.038142	0.025619751	281
	ultima	-0.010866	0.005356	0.001503	0.018054	0.027426937	255

Both two-syllable and three-syllable words do not especially indicate prominence for the penult (see Figure 3, comparing the left-right overall coefficient for words of length 2 (black), 3 (red) and 4 (blue)).

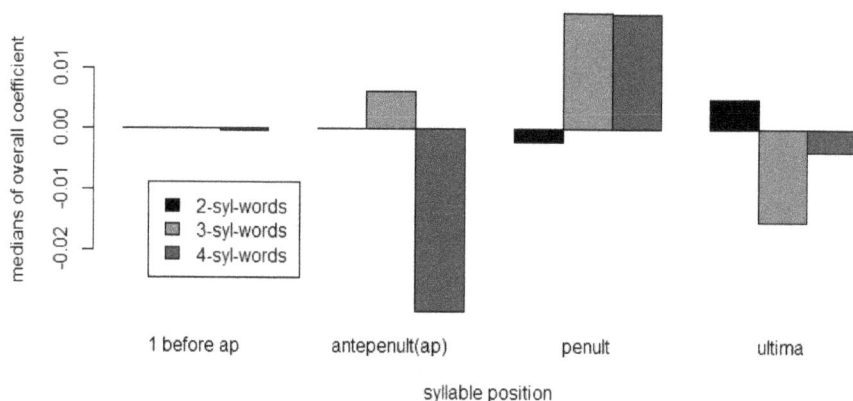

Figure 3: Barplots comparing the medians of the overall left-right coefficient for words of syllable length 2 (black), 3 (red) and 4 (blue), ordered according to syllable position in the word from the right word boundary. For 4-syllable words: N (1 before antepenult) = 31; N (antepenult) = 43 (4-syl words); N (penult) = 44; N (ultima) = 28. For 3-syllable words: N (antepenult) = 71; N (penult) = 110; N (ultima) = 72. For 2-syllable words: N (penult) = 105; N (ultima) = 116

The medians for all positions are more or less the same in 2-syllable words, and in 3-syllable words the median of the penult is the highest, but not by much. Not much indication, either, for a stronger realization of the initial syllable. However, in 4-syllable words, the picture changes (see Figure 3). Here, the median of the penult is visibly higher than that of its surrounding positions.

The initial syllable is also stronger in its realization than the ultimate and antepenult. This would give some support to the proposal of a primary prominence on the penultimate, and a secondary prominence on the initial or every second syllable from it (which of the two cannot be determined here), or one where prominence is assigned metrically to every second syllable in a unit. It has to be kept in mind however, that the ratios obtained here are again very small overall, indicating differences in the realizational strength of the syllables of at most 10–15 %.

4.3 Different parameters

We will now explore the factors contributing to the values of the overall realizational coefficient, i.e. the three acoustic parameters it consists of, duration, F0 and intensity. We will see how they support the finding of the penultimate syllable receiving word-level prominence.

4.3.1 F0

There are several ways in which F0 can reasonably influence realizational strength. Leaving other things aside, an interesting difference arises between the relative measurements of mean F0 per syllable and pitch range per syllable divided by their adjacent syllables. See Figure 4 showing the values for pitch range (dark blue) and mean F0 (red) per syllable, both in words of length 4.

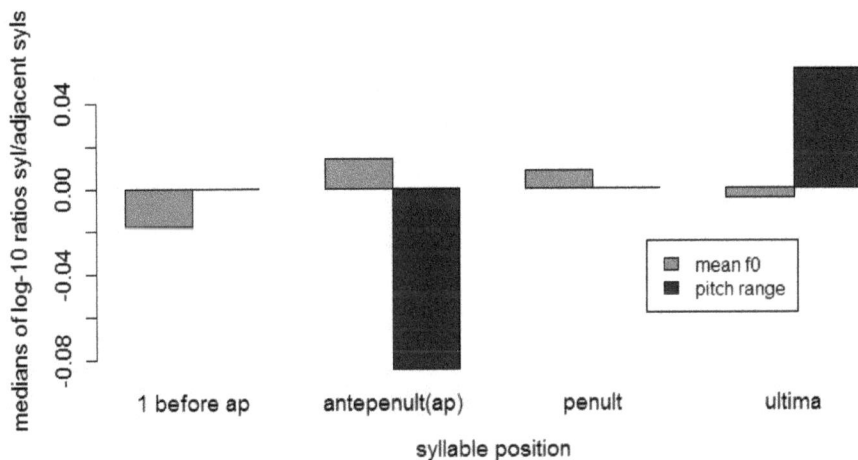

Figure 4: Barplots comparing the medians of the left-right pitch range (dark blue) and mean F0 (red) coefficients for words of syllable length 4, ordered according to syllable position in the word from the right word boundary. N (1 before antepenult) = 31; N(antepenult) = 43; N (penult) = 44; N (ultima) = 28

While the values for pitch range seem to display an alternating pattern, with the ultima realizing the largest range in comparison with adjacent syllables, the antepenult the least, and the penult and initial syllable being more or less equal, the values for plain F0 form a sort of arc, with low values at the edges and high ones in the two middle positions. These two results are what would be expected if the actual F0 pattern was that of a rise on the initial syllable, a plateau on the intervening one(s), and a drop on the penult (and/or ultima, see below).

This ties in with observations we made inspecting the corpus individually: the main tonal movements seem to be a fall on the penult, often combined with a severe reduction of the last syllable, and a less pronounced initial rise. At the phrase level, a similar pattern manifests, of a (phrase-)initial rise, slow down-trend throughout the phrase and additional movement on the penultimate and last syllable (see Figure 5 as a good example of the overall persisting pattern) – note that there is considerable variance on the values of the last two syllables of the phrase, likely due to additional phrase-final movement used to encode asser-tions and questions, or finalizations and continuations. Comparing the F0 values for the phrase and word levels, there is an indication that a considerable falling movement often takes place over the last three syllables - but this is the case for both words and phrases, so it is hard to tell whether it is indeed a word- or a phrase-level effect.

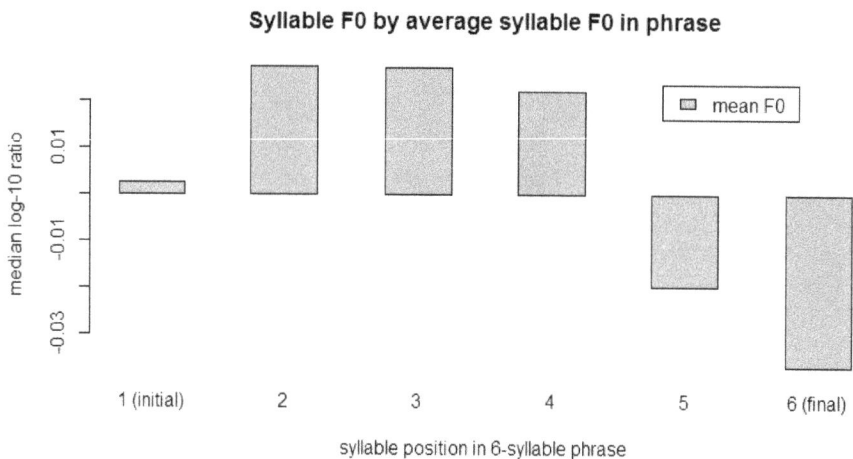

Figure 5: Barplots of median log-10 ratios of mean F0 per syllable di-vided by average mean F0 per syllable in phrases of syllable length 6, ordered according to syllable position in the phrase from left to right. N (1/initial) = 13; N (2) = 15; N (3) = 15; N (4) = 15; N(5) = 15; N (6/final) = 15

At least at the phrase-level, the shape of the overall movement can be taken as good evidence for phrasing in the domain of something like an intonational phrase – i.e. as evidence that what has here been labeled "phrase" indeed largely captures a phrase in the phonological sense. If the findings of a similar intonational shape across the word or a unit approximating it in size turned out to be robust, this would count as evidence for a lower-level type phrase as well. Whether this lower-level domain corresponds to the word or rather a small phrase above the morphosyntactic word such as an extended NP with preceding adjectives or a PP with embedded Noun, is another question.

4.3.2 Duration

Our variety of Quechua uses vowel length to distinguish meanings both at the level of lexemes and that of grammatical suffixes, for example *wata* 'year' vs. *waːta* 'domestic animal" vs. *waːtaː* (keep.animals.1s) 'I keep it [i.e. an animal]' (cf. Parker 1976: 51). As can be seen from these examples and from the literature, the positioning and multiple occurrence of such lengthened syllables is not constrained at the word level. However, when a syllable that has a long nucleus and is open is combined with a suffix beginning with two consonants, the first of those becomes the coda of the first syllable, and the vowel is said to be shortened (CVː + CCV -> CVC.CV, with the exceptions of nominal roots ending in a long vowel and the vowel lengthening used to encode verbal first person) in order to conform to a maximal syllable structure of CVC or CVː (cf. Parker 1976: 51–52). Nonetheless, as already mentioned, in our data we find a large number of instances of severely reduced word- or phrase-final syllables, which effectively yields spoken "super heavy" final syllables with structures like CVCC or CVːCC from a combination of the penult with this reduced final syllable. Hence it seems that often, the difference between long and short vowels manifests as unreduced but short vs. fully elided vowels. Apart from contravening proposed constraints on the syllable structure of our variety of Quechua, this process of course also has the effect of shifting syllable position from the right word boundary one step to the right (the "original" penult with the reduced final syllable becoming the "new" final syllable). In this situation, our expectation is not to find a straightforward encoding of a fixed prominent position at the word level by means of duration. Indeed, the results of plotting the left-right-coefficient for duration against syllable position from the right word boundary are very similar to those of the overall coefficient already discussed: basically no large outstanding differences between the positions, especially between penult and ultima (see Figure 2). This changes again when only considering words of length 4, but more interestingly, syllable structure has a much stronger effect: Figure 6 compares the same measurements restricted to syllables of the form CV (orange) to those of the form CVC (purple).

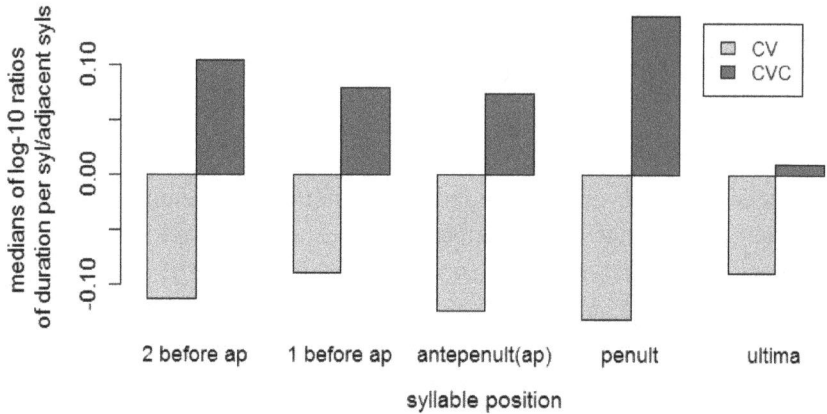

Figure 6: Barplots comparing medians of log-10 ratios of the left-right coefficient for duration between CV-syllables (orange) and CVC-syllables (purple), ordered according to syllable position in the word from the right word boundary. For CV-syllables: N (2 before antepenult) = 7; N (1 before antepenult) = 28; N (antepenult) = 67; N (penult) = 126; N (ultima) = 119. For CVC-syllables: N (2 before antepenult) = 4; N (1 before antepenult) = 7; N (antepenult) = 41; N (penult) = 84; N (ultima) = 79

Penults of the form CVC seem to be much longer than their surrounding syllables in comparison with penults of the form CV. Note also that the scale of the y-axis here indicates much larger differences than e.g. in the overall results (Figure 2). Consider here that we cannot tell whether the adjacent syllables for each individual syllable of this form also had the same form, thus it is possible that all of the penultimate CVC syllables were surrounded by syllables of shorter structure. If that were the case however, it would suggest a distribution of CVC-syllables sensitive to syllable position within the word, which would contradict Parker's description and would be interesting in itself. However, it would also be the case that a large share of the syllables in word final position annotated here as CVC are the product of final syllable reduction and are thus "former" penults. Thus, if a process existed to produce penults of the form CVC, it would work against that one producing final syllables of that form. In fact, many of the CVC-penults might actually have ended up as final syllables in this data, but the relative length distinction persists. It is thus plausible that syllables in penulti-mate position receive some kind of prominence that is realized at least partially through duration, but that this is often obscured by the length difference realized on behalf of syllable structure. As with all findings presented here, this one also needs to be supported by further analysis of a larger dataset.

4.3.3 Intensity

Intensity is usually not a very good correlate of metrical prominence in most languages, although it was once thought to be the main correlate in languages with word-level stress (Beckman 1986). Here, it presents an interesting addition to the results so far: From Figure 2, we can see that of all measures of realizational strength we have looked at so far, intensity (green) shows the penult to stand out from the other positions most clearly without the application of any further con-ditions. However, looking at the scale for the y-axis in Figure 2, we can see that none of the parameters there reach a median value above 0.04 (corresponding to a ratio of 1.096478 to 1), so also the strength of the effect of intensity here should not be overestimated.

4.4 Information structural categories

In many proposals, information structural categories play an important role for the assignment of prominence at a high level of prosodic structure. Especially, the category of focus is often associated with a particular pitch accent (Büring 2012, among many others) and many language specific annotation systems (To-BIs) implementing the autosegmental-metrical model of intonation (Pierrehum-bert 1980) include different intonational categories for different kinds of foci such as information focus and contrastive focus, including the ToBI for peninsular Spanish Sp_ToBI (Beckman et al. 2002; Estebas-Vilaplana & Prieto 2008). An ad-ditional assumption that has been proven empirically for many languages is that such high-level prominence markings of foci occur at the same site as other word- or phrase-level prominences, i.e. that a focused word will receive a particular ac-centual prominence on the syllable that is metrically already most prominent. Several recent proposals have cast the universality of this claim into doubt (cf. Kügler & Genzel 2012; Féry 2013). It seems to be the case that at least in some lan-guages, the hierarchy of focus strength proposed in Féry (2013: 688–690), going from broad information focus to narrow corrective focus necessitates a realiza-tion via marked prosody only at higher points of the scale. It is nevertheless promising to look for loci of prominence via information structural categories. It comes as somewhat of a surprise, then, that no clear overall results are obtained when applying this difference in labeling. Reasons for this might lie in the relatively broad labeling decision regarding focus (see §3.3.2), which might have to be refined for further studies, adopting Féry's hierarchy of focus strength, and which could allow for too much variation, or in the sample size. The same holds for the difference between those syllables labelled as "given", and those labelled as "new", and again speculation about reasons for this will lead us most immediately to categories labelled too broadly and the small sample size. However, a distinction that does yield interesting results is the one between topic and comment. See Figure 7 for a comparison of the values for topic (dark green) and comment (blue). Why this is the one information structural category yielding mentionable results (again favoring the penultima), is at this stage open to speculation. A possible factor might be that topics that are fully realized are often contrastive topics or topic shifts and hence focal in the sense that they evoke salient alternatives; the way the data was annotated has a bias towards labeling parts of utterances of comment insofar as that utterances without realized topics were labelled as "comment" (and not e.g. as "thetic"), so "topic" might actually often label a subset of focused parts of speech, namely those focused contrastively. Contrastive foci rank relatively high in Féry's hierarchy of focus strength and are thus more likely to be realized with marked prosody in her account.

A related explanation might be that realized topics are often only nominal constituents, again making them a more "narrow" label. Both these explanations receive incidental support by the fact that there is a total of 466 syllables labelled "comment" in the sample used versus only 235 labelled "topic". Further investigation into this is again needed.

5 Discussion – what we've got, what needs to be done and what's feasible

The results we have obtained so far are promising in that they demonstrate that it is indeed possible with this method to say something about consistent positions of realizational strength in a language where phonological prominence patterns are unknown, thus providing an empirical basis for hypotheses about these positions and the processes affecting their realization. The most convincing result for the utterances analyzed in this pilot corpus is that of prominence on the penult of the (prosodic) word, as demonstrated by the overall coefficient for 4-syllable words and under the condition topic and pitch range; duration when controlled for syllable structure and intensity overall. A second result is that of a possible

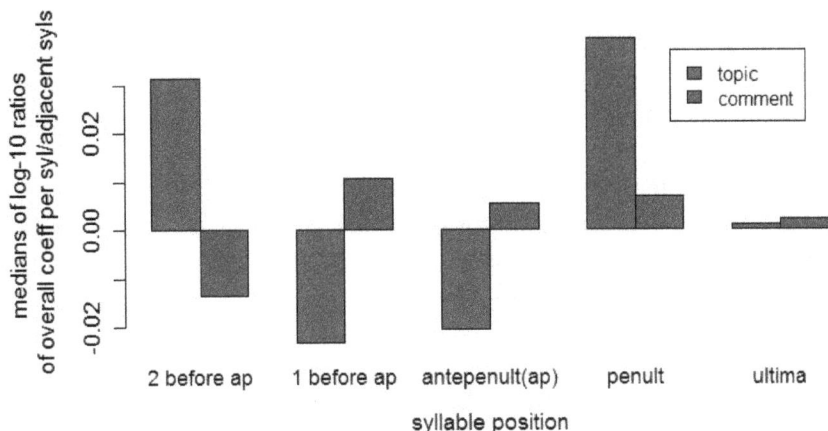

Figure 7: Barplots comparing medians of log-10 ratios of the overall left-right coefficient between syllables labeled "topic" (dark green) and "comment" (blue), ordered according to syllable position in the word from the right word boundary. For "topic": N (2 before antepenult) = 5; N (1 before antepenult) = 15; N (antepenult) = 37; N (penult) = 93; N (ultima) = 84. For "comment": N (2 before antepenult) = 6; N (1 before antepenult) = 33; N (antepenult) = 97; N (penult) = 180; N (ultima) = 194

secondary prominence on the initial syllable, as indicated by the overall and pitch range coefficient on 4-syllable words, and that for duration of CVC syllables. The most general caution regarding any of these hypotheses concerns the size and lack of balance of the corpus, and the consequent lack of any inferential statistics corroborating the general applicability of the results' predictions. We intend to improve upon this state of affairs, with a follow-up study on a larger sample. More specific limitations are discussed in the following. It would be useful to test the method as explained here on a comparable corpus of a language where prominence positions are well known, such as peninsular Spanish.[10] This is also something we intend to remedy in the future. Comparable research, reported on in Pamies Bertrán (1994 and especially 1996), has also used a coefficient composed of ratios of one acoustic parameter for one syllable by that of its neighbors to study acoustic realization of prominent positions in several languages where these positions are known. Although the calculations used to derive at his results,

---

[10]We thank Paolo Roseano for this and several other very useful suggestions on how to improve this work.

described in Pamies Bertrán (1996: 27–29), remain somewhat vague, the results themselves are similarly promising in that they suggest a general realization of prominences by a combination of these cues and a compensatory mechanism between them that is at work to differing degrees in the different languages under his discussion. His sample size for each of the seven languages analyzed (Catalan, English, French, Italian, Portuguese (lumping European and Brazilian Portuguese together, which we find questionable from a prosodic point of view), Russian and Spanish) is even smaller than ours for Quechua, hence the same general limitations apply. However, one very consistent result of his (reported on at greater length for Spanish in Pamies Bertrán 1994) is that prominent positions adjacent to each other ("acentos contiguous" in his terminology, "stress clash" more generally) do not allow for a consistently strong realization by any of the parameters. This has a possible bearing on our results as well, since it might help explain why no good results could be obtained in almost any condition for 2- and 3-syllable words. This would follow immediately if both the penult and the initial syllable were indeed prominent, creating clashes to be resolved by the phonetic realization (see also Hintz 2006 for a similar observation on a central Quechua variety very close to ours). It would especially be the case if what is seen as realizationally strong in the initial is mainly a rise in F0, whereas being a combination of a fall in F0 plus intensity and optional durational prominence in the penult; the rises and falls would conflict in 2-syllable words and create movements that cannot be disentangled by this method alone. This is one of the more specific limitations of this method, i.e. that in the domain of intonation it cannot properly differentiate between such phenomena as late and early peaks. The comparison of the coefficients for mean F0 and pitch range does allow for some more fine-grained intonational profiling of words of a given length, but it cannot resolve the issue of consistently late peaks versus peaks within the accented syllable by itself. Another related issue is that of reduction and prosodic phrasing. While in theory it would be possible to calculate mean constellations of F1–F2 for each intended vowel type in the corpus and then calculate their reduction by centralization by measurement of Euclidean distances from that mean and their durational reduction for each individual vowel token, in practice this would mean individually checking each vowel due to issues in automatic formant measurement in Praat, greatly reducing the advantage of automatization this method aims at. Hence, the clearly existing reduction processes in our variety of Quechua are not very well captured by this method. However, they are prime candidates as indicators for prosodic boundaries and hence very important to our general endeavor of determining prominence positions. To sum up and refine our desires for further investigations, they should therefore consist of acoustic measurements of the kind described here on a larger corpus of utterances where reductions are annotated as prosodic boundaries, preferably on ones of syllable length 4 and greater in order to better disentangle primary and secondary prominences and their differing realizations.

Acknowledgments

The research presented here has been conducted as part of the DFG-funded project *Zweisprachige Prosodie: Rhythmus, Metrik und Intonation zwischen Spanisch und Quechua* at FU Berlin. As part of this project, we undertook a fieldtrip to Huari, Conchucos, Peru in the summer of 2015, from which the data used in this research stems. We very gratefully acknowledge the support of the Deutsche Forschungsgemeinschaft and would also like to thank the speakers we recorded for their time and willingness to participate in our experiments.

References

Abaurre, Maria B. & Charlotte Galves. 1998. As diferenças rítmicas entre o Português Europeu e o Português Brasileiro: uma abordagem otimalista e minimalista. The rhythmic differences beween European Portuguese and Brazilian Portuguese. *Documentação de Estudos em Lingüística Teórica e Aplicada* 14(2). 377–403.

Adelaar, Willem F. H. 1977. *Tarma Quechua: Grammar, Texts, Dictionary*. Lisse: Peter de Ridder.

Anderson, Anne H., Miles Bader, Ellen Gurman Bard, Elizabeth Boyle, Gwyneth M. Doherty, Simon Garrod, Stephen Isard, Jacqueline Kowtko, Jan McAllister, Jim Miller, Catherine Sotillo, Henry S. Thompson & Regina Weinert. 1991. The HCRC Map Task Corpus. *Language and Speech* 34. 351–366.

Auer, Peter. 1993. *Is a rhythm-based typology possible?: A study of the role of prosody in phonological typology* (KontRI Working Paper 21). Konstanz: Universität Konstanz.

Auer, Peter. 2001. Silben- und akzentzählende Sprachen. In Martin Haspelmath, Ekkehard König, Wulf Oesterreicher & Wolfgang Raible (eds.), *Language typology and language universals // Sprachtypologie und sprachliche Universalien // La typologie des langues et les universaux linguistiques: An international handbook // Ein internationales Handbuch // Manuel international*, vol. 2, 1391–1399. Berlin, New York: de Gruyter.

Aurrekoetxea, Gotzon, Iñaki Gaminde, Leire Gandarias & Aitor Iglesias. 2012. Prosodic Variation in the Basque Language: Stress Areas. In Xosé A. álvarez Pérez (ed.), *Proceedings of the International Symposium on Limits and Areas in Dialectology (LimiAr), Lisbon, 2011*. Lisboa.

Austin, John L. 1962. *How to Do Things with Words: The William James Lectures delivered at Harvard University in 1955*. Oxford: Oxford University Press.

Baumann, Stefan. 2006. *The Intonation of Givenness: Evidence from German*. Tübingen: Niemeyer.

Becker, Thomas. 1996. Zur Repräsentation der Vokallänge in der deutschen Standardsprache. *Zeitschrift für Sprachwissenschaft* 15(1). 3–21.

Beckman, Mary E. 1986. *Stress and non-stress accent* (Netherlands Phonetic Archives 7). Dordrecht: Foris.

Beckman, Mary E., Manuel Díaz-Campos, Julia Tevis McGory & Terrell A. Morgan. 2002. Intonation across Spanish, in the Tones and Break Indices framework. *Probus. International Journal of Latin and Romance Linguistics* 14(1). 9–36.

Boersma, Paul & David Weenink. 2017. *Praat: Doing phonetics by computer [Computer program]*. Version 6.0.30. http://www.praat.org/.

Bolinger, Dwight. 1989. *Intonation and its uses: Melody in grammar and discourse*. London [etc.]: Edward Arnold.

Büring, Daniel. 2012. Focus and Intonation. In Gillian Russell & Delia G. Fara (eds.), *Routledge companion to philosophy of language (Routledge Philosophy Companions)*, 103–115. New York, NY: Routledge.

Chafe, Wallace L. 1976. Givenness, contrastiveness, definiteness, subjects, topics and point of view. In Charles N. Li (ed.), *Subject and topic*, 27–55. New York: Academic Press.

Dauer, Rebecca. 1983. Stress-timing and syllable-timing reanalyzed. *Journal of Phonetics* 11. 51–62.

Delforge, Ann M. 2008. Unstressed Vowel Reduction in Andean Spanish. In Laura Colantoni & Jeffrey Steele (eds.), *Selected Proceedings of the 3rd Conference on Laboratory Approaches to Spanish Phonology*, 107–124. Somerville, MA: Cascadilla Proceedings Project.

Delforge, Ann M. 2011. Vowel Devoicing in Cusco Collao Quechua. In Wai-Sum Lee & Eric Zee (eds.), *Proceedings of the 17th International Congress of Phonetic Sciences*, 556–559. Hong Kong: City University of Hong Kong.

Dufter, Andreas. 2003. *Typen sprachrhythmischer Konturbildung* (Linguistische Arbeiten 475). Tübingen: Niemeyer.

Estebas-Vilaplana, Eva & Pilar Prieto. 2008. La notación prosódica del español: una revisión del Sp_ToBI. *Estudios de fonética experimental* 17. 263–283.

Féry, Caroline. 2013. Focus as prosodic alignment. *Natural Language & Linguistic Theory* 31(3). 683–734.

Gómez Rendón, Jorge. 2006. Interpersonal aspects of evidentiality in Ecuadorian Quechua. In Silke Hamann & Roland Pfau (eds.), *ACLC Working Papers*, vol. 1, 37–50. Amsterdam: ACLC.

Grice, Martine, D. Robert Ladd & Amalia Arvaniti. 2000. On the place of phrase accents in intonational phonology. *Phonology* 17(2). 143–185.

Grice, Martine & Michelina Savino. 1997. Can pitch accent type convey information status in yes-no questions? In Kai Alter, Hannes Pirker & Wolfgang Finkler (eds.), *Concept to Speech Generation Systems: Proceedings of a Workshop in conjunction with 35th Annual Meeting of the Association for Computational Linguistics*, 29–38. Madrid: Universidad Nacional de Educación a Distancia.

Hayes, Bruce. 1995. *Metrical stress theory: Principles and case studies.* Chicago: University of Chicago Press.

Hintz, Daniel. 2000. *Caracteristicas distintivas del quechua de Corongo.* Lima: Instituto Lingüistico de Verano.

Hintz, Diane M. 2006. Stress in South Conchucos Quechua: A Phonetic and Phonological Study. *International Journal of American Linguistics* 72(4). 477–521.

Hualde, José Ignacio, Gorka Elordieta, Iñaki Gaminde & Rajka Smiljanic. 2008. From pitch accent to stress accent in Basque. In Carlos Gussenhoven & Natasha Warner (eds.), *Laboratory Phonology 7 (Phonology and phonetics 4-1)*, 547–584. Berlin, New York: Mouton de Gruyter.

Hyman, Larry M. 2009. How (not) to do phonological typology: The case of pitch-accent. *Language Sciences* 31(2–3).

Hyman, Larry M. 2014. Do All Languages Have Word Accent? In Harry van der Hulst (ed.), *Word stress: Theoretical and typological issues*, 56–82. Cambridge: Cambridge University Press.

Ka, Omar. 1989. Wolof Syllable Structure: Evidence from a Secret Code. In Joyce Powers & Kenneth d. Jong (eds.), *Proceedings of the Fifth Eastern States Conference on Linguistics*, 261–274. Columbus, Ohio.

Ka, Omar. 1994. *Wolof Phonology and Morphology.* Lanham, Maryland: University Press of America.

Krifka, Manfred. 2007. Basic Notions of Information Structure. In Caroline Féry, Gisbert Fanselow & Manfred Krifka (eds.), *Interdisciplinary Studies on Information Structure: The notions of information structure* (Working Papers of the

SFB 632 Interdisciplinary Studies on Information Structure 6), 13–56. Potsdam: Potsdam: Universitäts-Verlag.

Kügler, Frank & Susanne Genzel. 2012. On the Prosodic Expression of Pragmatic Prominence: The Case of Pitch Register Lowering in Akan. *Language and Speech* 55(3). 331–359.

Liberman, Mark & Alan S. Prince. 1977. On Stress and Linguistic Rhythm. *Linguistic Inquiry* 8(2). 249–336.

Muntendam, Antje G. 2010. *Linguistic Transfer in Andean Spanish: Syntax or Pragmatics?* Urbana-Champaign: University of Illinois at Urbana-Champaign dissertation.

Muntendam, Antje G. 2012a. Information structure and intonation in Andean Spanish. In *LSA Annual Meeting Extended Abstracts 3*.

Muntendam, Antje G. 2012b. *Bilingual intonation: a case study of Andean Spanish.* Bangor: Wales.

Muntendam, Antje G. & Francisco Torreira. 2016. Focus and prosody in Spanish and Quechua: Insights from an interactive task. In Meghan E. Armstrong, Nicholas Henriksen & Maria d. M. Vanrell (eds.), *Intonational Grammar in Ibero-Romance: Approaches across linguistic subfields*, 69–89. Amsterdam: John Benjamins.

Muysken, Pieter. 1995. Focus in Quechua. In Katalin é Kiss (ed.), *Discourse configurational languages*, 375–393. Oxford: Oxford University Press.

Muysken, Pieter & Antje G. Muntendam. 2016. Interfacing interfaces: Quechua and Spanish in the Andes. In Susann Fischer & Christoph Gabriel (eds.), *Manual of Grammatical Interfaces in Romance*, 607–633. Berlin, Boston: de Gruyter Mouton.

O'Rourke, Erin. 2005. *Intonation and Language Contact: A Case Study of two Varieties of Peruvian Spanish.* Urbana-Champaign: University of Illinois dissertation.

O'Rourke, Erin. 2007. Intonation in Quechua: Questions and Analysis. In Jürgen Trouvain & William J. Barry (eds.), *ICPhS XVI, Saarbrücken Germany, 6 - 10 August 2007: 16th international congress of phonetic sciences*. Saarbrücken.

O'Rourke, Erin. 2008. Correlating Speech Rhythm in Spanish: Evidence from Two Peruvian Dialects. In Joyce Bruhn de Garavito & Elena Valenzuela (eds.), *Selected proceedings of the 10th Hispanic Linguistics Symposium*, 276–287. University of Western Ontario.

O'Rourke, Erin. 2009. Phonetics and phonology of Cuzco Quechua declarative intonation: An instrumental analysis. *Journal of the International Phonetic Association* 39(3). 291–312.

O'Rourke, Erin. 2010. Dialect Differences and the Bilingual Vowel Space in Peruvian Spanish. In Marta Ortega-Llebaria (ed.), *Selected proceedings of the 4th Conference on Laboratory Approaches to Spanish Phonology*, 20–30. Somerville, MA.

O'Rourke, Erin. 2012. The realization of contrastive focus in Peruvian Spanish intonation. *Lingua* 122(5). 494–510.

Pamies Bertrán, Antonio. 1994. Los acentos contiguos en español. *Estudios de fonética experimental* 6. 91–111.

Pamies Bertrán, Antonio. 1996. Consideraciones sobre la marca acústica del acento fonológico. *Estudios de fonética experimental* 8. 11–49.

Parker, Gary. 1976. *Gramática quechua: Ancash-Huailas*. Lima: Ministerio de Educación.

Pierrehumbert, Janet B. 1980. *The phonology and phonetics of English intonation*. Bloomington: MIT dissertation.

R Core Team. 2016. *R: A Language and Environment for Statistical Computing*. R Foundation for Statistical Computing. Vienna, Austria. https://www.R-project.org/.

Reich, Uli. 2002. *Freie Pronomina, Verbalklitika und Nullobjekte im Spielraum diskursiver Variation des Portugiesischen in São Paulo* (Romanica Monacensia 62). Tübingen: Narr.

Reich, Uli & Martin Rohrmeier. 2014. Batidas latinas: On rhythm and meter in Spanish and Portuguese and other forms of music. In Javier Caro Reina & Renata Szczepaniak (eds.), *Syllable and word languages*, 391–420. Berlin: de Gruyter.

Rialland, Annie & Stéphane Robert. 2001. The Intonational System of Wolof. *Linguistics* 39(5). 893–939.

Rooth, Mats. 1992. A theory of focus interpretation. *Natural Language Semantics* 1(1). 75–116.

Searle, John R. 1969. *Speech Acts: An Essay in the Philosophy of Language*. Cambridge: Cambridge University Press.

Trager, George L. 1945. Analysis of a Kechuan Text. *International Journal of American Linguistics* 11(2). 86–96.

Trubeckoj, Nikolaj S. 1939. *Grundzüge der Phonologie: Publié avec l'appui du Cercle linguistique de Copenhague et du ministère de l'instruction publique de la République tchéco-slovaque*. Vol. 7 (Travaux du Cercle Linguistique de Prague). Prag.

Vallduví, Enric. 1992. *The informational component*. New York: Garland.

van der Hulst, Harry. 1999. Word accent. In Harry van der Hulst (ed.), *Word prosodic systems in the languages of Europe*, vol. 20 (Empirical approaches to language typology 4), 3–115. Berlin, New York: Mouton de Gruyter.

van der Hulst, Harry. 2010. Word accent systems in the languages of Europe. In Rob Goedemans, Harry van der Hulst & Ellen van Zanten (eds.), *A survey of word accentual patterns in the languages of the world*, 429–507. Berlin: de Gruyter.

van Rijswijk, Remy & Antje G. Muntendam. 2014. The prosody of focus in the Spanish of Quechua-Spanish bilinguals: A case study on noun phrases. *International Journal of Bilingualism* 18(6). 614–632.

Voisin-Nouguier, Sylvie. 2002. *Relations entre fonctions syntaxiques et fonctions sémantiques en wolof*. Lyon: Université Lumière Lyon dissertation.

Weber, David J. 1986. Information Perspective, Profile and Patterns in Quechua. In Wallace L. Chafe & Johanna Nichols (eds.), *Evidentiality: The linguistic coding of epistemology* (Advances in discourse processes 20), 137–155. Norwood, N.J.: Ablex publishing corporation.

Wetzels, Leo & Sérgio Meira. 2010. A Survey of South American stress systems. In Rob Goedemans, Harry van der Hulst & Ellen van Zanten (eds.), *A survey of word accentual patterns in the languages of the world*, 313–380. Berlin: de Gruyter.

Wittenburg, Peter, Hennie Brugman, Albert Russel, Alex Klassmann & Han Sloetjes. 2006. ELAN: A Professional Framework for Multimodality Research. In Nicoletta Calzolari, Khalid Choukri, Aldo Gangemi, Bente Maegaard, Joseph Mariani, Jan Odijk & Daniel Tapias (eds.), *Proceedings of the 5th International Conference on Language Resources and Evaluation (LREC'06)*, 1556–1559. Genoa, Italy.

Wölck, Wolfgang. 1972. *Especificación y foco en quechua*. San Marcos.

Yip, Moira. 2002. *Tone*. Cambridge: Cambridge University Press.

Chapter 5

On the role of prosody in disambiguating wh-exclamatives and wh-interrogatives in Cosenza Italian

Olga Kellert

Georg-August-Universität Göttingen

Daniele Panizza

Georg-August-Universität Göttingen

Caterina Petrone

Laboratoire Parole et Langage, Aix-Marseille Université

This work investigates the role of prosody in the perception of *wh*-exclamatives and (information-seeking) *wh*-interrogatives in Cosenza Italian, a Southern Italian variety spoken in Calabria. Following recent research on prosody, we use a two-alternative forced-choice identification task in combination with reaction time measurements, as reaction times have been used as a better substitute of discrimination scores to investigate categorical perception of prosodic contrasts. Here, this methodology is preferred to more difficult offline tasks (e.g. the gating paradigm) to test to what extent phonetic/phonological cues distributed over the utterance might guide listeners' responses during sentence type identification. Our results show that listeners identify the two sentence types after the end of the utterance in most of the trials, not before it. This suggests that prosodic cues that occur before the end of the utterance (e.g. in the prenuclear section of the intonational contour) are not strong enough by themselves to guide the pragmatic interpretation of the utterances. Furthermore, our study shows that exclamatives are processed faster than interrogatives, but this effect disappears when segmental duration is taken into account.

Olga Kellert, Daniele Panizza & Caterina Petrone. 2018. On the role of prosody in disambiguating wh-exclamatives and wh-interrogatives in Cosenza Italian. In Ingo Feldhausen, Jan Fliessbach & Maria del Mar Vanrell (eds.), *Methods in prosody: A Romance language perspective*, 165–188. Berlin: Language Science Press. DOI:10.5281/zenodo.1441343

Olga Kellert, Daniele Panizza & Caterina Petrone

1 Introduction

While in languages such as English, *wh*-exclamatives and information-seeking *wh*-interrogatives (hereafter "*wh*-interrogatives") are syntactically differentiated (e.g. *How many books you have read!* vs. *How many books have you read?*), in Italian the two sentence types are syntactically the same:

(1) Italian *wh*-exclamatives

  Quanti   romanzi ha scritto la tua amica!
  How many novels   has written the your friend

  'How many novels your friend wrote!'

(2) Italian *wh*-interrogatives

  Quanti   romanzi ha scritto la tua amica?
  How many novels   has written the your friend

  'How many novels did your friend write?'

  Studies on different languages have already shown that when syntactic structure is ambiguous, listeners mainly rely on prosodic information to identify exclamatives and interrogatives (cf. Batliner 1988; Eady & Cooper 1986; Sorianello 2011; 2012; Gyuris et al. 2013).

  However, it is still unclear to what extent temporally distributed phonological/phonetic properties are exploited by listeners for sentence-type identification. Consider the Italian examples in (1) and (2). The prosodic cues that determine the exclamative/interrogative meaning of these sentences could be contained in the *wh*-phrase ('how many novels'), in the verb phrase ('has written'), or in the final subject phrase ('your friend'). In the variety spoken in Cosenza (Southern Italy), *wh*-exclamatives and *wh*-interrogatives contain different prosodic cues in both the prenuclear region (i.e. at the beginning of the intonation contour) and in the nuclear region (i.e., at the end of the intonation contour). *wh*-exclamatives exhibit a %H at the left edge of the intonational phrase, which is absent in *wh*-interrogatives (where a prenuclear accent H* is produced on the *wh*-constituent; see Sorianello 2012 and §2 for details). Furthermore, the two sentence types are differentiated in the nuclear-accent choice associated with the verb phrase (L* in *wh*-exclamatives vs. L+H* in *wh*-interrogatives; ibid.).

  Our study, focusing on Cosenza Italian, addresses two main questions. First, we ask whether listeners rely on the nuclear information alone or whether the prenuclear region also contributes to the perception of sentence type. Given that %H might differ from the prenuclear H* in many F0 dimensions (such as tonal alignment and pitch excursion), we hypothesize that listeners should be able to discriminate the two sentence types from the beginning.

This question is linked to the issue in intonation research of how intonational meaning is created. The Autosegmental-Metrical (AM) framework assumes that the nuclear pitch accent is merely the last accent within a specific major prosodic phrase (cf. Ladd 2008 for a review). The overall meaning of a tune results from the independent contributions of its freely combinable, morpheme-like sub-parts, which include pitch accents and edge tones (Pierrehumbert & Hirschberg 1990). Despite this compositional-based approach to tune meaning, work within the AM theory often regards the nucleus – more or less implicitly – as the semantic "heart" of the tune. Hence, the current study searches for the meaning contribution of the prenuclear region and its potential interaction with the nuclear tune.

Furthermore, we ask whether the processing of the intonational contour is similar between the two sentence types or whether some cues are more salient in one sentence type than in the other. The %H is a marked pattern in Italian, since its use is restricted to a few contexts (including the *wh*-exclamatives). It also exhibits enhanced pitch excursion, which renders it perceptually salient (Sorianello 2012). Hence, we hypothesize that the intonation of *wh*-exclamatives should be processed and identified much faster than the intonation of *wh*-interrogatives.

Concerning methodology, we employ an experimental design that involves an identification task with measurement of reaction times. Identification tasks have been already used in combination with reaction times (RTs) in prosody research, especially within the categorical perception paradigm (Chen 2003; Falé & Faria 2006; Niebuhr 2007; Feldhausen et al. 2011, among others). Reaction times are believed to reflect task difficulty (Massaro 1987) and they have been used as a substitute for discrimination scores to test whether the perception of prosodic contrasts is categorical or gradient (Chen 2003; Niebuhr 2007). This methodology has been applied to contrasts at the level of pitch accents (Chen 2003; Niebuhr 2007; Feldhausen et al. 2011), prosodic boundaries (Schneider 2011; Petrone et al. 2017), and global phonetic cues (such as pitch range; see Borràs-Comes et al. 2010). The studies in question are all based on manipulated stimuli. Given a continuum of manipulated stimuli, it is generally supposed that, in the case of categorical boundary perception, reaction times should be long at the location corresponding to the category boundary and short in other parts of the continuum. In contrast, a gradual increase in reaction time with proximity to the boundary might reflect a gradual increase of the ambiguity of the stimuli, pointing to a more gradient boundary perception. In the current study, we will measure identification scores and reaction times in response to natural (not manipulated) stimuli as a first step in the investigation of an understudied prosodic contrast, i.e. the contrasts between *wh*-exclamatives and *wh*-interrogatives.

The structure of the paper is as follows: After a short review of the literature on *wh*-exclamatives and *wh*-interrogatives (§2), the goals of the study will be stated (§3) and a description of the experiment will be given (§4 and §5). The findings will be discussed in §6. Finally, the benefits and the challenges of the chosen methodology will be discussed in §7.

2 Previous investigations of the prosody of *wh*-exclamatives and *wh*-interrogatives

Prosodic characteristics of *wh*-interrogatives have been extensively studied in many languages (e.g. Zeng et al. 2004; Hedberg et al. 2010; Vanrell 2013). Concerning Italian, one of the most typical intonational characteristics of *wh*-interrogatives is the presence of utterance-final F0 fall (Chapallaz 1964; Avesani 1995; Sorianello 2011). However, the intonational pattern of *wh*-interrogatives can vary in many respects depending on their pragmatic function (e.g. rhetorical vs. information-seeking; see Hedberg et al. 2010) and on the regional variety (see Avesani 1995; Sorianello 2011; Gili Fivela et al. 2015, among others). In particular, in Cosenza Italian, the nuclear accent of information-seeking *wh*-interrogatives is associated with a rising accent L+H* followed by a low boundary tone L% (see Sorianello 2011; Sorianello et al. 2011).

Differently from *wh*-interrogatives, research on prosody of *wh*-exclamatives is cross-linguistically scarce (see Batliner 1988; Sorianello 2011; Gyuris et al. 2013). Studies so far have rather focused on the syntactic and semantic differences between *wh*-exclamatives and *wh*-interrogatives (see Zanuttini & Portner 2003; Castroviejo 2006, among others). *wh*-exclamatives and *wh*-interrogatives would mainly differ with respect to factivity, i.e., exclamatives imply a true proposition and interrogatives do not. Zanuttini & Portner (2003) deduce the factivity of *wh*-exclamatives from two considerations. First, exclamatives (including *wh*-exclamatives) can be embedded under factive predicates only (Zanuttini & Portner 2003: 46):

(3)   Mary knows/*thinks/*wonders how very cute Mario is.

Furthermore, *wh*-exclamatives can never be used as questions and never induce a response from the interlocutor:

(4)   a. A: How tall is Mary? B: 1.80.

     b. A: How tall Mary is! B: #1.80.

Some studies have shown that prosodic information alone might be used to distinguish (*wh*- and non-wh) exclamatives from other sentence types. Exclamatives have been claimed to be cross-linguistically characterized by an initial extra-high pitch followed by a falling intonation contour (see O'Connor & Arnold 1961 for English; Delattre 1966 for French; D'Eugenio 1976 for Italian; Batliner 1988 for German). However, in some languages, such as Hungarian, exclamatives are instead characterized by an initial low pitch (a low boundary tone; see Gyuris et al. 2013). Concerning the nuclear region, Gyuris et al. (2013) found that Hungarian listeners classified acoustic stimuli as exclamatives and not as interrogatives if they included nuclear pitch accents with rising F0 pattern; delayed peaks; and a combination of low initial boundary tones and rising accents.

Concerning Cosenza Italian, Sorianello (2011) provides a phonological analysis of both *wh*-exclamatives and *wh*-interrogatives (see also Gili Fivela et al. (2015: 182) on *wh*-interrogatives in Cosenza Italian and other Italian varieties). The two sentence types are characterized by the same ending, i.e., a L-L% tonal sequence (see Figure 1 and Figure 2). However, they are differentiated phonologically in the regions preceding the utterance's final fall, i.e., both at the left edge of the intonational phrase (IP) and within the nuclear region. First, the initial part of *wh*-exclamatives is marked by a high boundary tone at the left edge of the IP (represented by %H in Figure 1), which is not present in *wh*-interrogatives (for %H in non-*wh*-exclamatives, see Sorianello 2012; Avesani 1995; Grice et al. 2005). *Wh*-interrogatives are characterized by a prenuclear accent L+ H* on the *wh*-constituent (see Figure 2). Moreover, the nuclear accent is specified differently, i.e., a low accent L* characterizes *wh*-exclamatives and a rising accent L+H* appears in *wh*-interrogatives. Along with the intonational cues, *wh*-exclamatives are also characterized by an extra lengthening of the duration of the nuclear-stressed syllable (Sorianello 2011).

While there are still no perception studies on *wh*-exclamatives in Cosenza Italian, there are studies of non-*wh*-exclamatives in other Southern varieties of Italian that suggest that the prenuclear region can contribute to their identification. In an experiment on Bari Italian, Sorianello (2012) used natural minimal pairs of non-*wh*-exclamatives and assertions, cutting the sentences at different temporal locations. This procedure is reminiscent of the gating procedure used in word-recognition research to investigate the uptake of acoustic-phonetic cues to segmental structure (Grosjean 1980; Lahiri & Marslen-Wilson 1991, inter alia; see Petrone & D'Imperio 2011 for an example of this technique applied to intonational contrasts). Sorianello (2012) found that listeners could identify non-*wh*-exclamatives when only the initial part of the contour was available. By contrast, the prenuclear contour did not seem to provide robust cues for identifying assertions. Thus, the prenuclear cues are not equivalent across sentence types.

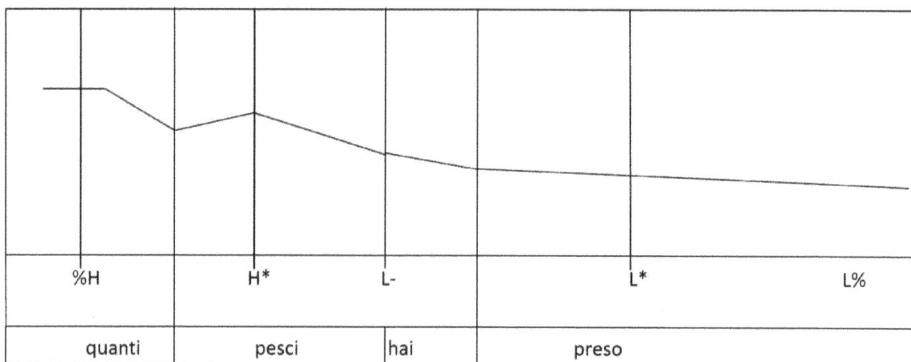

%H	H*	L-		L*	L%
quanti	pesci	hai		preso	

Figure 1: Our schematized version after Sorianello´s (2011: 316) representation of *Quanti pesci hai preso!* 'How many fishes you took!'

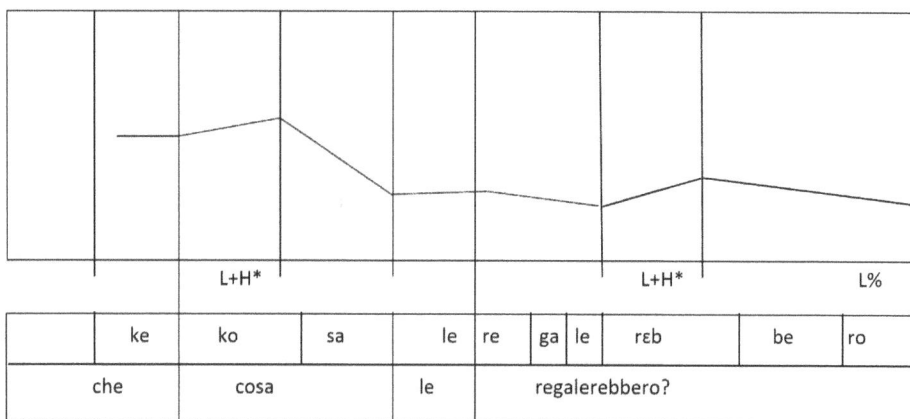

	L+H*						L+H*		L%
ke	ko	sa	le	re	ga	le	rɛb	be	ro
che	cosa		le			regalerebbero?			

Figure 2: Our schematized version after the representation of Information-seeking *wh*-interrogative: *Che cosa le regalerebbero?* 'What would they give her as a present?' in (Gili Fivela et al. 2015: 182)

3 Goals of the study

The main goal of this study is to determine if prosodic cues play an important role in the disambiguation of *wh*-exclamatives and *wh*-interrogatives in Cosenza Italian. Given the phonetic/phonological contrasts between the two sentence types that were described in §2, listeners should be capable of distinguishing *wh*-interrogatives from *wh*-exclamatives on the basis of prosody (Hypothesis 1).

In particular, we seek to determine to what extent phonetic/phonological cues distributed over the utterance might guide listeners' responses. Given that the contrast between *wh*-exclamatives and *wh*-interrogatives should be noticeable already in the prenuclear region (Sorianello 2011), we expect listeners to identify both sentence types before they hear the end of the sentence, with differences in the nuclear accent further helping perceptual disambiguation (Hypothesis 2).

Finally, we investigate the existence of potential differences in the processing of the two sentence types. Our hypothesis is that these processing differences do exist, since *wh*-exclamatives but not *wh*-interrogatives show a high boundary tone right at the beginning of the utterance, which is marked in Italian (i.e. %H at the left edge of the intonational phrase) (see Sorianello 2011). We thus assume that the intonation of *wh*-exclamatives should be processed and identified much faster than the intonation of *wh*-interrogatives (Hypothesis 3).

In order to test the three hypotheses, we conducted a two-alternative forced-choice identification task combined with measurement of reaction times. Our expectation was that identification scores should depend on differences in prosody between the two sentence types. Specifically, cues in the prenuclear region should enable disambiguation between *wh*-exclamatives and *wh*-interrogatives, even though robust identification is only expected after the listener hears the entire utterance. Moreover, longer reaction times are expected to indicate higher uncertainty with respect to sentence-type identification, which should then be associated with lower identification scores in the identification task.

4 Experiment

4.1 Experimental stimuli

We constructed 20 pairs of morpho-syntactically and lexically identical *wh*-exclamatives and *wh*-interrogatives (like those in 1 and 2). Each target sentence had a syntactic structure as in (5): a complex *wh*-constituent (i.e., *quanti* 'how many' + noun); a verb phrase consisting of an auxiliary and a past participle; and a nominal constituent including a grammatical subject. (The definite article preceding the subject constituent was omitted in the case of immediate family members, as typical in Italian.)

(5) Stimuli

[Quanti   romanzi] [ha scritto] [la tua   amica]
how many novels   has written the your friend

'How many novels your friend wrote!' or

'How many novels did your friend write?'

In order to elicit different intonation patterns in *wh*-exclamatives and *wh*-interrogatives, we embedded the stimuli in pragmatic contexts that only matched one or the other sentence type, such as in (6) and (7):

(6) *wh*-exclamative context: Your mother tells you that her friend spent 10 years of her life writing novels and shows you a list of her books. You exclaim:

Quanti   romanzi ha scritto la tua amica!
how many novels   has written the your friend

'How many novels your friend wrote!'

(7) *wh*-interrogative context: Your mother tells you that her friend spent 10 years of her life writing novels. You ask your mom:

Quanti   romanzi ha scritto la tua amica?
how many novels   has written the your friend

'How many novels did your friend write?'

The sentences were produced by a 38-year-old female speaker from Cosenza. The speaker silently read the contexts and then uttered the sentences aloud. She was instructed to produce the sentences in a natural way.[1] No instructions were given as to what specific prosodic pattern to use in sentence production. The 40 target sentences were presented randomly and interspersed with 20 fillers: non-*wh*-interrogatives and non-*wh*-exclamatives such as 'Do you like coffee?' 'Open the door!' and 'I came late today' (a yes-no interrogative, an imperative, and a declarative, respectively). A complete list of the experimental target sentences and the fillers is given in the Appendix.

---

[1]The discourse context was only presented in the production of the stimuli, to elicit a specific intonation contour, not in the identification task, since it would bias the responses of the listeners.

For the perception experiment, *wh*-exclamatives and *wh*-interrogatives constituted our auditory target stimuli. For each sentence, we identified four critical points or "marks" (M) at sequential temporal locations: M1 = the beginning of the utterance; M2 = the end of the *wh*-constituent; M3 = the end of the verb phrase; and M4 = the end of the subject constituent, which is also the end of the utterance. In example (8) below, M1 is represented by an opening bracket and M2–M4 by closing brackets.

(8) [=M1 Quanti   romanzi]=M2 ha scritto]=M3 la   tua   amica]=M4
      how many novels   has written   the your friend

'How many novels your friend wrote!' or

'How many novels did your friend write!'

The four marks divided the experimental sentences into three regions. The initial region, between M1 and M2, consisted of the *wh*-constituent (e.g. *Quanti romanzi*); the middle region, between M2 and M3, consisted of the verb phrase (e.g. *ha scritto*); and the final region, from M3 to M4, consisted of the subject phrase at the end of the utterance (e.g. *la tua amica*).

4.2 Tasks and procedure

Since it has been shown that there are durational differences between the two sentence types (cf. Sorianello 2011), something that was also clear from an initial analysis of our data, we measured the duration of each region. Statistical analysis of the duration showed that the initial region was significantly longer in the exclamative condition than in the interrogative one (on average, excl. = 616 ms vs. inter. = 546 ms, p < .01). The verb phrase was not significantly different between the two conditions (excl. = 592 ms vs. inter. = 604 ms, p = .40). The final subject phrase was longer in the exclamative condition (excl. = 933 ms vs. inter. = 751 ms, p < .001). Given that the duration of different regions seemed to play a crucial role in identification, this parameter was included as a variable in the statistical models (see §6).

Eighteen monolingual Italian native speakers (aged between 19 and 34 years) participated in the perception study and were reimbursed for their time. The group was composed of 10 women and 8 men. They were all from the Cosenza area and were either university students or employees at the *Università della Calabria*, in Cosenza. They reported no hearing problems.

Participants were asked to report which sentence type (*wh*-exclamative vs. *wh*-interrogative) better matched their auditory impression of the sentence. They were instructed to carefully listen to the stimuli and to press a button as soon as they were certain of the sentence type.

This instruction was given in order to elicit as many early responses as possible, to enable us to check whether listeners could identify the sentence type before the end of the utterance (e.g. just from hearing the initial region, or the initial and middle regions). Before the experiment, listeners had a short practice session, with four practice sentences to identify. They did not receive any feedback on their answers.

The identification task lasted about 10 minutes for each listener. Their responses and reaction times (measured from the offset of the stimulus) were recorded. Stimulus presentation and response collection were performed by an open-source toolkit based on the Python module Pygame (cf. Peirce 2007 for an overview of PsychoPy, a toolkit based on the same system).[2]

Each trial began with a written question to the participant/listener asking if they were ready to start. A beep was used to signal that an utterance was about to start, in order to draw the participant's attention to the stimulus. The session began with the presentation of the auditory stimulus. For each listener, the identification task was broken into two blocks of 30 sentences, with some stimuli repeated in the second block. The goal of this manipulation was to check whether repetition of the same sentences influenced reaction times (Bentin & McCarthy 1994). Block 1 contained 10 *wh*-exclamative sentences and 10 *wh*-interrogative sentences that were not lexically identical ("non-minimal-pair condition"). Stimuli were presented in random order and interspersed with 10 fillers (non-*wh*-exclamatives and non-*wh*-interrogatives). Block 2 also contained 10 *wh*-exclamatives, 10 *wh*-interrogatives, and 10 fillers. This time, 5 of the 10 *wh*-exclamatives were lexically identical to 5 of the 10 *wh*-interrogatives presented in the first block, and likewise 5 of Block 2's *wh*-interrogatives were lexically identical to 5 of Block 1's *wh*-exclamatives. In other words, each participant heard 10 sentences under both the exclamative and the interrogative condition ("minimal-pair condition", e.g. 'How many novels has your friend written?' vs. 'How many novels your friend has written!'). In total, then, each participant heard 60 sentences: 20 *wh*-exclamatives, 20 *wh*-interrogatives, and 20 fillers. The stimuli were divided into four counter-balanced lists, to which listeners were randomly assigned. Listeners were tested one at a time in a quiet room.

---

[2]The module can be downloaded for free together with the data from this experiment (danielepanizza.org/pages/programming).

5 Statistical analysis and results

Before going into detail regarding the statistical analysis, we summarize our results with respect to the hypotheses we formulated in section 3. Our results show that:

Hypothesis 1 is confirmed. Listeners are very accurate in distinguishing *wh*-exclamatives from *wh*-interrogatives solely on the basis of prosody.

Hypothesis 2 is partially confirmed. Listeners can distinguish between these two sentence types before they hear the end of the sentence, but this pattern is very rare in our data; much more often, listeners identified the sentence type after the end of the sentence.

Hypothesis 3 is partially confirmed. Listeners are faster at identifying *wh*-exclamatives than *wh*-interrogatives. However, this effect is the result of durational differences between the two sentence types, so that the processing advantage for *wh*-exclamatives disappears when the segmental duration is taken into account.

5.1 Identification task

Accuracy of sentence-type identification was very high in both experimental conditions. Listeners correctly identified exclamatives in 93.4% of the trials and interrogatives in 93.7% of the trials. Although listeners were instructed to make their choice as soon as possible, the great majority of responses were provided after the end of the utterance ("late" responses: 90.7% for *wh*-exclamatives and 92.0% for *wh*-interrogatives). As shown in Table 1, in only 31 trials in the *wh*-exclamative condition and 27 trials in the *wh*-interrogative condition did listeners provide "early" responses (i.e., before the end of the utterance). Early responses were mostly correct, suggesting that some listeners are indeed able to discriminate the prosody of the two sentence types before the end of the utterance. For *wh*-exclamatives, the error rate for early responses was 19% compared to 5% for late responses, while for *wh*-interrogatives, the error rates were 4% for early responses and 6% for late responses. These results suggest that listeners were more prone to error when providing an early answer in response to *wh*-exclamatives than to *wh*-interrogatives. However, the difference between correct and incorrect early responses could not be assessed statistically because of the low number of observations.

We ran a generalized linear mixed model (GLMM) in order to analyze the accuracy of late responses. We adopted *sentence type* (interrogative vs. exclamative) and *block* (Block 1 vs. Block 2) as fixed factors and *item* (i.e. the lexical material) and *participant* as random factors, with maximal random-effect structure (cf. Barr et al. 2013), that is, with the greatest possible number of free slopes and intercepts on both random factors, provided that the model converges. From this model, no significant difference in the accuracy of identification was revealed between *wh*-exclamative and *wh*-interrogative conditions (β = 0.11, z = 0.32, p = .75). The factor *block* was also not significant (β = 0.26, z = 0.81, p = .42), i.e., there was no effect of the repetition of the lexical material on the accuracy of the responses. A subsequent model was run with *sentence type* (interrogative vs. exclamative) and *response type* (early vs. late response) as fixed factors. The model confirmed no significant effects for *sentence type* for early responses (estimate = 1.65, z = 1.24, p = .21).

Table 1: Responses given in each time region.

	Exclamative condition		Interrogative condition	
	Correct	Incorrect	Correct	Incorrect
Initial region M1-M2	0	0	0	0
Middle region M2-M3	1	0	0	0
Final region M3-M4	24	6	26	1
After M4	289	16	290	20

5.2 Reaction Times (RTs)

We ran a statistical analysis on the RTs obtained from the identification task. Prior to the analysis, incorrect answers for both early and late responses were excluded and a logarithmic transformation was applied to the RTs to achieve a normal distribution (cf. Baayen 2008). The dependent variable was the RTs measured relative to the end of the sentence, which was positive for the trials in which listeners provided late responses and negative for the trials in which they provided early responses. After the logarithmic transformation, we excluded two outliers presenting a value that was greater than 3 standard deviations.

Statistical assessment was accomplished by applying a linear mixed model (LMM) to the RTs. We adopted *sentence type* as the main factor of interest and *item* and *participant* as random factors, with maximal random-effects structure (cf. Barr et al. 2013). We also checked whether the factor *block* had any effect on RTs. The LMM showed a non-significant effect of *block*, i.e., repetition of sentences did not have any influence on RTs (β = 0.03, t = −0.12, p = .91). Furthermore, there was no interaction between *sentence type* and *block* (β = 0.03, t = −0.08, p = .43). This allowed us to drop the factor *block* from the remaining analyses. Instead, there was a difference across *sentence type*, with the *wh*-exclamatives being identified faster than the *wh*-interrogatives. In the exclamative condition, listeners took 525 ms on average from the end of the sentence to provide a correct response, whereas they took 639 ms in the interrogative condition. This difference is statistically significant (β = 0.07, t = 3.43, p = .01). In the next round of analyses, we checked whether RTs were different across the two sentence-type conditions, taking into account both early and late responses. When listeners provided an early response, they pressed the button on average 259 ms before the end of the sentence in the exclamative condition vs. 239 ms before the end of the sentence in the interrogative condition. When listeners answered after the end of the sentence, they took on average 604 ms in the exclamative condition vs. 718 ms in the interrogative condition. The statistical significance of these differences was assessed by running a LMM with *sentence type* (*wh*-exclamative vs. *wh*-interrogative) and *response type* (early vs. late responses) as fixed factors and *item* and *participant* as random factors, with random slopes and intercepts. We found significant differences involving both *sentence type* and *response type*. The effect of *response type* was significant, as expected (β = 0.06, t = 3.52, p = .01). The effect of *sentence type* was also significant for late responses (β = 1.2, t = 19.42, p = .01). However, the interaction between *sentence type* and *response type* was not significant (β = 0.11, t = 0.83, p = .42). This last result should be interpreted with caution, in that the number of observations involving early responses was very low (see Table 1). Figure 3 presents RTs across *sentence type*, in separate plots for early and late responses. As can be seen, RTs are different for late responses, while they are very similar for early responses.

Given that the duration of the stimuli was different across the two sentence types (see §4), we conducted another analysis that included the durations of the initial region (the *wh*-phrase), the middle region (the verb phrase), and the final region (the subject phrase) as covariates. This analysis addressed the question of whether the difference in RT between *wh*-exclamatives and *wh*-interrogatives revealed by the above analyses was actually caused by *sentence type* or whether it was an epiphenomenon resulting from the durational differences between the component regions of the *wh*-exclamatives and the *wh*-interrogatives. An LMM

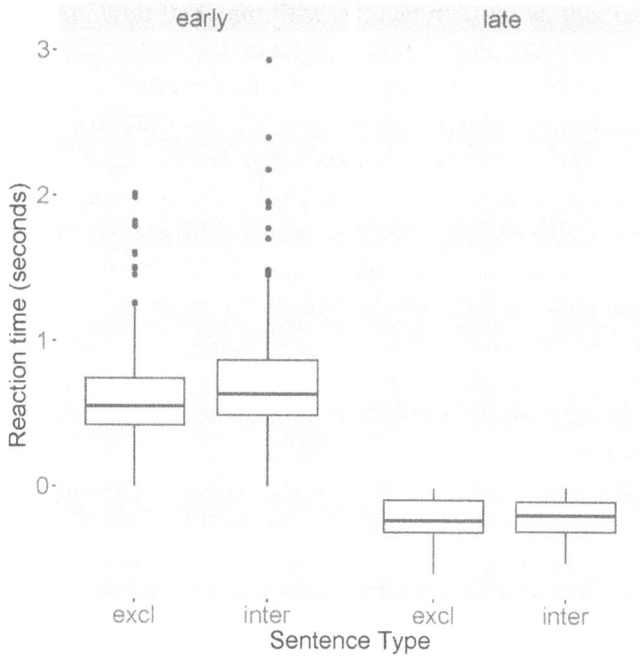

Figure 3: Reaction times (seconds) across *sentence type* and *response type*. The "0" value on the y-axis represents the end of the utterance, positive values represent RTs for responses given after the end of the utterance, and negative RTs correspond to responses given before the end of the utterance.

with *sentence type, response type,* and duration of *initial region, middle region,* and *final region* as fixed factors and *item* and *participant* as random factors yields the following results. There is no significant difference across *sentence type* ($\beta = 0.01$, $t = -0.77$, $p = .44$) nor is there any interaction between *sentence type* and *response type* ($\beta = 0.1$, $t = -1.08$, $p = .28$). Instead, *response type* ($\beta = 1.2$, $t = 21.9$, $p < .001$), *initial region* ($\beta = -0.31$, $t = -4.15$, $p < .001$), *middle region* ($\beta = -0.23$, $t = -2.56$, $p < .02$) and *final region* ($\beta = -0.33$, $t = -5.51$, $p < .001$) are significant. Hence, the results of this analysis show that the duration of each of the three regions of the sentence is a significant predictor of *reaction times,* while the main factor of our experimental design, *sentence type,* is not significant.

6 Discussion and conclusions

The identification task has shown that (Cosenza) Italian listeners are capable of distinguishing between *wh*-exclamatives and *wh*-interrogatives on the basis of prosody. The fact that listeners gave correct responses for both *wh*-exclamatives and *wh*-interrogatives in more than 90% of trials indicates that there must be some prosodic marker that guides listeners' judgments. Furthermore, this experiment was a preliminary attempt to find out whether prenuclear cues (like the %H vs H* difference at the left edge of the IP) might be used for the purpose of pragmatic interpretation. The fact that our experiment elicited some early responses, roughly to the same degree in *wh*-exclamatives (8.3%) and *wh*-interrogatives (9%), is compatible with the hypothesis that listeners can employ prosodic information either in the nuclear region or in the prenuclear region to identify the sentence type. However, our results strongly support the hypothesis that the most relevant phonetic/phonological cues for sentence-type disambiguation are located at the end of the utterance, given that a) listeners gave their responses mostly (in more than 90% of the cases) after the end of utterance; b) the early responses were provided on average about 200 ms before the end of the utterance and more than 2 seconds after the offset of the region containing the nuclear cues; and c) phonetic/phonological cues of the final region significantly affected the RTs.

However, the fact that the duration of the initial and middle regions also significantly affected RT is strongly indicative that prosodic information in the prenuclear section might be exploited by listeners in identifying sentence type. If we take into account this last result, we might interpret the high rate of late responses as a result of listeners' insecurity about their decision. Given that they were instructed to be both fast and accurate, listeners may have collected phonetic/phonological cues while listening to the utterance in order to increase the probability of a reliable response.[3]

To conclude, our study has yielded important preliminary results concerning the identification and processing of *wh*-exclamatives and *wh*-interrogatives on the basis of prosody in Cosenza Italian. Listeners wait until the end of the utterance to respond in most but not all of the trials, thus suggesting that prosodic cues in the prenuclear contour are not strong enough by themselves to guide the pragmatic interpretation of the utterances in an unambiguous way. Furthermore, our study indicates that *wh*-exclamatives are processed faster than *wh*-interrogatives, but this effect disappears when the duration of different segmental regions of the utterance is taken into account.

---

[3]We thank a reviewer for pointing out this hypothesis to us.

7 Benefits and challenges of the chosen method

By combining an identification task with reaction time measurements, we measured not only accuracy in prosodic disambiguation (through the identification scores) but we also provided additional information about when exactly sentence-type identification takes place and whether one sentence type is more difficult to process than another (through reaction times).

We preferred this method to other offline tasks like the gating paradigm. In a gating paradigm, fragments of speech are presented to listeners in an order of increasing duration. Listeners usually have to identify these fragments and to rate their level of confidence. This method allows to obtain the location of the phonetic or phonological cue that is responsible for the correct identification (Prieto 2012). The gating paradigm has already been used in prosody research, particularly for investigating the contribution of the prenuclear contour to tune meaning (e.g. Petrone 2008; Petrone & D'Imperio 2011; Sorianello 2012; Prieto 2012). One potential concern about this task is that stimuli consist in short pieces of artificially cut utterances, which might sound unnatural to listeners. Hence, the identification task might be more difficult to be accomplished. Furthermore, such a paradigm does not allow to track the continuous time course of utterance interpretation.

In the current study, we tried to overcome these concerns by using uncut stimuli, for which we tracked the course of utterance interpretation by means of reaction times. This seemed to us a simple technique that might be well suited for preliminary investigation of prosodic contrasts, such as the prosodic differences between *wh*-exclamatives and *wh*-interrogatives. However, our method did not clearly say whether the relevant phonological cues for sentence-type identification are included in the prenuclear region of the utterance or in the nuclear region. A potential problem with measuring RTs in an identification task in which listeners have to press a button is that there is a time delay between sentence-type identification and the response reaction (i.e., pressing the button). To address this issue, alternative methods for registering the response reaction could be implemented.

Online methods like eye-tracking or mouse tracking could be used (Marslen-Wilson et al. 1992; Pynte & Prieur 1996; Tomlinson & Fox Tree 2011; Warren 2014). In particular, a methodological challenge concerning eye-tracking would be to develop a paradigm to investigate the time course of processing of intonational meaning (i.e., taking into account the meaning contribution of the prenuclear and nuclear sections) during visual search. For instance, in a study on American

English, Heeren et al. (2015) created a "targeted language game" by which an indirect association between different sentence types (questions and statements) and referents (objects on a visual display) is created. Analysis of gazes demonstrated that listeners can make an immediate use of the nuclear accents and boundary tones in processing questioning vs. asserting utterances. Their stimuli were however limited to less typical syntactic constructions of American English (elliptical utterances only containing the nucleus), so the contribution of the prenuclear section was unclear. In an eye-tracking experiment on French, Petrone et al. (2016) combined long utterances produced with different degrees of commitment (as signaled by prosody: yes/no questions vs. incredulity questions) with pictures showing the corresponding facial expressions. Results indicated that French listeners can make immediate use of prenuclear cues for processing speaker commitment and that the effect of nuclear and prenuclear cues may vary across different utterance types. This kind of results encourages us to use the visual world paradigm to assess the use of intonation during sentence modality processing.

With regard to stimuli selection, the current experiment is based on natural stimuli and does not allow us to distinguish which acoustic marker contributed to listeners' relatively high performance on sentence-type disambiguation at the end of the utterance. Our speaker produced *wh*-exclamatives and *wh*-interrogatives based on specific pragmatic contexts, but she was not asked to produce a specific set of intonation contours.

In future studies, we will investigate the influence of intonational cues (edge tones and pitch accents) by controlling for the tonal structure of the target sentences. When looking at intonational cues, durational differences could be controlled for by using resynthesized stimuli with similar segmental duration for *wh*-exclamatives and *wh*-interrogatives. Furthermore, a continuum of resynthesized stimuli could be used in order to determine whether the prosodic parameters under investigation are perceived in a categorical or gradient manner (see Niebuhr 2007).

Appendix: Data Set

Table 2: Itemlist_Fillers

Vieni stasera?	'Will you come tonight?'
Mi fai un caffè?	'Would you prepare me a coffee?'
Apriresti la finestra?	'Would you open the window?'
Piove tanto?	'Does it rain a lot?'
Sei bella?	'Are you beatiful?'
Mi daresti il tuo numero?	'Would you tell me your number?'
Perchè piangi?	'Why do you cry?'
Hai visto il mio ragazzo?	'Did you see my boyfriend?'
Hai 25 anni?	'Are you 25 years old?'
Sei una stronza!	'You are stupid?'
C´è qualcuno al telefono!	'There is someone on the phone!'
Forse hai ragione!	'Maybe you are right!'
Sei una persona speciale!	'You are a special person!'
Vieni sta sera!	'Come tonight!'
Guarda 'sto video!	'Watch this video!'
Sei bellissima!	'You are beautiful!'

Table 3: Duration markers according to target sentences (Interrogatives)

Target sentences	Placement of dur. markers (sec)			
	M1	M2	M3	M4
Quanti romanzi ha scritto la tua amica 'How many novels did your friend write?'	1.052	1.733	2.252	3.127
Quanti libri ha pubblicato il tuo professore 'How many books did your professor publish?'	1.367	1.828	2.507	3.596
Quante sigarette ha fumato papa 'How many cigarettes did Dad smoke?'	1.219	1.926	2.595	3.074
Quanti paesi ha visto tua sorella 'How many countries did your sister see?'	1.141	1.651	2.138	2.847
Quante cose ha aggiustato tuo padre 'How many things did your father adjust?'	1.421	1.996	2.587	3.169
Quante birre ha bevuto la tua amica 'How many beers did your friend drink?'	0.999	1.490	2.052	2.747
Quanti chili ha perso tuo nipote 'How many kilos did your nephew loose?'	0.895	1.351	1.870	2.613
Quanti corsi ha seguito tua sorella 'How many lectures did your sister take?'	1.094	1.577	2.222	3.069
Quanta torta ha mangiato tua sorella 'How much cake did your sister eat?'	1.090	1.618	2.222	3.059
Quanti libri ha comprato tuo padre 'How many books did your father buy?'	0.809	1.285	1.965	2.710
Quanti soldi ti ha dato tuo padre 'How much money did your father give you?'	1.186	1.778	2.280	2.935
Quanti vestiti ha disegnato il tuo amico 'How many clothes did your friend design?'	1.049	1.684	2.285	3.100
Quanti pesci ha pescato tuo fratello 'How much fish did your brother catch?'	1.130	1.626	2.249	3.113
Quanti cd ha inciso tuo zio 'How many discs did your uncle record?'	1.124	1.739	2.256	3.013
Quante arance ha raccolto tuo nonno 'How many oranges did your grandfather collect?'	1.335	1.860	2.494	3.169
Quanti quadri ha dipinto tua zia 'How many paintings did your aunt paint?'	1.197	1.688	2.325	3.055
Quanti dolci ha preparato tua madre 'How many sweets did your mother prepare?'	1.230	1.751	2.402	3.149
Quanti fiori ha piantato tua nonna 'How many flowers did your grandmother plant?'	1.413	1.887	2.492	3.255
Quante farfalle ha catturato tuo fratello 'How many butterflies did your brother capture?'	0.624	1.266	1.926	2.759
Quante scarpe ha comprato tua zia 'How many shoes did your aunt buy?'	1.219	1.780	2.476	3.063

Table 4: Duration markers according to target sentences (Exclamatives)

Target sentences	Placement of dur. markers (sec)			
Quanti romanzi ha scritto la tua amica 'How many novels your friend wrote!'	1.286	1.985	2.575	3.438
Quanti libri ha pubblicato il tuo professore 'How many books your professor published!'	1.087	1.655	2.356	3.570
Quante sigarette ha fumato papa 'How many cigarettes Dad smoked!'	1.098	1.960	2.737	3.348
Quanti paesi ha visto tua sorella 'How many countries your sister saw!'	1.076	1.600	2.062	2.970
Quante cose ha aggiustato tuo padre 'How many things your father adjusted!'	1.030	1.553	2.235	3.044
Quante birre ha bevuto la tua amica 'How many beers your friend drunk!'	1.097	1.619	2.174	3.180
Quanti chili ha perso tuo nipote 'How many kilos your nephew lost!'	0.891	1.307	1.800	2.673
Quanti corsi ha seguito tua sorella 'How many lectures your sister took!'	1.207	1.766	2.237	3.237
Quanta torta ha mangiato tua sorella 'How much cake your sister ate!'	1.068	1.645	2.158	3.032
Quanti libri ha comprato tuo padre 'How many books your father bought!'	0.686	1.420	2.068	3.147
Quanti soldi ti ha dato tuo padre 'How much money your father gave you!'	1.037	1.803	2.265	3.062
Quanti vestiti ha disegnato il tuo amico 'How many clothes your friend designed!'	0.942	1.828	2.454	3.361
Quanti pesci ha pescato tuo fratello 'How much fish your brother catch!'	2.031	2.638	3.213	4.245
Quanti cd ha inciso tuo zio 'How many discs your uncle recorded!'	1.143	1.886	2.346	3.226
Quante arance ha raccolto tuo nonno 'How many oranges your grandfather collected!'	1.750	2.301	2.884	3.789
Quanti quadri ha dipinto tua zia 'How many paintings your aunt painted!'	1.711	2.214	2.828	3.753
Quanti dolci ha preparato tua madre 'How many sweets your mother prepared!'	1.482	2.028	2.671	3.680
Quanti fiori ha piantato tua nonna 'How many flowers your grandmother planted!'	1.335	1.802	2.463	3.486
Quante farfalle ha catturato tuo fratello 'How many butterflies your brother captured!'	0.803	1.457	2.129	3.141
Quante scarpe ha comprato tua zia 'How many shoes your aunt bought!'	1.054	1.670	2.316	3.240

References

Avesani, Cinzia. 1995. ToBIt. Un sistema di trascrizione per l'intonazione italiana. In Gianni Lazzari (ed.), *Metodologie di analisi e di descrizione delle caratteristiche prosodiche e intonative dell'italiano. Atti delle V Giornate di Studio del Gruppo di Fonetica Sperimentale (A.I.A.)* Vol. XXII, 85–98. Povo (TN), Italy.

Baayen, R. Harald. 2008. *Analyzing linguistic data: A practical introduction to statistics using R.* Cambridge: Cambridge University Press.

Barr, Dale, Roger Levy, Christoph Scheepers & Harry J. Tily. 2013. Random effects structure for confirmatory hypothesis testing: Keep it maximal. *Journal of Memory Language* 68. 255–278.

Batliner, Anton. 1988. Produktion und Prädikation. Die Rolle intonatorischer und anderer Merkmale bei der Bestimmung des Satzmodus. In Hans Altmann (ed.), *Intonationsforschungen,* 207–221. Tübingen: Niemeyer.

Bentin, Shlomo & Gregory McCarthy. 1994. The effects of immediate stimulus repetition on reaction time and event-related potentials in tasks of different complexity. *Journal of Experimental Psychology. Learning, Memory, and Cognition* 20(1). 130–149.

Borràs-Comes, Joan, Maria del Mar Vanrell & Pilar Prieto. 2010. The role of pitch range in establishing intonational contrasts in Catalan. In Mark Hasegawa-Johnson et al. (ed.), *Proceedings of the 5th International Conference on Speech Prosody.* Chicago, IL.

Castroviejo, Elena. 2006. *Wh-Exclamatives in Catalan.* Universitat de Barcelona PhD.

Chapallaz, Marguerite. 1964. Notes on the Intonation of Questions in Italian. In D. Abercrombie, D. B. Fry, P. A. D. MacCarthy, N. C. Scott & J. L. M. Trim (eds.), *In Honor of Daniel Jones,* 306–312. Longman.

Chen, Aoju. 2003. Reaction time as an indicator to discrete intonational contrasts in English. In *Proceedings of Eurospeech 2003,* 97–100. Geneva.

D'Eugenio, Antonio. 1976. The intonation systems of Italian and English. *Rassegna Italiana di Linguistica Applicata* 8(1). 57–85.

Delattre, Pierre. 1966. Les 10 intonations de base du français. *The French Review* 40(1). 1–14.

Eady, Stephen J. & William E. Cooper. 1986. Speech intonation and focus location in matched statements and questions. *Journal of the Acoustical Society of America* 80. 402–415.

Falé, Isabel & Isabel Hub Faria. 2006. Categorical perception of intonational contrasts in European Portuguese. In Rüdiger Hoffmann & Hansjörg Mixdorff (eds.), *Proceedings of the 3rd International Conference on Speech Prosody*, 69–72. Dresden.

Feldhausen, Ingo, Andrea Pešková, Elena Kireva & Christoph Gabriel. 2011. Categorical perception of Porteño nuclear accents. In *Proceedings of the 17th International Congress of Phonetic Sciences*, 17–21. Hong Kong.

Gili Fivela, Barbara, Cinzia Avesani, Marco Barone, Giuliano Bocci, Claudia Crocco, Mariapaola D'Imperio, Rosella Giordano, Giovanna Marotta, Michelina Savino & Patrizia Sorianello. 2015. Varieties of Italian and their intonational phonology. In Sónia Frota & Pilar Prieto (eds.), *Intonation in Romance*, 140–197. Oxford University Press.

Grice, Martine, Mariapaola D'Imperio, Michelina Savino & Cinzia Avesani. 2005. Strategies for Intonation Labelling across Varieties of Italian. In Sun-Ah Jun (ed.), *Prosodic Typology. The Phonology of Intonation and Phrasing*, 362–389. Oxford: Oxford University Press.

Grosjean, François. 1980. Spoken word recognition processes and the gating paradigm. *Perception & Psychophysics* 28. 267–283.

Gyuris, Beáta, Katalin Mády & Ádám Szalontai. 2013. *Experimental investigations on the prosody of Hungarian exclamatives*. Research Institute for Linguistics, Hungarian Academy of Sciences, Budapest, 30 May, 2013.

Hedberg, Nancy, Juan M. Sosa, Emrah Görgülü & Morgan Mameni. 2010. The prosody and meaning of wh-questions in American English. In Mark Hasegawa-Johnson et al. (ed.), *Proceedings of the 5th International Conference on Speech Prosody*. Chicago, Illinois.

Heeren, Willemijn F. L., Sarah A. Bibyk, Christine Gunlogson & Michael K. Tanenhaus. 2015. Asking or Telling–Real-time Processing of Prosodically Distinguished Questions and Statements. *Language and Speech* 58(4). 474–501. DOI:10.1177/0023830914564452

Ladd, D. Robert. 2008. *Intonational phonology*. 2nd edition. Cambridge: Cambridge University Press.

Lahiri, Aditi & William Marslen-Wilson. 1991. The mental representation of lexical form. A phonological approach to the recognition lexicon. *Cognition* 38. 245–294.

Marslen-Wilson, William, Lorraine K. Tyler, Paul Warren, Paula Grenier & Catherine S. Lee. 1992. Prosodic effects in minimal attachment. *Quarterly Journal of Experimental Psychology* 45. 73–87.

Massaro, Dominic W. 1987. *Speech perception by ear and eye. A paradigm for psychological inquiry*. Mahwah, NJ, USA: Erlbaum.

Niebuhr, Oliver. 2007. Categorical perception in intonation. A matter of signal dynamics? In *Proceedings of the 8th Annual Conference of the International Speech Communication Association 2007 (INTERSPEECH 2007)*, 109–112. Antwerp, Belgium: Curran Associates, Inc.

O'Connor, Joseph D. & Gordon Frederick Arnold. 1961. *Intonation of colloquial English: A practical handbook.* 1. publ. London: Longman.

Petrone, Caterina. 2008. *From targets to tunes. Nuclear and prenuclear contribution in the identification of intonation contours in Italian.* Laboratoire Parole et Langage, Université de Provence PhD.

Petrone, Caterina & Mariapaola D'Imperio. 2011. From Tones to Tunes: Effects of the f0 Prenuclear Region in the Perception of Neapolitan Statements and Questions. In Sónia Frota, Gorka Elordieta & Pilar Prieto (eds.), *Prosodic Categories: Production, Perception and Comprehension* (Studies in natural language and linguistic theory), 207–230. Dordrecht: Springer Netherlands.

Petrone, Caterina, Alessandra Lo Nobile, Christelle Zielinsky & Kiwako Ito. 2016. The role of prosody in processing speaker commitment in French. In Jonathan Barnes, Alejna Brugos, Stefanie Shattuck-Hufnagel & Nanette Veilleux (eds.), *Proceedings of the 8th International Conference on Speech Prosody.* Boston, USA. https://hal.archives-ouvertes.fr/hal-01462229.

Petrone, Caterina, Hubert Truckenbrodt, Caroline Wellmann, Julia Holzgrefe-Lang, Isabell Wartenburger & Barbara Höhle. 2017. Prosodic boundary cues in German. Evidence from the production and perception of bracketed lists. *Journal of Phonetics* 61. 71–92.

Pierrehumbert, Janet B. & Julia B. Hirschberg. 1990. The Meaning of Intonational contours in the Interpretation of Discourse. In Philip R. Cohen, Jerry Morgan & Martha E. Pollack (eds.), *Intentions in Communication*, 271–311. Cambridge MA: MIT Press.

Prieto, Pilar. 2012. Experimental methods and paradigms for prosodic analysis. In Abigail C. Cohn, Cécile Fougeron & Marie K. Huffman (eds.), *The Oxford Handbook of Laboratory Phonology* (Oxford Handbooks in Linguistics), 528–538. Oxford: Oxford University Press.

Pynte, Joel & Benedicte Prieur. 1996. Prosodic breaks and attachment decisions in sentence parsing. *Language and Cognitive Processes* 11. 165–191.

Schneider, Edgar W. 2011. *English around the world. An introduction.* Cambridge: Cambridge University Press.

Sorianello, Patrizia. 2011. Aspetti prosodici e pragmatici dell'atto esclamativo. *Studi Linguistici e Filologici Online* 9. 287–332.

Sorianello, Patrizia. 2012. A prosodic account of Italian exclamative sentences. A gating test. In Qi-uwu Ma, Hongwei Ding & Daniel Hirst (eds.), *Proceedings of the 6th International Conference on Speech Prosody*, vol. 1, 298–301. Shanghai, China: Tongji University Press.

Sorianello, Patrizia, Riccardo Giordano & Caterina Petrone. 2011. *L'Italiano parlato a Cosenza*. PPt presented at the workshop ToBI Italiano CRIL, Lecce.

Tomlinson, John M. & Jean E. Fox Tree. 2011. Listeners' comprehension of uptalk in spontaneous speech. *Cognition* 119(1). 58–69.

Vanrell, Maria del Mar. 2013. Pitch accent types and the perception of focus in Majorcan Catalan wh-questions. In Sylvie Hancil & Daniel Hirst (eds.), *Prosody and Iconicity*, vol. 13 (Iconicity in Language and Literature), 127–148. Amsterdam: John Benjamins Publishing Company. DOI:10.1075/ill.13.07van

Warren, Paul. 2014. Sociophonetic and prosodic influences on judgements of sentence type. In Jennifer Hay & Emma Parnell (eds.), *Proceedings of the 15th Australasian International Conference on Speech Science and Technology*, 185–188. Christchurch.

Zanuttini, Rafaela & Paul Portner. 2003. Exclamative Clauses at the Syntax-Semantics Interface. *Language* 79(1). 39–81.

Zeng, Xiao-Li, Philippe Martin & Georges Boulakia. 2004. Tones and intonation in declarative and interrogative sentences in Mandarin. In *Proceedings of the International Symposium on Tonal Aspects of Languages: With Emphasis on Tone Languages, Beijing, China, March 28-31*, 235–238.

Part III

Elicitation methods

Chapter 6

The Discourse Completion Task in Romance prosody research: Status quo and outlook

Maria del Mar Vanrell
Universitat de les Illes Balears

Ingo Feldhausen
Goethe-Universität Frankfurt am Main

Lluïsa Astruc
The Open University

The growing interest in the interfaces of prosody with other areas, notably pragmatics, has led to an interesting cross-fertilization of methods such as the *Discourse Completion Task* (DCT). In this chapter, we review previous and ongoing work in which the DCT method has been used to research Romance prosody. First, we introduce the design of the DCT used in pragmatics. After that, we discuss the design of the DCT used in Romance prosody and examine the strengths and weaknesses of the DCT method. Finally, we propose modifications and show how the DCT method can be further strengthened. All in all, we conclude that the DCT is an adequate method to research Romance prosody (as well as the prosody of other languages) and that future research should continue to consider how to further refine and improve this data collection instrument.

1 Introduction

The Discourse Completion Task (henceforth DCT) is a relatively new method in prosodic research adopted from the field of pragmatics, where it has been used

Maria del Mar Vanrell, Ingo Feldhausen & Lluïsa Astruc. 2018. The Discourse Completion Task in Romance prosody research: Status quo and outlook. In Ingo Feldhausen, Jan Fliessbach & Maria del Mar Vanrell (eds.), *Methods in prosody: A Romance language perspective*, 191–227. Berlin: Language Science Press. DOI:10.5281/zenodo.1441345 for decades for both research and assessment. Due to the numerous advantages of this method (see §2 below for details), the DCT has found a place in the field of prosody. It is time now to take a step back and assess the strengths and weaknesses of the DCT before considering how it can be improved and strengthened in future studies.

1.1 Research paradigms in empirical research in prosody

To place the DCT within the repertoire of empirical methods available in prosody, we need to imagine a hypothetical continuum of varying degrees of researcher interference ranging from correlational to experimental research (see Figure 1).[1] The DCT would find its place in the middle of this continuum.

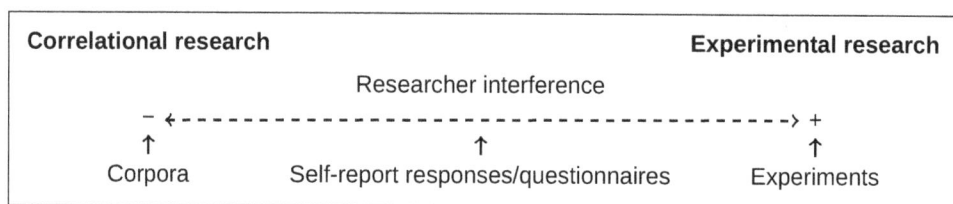

Figure 1: Diagram illustrating the continuum between correlational and experimental research.

As we see in Figure 1, empirical research in prosody encompasses both correlational and experimental research. The difference between these types of research is that in correlational studies the researcher observes what naturally goes on in the world with little or no direct interference by the researcher. S/he tries to determine if a relationship or covariation exists between two variables, such as different types of intonational patterns and different dialects, for example. Experimental research, in contrast, aims to isolate cause and effect by manipulating one or more variable/s to assess the effect of such manipulation on another variable, the dependent variable.

In the continuum shown in Figure 1, corpora composed of spontaneous speech would occupy the left-hand end, which would also correspond to the most ecologically valid data.[2] Some of the speech corpora used in prosody research are

---

[1]Different criteria can be used to classify the methodological approaches to prosody research. For instance, Niebuhr & Michaud (2015) propose the following five dimensions: (i) degree of control over experimental variables (which broadly corresponds with the proposal defended in this paper), (ii) event density or the number of tokens per time unit, (iii) expressiveness, (iv) communicative intention, and (v) homogeneity of behavior.

[2]Ecological validity refers to an experimental condition in which the methods, the materials and the setting are as natural as possible, that is, close to the real world.

the ICE-GB corpus (Wichmann & Cauldwell 2003), the Boston database of FM radio news speech (Ostendorf et al. 1995), the CALLHOME corpus (Ogden 2006), the Spontal corpus (Edlund et al. 2010) and the Map Task corpus (Anderson et al. 1991). For Romance languages specifically, we should mention the ESTER corpus for French media speech (Gravier et al. 2004), the corpus of casual French (Torreira & Ernestus 2010), the Glissando corpus (Garrido et al. 2013) for Catalan and Spanish and the Val.es.co corpus (Cabedo Nebot & Pons 2013) for Spanish (for further details see Delais-Roussarie 2008; Post & Nolan 2012; Delais-Roussarie & Yoo 2014).

The use of large corpora in prosody research has had an effect on other research in the development of speech processing software, statistical procedures to assess the reliability of auditory analyses, and the development of online tools for sharing data with the research community and general public. One of the outcomes of research using large corpora is the development of automatic procedures to detect prominence, phrase boundaries and tonal events (that is, peaks and valleys), such as Analor (Avanzi et al. 2010), ModProso, SegProso (Garrido 2013a; 2013b) or the ProsodyDescriptor (Barbosa 2013). Different tests have been proposed to assess intertranscriber reliability such as the pairwise transcriber agreement and the kappa statistic (Cohen kappa and Fleiss kappa) (Brennan & Prediger 1981; Yoon et al. 2004; Randolph 2008; Mo et al. 2008; Escudero et al. 2012, among others).

New tools have also been developed to make corpora available on the Internet. One of the most recent such projects in the field of Romance intonation is the *Interactive Atlas of Romance intonation* (Prieto et al. 2010–2014). The *Atlas* uses interactive maps of Europe and the Americas to display audio and video data collected using a Map Task and a questionnaire in the form of a DCT (see discussion below). The *Atlas* follows a line of research that has a long tradition within Romance linguistics (Geckeler & Dietrich 2003: 55). These *language atlases* mainly concentrate on segmental phonetics and phonology, morphology, and the lexicon, and date back to the *Deutscher Sprachatlas* (DSA, Georg Wenker 1876–1888 in Germany) and the *Atlas linguistique de la France* (ALF, Gilliéron & Edmont 1902-1910); see Goebl (1992) or Auer & Schmidt (2010) for an overview. At the end of the last century, these atlases also started to appear in digital form (e.g. Goebl 1998; Kattenbusch et al. 1998–2016). The recent technological revolution has resulted in the widespread availability of devices and software to collect and display data. As a consequence, it is easier for language atlases to include spontaneous speech. A challenge for future research would be to combine different types of atlases in order to provide linguistic information from different linguistic modules in one and the same interactive atlas.

At the other end of the continuum lies experimental research (see Figure 1). As discussed above, experimental research involves the manipulation of a variable or variables to measure their possible effect upon another variable, the dependent variable. Some common dependent variables used in experimental research are behavioral measures and physiological responses. In behavioral experiments responses are produced automatically, without conscious thought. Participants typically sit at a computer where they receive visual or auditory stimuli and press buttons in response.[3] The researcher then counts the number of times a particular response occurs. Within this approach in prosody, we find paradigms such as the Categorical Perception paradigm (e.g. Kohler 1987; Ladd & Morton 1997; Chen 2003; Schneider et al. 2006; Feldhausen et al. 2011; Vanrell 2011), the Gating paradigm (e.g. Hadding-Koch & Studdert-Kennedy 1964; van Heuven & Haan 2002; Vion & Colas 2006; Face 2007; Petrone & D'Imperio 2011; Crespo-Sendra 2011, among others), the imitation task (Pierrehumbert & Steele 1989; Dilley 2005; Dilley & Brown 2007; Vanrell 2011), and the Priming paradigm (Cutler 1986; Jun & Bishop 2015) (all used with adults) or the Head-turn preference procedure (Jusczyk et al. 1993) (used mainly with children of 6–12-months old).

Sometimes these paradigms can also be combined with reaction time measurements (Chen 2003; Feldhausen et al. 2011), i.e. the speed with which someone reacts to a stimulus. Examples of physiological responses include acoustic (F0, local or global duration) and articulatory analyses of speech productions (see Prieto et al. 1995; Arvaniti et al. 1998; Frota 2002 for acoustic and articulatory analysis; and see D'Imperio et al. 2007; Mücke et al. 2006; Stella et al. 2014 and Gili Fivela, this volume, for articulatory analyses). Of particular interest are methods which have been applied only recently to prosody research and which measure brain activity (Event Related Potentials (ERPs) and Brain Imaging Techniques (fMRI); see Kaiser 2006 for details) and patterns of attention in babies and adults (Eye-tracking paradigm; see Watson et al. 2006 for details). For an overview of the experimental methods and paradigms for prosodic analysis see Sudhoff et al. (2006), Prieto (2012), and Niebuhr & Michaud (2015), among others. Differences between read and spontaneous speech are addressed in Llisterri (1992); Beckman (1997); Face (2003); Xu (2010), and Wagner et al. (2015), among others. A comprehensive overview of research methods in linguistics from a more general point of view, including experimental methods, is provided in Podesva & Sharma (2013).

Halfway between correlational and experimental research are self-report responses and questionnaires (Figure 1), and among these, the DCT. These methods

---

[3]This is a very general definition that includes different types of behavioral experiments (please see Gili Fivela, this volume, for a more precise classification).

have been borrowed from research in pragmatics, where they have been commonly used to research and assess language learners' pragmatic development. Self-report responses/questionnaires typically take the form of a survey or questionnaire in which the respondents read the questions and select a response based on their attitudes or beliefs. Researcher interference can be regarded as medium, since some variables can be tightly controlled but the respondents still have the freedom to answer in a very natural way. According to Kasper & Rose (2002), three different categories can be distinguished: oral and written self-reports, measures of spoken interaction, and questionnaires.

Oral and written-self reports can be further classified into interviews, think-aloud protocols and diaries (less commonly used). Interviews are used to tap into "the participants' long-term memories of generalized knowledge states, attitudes or past events" (Kasper & Rose 2002: 107). Think-aloud protocols basically require participants to verbalise their thinking processes as they are performing a specific task. They can take place simultaneously with a DCT, for example, but they can also be used retrospectively (Cohen & Olshtain 1993; Robinson 1992). They can also be audio- or video-recorded.

Regarding measures of spoken interaction, an important distinction should be made between elicited conversations and role-plays. In elicited conversations the participants do not take on roles different from their own, whereas in role-plays they are asked to take on specified roles (Kasper & Rose 2002). By adopting different roles, the influence of power, distance and degree of imposition (Brown & Levinson 1987) that motivate specific linguistic choices can be explored.

Three different types of questionnaires can be distinguished: DCT, multiple choice questionnaires and scaled-response formats. In DCTs, participants are presented with short (usually written, although not necessarily) role-plays based on everyday situations designed to elicit specific speech acts. They are required to complete a turn of dialogue for each item (Barron 2003). Multiple choice questionnaires present items containing a question and different alternatives, from which the participants must choose the most appropriate one. These questionnaires are often used to gather information about pragmatic production and comprehension (Kasper & Rose 2002). In scaled-response formats, the participants judge the degree of appropriateness (also the degree of power, distance, imposition, etc.) of a particular item in a specific context using a Likert scale.

1.2 The *Discourse Completion Task* in research on pragmatics

A DCT is defined as a questionnaire which can be administered either orally or in writing and describes different scenarios designed to elicit the desired speech act. Informants respond by completing a turn of dialogue (Kasper & Dahl 1991; Brown 2001). What sets this methodology apart from other contextualized elicitation tasks is that the prompt usually contains not only foreground and background information about the current event but also information on the social distance between the interlocutors. Typically, five different types of DCT are distinguished (Nurani 2009). In the classic format, the prompt finishes with a reply, whereas in the second type, the dialogue is initiated by the interlocutor and no reply is offered (see (1) and (2), respectively). In the third type, there are neither interlocutor initiations nor replies, and participants are completely free to respond however they wish, though they must give a verbal response (the *open item-verbal response only construction*, see (3)). In the fourth format, the *open item free response construction* (see (4)), participants can give either a verbal or a non-verbal response, or even no response at all. The fifth type is similar to the open item-verbal response format, but includes detailed situational background (see (5)); both an old and a new version exist, which differ in the details given in the prompt.

(1) *Classic format:* Walter and Leslie live in the same neighborhood, but they only know each other by sight. One day, they both attend a meeting held on the other side of town. Walter does not have a car but he knows Leslie has come in her car.
Walter: _____
Leslie: I'm sorry but I'm not going home right away.
(Blum-Kulka et al. 1989)

(2) *Dialogue construction:* Your advisor suggests that you take a course during summer. You prefer not to take classes during the summer.
Advisor: What about taking a course in the summer?
You: _____
(Bardovi-Harlig & Hartford 1993)

(3) *Open item-verbal response only:* You have invited a very famous professor to an institutional dinner. You feel extremely hungry, but someone starts speaking and nobody has started eating yet, because they are waiting for the guest to start. You want to start having dinner. What would you say?
(Safont-Jordà 2003)

(4) *Open item free response construction:* You are the president of the local chapter of a national hiking club. Every month the club goes on a hiking

trip and you are responsible for organizing it. You are on this month's trip and have borrowed another member's hiking book. You are hiking by the river and stop to look at the book. The book slips from your hand, falls in the river and washes away. You hike on to the rest stop where you meet up with the owner of the book.

You: _____

(Hudson et al. 1995)

(5) *Old version:* A student in the library is making too much noise and disturbing other students. The librarian decides to ask the student to quiet down. What will the librarian say?

(Billmyer & Varghese 2000)

New version: It is the end of the working day on Friday. You are the librarian and have been working in the University Reverse Room for two years. You like your job and usually the Reverse Room is quiet. Today, a student is making noise and disturbing other students. You decide to ask the student to quiet down. The student is a male student who you have often seen work on his own in the past two months, but today he is explaining something to another student in a very loud voice. A lot of students are in the library and they are studying for their midterm exams. You notice that some of the other students are looking in his direction in an annoyed manner. What would you say?

(Billmyer & Varghese 2000)

DCT methods have a long history in pragmatics, and though their reliability and validity have been the subject of much discussion in this field, they have yet to be reviewed in the field of prosody. According to Nurani (2009) and Cyluk (2013), some of the strengths of this method for pragmatics research include the possibility of collecting a large amount of data in a short time, the control of contextual variables and demographic information, and the possibility to compare two or more languages. Compared to natural speech, the use of a DCT elicits a prototypical response, whereas natural data is more likely to trigger less common items (Kwon 2004). Researchers have also argued that DCT methods are limited in terms of the authenticity of the situations, with interactions being much simpler than in real conversations and with responses to the scenarios that may not correspond with what speakers would actually say in real life. Additionally, it has been noted that traditional written DCTs used in pragmatics research do not collect or analyze the use of non-verbal features such as gestures or facial expressions, as well as paralinguistic elements such as pitch and intonation (Cyluk 2013, which in turn cites Kasper 2000: 326). Scholars seem to agree that the validity and reliability of this method should be evaluated in terms of the objectives of the investigation. Thus, the DCT is an effective method when the aim of the study is "to inform about the speakers' pragmalinguistic knowledge of the strategic and linguistic forms by which communicative acts can be implemented, and about their sociopragmatic knowledge of the context factors under which particular strategies and linguistic choices are appropriate" (Kasper 2000: 329), but should be avoided if the focus is on conversational interaction.

Acknowledging that the DCT has, as does every data collection method, advantages and disadvantages, scholars have focused on possible ways to strengthen the design of a typical DCT. Possibilities range from enriching the contextual detail of DCT prompts (Billmyer & Varghese 2000; Rose 2000; Cohen & Shively 2003; Schauer 2004; McLean 2005, among others) to the use of two or more methods (triangulation) (Wiersma 1986) to verify the validity of the data while reducing possible task bias.

In this chapter we will review previous and ongoing work in which the DCT has been applied to Romance prosody. First, we will analyze the design of DCTs applied to this field, before examining their strengths and weaknesses while considering their reliability/validity. Finally, we will discuss some of the modifications proposed in the literature and suggest a few other improvements.

2 Use of the DCT in Romance prosody research

In this section, we review some of the studies that have applied the DCT to Romance prosody as a data collection instrument. In doing so we highlight the strengths and weaknesses attributed to the DCT in these studies and add considerations of our own. We do not intend to offer an exhaustive literature review, which would be impossible, given the increasing popularity of this method in this field. Rather, we will concentrate on studies that clearly address issues regarding the validity or reliability of the method. Table 1 provides the reader with a summary of the method's strengths and weaknesses explored in this section.

The DCT has been applied to different fields of research on Romance prosody such as intonational phonology (Prieto 2001; Prieto & Cabré 2007–2012; Prieto & Roseano 2010; 2009–2013; Brehm et al. 2014; Frota & Prieto 2015a; Roseano et al. 2015; Huttenlauch et al. 2016), language contact (Sichel-Bazin & Meisenburg 2015), L2 acquisition (Craft 2015; Astruc & Vanrell 2016), sociophonetics (Mascaró & Roseano 2015), prosody and its interfaces (Vanrell & Fernández-Soriano 2014; Vanrell et al. 2014b,a; Elvira García et al. 2017; Sánchez-Alvarado 2018; Hut-

Table 1: Main strengths and weaknesses attributed to DCT used in the context of Romance prosody.

Strengths	Weaknesses
Collection of large amount of data within a short period of time.	Situations not always easily to understand (which may lead to rising contours meaning "Did I do it well?" or to contours expressing obviousness).
Elicitation of comparable (semi-) spontaneous data across speakers and varieties.	The intonational patterns obtained may not always coincide with those previously found.
Feasible for older and illiterate people.	Elicitation of less trivial speech acts can be difficult.
Little and easily transportable recording equipment is required.	Cultural differences or social / psychological factors may arise.
Control of both the context (pragmatic and politeness factors) and relevant aspects of the target sentence (stress pattern, sentence type and segmental and syntactic structure).	The range of situations may not portray the variety of language uses in real situations.
Interface phenomena (such as syntax and prosody, word order and information structure or pragmatics, etc.) can be easily addressed.	The DCT does not allow for scripted speech (and thus cannot easily address research questions that need predetermined answers).
The task can be used for studies on monolingual speakers (L1) and (different types of) bilingual speakers (L2, 2L1, eL2, heritage speakers...).	Each context allows for only one answer; it is not possible to assess how felicitous other sentences would be in the same context.
Allows the speaker to freely utter any response as long as it fits the situation evoked by the prompt.	Establishing different contexts may be difficult in case in which the pragmatic differences between contexts are unclear.

tenlauch et al. 2018), Politeness theory (Astruc et al. 2011; Astruc & Vanrell 2016; Borràs-Comes et al. 2015) and visual prosody (Cruz et al. 2015; González-Fuente et al. 2015; Gili Fivela, this volume). The Romance languages explored through the use of this method include Catalan, French, Friulian, Italian, Occitan, Portuguese, Romanian, Sardinian and Spanish.

As far as we know, the DCT was first applied to Romance prosody research by Prieto (2001), who worked on the intonation of absolute questions in different varieties of Catalan. Later on, the DCT was used by Prieto & Cabré (2007–2012) to collect data for the *Interactive Atlas of Catalan intonation*. According to the authors and collaborators of the *Interactive Atlas of Catalan Intonation*, one of the clear advantages of using this method is that it allows the researcher to collect semi-spontaneous speech within a short period of time, while still controlling for the stress pattern (stress on the penultimate or antepenultimate syllable) of the last word in the utterance, segmental structure (use of sonorants), and sentence type of the target utterances. The questionnaire was designed to elicit different sentence types (statements, questions, commands and requests, and vocatives), which contained mostly voiced segments so that the resulting F0 contour was generated with no interruptions (i.e., *Sí, dona, d'en Jaume!* 'Obviously! It's Jaume's!'). In addition, the last word of the utterance always contained the stress on the penultimate or antepenultimate syllable (to provide more room for tonal realization). It was administered orally to 145 females aged between 20 and 45 coming from 70 different Catalan locales from distinct dialectal areas (Alguer Catalan, Balearic Catalan, Central Catalan, Northwestern Catalan, Northern Catalan and Valencian). Importantly, the questionnaire was adapted to each dialect and the researcher administering the questionnaire was a native speaker of the dialect under investigation. The researcher explained each context to the participant. After the participant produced the sentence, the researcher checked whether the utterance agreed with the proposed utterance type and intention. Most of the situations were of the *open item-verbal response only* type (see Introduction), although in some cases the informant was provided with an interlocutor initiation and, in one specific case, with a picture. Until then, the data collection instruments used in Romance prosody research consisted either of read speech or tasks designed to elicit spontaneous speech such as the Map Task methodology (see Grice & Savino 2003, among others). In this way, the DCT developed for the *Interactive Atlas of Catalan Intonation* constituted a significant improvement in data collection in Romance and has prompted a variety of studies to follow the same approach (Prieto & Roseano 2010; Brehm et al. 2014; Frota & Prieto 2015b; Sichel-Bazin & Meisenburg 2015).

Other merits attributed to DCT by Sichel-Bazin & Meisenburg (2015) include allowing for the elicitation of comparable spontaneous data across speakers and varieties, its feasibility for older and illiterate people (since the questionnaire was administered orally) and its minimal requirements in recording equipment. Sichel-Bazin & Meisenburg (2015) investigated the consequences of language contact on the prosody of Occitan and French. Given the objectives of the project as well as the need to consider the precarious sociolinguistic situation of Occitan, the data collection instrument needed to meet a number of conditions: it should elicit comparable spontaneous data across speakers and varieties, it should be feasible for older and illiterate people, and it should allow the researcher to obtain as many different intonational contours as possible. In addition, Occitan speakers should preferably be recorded at their homes, where they would feel comfortable speaking the language. Easily transportable recording equipment would be required for this purpose. One of the methodologies used was a DCT questionnaire that consisted of 29 situations with different semantic and pragmatic meanings. This was administered to 81 speakers of Northern French, 95 speakers of Southern French and 83 speakers of Occitan. The use of the DCT allowed for the time-efficient collection of data from older participants in their own homes. Some of the problems encountered by the researchers were general issues arising due to the environment in which the survey was conducted: interruptions by people coming into the room where the recording was made or other noises in the homes of the speakers.

This data collection method enables the researcher not only to control the pragmatic structure (polarity, speaker bias towards the proposition and politeness factors) of the context but also the syntactic pattern (clause type or type of verbs or subjects) of the target sentence. Vanrell & Fernández-Soriano (2014) investigated how prosody interacts with word order in the expression of interrogativity in different varieties of two Ibero-Romance languages, Catalan and Spanish. One hundred and thirty questionnaire items were designed by controlling factors of the target sentence such as the type of interrogative (direct/indirect polar and wh-questions), type of verb (copulative, transitive, unaccusative and unergative), type of subject (nominal, pronominal or the second person formal *vostè/usted*), degree of presupposition (information- and confirmation polar questions, and tag questions) and the presence of external interrogative adverbials of the type *how come* (Rizzi 2001). The questionnaire was administered to 14 informants from different Catalan and Spanish dialectal areas. One of the clear strengths of this method is that it can reconcile the two perspectives, prosodic and syntactic, when dealing with dialectal variation. In Vanrell et al. (2014b), the interplay between lexicon, syntax, intonation and pragmatics in Sardinian polar questions was investigated. A questionnaire containing 10 items was designed in which three different bias conditions (neutral, epistemic and evidential) with positive and negative polarities (conveying the speaker bias towards either a positive or negative answer) were manipulated. Neutral situations were not biased towards a positive or a negative response. In the epistemic situations, "the speaker's bias was based on beliefs or expectations or what s/he would assume to be a norm", whereas the evidential situations "were based on evidence available in the immediate context of the conversation" (Vanrell et al. 2014b: 4). Eleven Sardinian female speakers, aged between 47 and 73, participated in the task.

DCT methods have also been used to research politeness intonation (see an introduction to Politeness Theory in Brown & Levinson 1987; see also Astruc et al. 2011; 2016; Borràs-Comes et al. 2015; Astruc et al. 2016). Astruc et al. (2011) and Astruc et al. (2016) examined how politeness in offers and requests is encoded by intonation in Central Catalan, a language with two distinct intonational contours for unbiased polar questions. The DCT method permitted the manipulation of social distance, power and the cost of the face-threatening act – the contextual variables identified as relevant in politeness research – in two steps: high versus low social distance, high versus low power difference, and high versus low cost. Sixteen scenarios were included in the questionnaire. The carefully controlled design allowed the researchers to conclude that the cost of the act determines the choice of intonation, whereas the power differential between participants may not be a relevant factor. The lack of statistically significant results in the case of the power differential variable could be due to the specific scenarios selected. Specifically, the authors state that "the high power scenario in the DCT presented a work-related situation in the public services context, which may have been interpreted by participants as less face-threatening than expected" (Astruc et al. 2016: 110). Therefore, a clear strength of the DCT is the possibility to manipulate the social variables relevant to politeness in two or more steps, whereas a drawback can be that designing effective scenarios requires thoughtful consideration and some degree of trial and error.

The findings in Astruc et al. (2016) are consistent with those in Astruc & Vanrell (2016), in which the DCT was applied to the field of L2 acquisition with the aim of comparing the interaction of politeness and intonational phonology in first and second language. The DCT questionnaire was used to elicit spoken data from 12 speakers of Mexican Spanish. The questionnaire contained 16 scenarios, of which eight were offers and eight requests, and controlled for social distance, the power of the hearer over the speakers and the cost of the face threatening act. Participants completed the survey three times. The first time they were asked to say anything they would say in a real situation. The second time they had to ask a question, while the third time they were asked to imagine that the hearer rejected their request (this last part has yet to be analysed). The rationale for a free response followed by a sentence-only response is to allow participants to immerse themselves in the scenarios, which should thus elicit responses that are more natural and appropriate to the context. Again, power was not found to be a relevant factor and the authors hypothesize that this may be due to changing conditions in the Mexican workplace (also confirmed by some participants): "[...] they commented in their interviews on the new tendency in the private sector to treat everybody as an equal ("no rank: we are a team"). In the public sector, differences in rank are felt to be more marked and people address each other using titles such as *licenciado* or *ingeniero* ('graduate' and 'engineer', respectively)" (Astruc et al. 2016: 22).

Borràs-Comes et al. (2015) investigated the pragmatic conditions underlying the choice of three vocative pitch contours in Central Catalan. The DCT allowed them to manipulate other relevant contextual variables such as physical distance and the insistence of the call, in addition to power and social distance. Their questionnaire contained 16 scenarios, and 20 participants (17 females and three males) took part in the experiment. The results obtained through the DCT questionnaire were complemented by an acceptability judgment task. A perception test was needed to confirm the results of the DCT data, as with this method "each participant could only produce one contour for a given communicative context, meaning that this methodology does not allow us to adequately assess how felicitous other possibilities would be in that specific context" (Borràs-Comes et al. 2015: 74–75).

In terms of weaknesses of the DCT, some authors (Sichel-Bazin & Meisenburg 2015; Vanrell & Fernández-Soriano Forthcoming; Vanrell et al. 2014b) note that speakers may struggle to understand the task, possibly giving rise to the use of rising contours meaning "Did I do it well?" or expressing obviousness. This latter effect has also been reported by Vanrell & Fernández-Soriano (Forthcoming) as a task-induced effect. According to them, through this final rise the participants might manifest their perplexity at having to reply to questions whose answers are evident from the visual stimuli used in their elicitation task.

Other scholars such as Uth (2014) had already recognized potential problems with the use of images to elicit language production. Asking the participants about what they see in the images can favor the marking of evidentiality (referring to a visual source of information) and also epistemicity (given that the answer is evident from the pictures). Following the same line of reasoning and according to personal communication with Francesc Ballone (28.09.2016), some of the questionnaire items used in Vanrell et al. (2014b) represented a challenge for the speakers in that they were very long and sometimes contained very specific details that might easily go unnoticed (see 6).

(6)　The city council has published a very nice booklet about the history of the Santu Pedru in Vincoli church and it is being distributed free of charge. A neighbor of yours goes to the city council to get one of them and you ask her to pick one up for you too. The problem is that sometimes she forgets things. When you see that she's coming back, ask her whether she's bringing one for you, presuming that she probably isn't.

There have also been concerns regarding the fact that the intonational patterns obtained through this method may not always coincide with those found in previous investigations using different methodologies. For instance, the nuclear patterns found in Italian yes-no questions are shown in Figure 5.10 in Gili Fivela et al. (2015: 169). The authors note that the patterns evident in this figure did not always coincide with those found in previous investigations in which a different methodology was used (i.e. Map Task dialogues). They attribute this difference to the elicitation method, which may induce "different types of assumption concerning the knowledge shared by the possible interlocutors" in the speakers (Gili Fivela et al. 2015: 168). It is also noted in Vanrell & Fernández-Soriano (2014) that the intonational results for Castilian Spanish yes-no questions do not conform with the predictions made by traditional studies such as Navarro Tomás (1944) and Quilis (1981), since the expected intonational pattern for Castilian Spanish yes-no questions would be L^* H% rather than $L+¡H^*$ L%. However, it is interesting to note that Vanrell & Fernández-Soriano's findings do agree with those of Henriksen et al. (2016), in which polar questions uttered in spontaneous speech are analysed. The authors argue that a possible explanation for this inconsistency could be that L^* H% contours are more common in formal speech situations (Henriksen 2013; Henriksen et al. 2016).

While the previous sections have mainly summarized comments on the strengths and weaknesses found in the literature, we would like to add additional considerations in what follows. In using DCTs in our research we have noticed some problems that must be addressed.

First, in order to elicit different speech acts, both the interviewer and the participant must establish a certain degree of participation. When reading the situation/context for a simple statement and uttering a corresponding response, neither the interviewer nor the participant need to expend much effort. However, when the speech act is less trivial, such as in the case of counterexpectational or rhetorical questions, the task is more complex for both participants. A counterexpectational question, for example, hinges on the fact that the participant utters the question with a certain degree of surprise. Consequently, it is important that the participant fully understands each scenario. In the questionnaires for the Intonation Atlases, for example, many different situations appeared one after another and the participant must get into the spirit of each new situation immediately.

Second, even if there is no rapid change between the different situations, a specific situation can still be challenging due to cultural circumstances. In their study on imperatives in Mexican Spanish, Brehm et al. (2014) created situations evoking short and long imperatives (imperatives consisting of one word, i.e. the verb, and imperatives consisting of the verb followed by an argument). All participants had initial difficulties in uttering imperatives, commenting that imperatives are considered to be very impolite and, as such, are seldom used. Thus, instead of saying ¡Dímelo! 'Tell me that!', the speakers seemed to prefer using an absolute question combined with the conditional, i.e., something like ¿Podrías decírmelo? 'Could you tell me that?'.[4] The authors then asked participants to ignore politeness conventions and reply using only imperatives. Thus, in addition to using the variety-specific lexicon (as mentioned above), researchers should also be aware of culture-dependent rules of politeness and other social factors. Furthermore, psychological factors such as introvert/extrovert, expressive/inexpressive, etc. as well as gender differences between the interviewer and the interviewee may also play a role (see a discussion about participant selection in Niebuhr & Michaud 2015: 22–23).

A third difficulty in setting up a successful DCT is that of establishing clear pragmatic boundaries between the different scenarios. While the difference between a neutral statement and a neutral wh-question or a vocative may be intuitively clear, the difference between different types of wh-questions (such as neutral and counterexpectational echo wh-questions; see, e.g., Huttenlauch et al. 2016) may not. For this reason, it is necessary to clearly define the pragmatic context most likely to elicit each intended speech act and to design each scenario according to these definitions.

---

[4]These observations match the results presented in Blum-Kulka et al. (1989), which demonstrate that different languages may use varying sentence types (imperatives, indirect requests, hints) to produce requests.

A standard question in experimental research is how to proceed when participants do not behave as expected:

(a) A participant may not understand a given scenario, and thus cannot provide a pragmatically appropriate response. If this concerns only one or two participants, their data can be withdrawn from the experiment. If this applies to the majority of the participants, however, the scenario might not be optimal and needs to be revised.

(b) A participant might give a non-corresponding answer, such as uttering *¿Podrías decirmelo?* 'Could you tell me that?' in a scenario which should elicit an imperative. In this case the interviewer might intervene and ask for the intended speech act. As described above, this can be more or less difficult.

(c) A participant may have replied adequately to the situation, but in doing so adds further material. An imperative, for example, could be followed by the interjection *por favor* 'please', as in the following Spanish example: *Mírala, por favor.* 'Please look at her'. Now the question arises as to whether the interjection can be discarded from the analysis. The question is relevant because studies such as Brehm et al. (2014) or Lausecker et al. (2014) have shown that the nuclear configuration of imperatives differs with respect to the position of the imperative verb (see also Prieto 2002 for the intonational difference between short and long declaratives). In sentence-final position there is a rising-falling contour (L+H* L%), while there is a low nuclear configuration with the verb in a non-final position (L* L%). The interjection prevents the imperative verb from occurring in sentence-final position, and as a consequence the nuclear contour changes. Again, the interviewer might intervene and ask the participant to avoid using interjections. Another possibility would be to create additional scenarios and discard non-optimal utterances from the analysis.

3 Strengthening the design of the DCT

3.1 Proposals for improving the DCT in pragmatic research

Different attempts have been made in pragmatics research to strengthen the design of the typical DCT (Billmyer & Varghese 2000; Rose 2000; Cohen & Shively 2003; Schauer 2004; McLean 2005). Billmyer & Varghese (2000) investigated the effects of the modification of DCT prompts used to elicit requests from native and non-native speakers of English. Modifications consisted of enhancing the prompt by adding information about social and contextual variables such as the gender of interlocutor, social distance, length of acquaintanceship, and setting and scene (time, place, circumstances and psychological), among others (p. 546). The results conclude that while enhancement did not generally affect the request strategy, it did result in significantly more elaborate requests (in terms of mean length of the speech act and the mean number of supportive moves) in both groups. In Rose (2000), three groups of primary school English students in Hong Kong completed a cartoon oral production task. Each scenario was depicted in a single-frame cartoon (see Figure 2) and was designed to elicit requests, apologies, and compliment responses. Data were also collected in Cantonese.

Figure 2: Pictures taken from the cartoon oral production task used in Rose (2000) (adapted).

According to the authors, the methods should be refined through metapragmatic assessment or thinking/talking about their specific productions (p. 56).

Cohen & Shively (2003) applied the multiple-rejoinder DCT, which involved participants reading not only the situations but also all of the replies. Twelve contexts were presented to the participants, each of them requiring either a request or an apology. The context was introduced in English, but then the conversational replies were introduced in the language of the research site (see (7), with replies in English as a matter of illustration). According to the authors, the multiple rejoinders aim to make the DCT "more reflective of the conversational turn-taking of natural speech" and should facilitate a more precise analysis of pragmatic language ability.

(7)   You completely forget a crucial meeting with the distinguished professor
       with whom you are doing an internship. An hour later you call him to
       apologize. The problem is that this is the second time you've forgotten
       such a meeting with your professor.
       Professor: What happened to you?
       You: _____
       Professor: I can imagine that you have a lot on your mind these days, but
       this is the second time you've missed a meeting you agreed to attend.
       You: _____
       Professor: Yes, indeed. I hope you won't forget it next time.
       You: _____
       Professor: I'm afraid I can't reschedule it for today. Let's try again next
       week at the same time.

A new tool, the Multimedia Elicitation Task (MET), was developed in Schauer
(2004) to investigate the acquisition of requests by German learners of English.
This tool was designed to ensure comparable audiovisual contextual information for every participant. An introductory slide preceded each MET scenario
telling participants what would happen in the scenario (e.g. asking a professor
to open a window, see Table 2). After 10 seconds, the actual scenario slide appeared providing participants with audiovisual information, first in the form of
a picture illustrating the situation and then as an audio description of the scenario (see Table 2). According to the author, the main methodological advantage
of using the Multimedia Elicitation Task is that it allows comparability across
various samples, while providing the researcher with the opportunity to use native speaker speech without the presence of an actual native speaker. Finally,
in McLean (2005), after students were given an introduction about pragmatics in
language learning, a set of DCTs were provided as the basis for group discussions
about situations requiring the use of speech acts such as requests, apologies, and
refusals. The main purpose of this activity was to encourage metapragmatic re-
flection, meaning to provide the students with an adequate context to think and
talk about how language can or cannot be used in a variety of situations. The
students were then asked to write personal DCTs for the class to discuss.

3.2 Proposals for improving the DCT in Romance prosody research

In this section we will address all of the weak points listed in Table 1 and discuss
the ways in which these potential problems can be circumvented. Then we will
review some recent studies in which the design of the DCT differs from those

Table 2: Scenario slide 1 for Scenario 1 taken from the MET task used in Schauer (2004). The source for the image is https://www.benjamins.com/#catalog/journals/eurosla.16/main.

Visual input	Audio input – Scenario 1
	You are attending a seminar. It is a very sunny day and the classroom is hot. The professor is standing near the window. You ask him to open it.

versions introduced in (1)–(5) and discuss ways in which the authors address weaknesses of the general methodology used in prosody research.

To ensure that the scenarios are easy to understand, the context should be concise and the relevant information should be mentioned explicitly and not merely introduced in passing. In addition, the use of pictures to elicit information bears the risk of providing the speaker with obvious information. For this reason, using images should be avoided. However, when pictures shall be used, obviousness can be reduced or even avoided when the scenario is created in such a way that the test subject 'thinks' that s/he is the only one who sees the picture, while the (imagined) interlocutor does not.

In light of recent technical developments, one could imagine a completely new way to provide the test subjects with DCT scenarios: virtual reality (VR; see Fox et al. 2009 for details on VR).[5] Using VR technologies, the test subject experiences a rich audiovisual context instead of a verbally presented scenario which depends on the imaginative powers of the researcher and the test subject. Let us imagine a DCT scenario evoking a *first contact call*: the subject experiences herself entering a house, while the voice of a virtual narrator explains that she is entering the flat of her friend Maria. Being in the virtual house, the test subject

---

[5]We would like to thank A. Muntendam, p.c., for bringing up the idea of VR.

sees that there is no one visible from the hall. The narrator asks her to call up to Maria, as she guesses that Maria is up in her room. After that, the test subject replies verbally as the scenario dictates. Previous psycholinguistic research has shown that VR creates an ecologically valid setting in which the test subject interacts with the virtual interlocutor in the way they would speak with human interlocutors (see Heyselaar et al. 2017; Peeters & Dijkstra 2017 and references cited therein). As in the typical DCT setting, the researcher still has control over the scenario with respect to pragmatic and politeness factors, stress patterns, etc. But VR, similarly to MET, additionally guarantees the repeatability of each scenario, since it does not depend on the quality of the involvement of the researcher – the virtual scenario is always the same. A crucial contrast to MET, however, is that VR provides the test subject with a complete audiovisual world with virtual agents and in which she does not see the laboratory surroundings. Even though using VR in linguistic research is relatively new, studies on speech rate and F0 (Gijssels et al. 2015; Staum Casasanto et al. 2010, respectively) show that VR can easily be used for prosodic research–a promising fact for virtual DCT scenarios.

As the intonational patterns obtained through this method may not always coincide with those previously found using other methodologies, we would like to point out that, while we understand the concerns, this does not necessarily imply that DCT is inadequate as a data collection instrument, but rather that we have elicited a wider or different set of patterns compared to previous research (in this sense we agree with Barbara Gili Fivela, personal communication, 02/2017).

As we saw in the previous section, the elicitation of speech acts is not always an easy task. We therefore recommend that the design of the contexts is carried out with care and attention to ensure that different speech acts are clearly differentiated. The full participation of the interviewer is fundamental; s/he should present the context in such a way that the participant feels immersed in the situation. If this is successful, the participant may confirm this feeling by smiling and nodding or, on the contrary, may make gestures of incomprehension (shoulder shrug, mouth turned down, etc.). Small adaptations of the situation to the context of the speaker (i.e. use of proper names of relatives/friends, specific places or festivals in the village/city, etc.) may be required and, as confirmed by Billmyer & Varghese (2000), can lead to a more adequate participation

Even when the contexts are carefully established, active directions may be needed to guide the recording process (such as asking the participants to temporarily ignore certain culture-dependent rules). Potential problems could be avoided if the interviewer is a native speaker of the language/variety under study or if a native speaker is present during the recording session. Otherwise, the researchers should try to be familiar with culture-dependent rules of politeness or other psychological/social factors. Furthermore, attention should be paid to the participant recruitment process (see above). An alternative to the presence of a native speaker could be the use of the Multimedia Elicitation Task (see Schauer 2004).

Previous proposals to strengthen the design of the DCT in Romance prosody research are rare and still very tentative. Recently, some studies have proposed modifications to the design of the DCT presented in (1)–(5) with the aim of overcoming existing limitations of the general methodology commonly used in prosody research (Elvira García et al. 2017; Sánchez-Alvarado 2018). Other proposals do not improve the DCT itself, but rather propose complementing the DCT with additional tasks (a technique known as *triangulation*), which can increase the validity/robustness of the results obtained through the DCT (Vanrell et al. 2014a; Borràs-Comes et al. 2015). A study by Sánchez-Alvarado (under review) represents a new approach in the study of the prosody-information structure interface in Romance. So far, most of the research on this topic had made use of picture-based tasks to elicit different focus constructions (see Gabriel 2007; Muntendam 2009; Vanrell & Fernández-Soriano 2013; Feldhausen & Vanrell 2014; 2015, among others). In her approach, Sánchez-Alvarado uses a contextualized sentence completion task based on the DCT. By using this technique, she aims to develop an elicitation method that can overcome one of the weaknesses of picture-based tasks, namely "the tendency shown by native speakers to respond with a single word" (Sánchez-Alvarado 2018 citing Ortega-Llebaria & Colantoni 2014). The questionnaire presented 25 items to 12 Asturian Spanish native speakers. Every context presented a scenario introducing an information gap to be filled by the participant (see 8). Importantly, only one of the possible responses was presented to the participants. This was done by creating three versions of the experiment. The prompt (such as 8) was the same for each experiment, but the predetermined response varied (8a, 8b, and 8c respectively). Although this proposal clearly represents an improvement to the methods used to explore the prosody-information structure interface in Romance, it implies moving away from a core concept of the DCT: allowing the speaker to freely utter whatever response she deems appropriate as long as it fits the situation evoked by the prompt. Sánchez-Alvaro already restricts this freedom by providing the speaker with a set of answers (i.e. predetermined parts of possible answers) and as a consequence, the speaker is less free in his/her answers. In this way, the DCT no longer offers the possibility of giving a free response, which is one of the defining features of this method, as argued by Kwon (2004).

(8) *Tu jefe te comenta que alguien pasó la noche en la oficina. No puedes
     ayudarle porque no sabes quién fue pero después, tu compañero te comenta
     que fue Andrea así que vuelves a la oficina del jefe y le dices...*
     'Your boss tells you that someone spent the night in the office. You
     cannot help him, because you do not know who it was but later your
     colleague tells you that it was Andrea, so you go back to the office and
     tell your boss?'
     a. *Andrea...*
     b. *Fue...* 'It was'
     c. *Pasó la noche en la oficina...* 'Spent the night at the office...'

A similar modification in the design of the DCT is used in (Elvira García et
al. 2017), who analyze the prosody of semi-dependent and independent clauses
with subordination marks in Peninsular Spanish (Castilian Spanish, Andalusian
Spanish and the variety of Spanish spoken in Barcelona). A questionnaire with
123 items was presented to 10 native speakers of Peninsular Spanish. The variation in their DCTs consisted of providing not only a pragmatic context but also
the lexical content of the utterance that participants were requested to produce.
To this end, each participant listened to the context, read the sentence appearing in the slide and, as soon as the slide disappeared, s/he performed a speech
act including the given information and using the intonation the speaker would
use in the same context (see 9). As in the previous case, this approach has the
advantage of eliciting very specific syntactic constructions (semi-dependent and
independent clauses with subordination marks), while still controlling for the
effects of pragmatic context. On the other hand, this proposal departs from the
original idea of the DCT by weakening speakers' freedom to answer in the way
they would like. In conclusion, it is up to the researcher to decide what matters
most: a careful control of the context and the syntactic structure of the target
sentence, or that the speaker has the freedom to answer as s/he wishes.

(9) Imagine that we are talking about a common friend, Lorena. You know
     for sure that Lorena eats vegetables in the afternoon. Imagine that I ask
     you "Did you know that Lorena eats chocolate every afternoon?"
     [A PowerPoint slide appears on the screen with an image of a girl eating
     vegetables and the sentence *¡Si merienda verdura!* 'Yes she eats
     vegetables'].

3.3 Proposals for complementing the DCT with further methods (triangulation)

Some proposals have been made towards the use of two or more methods (triangulation) to verify the validity of the data collected through DCT questionnaires while reducing possible task bias. For instance, Vanrell et al. (2014a) investigated the type of meaning encoded in yes-no questions through the combination of the question particle *que* 'that' and the nuclear pattern L+H* L% in Majorcan Catalan yes-no questions with the objective of understanding any temporal information related to this meaning. The DCT they created involved scenarios containing two evidential conditions ((i) inferred direct evidential and (ii) hearsay) and a non-evidential situation. Their questionnaire consisted of 12 situations, which were presented to 15 speakers. The results were quite convincing in showing that direct evidential contexts elicit the production of the L+H* L% pattern headed by a question particle. Two additional experiments were carried out to further explore the degree of perceived appropriateness of the target intonational patterns to different pragmatic contexts as well as the information source at the time at which the evidence was available. The first additional experiment consisted of an acceptability task to rate the degree of appropriateness of the target intonational patterns to different evidential conditions. For the second additional experiment a multiple-choice questionnaire was created asking the subjects to answer two questions related to the information source (heard, seen, heard/seen, I don't know) and the time of the evidence (just now, a few hours ago, yesterday, I don't know). The results obtained through these three methods allowed the authors to conclude that three types of information are encoded in *que*_L+H* L% questions: sentence modality, inference through direct evidence and immediate evidence (Vanrell et al. 2014a: 1025).

After the production experiment, Borràs-Comes et al. (2015) also conducted a perception experiment based on the acceptability judgment task. Seventy-two speakers of Central Catalan were asked to rate the degree of adequacy between a vocative uttered with a specific intonational contour and its preceding discourse context. The results obtained in production were confirmed by those obtained in perception. Other proposals have been made in a more informal way. Andrea Pešková has indicated via personal communication (29.08.2016) that, in her experience, informants are able to correct/refine their own productions. Thus, a possible method to double-check the productions obtained through a DCT would be to use think-aloud protocols or some form of metapragmatic assessment. After being recorded answering to the DCT scenarios, participants could listen to the utterances they produced in a second session and reflect on them.

3.4 Summary

In the previous sections we have reviewed the weaknesses of the different DCT methods commonly used in prosodic research and we have discussed possible ways to strengthen them. We offer a summary of these discussions in Table 3.

4 Conclusions

In this paper we have reviewed some studies that have applied the DCT to Romance prosody as a data collection instrument. We have concentrated on those studies that have addressed issues regarding the validity or reliability of the method as well as those that propose modifications to the design of the DCT. Our analysis has been organized according to the strengths and weaknesses identified by different scholars in applying this instrument to Romance prosody research. Finally, we have discussed the few studies that have used modified versions of the DCT design described in (1–5) or have added supplementary tasks.

All of the studies discussed in this chapter confirm that some of the strengths of the DCT lie in its flexibility and adequacy for: 1) obtaining semi-spontaneous speech within a short period of time, 2) eliciting comparable spontaneous data across speakers and varieties, 3) working with older and illiterate people, 4) requiring little and easily transportable equipment, 5) controlling both the context (pragmatic and politeness factors) and the target sentence (stress pattern, sentence type and segmental and syntactic structure), 6) easily addressing interface phenomena, 7) being feasible for monolingual and bilingual speakers, and 8) allowing spontaneity in the responses.

Despite these considerable strengths, attention should be devoted to the following possible drawbacks: 1) the fact that some speakers may not understand the task, leading to the appearance of rising contours meaning "Did I do it well?" and/or expressing obviousness, 2) the intonational patterns found may not always coincide with previous investigations using a different methodology, 3) the elicitation of less trivial speech acts can be a difficult task, 4) cultural differences or psychological/social factors may arise, 5) the range of situations can be limited and may not portray the richness of language uses in real situations, 6) collecting the target sentences always implies a free choice in the answers, 7) each context allows for only one answer and, for that reason, this method does not allow to assess the felicity of other possibilities realized in the same context, and 8) setting up the different contexts may be challenging.

Table 3: Main weaknesses attributed to DCT used in the context of Romance prosody and proposals for how to address these issues.

Weaknesses	Improvements
Scenarios that are natural and easy to understand are notoriously difficult to create. Difficulties in interpreting specific scenarios may lead to rising contours meaning "Did I do it well?" or to contours expressing obviousness.	Scenarios should be carefully crafted, the context should be brief but concise, and the relevant information should be explicitly mentioned so that no information is introduced merely in passing. The use of images depicting information to be elicited should be very carefully crafted or avoided. Using VR helps to create ecologically valid settings and might help to create authentic and understandable scenarios.
The intonational patterns obtained with this method may not always coincide with those described in previous studies.	(see discussion in §2)
Elicitation of less trivial speech acts can be difficult.	Care and attention are necessary in the design of the scenarios to ensure that the different speech acts are not mixed. Involvement on the part of the interviewer and small adaptations should guarantee that the participant fully immerses herself in the task.
Cultural differences or social / psychological factors may arise.	Awareness on the part of the interviewer and readiness to intervene; for instance, asking the participants to ignore certain culture-dependent conventions.
The range of scenarios may not portray the variety of language uses in real situations.	This is a limitation in pragmatics but less so in prosodic research, where the focus lies on eliciting prototypical answers from a variety of speakers rather than on assessing the pragmatic repertoire of any given individual.
Collecting the target sentences always implies a certain degree of free choice in the answers chosen by the speakers. The DCT does not allow for scripted speech (and thus cannot easily address research questions that need predetermined answers).	(see discussion in §3.2)
Each scenario allows for only one answer.	This problem could be circumvented by providing the speaker with different situations evoking the same communicative context. The speaker would have different tokens of the same context and can utter different answers. Alternatively, further methods can be used (triangulation).
Setting up the different contexts might be difficult in cases in which the pragmatic differences between contexts are unclear.	A clear definition of the required speech acts is needed and the context should be carefully established according to these definitions. Pilot studies might help to figure out which contexts work well.

In the present chapter we have also proposed some improvements to ameliorate the weaknesses we have named. These include the following: 1) the scenarios should be carefully crafted, the context should be brief and concise and the use of images depicting the information to be elicited should be avoided, 2) special effort should be invested so that the participant feels immersed in the task, 3) the interviewer should be aware that cultural or social/psychological differences may arise and should be ready to intervene when necessary, 4) triangulation should be considered as a way to reduce possible task bias, and 5) the different speech acts should be clearly defined.

We believe that the DCT is definitely an adequate method for eliciting features such as pitch and intonation (contrary to what had been argued in Kasper 2000), although further research is needed to directly address the validity/reliability of the method in prosody research. In the words of Lusia M. Nurani: "The investigation of the DCT's design will bring about a reassessment of instrument design which will lead to the improvement to the usefulness of DCT"(Nurani 2009: 676). This applies not only to research in pragmatics, but is also particularly relevant for research in prosody as well as for advancing the field of language testing in general.

Acknowledgments

This paper has benefited from the comments offered by the participants in a session created in Academia.edu. We are grateful to the participants (Marco Barone, Ander Egurtzegi, Wendy Elvira-García, Barbara Gili Fivela, Guillermo González Campos, Andrea Pešková, Melanie Uth) for the time devoted to reading and discussing our manuscript. Our gratitude also goes to the participants of the session on "Prosody and Conceptual Variation" at the 35th Romanistentag – the biannual conference of the German Society of Romance Philology (Zürich, 8–12 October 2017) for their important comments and remarks. The second author would also like to thank the students of his class on intonation in Spanish (summer term 2016) for their feedback on the method. Our further gratitude goes to Julia Otto, the student assistant of the second author, for her help with the references. This research has been partially funded by the Spanish government via projects FFI2016-76245-C3-1-P and FFI2017-87699-P (Ministerio de Economía, Industria y Competitividad). We would also like to thank the two anonymous reviewers for their valuable comments for improving the quality of the paper. All errors are our own.

References

Anderson, Anne H., Miles Bader, Ellen Gurman Bard, Elizabeth Boyle, Gwyneth M. Doherty, Simon Garrod, Stephen Isard, Jacqueline Kowtko, Jan McAllister, Jim Miller, Catherine Sotillo, Henry S. Thompson & Regina Weinert. 1991. The HCRC Map Task Corpus. *Language and Speech* 34. 351–366.

Arvaniti, Amalia, D. Robert Ladd & Ineke Mennen. 1998. Stability of tonal alignment: the case of Greek prenuclear accents. *Journal of Phonetics* 26. 3–25.

Astruc, Lluïsa & Maria del Mar Vanrell. 2016. Intonational phonology and politenes in L1 and L2 Spanish. *Probus. International Journal of Latin and Romance Linguistics* 28(1). 91–118. Special issue "Language Acquisition in the 21st Century: Theory and Methodology".

Astruc, Lluïsa, Maria del Mar Vanrell & Pilar Prieto. 2011. *Offering questions in Catalan – the phonetic and phonological encoding of politeness.* Paper presented at Phonetics and Phonology in Iberia. Tarragona.

Astruc, Lluïsa, Maria del Mar Vanrell & Pilar Prieto. 2016. Intonational phonology and pragmatics: The intonation of offers in Catalan. In Meghan E. Armstrong, Nicholas Henriksen & Maria del Mar Vanrell (eds.), *Intonational grammar in Ibero-Romance: Approaches across linguistic subfields*, 91–114. Amsterdam: John Benjamins.

Auer, Peter & Jürgen Erich Schmidt (eds.). 2010. *Language and Space. An International Handbook of Linguistic Variation.* Vol. 1 (Theories and Methods). Berlin: Mouton de Gruyter.

Avanzi, Mathieu, Anne Lacheret-Dujour & Bernard Victorri. 2010. A corpus based learning method for prominence detection in spontaneous speech. In Mark Hasegawa-Johnson (ed.), *Proceedings of the 5th International Conference Speech Prosody.* Chicago, IL.

Barbosa, Plínio Almeida. 2013. Semi-automatic and automatic tools for generating prosodic descriptors for prosody research. In *Proceedings of Tools and Resources for the Analysis of Speech Prosody (TRASP)*, 86–89. Aix-en-Provence.

Bardovi-Harlig, Kathleen & Beverly S. Hartford. 1993. Refining the DCTs: Comparing open questionnaires and dialogue completion tests. In Lawrence Bouton & Yamuna Kachru (eds.), *Pragmatics and Language Learning, Selected papers presented at the Annual Meeting of the International Conference on Pragmatics and Language Learning*, vol. 4, 143–165. Urbana, Illinois: University of Illinois at Urbana-Champaign.

Barron, Anne. 2003. *Acquisition in interlanguage pragmatics: Learning how to do things with words in a study abroad context.* Amsterdam: John Benjamins.

Beckman, Mary E. 1997. A Typology of Spontaneous Speech. In Yoshinori Sagisaka, Nick Campbell & Norio Higuchi (eds.), *Computing Prosody. Computational Models for Processing Spontaneous Speech*, 7–26. New York: Springer.

Billmyer, Kristine & Manka Varghese. 2000. Investigating instrument-based pragmatic variability: Effects of enhancing discourse completion tests. *Applied Linguistics* 21. 517–552.

Blum-Kulka, Shoshana, Juliane House & Gabriele Kasper. 1989. Investigating crosscultural pragmatics: An introductory overview. In Shoshana Blum-Kulka, Juliane House & Gabriele Kasper (eds.), *Cross-cultural Pragmatics. Requests and Apologies*, 1–34. Norwood (NJ): Ablex.

Borràs-Comes, Joan, Rafèu Sichel-Bazin & Pilar Prieto. 2015. Vocative intonation preferences are sensitive to politeness factors. *Language and Speech* 58(1). 68–83.

Brehm, Annika, Alina Lausecker & Ingo Feldhausen. 2014. The Intonation of Imperatives in Mexican Spanish. In Susanne Fuchs, Martine Grice, Anne Hermes, Leonardo Lancia & Doris Mücke (eds.), *Proceedings of the 10th International Seminar on Speech Production (ISSP)*, 53–56. Cologne. Germany.

Brennan, Robert L. & Dale J. Prediger. 1981. Coefficient Kappa: Some uses, misuses, and alternatives. *Educational and Psychological Measurement* 41. 687–699.

Brown, James D. 2001. Pragmatics tests: Different purposes, different tests. In Kenneth R. Rose & Gabriele Kasper (eds.), *Pragmatics in Language Teaching*, 301–325. Cambridge: Cambridge University Press.

Brown, Penelope & Stephen C. Levinson. 1987. *Politeness: Some Universals in Language Usage* (Studies in Interactional Sociolinguistics). Cambridge: Cambridge University Press.

Cabedo Nebot, Adrián & Salvador Pons. 2013. *Corpus Val.Es.Co 2.0*. http://www.valesco.es.

Chen, Aoju. 2003. Reaction time as an indicator to discrete intonational contrasts in English. In *Proceedings of Eurospeech 2003*, 97–100. Geneva.

Cohen, Andrew D. & Elite Olshtain. 1993. The production of speech acts by EFL learners. *TESOL Quarterly* 27(1). 33–56.

Cohen, Andrew D. & Rachel L. Shively. 2003. Measuring speech acts with multiple rejoinder DCTs. *Language Testing Update* 32. 39–42.

Craft, Jessica. 2015. *The Acquisition of Intonation by L2 Spanish Speakers While on a Six Week Study Abroad Program in Valencia, Spain*. Tallahassee, Florida: Florida State University Master Thesis.

Crespo-Sendra, Verònica. 2011. *Aspectes de l'entonació del valencià*. Barcelona: Universitat Pompeu Fabra PhD.

Cruz, Marisa, Marc Swerts & Sónia Frota. 2015. Variation in tone and gesture within language. In *Proceedings of the 18th International Congress of Phonetic Sciences. The Scottish Consortium for ICPhS 2015*. Glasgow, UK. Paper 0452.

Cutler, Anne. 1986. Forbear is a homophone: Lexical prosody does not constrain lexical access. *Language and Speech* 29. 201–220.

Cyluk, Agnieszka. 2013. Discourse completion task: Its validity and reliability in research projects on speech acts. *Anglica. An International Journal of English Studies* 22(2). 101–112.

D'Imperio, Mariapaola, Robert Espesser, Hélène Loevenbruck, Caroline Menezes, Noël Nguyen & Pauline Welby. 2007. Are tones aligned with articulatory events? Evidence from Italian and French. In Jennifer Cole & José Ignacio Hualde (eds.), *Laboratory phonology 9*, vol. 4-3 (Phonology and phonetics), 577–608. Berlin: Mouton de Gruyter.

Delais-Roussarie, Elisabeth. 2008. Corpus et données en prosodie et en phonologie post-lexicale: forme et statut. *Languages* 171(3). 60–76.

Delais-Roussarie, Elisabeth & Hiyon Yoo. 2014. Corpus and research in phonetics and phonology: Methodological and formal considerations. In Jacques Durand, Ulrike Gut & Gjert Kristoffersen (eds.), *Handbook of Corpus Phonology*, 193–214. Oxford: Oxford University Press.

Dilley, Laura C. 2005. *The phonetics and phonology of tonal systems*. Cambridge, MA: Massachusetts Institute of Technology PhD.

Dilley, Laura C. & Meredith Brown. 2007. Effects of pitch range variation on F0 extrema in an imitation task. *Journal of Phonetics* 35(4). 523–551.

Edlund, Jens, Jonas Beskow, Kjell Elenius, Kahl Hellmer, Sofia Strömbergsson & David House. 2010. Spontal: a Swedish spontaneous dialogue corpus of audio, video and motion capture. In Nicoletta Calzolari, Khalid Choukri, Bente Maegaard, Joseph Mariani, Jan Odijk, Stelios Piperidis, Mike Rosner & Daniel Tapias (eds.), *Proceedings of the 7th International Conference on Language Resources and Evaluation (LREC'10)*, 2992–2995. Valletta, Malta.

Elvira García, Wendy, Paolo Roseano & Ana María Fernández Planas. 2017. Prosody as a cue for syntactic dependency. Evidence from dependent and independent clauses with subordination marks in Spanish. *Journal of Pragmatics* 109. 29–46.

Escudero, David, Lourdes Aguilar, Maria del Mar Vanrell & Pilar Prieto. 2012. Analysis of intertranscriber consistency in the Cat_ToBI prosodic labelling system. *Speech Communication* 54(4). 566–582.

Face, Timothy L. 2003. Intonation in Spanish declaratives: Differences between lab speech and spontaneous speech. *Catalan Journal of Linguistics* 2. 115–131.

Face, Timothy L. 2007. The role of intonational cues in the perception of declaratives and absolute interrogatives in Castilian Spanish. *Estudios de Fonética Experimental* 16. 185–225.

Feldhausen, Ingo, Andrea Pešková, Elena Kireva & Christoph Gabriel. 2011. Categorical perception of Porteño nuclear accents. In *Proceedings of the 17th International Congress of Phonetic Sciences*, 17–21. Hong Kong.

Feldhausen, Ingo & Maria del Mar Vanrell. 2014. Prosody, Focus and Word Order in Catalan and Spanish: An Optimality Theoretic Approach. In Susanne Fuchs, Martine Grice, Anne Hermes, Leonardo Lancia & Doris Mücke (eds.), *Proceedings of the 10th International Seminar on Speech Production (ISSP)*, 122–125. Köln (Germany).

Feldhausen, Ingo & Maria del Mar Vanrell. 2015. Oraciones hendidas y marcación del foco estrecho en español: una aproximación desde la Teoría de la Optimidad Estocástica. *Revista Internacional de Lingüística Iberoamericana* 13(2). 39–60.

Fox, Jesse, Dylan Arena & Jeremy N. Bailenson. 2009. Virtual Reality: A survival guide for the social scientist. *Journal of Media Psychology* 21(3). 95–113. DOI:10.1027/1864-1105.21.3.95

Frota, Sónia. 2002. Tonal association and target alignment in European Portuguese nuclear falls. In Carlos Gussenhoven & Natasha Warner (eds.), *Laboratory Phonology 7*, 387–418. Berlin: Mouton de Gruyter.

Frota, Sónia & Pilar Prieto (eds.). 2015a. *Intonation in Romance*. Oxford: Oxford University Press.

Frota, Sónia & Pilar Prieto. 2015b. Intonation in Romance: Systemic similarities and differences. In Sónia Frota & Pilar Prieto (eds.), *Intonation in Romance*, 392–418. Oxford: Oxford University Press.

Gabriel, Christoph. 2007. *Fokus im Spannungsfeld von Phonologie und Syntax: Eine Studie zum Spanischen*. Frankfurt am Main: Vervuert.

Garrido, Juan María. 2013a. ModProso: A Praat-Based tool for F0 Prediction and Modification. In *Proceedings of TRASP 2013*, 38–41.

Garrido, Juan María. 2013b. SegProso: A Praat-Based tool for the Automatic Detection and Annotation of Prosodic Boundaries. In *Proceedings of TRASP 2013*, 74–77.

Garrido, Juan María, David Escudero, Lourdes Aguilar, Valentín Cardeñoso, Emma Rodero, Carme de-la-Mota, César González, Carlos Vivaracho, Sílvia Rustullet, Olatz Larrea, Yesika Laplaza, Francisco Vizcaíno, Eva Estebas Mercedes Cabrera & Antonio Bonafonte. 2013. Glissando: A corpus for multidisciplinary prosodic studies in Spanish and Catalan. *Language Resources and Evaluation* 47(4). 945–971.

Geckeler, Horst & Wolf Dietrich. 2003. *Einführung in die französische Sprachwissenschaft. Ein Lehr- und Arbeitsbuch.* Berlin: ESV.

Gijssels, Tom, Laura Staum Casasanto, Kyle Jasmin, Peter Hagoort & Daniel Casasanto. 2015. Speech Accommodation Without Priming: The Case of Pitch. *Discourse Processes* 53(4). 233–251. DOI:10.1080/0163853X.2015.1023965

Gili Fivela, Barbara. 2018. Multimodal analyses of audio-visual information: Some methods and issues in prosody research. In Ingo Feldhausen, Jan Fliessbach & Maria del Mar Vanrell (eds.), *Methods in prosody: A Romance language perspective* (Studies in Laboratory Phonology), 83–122. Berlin: Language Science Press.

Gili Fivela, Barbara, Cinzia Avesani, Marco Barone, Giuliano Bocci, Claudia Crocco, Mariapaola D'Imperio, Rosella Giordano, Giovanna Marotta, Michelina Savino & Patrizia Sorianello. 2015. Varieties of Italian and their intonational phonology. In Sónia Frota & Pilar Prieto (eds.), *Intonation in Romance*, 140–197. Oxford University Press.

Gilliéron, Jules & Edmond Edmont. 1902-1910. *Atlas linguistique de la France (ALF)*. Vol. 10. Paris: Champion.

Goebl, Hans. 1992. Die Sprachatlanten der europäischen Romania. In Klaus Beitl & Isac Chiva (eds.), *Wörter und Sachen. österreichische und deutsche Beiträge zur Ethnographie und Dialektologie Frankreichs*, 249–290. Vienna: Österreichische Akademie der Wissenschaften.

Goebl, Hans. 1998. *Sprachatlas des Dolomitenladinischen und angrenzender Dialekte.* Wiesbaden: Dr. L. Reichert Verlag. 1. Teil (ALD I). 4 Kartenbände, 3 Indexbände, 3 CD-ROM.

González-Fuente, Santiago, Susagna Tubau, Maria Teresa Espinal & Pilar Prieto. 2015. Is there a universal answering strategy for rejecting negative propositions? Typological evidence on the use of prosody and gesture. *Frontiers in Psychology* 6(899).

Gravier, Guillaume, Jean-François Bonastre, Sylvain Galliano, Edouard Geoffrois, Kevin McTait & Khalid Choukri. 2004. The ESTER evaluation campaign of rich transcription of French broadcast news. In *Proc. Language Evaluation and Resources Conference*, 885–888.

Grice, Martine & Michelina Savino. 2003. Map Tasks in Italian: Asking questions about Given, Accessible and New Information. *Catalan Journal of Linguistics* 2. 153–180.

Hadding-Koch, Kerstin & Michael Studdert-Kennedy. 1964. An experimental study of some intonation contours. *Phonetica* 11. 175–185.

Henriksen, Nicholas. 2013. Style, prosodic variation, and the social meaning of intonation. *Journal of the International Phonetic Association* 43. 153–193.

Henriksen, Nicholas, Meghan E. Armstrong & Lorenzo García-Amaya. 2016. The intonational meaning of polar questions in Manchego Spanish spontaneous speech. In Meghan E. Armstrong, Nicholas Henriksen & Maria del Mar Vanrell (eds.), *Intonational Grammar in Ibero-Romance: Approaches across linguistic subfields*, 181–206. Amsterdam: John Benjamins.

Heyselaar, Evelien, Peter Hagoort & Katrien Segaert. 2017. In dialogue with an avatar, language behavior is identical to dialogue with a human partner. *Behavior research methods* 49(1). 46–60. DOI:10.3758/s13428-015-0688-7

Hudson, Thom, Emily Detmer & James D. Brown. 1995. *Developing prototypic measures of cross-cultural pragmatics*. Honolulu: Second Language Teaching & Curriculum Center, University of Hawaii at Manoa.

Huttenlauch, Clara, Sophie Egger, Daniela Wochner & Ingo Feldhausen. 2016. The intonation of echo wh-questions in Ecuadorian Spanish. In Jonathan Barnes, Alejna Brugos, Stefanie Shattuck-Hufnagel & Nanette Veilleux (eds.), *Proceedings of the 8th International Conference on Speech Prosody*, 385–389. Boston (USA).

Huttenlauch, Clara, Ingo Feldhausen & Bettina Braun. 2018. The purpose shapes the vocative - Prosodic realisation of Colombian Spanish vocatives. *Journal of the International Phonetic Association* 48(1). 33–56.

Jun, Sun-Ah & Jason Bishop. 2015. Priming implicit prosody: Prosodic boundaries and individual differences. *Language and Speech* 58(4). 459–473.

Jusczyk, Peter W., Anne Cutler & Nancy J. Redanz. 1993. Infants' preference for the predominant stress patterns of English words. *Child Development* 64(3). 675–687.

Kaiser, Elsi. 2006. Experimental Paradigms in Psycholinguistics. In Stefan Sudhoff, Denisa Lenertov, Roland Meyer, Sandra Pappert, Petra Augurzky, Ina Mleinek, Nicole Richter & Johannes Schließer (eds.), *Methods in Empirical Prosody Research*, 135–168. New York: Walter de Gruyter.

Kasper, Gabriele. 2000. Data collection in pragmatics research. In Helen Spencer-Oatey (ed.), *Culturally Speaking: Managing Rapport through Talk across Cultures*, 316–369. London: Continuum.

Kasper, Gabriele & Merete Dahl. 1991. Research methods in interlanguage pragmatics. *Studies in Second Language Acquisition* 13(2). 215–247.

Kasper, Gabriele & Kenneth R. Rose. 2002. *Pragmatic development in a second language.* Vol. 52 (Language Learning Monograph Series). Oxford: Wiley-Blackwell.

Kattenbusch, Dieter, Carola Köhler, Marcel Lucas Müller & Fabio Tosques. 1998–2016. *Vivaldi - Vivaio Acustico delle Lingue e dei Dialetti d'Italia.* http://www2.hu-berlin.de/vivaldi/.

Kohler, Klaus. 1987. Categorical pitch perception. In *Proceedings of the 11th International Congress of Phonetic Sciences (ICPhS)*, 331–333. Tallinn.

Kwon, Jihyun. 2004. Expressing refusals in Korean and in American English. *Multilingua* 23. 339–364.

Ladd, D. Robert & Rachel Morton. 1997. The perception of intonational emphasis: continuous or categorical? *Journal of Phonetics* 25. 313–342.

Lausecker, Alina, Annika Brehm & Ingo Feldhausen. 2014. Intonational Aspects of Imperatives in Mexican Spanish. In Nick Campbell, Dafydd Gibbon & Daniel Hirst (eds.), *Proceedings of the 7th International Conference on Speech Prosody*, 683–687. Dublin, Ireland.

Llisterri, Joaquim. 1992. *Speaking styles in speech research.* ELSNET/ESCA/SALT Workshop on Integrating Speech and Natural Language. Dublin, Ireland. http://liceu.uab.es/~joaquim/publicacions/SpeakingStyles_92.pdf.

Mascaró, Ignasi & Paolo Roseano. 2015. Un canvi entonatiu en curs: Les interrogatives absolutes entre els adolescents menorquins. *Randa* 74. 139–153.

McLean, Terence. 2005. 'Why no tip?': Student-generated DCTs in the ESL classroom. In Donna Tatsuki (ed.), *Pragmatics in language learning, theory, and practice*, 150–156. Tokyo: Pragmatics Special Interest Group of the Japan Association for Language Teaching.

Mo, Yoonsook, Jennifer Cole & Eun-Kyung Lee. 2008. Naïve listeners' prominence and boundary perception. In P. A. Barbosa, S. Madureira & C. Reis (eds.), *Proceedings of the 4th International Conference on Speech Prosody*, 735–736. Campinas, Brazil.

Mücke, Doris, Martine Grice, Johannes Becker, Anne Hermes & Stefan Baumann. 2006. Articulatory and Acoustic Correlates of Prenuclear and Nuclear Accents. In Rüdiger Hoffmann & Hansjörg Mixdorff (eds.), *Proceedings of the 3rd International Conference on Speech Prosody*, 297–300. Dresden.

Muntendam, Antje G. 2009. *Linguistic transfer in Andean Spanish: Syntax or pragmatics?* Urbana, Illinois: University of Illinois PhD.

Navarro Tomás, Tomás. 1944. *Manual de entonación española.* New York: Hispanic Institute.

Niebuhr, Oliver & Alexis Michaud. 2015. Speech data acquisition: The underestimated challenge. *KALIPHO – Kieler Arbeiten zur Linguistik und Phonetik* 3. 1–42.

Nurani, Lusia M. 2009. Methodological issue in pragmatic research: is discourse completion test a reliable data collection instrument? *Jurnal Sosioteknologi* 17(8). 667–678.

Ogden, Richard. 2006. Phonetics and social action in agreements and disagreements. *Journal of Pragmatics* 38. 1752–1775.

Ortega-Llebaria, Marta & Laura Colantoni. 2014. L2 English Intonation. *Studies in Second Language Acquisition* 36(2). 331–353.

Ostendorf, Mari, Patti Price & Stefanie Shattuck-Hufnagel. 1995. *The Boston University radio news corpus*. Tech. rep. Boston University.

Peeters, David & Ton Dijkstra. 2017. Sustained inhibition of the native language in bilingual language production: A virtual reality approach. *Bilingualism: Language and Cognition* 6. 1–27. DOI:10.1017/S1366728917000396

Petrone, Caterina & Mariapaola D'Imperio. 2011. From Tones to Tunes: Effects of the f0 Prenuclear Region in the Perception of Neapolitan Statements and Questions. In Sónia Frota, Gorka Elordieta & Pilar Prieto (eds.), *Prosodic Categories: Production, Perception and Comprehension* (Studies in natural language and linguistic theory), 207–230. Dordrecht: Springer Netherlands.

Pierrehumbert, Janet B. & Shirley Steele. 1989. Categories of tonal alignment in English. *Phonetica* 46. 181–196.

Podesva, Robert J. & Devyani Sharma (eds.). 2013. *Research methods in linguistics*. Cambridge: Cambridge University Press.

Post, Brechtje & Francis Nolan. 2012. Data collection for prosodic analysis of continuous speech and dialectal variation. In Abigail C. Cohn, Cécile Fougeron & Marie K. Huffman (eds.), *The Oxford Handbook of Laboratory Phonology*, 538–547. Oxford: Oxford University Press.

Prieto, Pilar. 2001. L'entonació dialectal del català: el cas de les frases interrogatives absolutes. In August Bover i Font, Maria-Rosa Lloret, Joseph Gulsoy, Victòria Alsina & Janet Ann DeCesaris (eds.), *Actes del novè col·loqui d'estudis catalans a Nord-Amèrica* (Biblioteca Abat Oliba), 347–377. Barcelona: Publ. de l'Abadia de Montserrat.

Prieto, Pilar. 2002. Tune-text association patterns in Catalan: An argument for a hierarchical structure of tunes. *Probus. International Journal of Latin and Romance Linguistics* 14. 173–204.

Prieto, Pilar. 2012. Experimental methods and paradigms for prosodic analysis. In Abigail C. Cohn, Cécile Fougeron & Marie K. Huffman (eds.), *The Oxford*

Handbook of Laboratory Phonology (Oxford Handbooks in Linguistics), 528–538. Oxford: Oxford University Press.

Prieto, Pilar, Joan Borràs-Comes & Paolo Roseano. 2010–2014. *Interactive Atlas of Romance Intonation*. http://prosodia.upf.edu/iari/. Accessed 2016-05-20.

Prieto, Pilar & Teresa Cabré. 2007–2012. *Atles interactiu de l'entonació del català*. http://prosodia.upf.edu/atlesentonacio/. Accessed 2016-05-20.

Prieto, Pilar & Paolo Roseano (eds.). 2010. *Transcription of Intonation of the Spanish language*. Munich: Lincom.

Prieto, Pilar & Paolo Roseano. 2009–2013. *Atlas interactivo de la entonación del español*. http://prosodia.upf.edu/atlasentonacion/. Accessed 2016-05-20.

Prieto, Pilar, Jan van Santen & Julia Hirschberg. 1995. Tonal alignment patterns in Spanish. *Journal of Phonetics* 23. 429–451.

Quilis, Antonio. 1981. *Fonética acústica de la lengua española*. Madrid: Gredos.

Randolph, Justus J. 2008. *Online Kappa Calculator*. http://justusrandolph.net/kappa/.

Rizzi, Luigi. 2001. On the position 'Int(errogative)' in the left periphery of the clause. In Guglielmo Cinque & Giampaolo Salvi (eds.), *Current studies in Italian syntax. Essays offered to Lorenzo Renzi*, 287–296. Amsterdam: Elsevier.

Robinson, Mary Ann. 1992. Introspective methodology in interlanguage pragmatics research. In Gabriele Kasper (ed.), *Pragmatics of Japanese as a native and target language* (Technical report 3), 27–82. Honolulu, Hawaii: Second Language Teaching & Curriculum Center, University of Hawaii at Manoa.

Rose, Kenneth R. 2000. An exploratory cross-sectional study of interlanguage pragmatic development. *Studies in Second Language Acquisition* 22. 27–67.

Roseano, Paolo, Ana Maria Fernández Planas, Wendy Elvira García, Ramon Cerdà Massó & Eugenio Martínez Celdrán. 2015. La entonación de las preguntas parciales en catalán. *Revista Española de Lingüística Aplicada* 28(2). 511–554.

Safont-Jordà, Maria Pilar. 2003. Metapragmatic awareness and pragmatic production of third language learners of English: A focus on request acts realizations. *The International Journal of Bilingualism* 7(1). 43–69.

Sánchez-Alvarado, Covadonga. 2018. The Realization of Focus in Asturian Spanish. *Journal of Portuguese Linguistics* 17(1). 1. DOI:10.5334/jpl.176

Schauer, Gila. 2004. May you speak louder maybe? Interlanguage pragmatic development in requests. In Susan H. Foster-Cohen, Michael Sharwood-Smith, Antonella Sorace & Ota Mitsuhiko (eds.), *EUROSLA Yearbook*, vol. 4, 253–272. Amsterdam: John Benjamins.

Schneider, Katrin, Britta Lintfert, Grzegorz Dogil & Bernd Möbius. 2006. Phonetic grounding of prosodic categories. In Stefan Sudhoff, Denisa Lenertové, RolandMeyer, Sandra Pappert, Petra Augurzky, Ina Mleinek, Nicole Richter & Johannes Schliesser (eds.), *Methods in Empirical Prosody Research*, 335–362. Berlin: De Gruyter.

Sichel-Bazin, Rafèu & Trudel Meisenburg. 2015. *Methodology for the study of prosody in language contact: Occitan and French*. Paper presented at Romanistentag 2015.

Staum Casasanto, Laura, Kyle Jasmin & Daniel Casasanto. 2010. Virtually accommodating: Speech rate accommodation to a virtual interlocutor. In S. Ohlsson & R. Catrambone (eds.), *Proceedings of the 32nd Annual Conference of the Cognitive Science Society*, 127–132.

Stella, Antonio, Maria del Mar Vanrell, Massimiliano Iraci, Pilar Prieto & Barbara Gili Fivela. 2014. Intergestural coordination between tonal and oral gestures in Catalan, Italian. In Susanne Fuchs, Martine Grice, Anne Hermes, Leonardo Lancia & Doris Mücke (eds.), *Proceedings of the 10th International Seminar on Speech Production*, 421–424. Cologne, Germany.

Sudhoff, Stefan, Denisa Lenertova, Roland Meyer, Sandra Pappert, Petra Augurzky, Ina Mleinek, Nicole Richter & Johannes Schließer (eds.). 2006. *Methods in empirical prosody research*. Vol. 3 (Language, Context, and Cognition). Berlin & New York: Walter de Gruyter.

Torreira, Francisco & Mirjam Ernestus. 2010. The Nijmegen corpus of casual Spanish. In Nicoletta Calzolari, Khalid Choukri, Bente Maegaard, Joseph Mariani, Jan Odijk, Stelios Piperidis, Mike Rosner & Daniel Tapias (eds.), *Proceedings of the 7th International Conference on Language Resources and Evaluation (LREC'10)*, 2981–2985. Valletta, Malta.

Uth, Melanie. 2014. Spanish preverbal subjects in contexts of narrow information focus: Non-contrastive focalization or epistemic-evidential marking? *Grazer Linguistische Studien* 81. 87–104.

van Heuven, Vincent J. & Judith Haan. 2002. Temporal distribution of interrogativiy markers in Dutch: A perceptual study. In Carlos Gussenhoven & Natasha Warner (eds.), *Papers in Laboratory Phonology 7*, vol. 4 (Phonology & Phonetics 1), 61–86. Berlin/New York: Mouton de Gruyter.

Vanrell, Maria del Mar. 2011. *The phonological relevance of tonal scaling in the intonational grammar of Catalan*. Barcelona: Universitat Autònoma de Barcelona PhD.

Vanrell, Maria del Mar, Meghan A. Armstrong & Pilar Prieto. 2014a. The role of prosody in the encoding of evidentiality in Catalan. In Nick Campbell, Dafydd

Gibbon & Daniel Hirst (eds.), *Proceedings of the 7th International Conference on Speech Prosody*, 1022–1025. Dublin, Ireland.

Vanrell, Maria del Mar, Francesc Ballone, Carlo Schirru & Pilar Prieto. 2014b. Intonation and its interfaces in Sardinian polar questions. *Loquens* 1(2). DOI:10.3989/loquens.2014.014

Vanrell, Maria del Mar & Olga Fernández-Soriano. Forthcoming. Language variation at the prosody-syntax interface: Focus in European Spanish. In Marco García García & Melanie Uth (eds.), *Focus Realization and Interpretation in Romance and Beyond* (Studies in language companion series). Amsterdam/Philadelphia: John Benjamins.

Vanrell, Maria del Mar & Olga Fernández-Soriano. 2013. Variation at the interfaces in Ibero-Romance. Catalan and Spanish prosody and word order. *Catalan Journal of Linguistics* 12. 243–282.

Vanrell, Maria del Mar & Olga Fernández-Soriano. 2014. Dialectal variation at the Prosody-Syntax interface: Evidence from Catalan and Spanish interrogatives. In Nick Campbell, Dafydd Gibbon & Daniel Hirst (eds.), *Proceedings of the 7th International Conference on Speech Prosody*, 253–282. Dublin, Ireland.

Vion, Monique & Annie Colas. 2006. Pitch Cues for the Recognition of Yes-no Questions in French. *Journal of Psycholinguistic Research* 35. 427–445.

Wagner, Petra, Jürgen Trouvain & Frank Zimmerer. 2015. In defense of stylistic diversity in speech research. *Journal of Phonetics* 48. 1–12.

Watson, Duane G., Christine A. Gunlogson & Michael K. Tanenhaus. 2006. On-line methods for the investigation of prosody. In Stefan Sudhoff, Denisa Lenertova, Roland Meyer, Sandra Pappert, Petra Augurzky, Ina Mleinek, Nicole Richter & Johannes Schließer (eds.), *Methods in Empirical Prosody Research*, 259–282. New York: Walter de Gruyter.

Wichmann, Anne & Richard Cauldwell. 2003. Wh-questions and attitude: the effect of context. In Andrew Wilson, Paul Rayson & Tony McEnery (eds.), *Corpus Linguistics by the Lune: A Festschrift for Geoffrey Leech*, 291–305. Frankfurt am Main: Peter Lang.

Wiersma, William. 1986. *Research Methods in Education: An Introduction*. Newton: Allyn & Bacon.

Xu, Yi. 2010. In defense of lab speech. *Journal of Phonetics* 38. 329–336.

Yoon, Tae-Jin, Sandra Chavarria, Jennifer Cole & Mark Hasegawa-Johnson. 2004. Intertranscriber reliability of prosodic labeling on telephone conversation using ToBI. In *Proceedings of the International Conference on Spoken Language Processing (Interspeech ICSA)*, 2729–2732. Jeju, South Korea.

Chapter 7

Describing the intonation of speech acts in Brazilian Portuguese: Methodological aspects

João Antônio de Moraes
Universidade Federal do Rio de Janeiro, CNPq

Albert Rilliard
LIMSI, CNRS, Université Paris-Saclay

This chapter details a methodology based on the notion of close-copy and equivalent-copy ('t Hart 1991), showing how systematic modifications of pitch contours using resynthesis techniques allow for testing the phonological and/or expressive nature of prosodic changes for speech-act performances. The methodology is illustrated with examples of prosodically performed speech acts in Brazilian Portuguese. A perception test shows that listeners are able to discriminate between these speech acts on prosodic cues alone. Then systematic modifications of their pitch contours are detailed and synthesized. Perceptual validation of these productions shows: (1) the relative importance of pitch versus intensity and duration for these expressions; and (2) the importance of each turning point along the stylized pitch contour, both in terms of pitch height and segmental anchoring. The results support the need for three pitch levels for the phonological description of speech acts in Brazilian Portuguese. They also show the importance of the segmental anchoring of valleys for the acceptability of contours.

1 Introduction

One of the central functions of intonation/prosody, along with phrasing and focalization, is the expression of the illocutionary force of utterances, which characterizes them as different speech acts. Classical works on the Speech Act theory

João Antônio de Moraes & Albert Rilliard. 2018. Describing the intonation of speech acts in Brazilian Portuguese: Methodological aspects. In Ingo Feldhausen, Jan Fliessbach & Maria del Mar Vanrell (eds.), *Methods in prosody: A Romance language perspective*, 229–262. Berlin: Language Science Press. DOI:10.5281/zenodo.1441347

(Austin 1962; Searle 1969; Vanderveken 1990; Alston 2000) have based their inventories of speech acts mostly on the existence of performative verbs. These works have relied upon written forms of language, and account for introspective representations of hypothetical examples. Within such approaches, prosody has been only incidentally mentioned as a potential tool in speech act performances. More recent works have asserted the importance of including oral and unscripted language productions for the description of speech acts (Cresti 2005; Moneglia 2011; Raso 2012; Tamoto & Kawabata 1998). Such an approach for describing language in its actual use puts emphasis on the role of intonation in conveying speech acts. In doing so, it notably shows the relevance of prosodic variants in the performance of sets of illocutions. This is done in situations where no other factors (whether morphosyntactic or lexical) can explain the given illocutionary force that is carried by an utterance, other than the peculiarities of its prosody. In Brazilian Portuguese, for instance, a number of directive acts may be distinguished by means of their prosodic patterns; a directive act is here understood as an attempt by the speaker to induce an action from the hearer (Searle 1979).

Works such as those pursued in the framework of the C-ORAL-ROM corpus (Cresti 2005; Moneglia 2011; Raso 2012) or by other research groups (e.g., Fontaney 1991; Culpeper et al. 2003; Moraes 2012) provide significant sources of knowledge on speech act performances, especially due to the "spontaneous" nature of the data on which they base their analysis (on this notion of "spontaneous speech", cf. Blanche-Benveniste & Bilger 1999). Because they study in detail occurrences of speech observed in context, they may derive and model their occurrence context, the relations between the speaker and the interlocutors, the speech act aims, etc. (see Kohler 2004). This allows, to some extent, for developing models of interactions based on the observation of performances unconstrained by theoretical or a priori views (but see Wagner et al. 2015, for another view on data selection). On the other hand, recognized features of such in-the-field speech productions are also characterized by low quality of the acoustic signal (compared to "lab speech"), as well as by unconstrained utterances. The use of such material makes it more difficult to perform strict comparisons of acoustic changes across studied categories. On the contrary, and as defended notably by Xu (2010), lab speech presents characteristics that are not found in unconstrained productions (such as strict control over the sources of variation, crucial for pursuing controlled psycholinguistic experimentation). Such properties of lab speech are primarily useful for (in)validating theoretical proposals, but it is desirable that various studies could be produced on the basis of typologically different types of spoken productions (Wagner et al. 2015).

We thus defend here the view that out-of-the-lab speech is of an indisputable interest in developing theories through the observation of recurrent patterns in the actual use of speech during situations of communication, and that such theoretical proposals may usefully be tested in controlled experimental settings (as has been done for example by Gussenhoven & Chen 2000; Boula de Mareüil et al. 2002; House 2005; D'Imperio et al. 2010; Vanrell et al. 2013; Borràs-Comes et al. 2015). Unconstrained recordings (in the Labovian tradition) may lead to observations that were not observed or described on the basis of constrained recordings (see for example the main perceptual correlates of smiled speech in Émond 2013, which contrast with those described by Tartter 1980). Lab speech, by its very nature of controlled recordings, reduces the variability of speech; the conclusions of studies based on such material thus have to be correlated to observations of unconstrained performances. This is notably true for inter-speaker variability (or said another way, of idiosyncratic strategies) that may be downplayed (or enhanced) by laboratory approaches based on a few subjects. Meanwhile, a careful selection of controlled parameters allows for repeatable experiments; the key here is in a number of studies that can vary some characteristics (or style, to follow the terminology in Wagner et al. 2015) of the recordings (type and structure of sentences, list and nature of speech acts, speakers' gender or dialectal origin, etc.), so as to gradually improve the understanding of the extent to which such cues may convey a given communicative function. Recurrent observations of a phenomenon back and forth in both controlled and uncontrolled circumstances are the best way to assert the robustness of theoretical observations – House (2005) being an example of such a methodology linking spontaneous and controlled utterances (see also Pešková, this volume, for similar observations).

The intonation of Portuguese has been well studied in the last decade, for both European Portuguese (EP) and Brazilian Portuguese (BP) varieties, including in its illocutionary dimensions, with works on the expressions of orders, requests, vocatives, or different kinds of questions, etc. (Moraes 2008; Frota 2014; Frota & Prieto 2015; Frota & Moraes 2016), or even from an explicit regional perspective (Frota et al. 2015). On the prosody of directive acts, and especially on the distinction between orders and requests, a number of studies have been done for BP (Bodolay 2009; Queiroz 2011; Rocha 2016; 2013), and fewer for the EP variety (Falé & Faria 2007). Previous works have shown that the prosodic patterns of such speech acts not only have different prosodic characteristics (Falé & Faria 2007), but are also recognized by hearers in a consistent way (Véliz 2004; Moraes 2008; Moraes & Rilliard 2014).

This paper describes a methodological process that allows the evaluation of the relative contribution of acoustic correlates of prosody, and the prototypicality of intonation contours, for the performance of a set of speech acts. To this aim, a resynthesis technique (implemented in Praat, Boersma & Weenink 2017), based on stylized contours, is used to systematically change some aspects of the prosodic characteristics of utterances. The perception of these controlled systematic changes allows for the discussion of modifications that challenge the interpretations of speech acts versus those that merely affect the quality of the perceived pitch contour (in the line of works such as Uldall 1960; Fónagy & Bérard 1972; and House 2005). Being decoded and interpreted by listeners, such prosodic modifications change the meaning of the verbal content, participating in the communicative meaning (Mahadin & Jaradat 2011; Nadeu & Prieto 2011; Portes et al. 2014; González-Fuente et al. 2015). Hence, by modifying the melodic contours for the pitch target's height and temporal alignment, and observing the perceptual effects of each change, we intend to show how this approach allows an evaluation of the extent to which changes are acceptable, that is, those that still carry a similar meaning as the original vs. changes that either bar access to the original speech act or change its interpretation. Changes of interpretation and acceptability address differences in the phonological meaning of prosodic contours, whereas changes of their perceived quality are merely circumstantial and/or expressive. In order to support the description of the process and give examples of possible findings, the paper bases the description of the method on a set of directive speech acts produced by speakers of Brazilian Portuguese from the Rio de Janeiro variety. As the paper focuses on the methodology and not on the linguistic description, only a restricted discussion will be given of these speech acts in this language variety (referring the interested reader to papers detailing these aspects), compared to other varieties of Portuguese, or other languages (Romance or not). Similarly, the authors believe that such an experimental process allows the researcher to tackle prosodic variation at a very early level, and then to interpret the phonological significance of some of the observed variants. For this reason, and before reaching strong conclusions, the experimental method will be applied to a variety of utterances from speakers of various regional and sociocultural origins. For the same reason, it is thought to be inconvenient to describe the observed speech acts using phonological tools before evaluating the distinctive nature of the variants.

This paper first describes a set of speech acts and their prosodic variation (Section 2.1), before presenting the concept of close-copy stylization (Section 2.2) aimed at keeping only perceptually relevant intonational variation for the targeted function; other prosodic parameters are described in Section 2.3. The perceptual evaluation of systematic changes introduced in such a close-copy stylization is then presented to show how experimental processes allow for the identification of relevant patterns for the various illocutionary performances under study (Section 3). The presented data are discussed in Section 4, before concluding on the pros and cons of this approach (Section 5).

2 A corpus of seven speech acts

2.1 Phonetic description

A corpus of 462 utterances, corresponding to seven speech acts, was recorded by two Brazilian Portuguese speakers (one female and one male) from Rio de Janeiro. We chose to record two speakers so as to capture some of the inter-speaker variation linked to the varying strategies allowed in the production of such speech acts. The perceptual validation of the speakers' productions shows that all were recognized (cf. infra), if differences in their performances were also observed. The targeted speech acts are labelled in BP as follows: *asserção* ('statement'), *interrogação* ('yes/no question'), *ordem* ('order'), *desafio* ('threat', 'challenge'), *alerta* ('warning'), *sugestão* ('suggestion', 'advice'), and *pedido* ('request'); the Brazilian Portuguese terms will be kept in the chapter to avoid misinterpretations based on the imperfect English translations. To clarify these terms, it is worth saying, following Searle (1979), that in the speech acts *ordem* and *pedido*, speaker S wants the hearer H to perform action A. In the case of *ordem*, S has a social position of authority over H and uses it while performing this speech act. In contrast, in *pedido*, S does not use or does not have a higher social position, while performing this speech act. In the *sugestão*, S believes A will benefit H, "advising" being telling someone what is best for her or him. In the *alerta*, S believes something that may not be in H's best interest could happen in case H would not do A, so S urges H to perform A for H's own good. In the *desafio*, S doesn't want H to perform A, and dares H to do so; in this sense, it is a sort of ironic order, as S wants the reverse of what she/he says, and threatens H in case she/he performs A. Finally, in the *interrogação*, S asks for information, and in the *asserção*, S transmits this information.

The mentioned speech acts were recorded on sentences of varying length: sentences of one, two, three, six, nine, and 12 syllables were used. For each length (except the one-syllable sentence), two sentences were proposed, ending respectively with a paroxytonic or an oxytonic word. This results in a set of 11 different

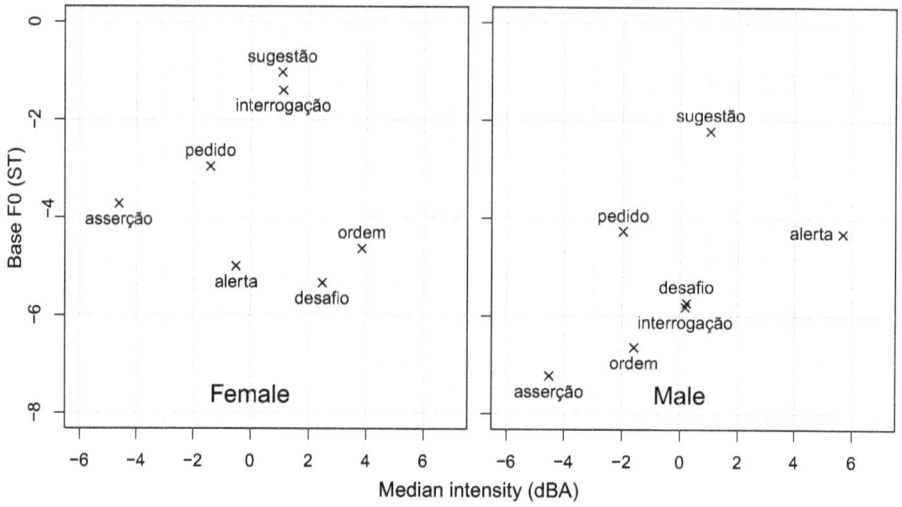

Figure 1: Position of each speech act in the (median intensity * base F0) plane, for each speaker (left: female, right: male).

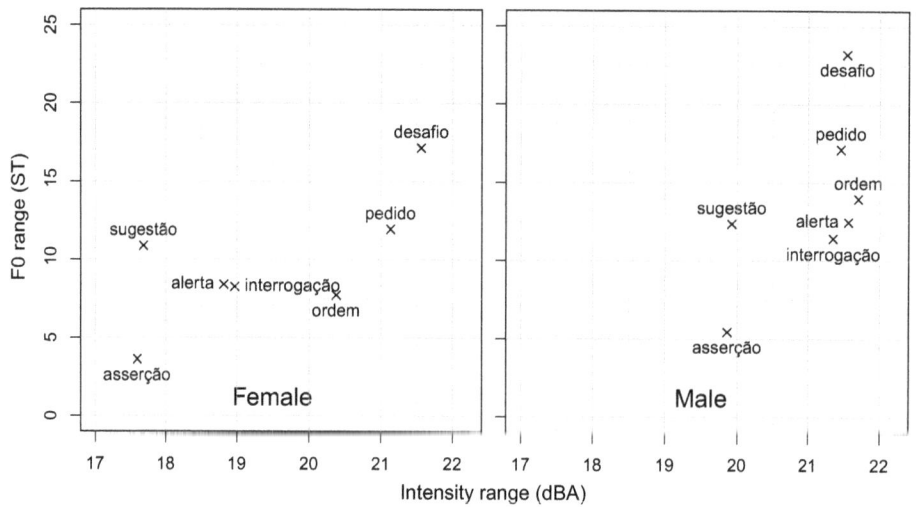

Figure 2: Position of each speech act in the (intensity range * F0 range) plane, for each speaker (left: female, right: male).

sentences (these data are based on structures similar to one that is presented in Moraes 2008, but presenting larger variation). Three repetitions of each of these sentences, for each speech act, were recorded by the two speakers. Before the recordings, each speaker was presented with the seven contexts and their communicative implications. They were then recorded, with the speaker and an experimenter monitoring the quality of the production, and recording again in case they were not satisfied with the performance.

The fundamental frequency (F0, expressed in semitones) and A-weighted intensity (expressed in dBA) of all the sentences were extracted for each 10 milliseconds of the recorded stimuli, using Praat (Boersma & Weenink 2017); values in unvoiced parts were discarded. A-weighted intensity was selected as a good correlate of the perceived vocal effort (cf. Liénard & Barras 2013; and similar measures in Traunmüller & Eriksson 2000).

Traunmüller & Eriksson (1995) introduced the notion of F0 base value, linked to the perceived register of a speaker's voice and differentiated from the size of the F0 excursion in the voice. They estimated the base value of a speaker as 1.43 standard deviation below the speaker's mean F0. Arantes & Eriksson (2014), building on this notion, have shown that the base value is a measure of preferred F0 (the frequency the speaker is more likely to use spontaneously) that stabilizes more rapidly over time compared to, for example, measures of central tendency like the mean or the median.

The F0 base value was thus estimated for each speaker and each speech act to estimate its register. The base value was measured as the 10th percentile of a speaker's F0 distribution in a given speech act – a close approximation of Traunmüller & Eriksson (1995) calculation, which also takes into account F0's skewness (cf. Arantes & Eriksson 2014: for a slightly different choice). The amplitude of pitch excursions in each speech act was estimated by calculating the difference between the 90th and the 10th percentile of F0. The median intensity was calculated to indicate the preferred effort used to perform a given speech act; the span of intensity (the difference between the 90th and the 10th percentiles of intensity) measures variation in intensity. The F0 and intensity measures were corrected for speaker-specific value by subtracting the speaker-specific values of (respectively) base F0 and median intensity from the raw measures.

Figure 1 presents the position of speech acts according to their median intensity and F0 base value. It thus represents the preferred pitch and average effort required for each speech act. Figure 2 presents the speech act's span in pitch and intensity – thus representing the acoustic variation linked to these expressions.

Figure 2 shows that both speakers are highly coherent in the prosodic changes they produce for each speech act: The distribution of F0 and intensity spans are the same – even if the male speaker uses a reduced span of intensity compared to the female speaker. In that figure, *asserção* ('statement') is performed with the most reduced prosodic change on both parameters, while other speech acts require more variation. Some of this variation is essentially produced as pitch changes; this is the case for *sugestão*, which shows an F0 span of around 10 semitones, but intensity changes are comparable to those observed in *asserção*. Speech acts of the *ordem* type are mostly performed via variation in the voice's strength, which could also induce pitch change in the male voice. The most extreme variation among speech acts for both speakers is represented by *desafio*, which shows very large pitch and intensity spans. *Pedido*, *interrogação* and *alerta* are in intermediate positions.

Contrary to F0 and intensity spans, both speakers show different uses of preferred pitch and effort for these speech acts (see Figure 1). A first difference is observed for *asserção*: These acts show the lowest base F0 for the male speaker, while they are at about the median pitch of the female speaker. This difference in pitch usage for the two speakers may be related to their gender, and linked to sociocultural representations. Given that she has a relatively high base pitch for *asserção*, the female speaker can lower it for the expressions of *alerta*, *desafio*, and *ordem*, despite producing them with a higher median intensity. Recall that intensity and F0 are correlated (Titze & Sundberg 1992; Liénard & Di Benedetto 1999; Traunmüller & Eriksson 2000); thus, lowering F0 while speaking louder requires a strong control on vocal folds and is expressively significant. The male speaker, already producing *asserção* near his lower (comfortable) pitch, shows an increased F0 for all expressions, including *ordem*, *desafio*, and *alerta* – also produced with a higher intensity. Note that both speakers also differ in the way they perform *ordem* and *alerta*: The female's expressions of *ordem* are louder (*ordem* also representing the loudest expression) than *alerta* while the reverse is observed for the male speaker (*alerta* being the loudest expression). One may speculate that these speech acts (*ordem*, *alerta* and *desafio*) are produced with a voice louder than *asserção* by both speakers–and that this louder voice leads mechanically to a higher pitch. This rise in pitch can be controlled by the female speaker, who uses for her neutral voice a rather high pitch, but not by the male speaker, thus limiting his pitch rise to the constraint given by a stronger effort. The increase in base F0 observed for the male speaker along these speech acts follows almost linearly the increase in intensity.

Comparatively, the increase in base F0 (from *asserção*) is more important than the increase in intensity in the cases of *sugestão* and *pedido*. *Sugestão*, which is performed with large pitch spans but few intensity changes, shows the highest F0 baseline (i.e., the highest "register") for both speakers, with an intensity around their median value. *Pedido* is halfway between *asserção* and *sugestão*. These two expressions may thus be focused on high pitch as an expressive marker, rather than on loud voice, as could be the case with *alerta*, *ordem*, and *desafio*. The expression of *interrogação* shows an increase in base pitch and intensity over statement for both speakers, but the pitch increase is more marked in the case of the female speaker.

These average values over several sentences allow one to understand some of the differences between the seven speech acts, but they do not capture the dynamic of pitch change along the linguistic structure of sentences. In order to have a better understanding of melodic contours and to see how they may be distinctive, the next sections will focus on the description of one sentence. The verb-object, six-syllable-long (six syllables only because of the crasis between the two /a/ at the middle of the sentence) and two-accent sentence *Destranca a gaveta* ('Unlock the drawer'), as produced by the female speaker, is used here to display the prosodic features linked to these speech acts. From the F0 estimations, close-copy stylizations of the intonation ('t Hart 1991) were hand-produced, thanks to Praat "modification" objects. Figures 3 to 9 present the close-copy obtained for one sentence, superimposed on a spectrogram, and a plot of the raw F0 values.

2.1.1 *Asserção* ('statement')

A sentence produced as a simple declarative *asserção* (see Figure 3), without any further expressive variation, shows a reduced F0 span (the middle 80% range spans 3.6 semitones for the female and 5.4 for the male speaker on the complete corpus), rising up to the first stressed syllable and then falling to the end of the sentence. In this configuration, the final stressed syllable bears a low level of F0 with a falling configuration, while the pre-stressed syllable has a higher pitch level. Post-stressed syllables show the lowest pitch levels, with lowest intensity and possibly devoicing or creak.

2.1.2 *Interrogação* ('Yes/No question')

The sentence produced as an interrogative speech act (*interrogação* – see Figure 4) shows a wider F0 span (the middle 80% range spans 8.2 semitones for the female and 11.4 for the male speaker on the complete corpus), presenting a double rising

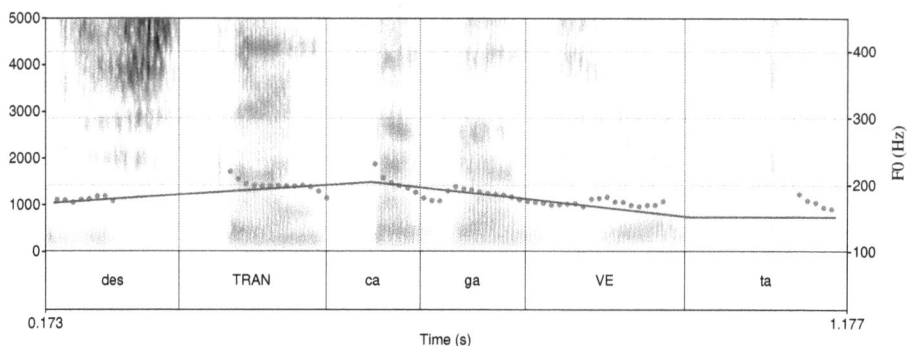

Figure 3: Representation of the sentence *Destranca a gaveta*, produced as a speech act of the *asserção* type – as in an answer to *O que ele faz quando chega em casa?* ('What does he do when he gets home?'): Spectrogram of the recorded sound (scale in Hertz on the left), measures of F0 estimated from the signal indicated by red dots and close-copy stylization by continuous straight blue lines (in Hz, right scale); the syllabic segmentation is indicated on the bottom tier.

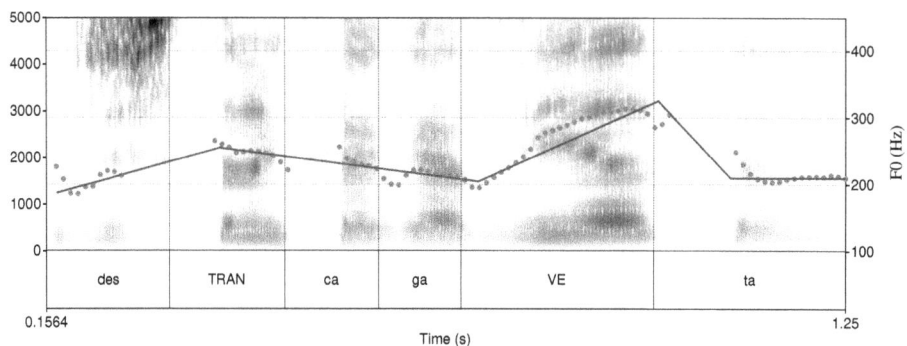

Figure 4. Representation of the sentence *Destranca a gaveta*, produced with a speech act of *interrogação*: Spectrogram of the recorded sound (scale in Hertz on the left), measures of F0 estimated from the signal indicated by red dots and close-copy stylization by continuous straight blue lines (in Hz, right scale); the syllabic segmentation is indicated on the bottom tier.

movement: The first (and the smallest) in the prenuclear position, and a second one in the nuclear position, reaching the highest level of the sentence in a rising movement along the final stressed syllable (not falling, like in *asserção*) – that is, the F0 peak has a late alignment. F0 then goes down on the potential post-stressed syllables. The valley between these two peaks is at its lowest at the end of the pre-stressed syllable.

2.1.3 *Ordem* ('order')

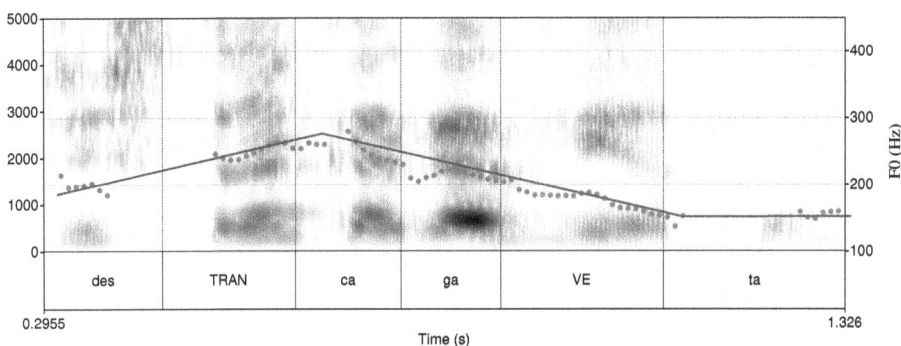

Figure 5: Representation of the sentence *Destranca a gaveta*, produced as a speech act of *ordem*: spectrogram of the recorded sound (scale in Hertz on the left), measures of F0 estimated from the signal indicated by red dots and close-copy stylization by continuous straight blue lines (in Hz, right scale); the syllabic segmentation is indicated on the bottom tier.

The expression of *ordem* (Figure 5) shows a rising–falling movement: F0 rises along the prenuclear part, reaching the sentence's highest level on the first stressed syllable, and then falls until the nuclear position; the pitch span reaches medium levels (the middle 80% range spans 7.7 semitones for the female and 14.0 for the male speaker on the complete corpus). The final stressed syllable is performed with a low pitch and a falling configuration, while the pre-stressed syllable has a higher pitch. Potential post-stressed syllables have the lowest F0 values.

2.1.4 *Desafio* ('threat, challenge')

Desafio, as *ordem* and *asserção*, also shows a global rising–falling F0 contour (Figure 6): The movement rises during the prenuclear part, up to the end of the first stressed syllable, and goes down until the nuclear position. Differing from *as-*

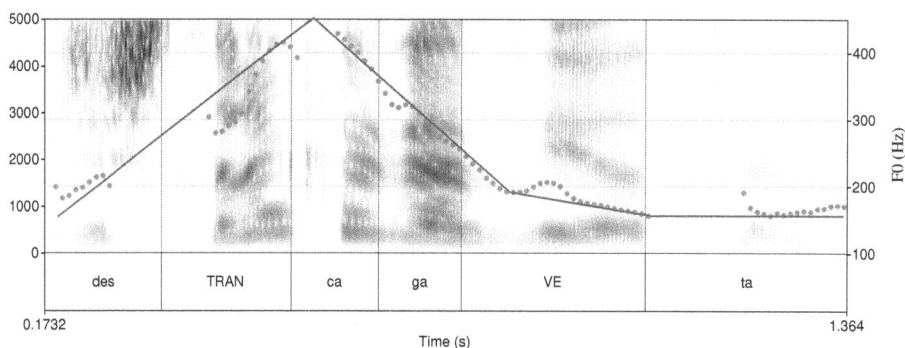

Figure 6: Representation of the sentence *Destranca a gaveta*, produced as a speech act of *desafio*: Spectrogram of the recorded sound (scale in Hertz on the left), measures of F0 estimated from the signal indicated by red dots and close-copy stylization by continuous straight blue lines (in Hz, right scale); the syllabic segmentation is indicated on the bottom tier.

serção and *ordem*, *desafio* receives the largest pitch span (the middle 80% range spans 17.1 semitones for the female and 23.2 for the male speaker on the complete corpus), with an especially high rise in the first stressed syllable. The final stressed syllable shows a falling configuration, at the end of the falling contour. The eventual post-stressed syllables receive the lowest F0 values. The change in the slopes of the falling contour on the pre-stressed syllables, compared to the stressed syllable, is not relevant as far as speech acts are concerned.

2.1.5 *Alerta* ('warning')

The intonation contour for the expression of *alerta* (Figure 7) may also be summarized as a rising–falling one, but it does not follow the same timing as those observed for *asserção*, *ordem* and *desafio*: Unlike those, the rise for *alerta* starts later, after the first stressed syllable, and ends just before the final stressed syllable. The F0 movement spans a notable F0 range (the middle 80% range spans 8.4 semitones for the female and 12.5 for the male speaker on the complete corpus). The pitch movement on the final stressed syllable is descending down to the post-stressed syllable, with a sharp fall at the beginning and an important lengthening of the stressed syllable (with a median duration in *alerta* of 0.551 and 0.604 seconds for the female and male speakers respectively, vs. median durations in *asserção* of 0.308 and 0.253 seconds for the female and male speakers). The potential post-stressed syllable continues this descending movement down to the lowest F0 in the sentence.

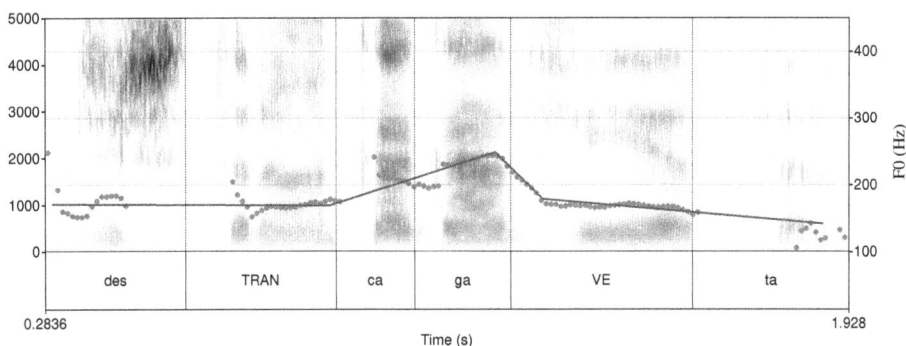

Figure 7: Representation of the sentence *Destranca a gaveta*, produced as an *alerta* speech act: Spectrogram of the recorded sound (scale in Hertz on the left), measures of F0 estimated from the signal indicated by red dots and close-copy stylization by continuous straight blue lines (in Hz, right scale); the syllabic segmentation is indicated on the bottom tier.

2.1.6 *Sugestão* ('suggestion')

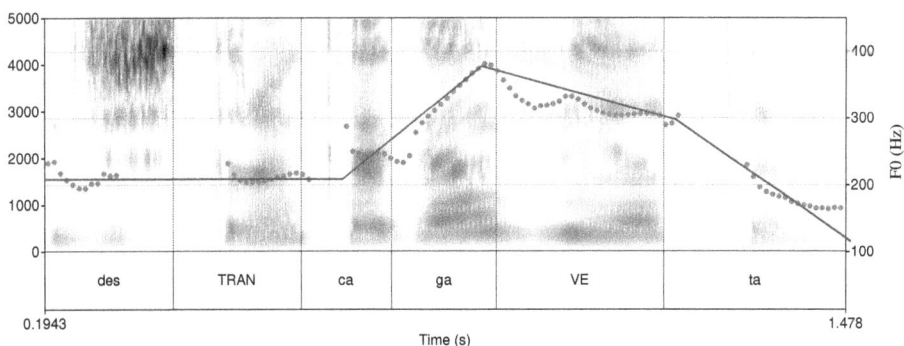

Figure 8: Representation of the sentence *Destranca a gaveta*, produced as a speech act of *sugestão*: Spectrogram of the recorded sound (scale in Hertz on the left), measures of F0 estimated from the signal indicated by red dots and close-copy stylization by continuous straight blue lines (in Hz, right scale); the syllabic segmentation is indicated on the bottom tier.

Expression of *sugestão* (Figure 8), like that for *alerta*, presents a rising–falling contour with a late rise, spanning the two unstressed syllables between the stress in prenuclear position, up to the final one. The melodic movement is wider than

241

for *alerta* (the middle 80% range spans 10.8 semitones for the female, and 12.4 for the male speaker on the complete corpus). After the F0 peak, the melodic movement shows a light fall on the stressed syllable that stays at a high level, and a steep fall on the post-stressed syllable, departing from *alerta*. *Sugestão* also departs from *alerta* in terms of lengthening – lacking the typical lengthening on the final stressed syllable observed in *alerta*.

2.1.7 *Pedido* ('request')

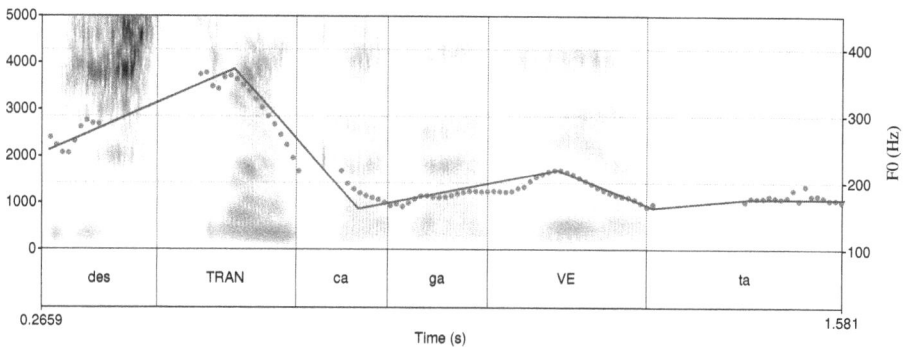

Figure 9: Representation of the sentence *Destranca a gaveta*, produced as a speech act of *pedido*: Spectrogram of the recorded sound (scale in Hertz on the left), measures of F0 estimated from the signal indicated by red dots and close-copy stylization by continuous straight blue lines (in Hz, right scale); the syllabic segmentation is indicated on the bottom tier.

Finally, the expression of *pedido* depicts a double rise (one on each stressed syllable, see Figure 9), and is similar in that respect to the *interrogação* expression. The first rise, on the stressed syllable at the prenuclear position, reaches the highest level – contrary to the *interrogação* contour. The second rise is located on the nuclear stressed vowel. Both peaks are located at the beginning of the vowels (early alignment), thus leading to a falling F0 contour during the stressed vowels. The valley between these two peaks is at its lowest at the end of the first post-stressed syllable; this also differs from the *interrogação* contour, with a much steeper slope in *pedido*, spanning the first stressed syllable and its post-stressed syllable, followed by a shallower rise up to the nuclear stress. The final post-stressed syllable bears a low tone. The F0 span is of 12.0 semitones for the female and 17.1 for the male speaker on the complete corpus (middle 80% range).

2.2 Close-copies of intonation contours

In order to explore similarities and differences between these contours, the notion of close-copy, developed by 't Hart and colleagues at IPO was used ('t Hart 1991). It basically consists of a straight-line stylization of the raw F0 contour, using as few straight lines as needed so as to obtain a perceptually indistinguishable stimulus. Close-copies were obtained here using the stylization capabilities of Praat (its "Stylize pitch" function, used with a threshold of two semitones), and then reaching a minimal number of straight lines by hand, thanks to a careful process of listening. This concept of close-copy is the basis of other processes of intonation stylization, which reach perceptually identical stimuli by means of, for example, quadratic splines (for MOMEL, cf. Hirst & Espesser 1993) or straight-line stylization of vocalic nucleus (the model of tonal perception proposed by d'Alessandro & Mertens 1995, implemented into the *Prosogram* by Mertens 2004). The lines that constitute the close-copies of each of these seven expressions are presented in Figures 3 to 9 (the straight lines that approximate the raw F0 estimation). The notion of equivalent-copy – the intonation contour of a close-copy simplified even more so as to reach a stimulus that, if not perceptually identical to the original, does not lead to any difference in its interpretation – is then used to simplify further the contours of these expressions.

The phonetic description of these seven speech acts (cf. the preceding part) leads to three types of contours:

1. rising–falling contours with a peak near the end of the prenuclear stressed syllable (and thus a rise during the first stress and a slope on the second stress);

2. rising–falling contours with a peak reached at the end of the pre-stressed syllable (nuclear stress) – and thus a rise along the unstressed part of the sentences between the stressed syllables; and

3. two-peak contours, observed on the two accented syllables (the details of these two-peak contours will be analyzed later).

These three categories of contours present equivalent-copies that share striking similarities – as well as some differences.

The first category regroups *asserção*, *ordem*, and *desafio* (Figure 10). They are distinguished mostly by the span of the F0 peaks, as one can observe in Figure 10, representing the time-normalized equivalent-copies of these three speech acts. The similarities of the three contours are obvious, as are their clear differences

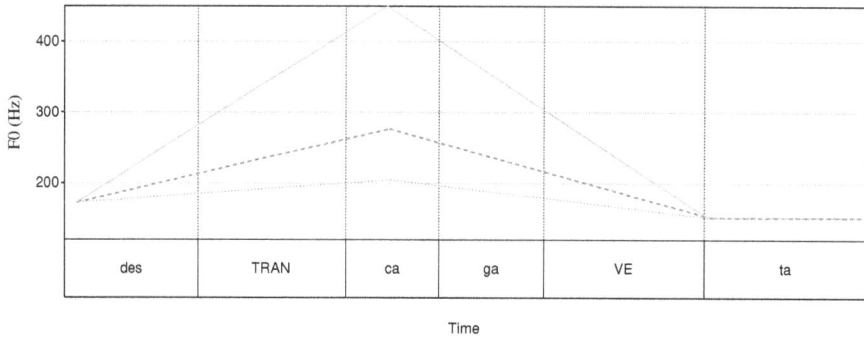

Figure 10: Equivalent-copies of the speech acts of *asserção* (dotted curve), *ordem* (dashed curve), and *desafio* (plain lines); the alignment of contours onto the phonetic segments is normalized to remove variation in timing between the expression and projected onto the segmentation of *asserção* (time-normalization is done at the level of syllable).

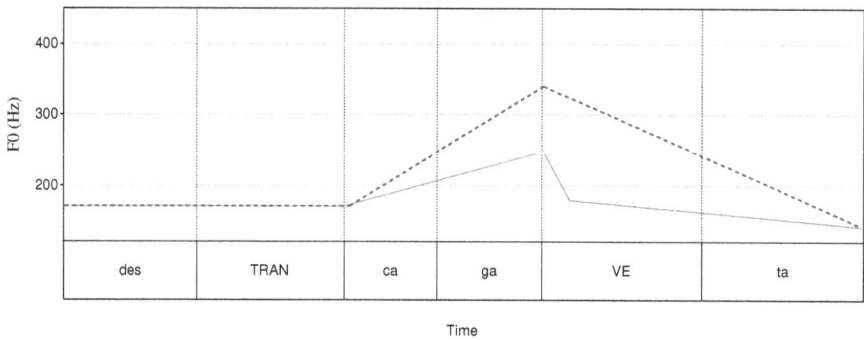

Figure 11: Equivalent-copies of the speech acts of *sugestão* (dashed curve) and *alerta* (plain lines); the alignment of contours onto the phonetic segments is normalized to remove variation in timing between the expression and projected onto the segmentation of *asserção* (time normalization is done at the level of syllable).

in terms of F0 spans. The alignment of the contours on the segmental content is comparable, as are the initial and final F0 levels of each contour.

The second category regroups the *sugestão* and *alerta* expressions, both of which have a rising–falling contour with a late rise, starting after the prenuclear stress, up to the nuclear stress. Figure 11 shows their two equivalent-copies. One can observe that the two rises differ, as between the expressions in the first group, in terms of pitch span but not in their segmental anchoring. The main difference, though, is linked with the falling parts, which mostly span the nuclear stressed syllable. *Sugestão* shows a continuous straight line from the beginning of the stressed syllable down to the end of the sentence, while *alerta* has a typical sharp F0 fall at the beginning of the stressed syllable (mostly on the consonant part), followed by a shallow slope through the stressed vowel, down to the end of the sentence.

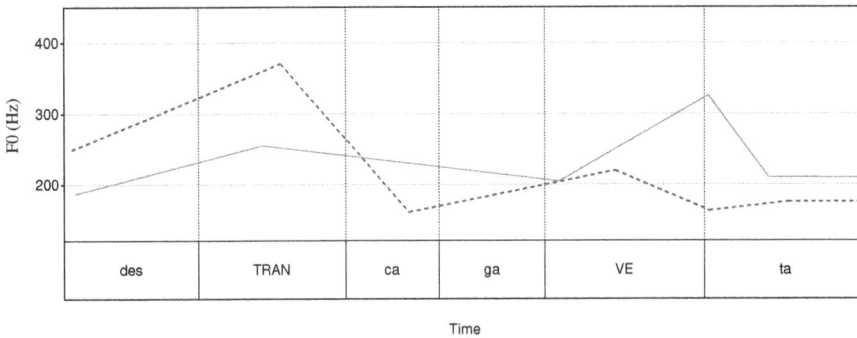

Figure 12: Equivalent-copies of the speech acts of *pedido* (dashed curve) and *interrogação* (plain lines); the alignment of contours onto the phonetic segments is normalized to remove variation in timing between the expression and projected onto the segmentation of *asserção* (time normalization is done at the level of syllable).

The third category, with *interrogação* and *pedido*, regroups two-peak contours, one on each stressed syllable (see Figure 12). Apart from the presence of peaks on these two syllables, the contours have many differences, including differences in pitch span (first peak higher for *pedido*, second for *interrogação*) and differences in segmental anchoring (the second peak of *interrogação* has a late alignment, while *pedido* is aligned to the start of the stressed vowel; the valley between the two peaks reaches its minimum at the start of the nuclear stressed syllable for *interrogação* but during the first prenuclear post-stressed syllable for *pedido*).

The determination of the equivalent-copies underlines the potential interest of two types of parameters in these performances: (1) the number of pitch levels; and (2) the segmental anchoring of peaks and valleys. These two parameters notably change the slopes, direction, and steepness on the stressed vowels.

2.3 Importance of other acoustic parameters of prosody

Equivalent-copies focus on the melodic contour as the main dimension to express such speech acts. If fundamental frequency is certainly a major parameter for prosodic expression, intensity and duration also play a role (see Kochanski et al. 2005, for example). To that end, the use of stylization is interesting, as the stylized melodic contours can be transferred onto another sentence, with a similar segmental content but different duration, intensity, and voice quality. This is achieved by mixing, for example, a sentence's melody – let's say with a *pedido* pitch contour – with the *asserção* sentence's segments, following the process schematized in Figure 13; the equivalent copy (thus the melodic contour) of *pedido* (lower left graph) is transferred onto the *asserção* (upper left graph), keeping a proportional segmental anchoring of straight lines' beginning and end at the syllable level. This is achieved thanks to Praat's "Manipulation" object, and the result is presented in the right graph. The resulting sound has the temporal, intensity, and articulation patterns of *asserção*, but the melodic contour of *pedido* (note that one may also have mixed the duration and intensity parameters using a similar procedure).

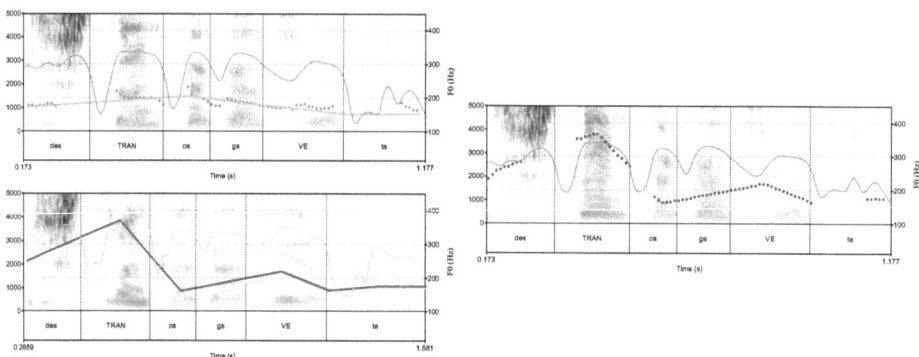

Figure 13: Schematic representation of transplanting the melodic contour of one sentence onto another: On the left, the two original sentences (top: *asserção*, bottom: *pedido*) showing the same segments but different prosodic parameters (each graph presents, over the spectrogram, the raw pitch in speckles, the intensity in curved lines, and the close-copy stylization of intonation in straight lines); on the right, the result of transplanting the melodic curve of *pedido* onto the segmental content of *asserção*.

3 Perception tests

To validate the importance of various aspects of the melodic contours described above, perception tests were carried out. The first test aimed to validate that each original performance expresses a speech act that is distinguishable from the others and recognized for what it was intended to express; a categorical perception test was thus run on the natural stimuli, the subjects having to judge the intended speech act among the five categories (*ordem*, *pedido*, *alerta*, *sugestão*, and *desafio* – the neutral *asserção* and *interrogação* were not part of the test).

3.1 Categorical recognition

The categorical recognition test was taken by 34 subjects, native speakers of BP, who had to identify the intended speech act among the five possible acts. The stimuli were based on five sentences with varying length (one, three, six, nine and 12 syllables), each sentence produced by one female speaker with the five speech acts (thus resulting in 25 stimuli). All sentences but the one with a single syllable were based on a final word bearing a paroxytonic stress. The percentages of correct recognition (presented in Figure 14) were then analyzed (complete results, based on more speakers and expressions, are presented in Moraes & Rilliard 2014). As recognition scores are binary data, a logistic regression was applied (following Baayen 2008: 196, and using R's glm() procedure; R Core Team 2016). The predictors used to fit the results were the presented speech act (five levels) and the support sentence (five levels), plus the interaction between both factors.

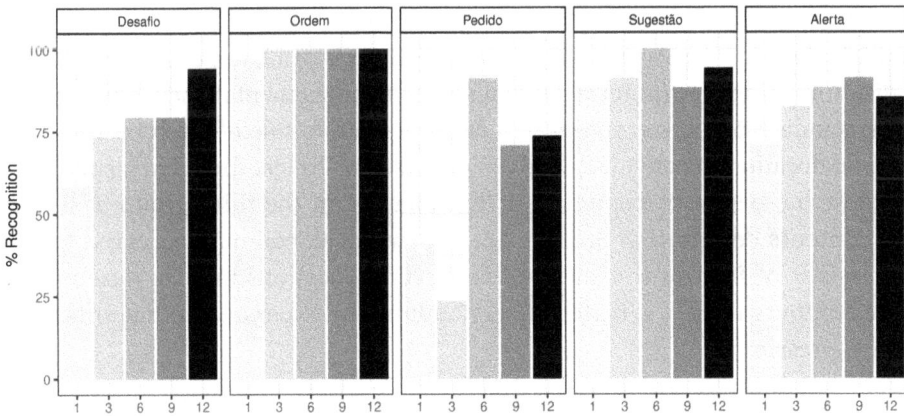

Figure 14: Bar graph representing the recognition percentages obtained by each of the 25 stimuli (five sentences performed with five speech acts); each box presents the results for one speech act, with the five sentences ranked by length.

Results of the logistic regression (see Table 1) show that all factors have a significant effect on the recognition of speech acts. The factor speech act has the largest effect, with *pedido* and *desafio* receiving the lowest recognition scores.

Table 1: Output of the logistic regression on the categorical perception results: Likelihood ratio test against the chi square distribution ($LR\chi^2$), degrees of freedom (df) and observed probability (p).

	$LR\chi^2$	df	p
Speech act	127.2	4	<0.0001
Sentence	46.8	4	<0.0001
Speech act * Sentence	27.7	16	<0.05

As one can observe in Figure 14, this is mainly due to the short sentences (one and three syllables long), and similarly, the effect of sentence length is mostly due to poor recognition scores in short sentences, mainly observed in the expressions of *pedido* and *desafio* (thus the significant interaction). From this set of sentences, the one that is analyzed in the preceding section is the six-syllable sentence, which receives high recognition scores for all speech acts.

3.2 Quality of the performance

The close-copy stylizations of the intonation pattern typical of each expression were produced from the six-syllable sentences (see Section 2). From such stylization, one may test two aspects of prosody: The perceptual importance of a given stylization parameter (in terms of melodic level or segmental anchoring) for the understanding of a given speech act, and the relative role of pitch versus intensity and duration in conveying a given expression. To test these two aspects, we will describe here a perception test that focuses on the third group of intonation contours described in Section 2.2: The two-peak contours observed for the expressions of *interrogação* and *pedido*. Several questions may be raised about these contours to have a better understanding of the parameters important for their expression:

- Minimum number of pitch levels useful for reproducing these expressions;

- Temporal anchoring of intonation contours regarding the segmental structure of the sentence;

- Importance of pitch versus the other prosodic dimensions (loudness, duration).

To test these three points, several resyntheses of the two close-copies were produced by altering various components of their structure:

- Transplanting the stylized intonation contour onto the neutral *asserção* sentence to remove any intensity and duration changes that could help in characterizing these two expressions.

- Averaging the pitch levels of the two expressions, for various parts of the contours, to test the extent to which the pitch level plays a role at a given position in the sentence.

- Changing the segmental anchoring of the pitch contours to observe whether the pitch alignment changes the understanding of expressions.

With such aims and modifications, 48 stimuli were produced (24 for each of the two speech acts), on the basis of the 12 modifications described hereafter, and resynthesized using either the original segmental information (from *pedido* or from *interrogação*), or the segmental information of *asserção*. The close-copy stylizations of *interrogação* ('yes/no question') and *pedido* ('request') are reproduced in Figure 15, with labels associated with each end of the stylized pitch segments; these points are modified in the following way:

M1: The original close-copy reproduction of both expressions.

M2: P1 averaged for frequency in both contours.

M3: P2 (initial peaks) averaged for frequency in both contours.

M4: P3 averaged for frequency in both contours.

M5: P4 (final peaks) averaged for frequency in both contours.

M6: P5 and P6 averaged for frequency in both contours.

M7: P3's segmental anchoring temporally averaged in both contours.

M8: P3's segmental anchoring inverted between the two contours (i.e., segmental anchoring of the *interrogação* sentence P3 replaced by that of *pedido*, and vice versa).

M9: P4's segmental anchoring inverted between the two contours (i.e., segmental anchoring of the *interrogação* sentence's final peak replaced by that of *pedido*, and vice versa).

M10: Averaging of frequency between both contours for each point in unaccented syllables (P1, P3, P5, P6).

M11: Averaging of frequency between both contours for each point (P1 to P6). Point P4b in the contour of *pedido* is given P5's averaged frequency.

M12: The same averaging process for frequencies as in the preceding modification, plus averaging of the segmental anchoring of unaccented syllables (P1, P3, P5, P6). The point P4b of *pedido* is removed. The two contours are similar for all their characteristics except for the segmental anchoring of peaks (P2, P4).

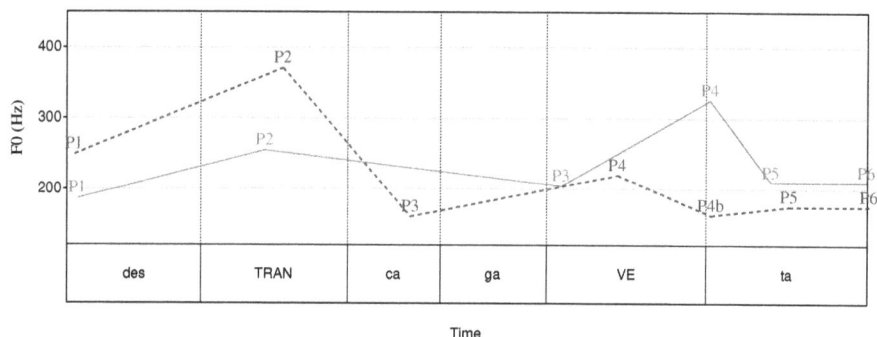

Figure 15: Target points of the close-copy stylization of *interrogação* (continuous line) and *pedido* (dashed line).

Table 2: Results of the analysis of variance run on the quality measure: Effect of each factor and interactions among factors. Columns present the degrees of freedom (df) of factors, the associated F value, the p-value, and effect size (η^2).

	df	F value	p	η^2
Modif	11	15.95	<0.0001	0.142
Speech act	1	17.95	<0.0001	0.017
Segment	1	192.22	<0.0001	0.154
Modif * Speech act	11	3.83	<0.0001	0.038
Modif * Segment	11	0.76	0.680	0.008
Speech act * Segment	1	2.16	0.142	0.002
Modif * Speech act * Segment	11	2.83	<0.01	0.029
Residuals	1056			

The 12 modifications (on two segmental substrates) obtained for *interrogação* (and *pedido*) were then presented to 23 subjects – speakers of Rio de Janeiro BP–who had to judge if each stimulus was a good performance for *interrogação* (and *pedido*), on a scale of 1 to 5. An analysis of variance was then run on these scores, with three factors: The type of modification imposed on the stimulus (12 levels), the segmental substrate used to synthesize the stimulus (two levels) and the original speech act (two levels). Interactions (double and triple) between these factors were also tested. The results are presented in Table 2.

The mean values of the quality judgments given to each stimulus are depicted in Figure 16. The reference level of a good quality for each expression is given by the two close-copies (M1) on the original segmental substrate. Post-hoc Tukey tests allowed for testing the significance of differences in quality perceived between pairs of modifications; they show the following significant differences:

- Among stimuli based on the original segmental substrate:
    - For *interrogação*: M8, M11, and M12 modifications received significantly lower scores than M1.
    - For *pedido*: M8, M9, M11, and M12 modifications received significantly lower scores than M1.

- Among stimuli based on the neutral substrate:
    - For *interrogação*: M5, M8, M11, and M12 modifications received significantly lower scores than M1 neutral.
    - For *pedido*: No modification received a significantly different score compared to M1 neutral.

- Between original and neutral-based M1 stimuli:
    - The difference between the two *interrogação* M1 modifications is not significant.
    - The difference between the two *pedido* M1 modifications is significant.

4 Discussion

Section 2 describes three categories of pitch contours, for speech acts in the Rio de Janeiro variety of Brazilian Portuguese. The first category bears a peak at the end of the prenuclear stress. Among the three performances of this category, *asserção* conveys a simple statement without imposition of the speaker onto the

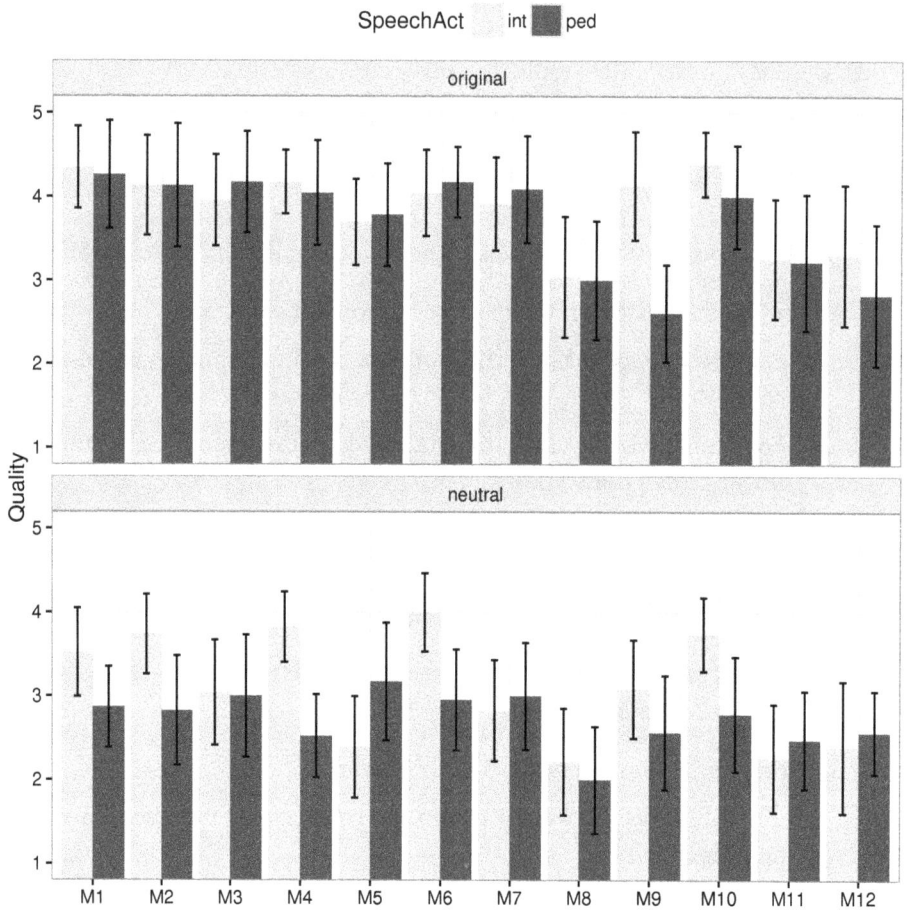

Figure 16: Bar graphs representing the mean quality given to each of the 48 stimuli (two speech acts with 12 modifications, resynthesized on twop segmental bases).

hearer. By expressing *ordem*, the speaker imposes on the listener her/his will. In *desafio*, the speaker dares the listener to perform something; the speaker does not want the hearer to perform this act. This could be interpreted under the terms of Brown & Levinson (1987) as three speech acts with varying threats to each inter-locutor's face: No threat for *asserção*; a threat to the negative face of the hearer with *ordem*; and, with *desafio*, a threat by the speaker to the negative face of the hearer to dare, challenging the positive face of the speaker. For the speech acts of *ordem* and *desafio*, the speaker and the hearer are in a relation of dominance, with the speaker having power over the hearer (Spencer-Oatey 1996). The second category regroups two contours with a peak observed later in the sentence (reaching its maximum at the beginning of the nuclear stress). These contours express directive speech acts (*sugestão* and *alerta*) with a speaker in a retracted position, showing less personal implication in the outcome compared to the preceding speech acts (there is no threat on the speaker's face in these cases). The third category regroups contours performed with two peaks, one at the prenu-clear and one at the nuclear position. These contours express two speech acts (*interrogação* and *pedido*) in which the speaker is somehow dependent on the listener. This could be interpreted as the speaker being in a lower position or having less power than the hearer (Spencer-Oatey 1996). For *interrogação*, the speaker is at least dependent on the hearer for having information (see the interpretation of a "desire for the goodwill of the receiver" given in Ohala 1994: 343).

Speech acts inside each of these three groups thus share similarities in shape and in meaning. In the first group of speech acts, there is an increased imposition of the speaker onto the hearer, linked to a more dominant behavior or position. This seems to be reflected in the pitch span – the wider the span, the stronger the imposition, following the mechanism of sound symbolism described by the *Effort Code* for authority (Gussenhoven 2004). The two speech acts of *ordem* and *desafio* are also performed with a relatively low base pitch (as compared to other speech acts; see Figure 1), in accordance with the *Frequency Code*'s predictions for dominant expressions (Ohala 1994). Such a need to keep the pitch low (in comparison with "neutral" pitch) may explain the difference between the strategies of the female and the male speakers regarding *ordem*. The female speaker has a base pitch for *asserção* (i.e., the more neutral speech act) close to the mean of her base pitches, while the male speaker's base pitch for *asserção* is low among his base pitches (see Figure 1). The female can lower her pitch while producing loud *ordem*; the male speaker has to refrain from getting very loud in perform-ing *ordem* if he wants to keep the base pitch relatively low – thus, the difference in median intensity and intensity span observed for *ordem* between these two speakers.

The importance of the localization of the maximum pitch along the sentence (early, during the prenuclear part, or late, during the nuclear part) opposes speech acts that impose more (for early peaks) or less (for late maximum peaks) on the hearer. Early peaks are typical of the involved directives of the first group and of *pedido* (the first peak of *pedido* is higher than the second, contrary to *interrogação*). Late peaks are typical of the second group (distanced directives) and of *interrogação*. Such an analysis is in conformity with the *Frequency Code*, which predicts that raised or rising pitch on an utterance would tend to carry a more submissive meaning (Ohala 1994). Distinctions inside these groups are made either in terms of power, imposition, or dominance (with the gradation of imposition levels presented in the first group) or in terms of shape for the second group (a sharp pitch fall after the peak vs. a plateau).

Then the importance of pitch alignment with the segmental substrate, the number of distinctive pitch levels, and the relative importance of other prosodic parameters (duration, intensity) required to adequately perform a given speech act have been investigated.

The relative importance of prosodic parameters in conveying such speech acts in Rio de Janeiro's variety of BP is tested in transferring the melodic contours onto the neutral segmental substrate. The scores given by listeners to the resulting stimuli show that pitch alone is sufficient to express the speech act of *interrogação* – while the duration and intensity play a significant role for *pedido*, in combination with F0. Duration is also mandatory in the expression of *alerta* (see Section 2.1.5), in which the important lengthening of the final stressed syllable goes along with the melodic contour (note that the importance of duration in this case is not formally tested in this paper). The use of other parameters for expressive speech acts, and typically intensity, is linked to the notion of *involvement* in speech described by Daneš (1994), which refers to the illocutionary strength of the associated speech acts and thus to vocal effort (Gussenhoven 2004). Intensity is known to be a primary correlate of increased vocal effort during speech production (Liénard & Di Benedetto 1999; Traunmüller & Eriksson 2000). But such changes are mostly linked to changes in the speaker's affective arousal (Goudbeek & Scherer 2010) and induce changes in the mean levels of parameters – that is, gradient differences derived from symbolic melodic gestures rather than conventional, arbitrary (hence phonological) signs (cf. Bolinger 1986).

If not the only expressive mean of prosody, melodic contours certainly bear a great deal of the prosodic speech acts' semantics in BP (Moraes & Rilliard 2014). In doing so, F0 variation expresses an additional meaning (a prosodic meaning because it is not necessarily expressed by morphosyntactic means) that changes the original utterance's literal meaning. This allows the speaker to address a question, a statement, an order, and so on, without resorting to lexicon. The codification of these prosodic speech acts obeys phonological rules depending on languages – if possibly derived from symbolic codes (Ohala 1983; Bolinger 1986). The validity of the results presented here is, of course, limited to the Rio de Janeiro variety (one may even call into question possible sociocultural variation). Meanwhile, this paper focuses on the methodological aspect, which may be used in further experiments to test the perception of these speech acts across dialectal varieties of BP – or EP. We may speculate, given existing descriptions (cf. the introduction) and the level of diffusion through media of Rio de Janeiro's variety of BP, that such speech acts will be recognized adequately within Brazil, showing variation comparable to the one observed within the two speakers described here (cross-gender variation, or for example variation due to personality; see Rilliard et al. 2016). Conversely, the EP varieties may show much different strategies, and possibly cross-cultural differences, in such performances – but this has to be tested.

The two speech acts analyzed in detail in Section 3.2 share a global similarity, each presenting two peaks, one on each stressed syllable. But these peaks have distinct features in terms of pitch height and segmental anchoring that allow listeners to recognize each speech act. The modifications of these characteristics introduced via a resynthesis technique allowed us to test the perceptual relevance of these features for the expression of the two speech acts (hence for this speaker).

For the speech act of *interrogação*, only modifications M8, M11, and M12 significantly lowered the perception score. For *pedido*, modification M9 also received low scores. Modification M8, by changing the segmental anchoring of the valley between the two peaks, basically smoothed the final rise of the *interrogação*'s melodic contour, and the slope of the first peak for the *pedido* contour. This shows that the F0 slope, and not only the peak anchoring, has a pertinent effect on perception. M11, averaging the pitch height of each point, removed the relative difference in height between the first and second peak. M12 removed even further information from M11, causing the two contours to be almost comparable except for the peaks' segmental anchoring. M9 inverted the segmental anchoring of the second peak; thus, the peak of *pedido* arose at the end of the stressed vowel while the peak of *interrogação* arose at the beginning of the stressed vowel. The M9 modification inverted the slope of the pitch contours on the last stressed vowel: It rose for *pedido*, and went down for *interrogação*. For the speech act of *interrogação*, the height of the final peak (compared to the first peak, the second being higher) and the steepness of this final peak's rise appear to be critical. For *pedido*, the critical characteristics are the relative height of the first peak (compared to the final peak, the second being lower), the steepness of the first peak's slope down the initial stress's vowel, and the direction of the slope on the final stress's vowel.

These results confirm the distinctive nature of the two contours beyond their two-peak categorization. Speech acts of *interrogação* in BP are characteristically recognized by their steep rise on the final stress syllable – at least in the Rio de Janeiro variety. Expressions of *pedido*, on the other hand, are characterized by two peaks on stressed syllables (the first higher than the second), with these vowels bearing falling melodic contours. This descending slope is typical of *asserção* and strong directive speech acts, while the two-peak configuration refers to *interrogação*. This mixture of characteristics may lead to the interpretation of *pedido*. The results of the experiment also shed light on the importance of the F0 slope's steepness, a factor that is linked to the anchoring of *both* peaks and valleys. The M11 modification having a perceptual effect (linked to the relevance of pitch differences between the two peaks' height), this result supports the need for at least three tonal levels in describing such melodic contour (one for valley, and two for peaks). Before concluding on the phonological differences existing between these potential three levels, more studies must be pursued, but the presented methodology allows for such strictly controlled perception tests.

5 Conclusions

The presented methodology allows one to investigate phonological differences conveyed by prosody at the speech act level. An application of this methodology was made on a corpus of seven prosodic speech acts in the Rio de Janeiro BP variety and shows that they can be perceptually distinguished. These seven speech acts are performed with three types of melodic contours: With a peak on the first stress, with a peak before the final stress, or with two peaks. The detailed characteristics of the contours in each group (their pitch span and height, their segmental anchoring, or the shape of their melodic contours) allowed listeners to distinguish each speech act. On the basis of a methodology using close-copy stylization and systematic changes in the constituents of these stylized contours, it has then been shown that the segmental anchoring of peaks and valleys, as well as the relative levels of peaks, has critical importance for the intonation of speech acts.

Typically, it is mandatory to have three levels of pitch register to describe the melodic contours conveying varying directive speech acts. Segmental anchoring of the stylized contours' valleys, on the inter-stress syllables, has an influence on the pitch slope and is thus important for the quality of the output. The melodic contour along the stressed syllables must be falling for *pedido*, while its direction is not mandatorily rising for BP interrogations; one may find falling contours on final stress for BP questions, as in confirmative yes-no questions or wh-questions (Moraes 2008). Such results may have implications (outside the focus of this paper) for phonological models of prosody, and typically within an autosegmental-metric approach (Ladd 2008), where it is customary to stick with two tone levels (see Face & Prieto 2007; D'Imperio et al. 2010).

References

't Hart, Johan. 1991. F0 stylization in speech: straight lines versus parabolas. *The Journal of the Acoustical Society of America* 90(6). 3368–3372.

Alston, William. 2000. *Illocutionary acts and sentence meaning*. Ithaca: Carnell University Press.

Arantes, Pablo & Anders Eriksson. 2014. Temporal stability of long-term measures of fundamental frequency. In *Proceedings of the 7th International Conference on Speech Prosody*, 1149–1152. Dublin, Ireland.

Austin, John L. 1962. *How to Do Things with Words: The William James Lectures delivered at Harvard University in 1955*. Oxford: Oxford University Press.

Baayen, R. Harald. 2008. *Analyzing linguistic data: A practical introduction to statistics using R*. Cambridge: Cambridge University Press.

Blanche-Benveniste, Claire & Mireille Bilger. 1999. Français parlé-oral spontané. Quelques réflexions. *Revue française de linguistique appliquée* 4(2). 21–30.

Bodolay, Adriana. 2009. *Pragmática da entonação: a relação prosódia/contexto em atos diretivos no Português*. Tese de Doutorado em Estudos Linguísticos, Universidade Federal de Minas Gerais dissertation.

Boersma, Paul & David Weenink. 2017. *Praat: Doing phonetics by computer [Computer program]*. Version 6.0.30. http://www.praat.org/.

Bolinger, Dwight. 1986. *Intonation and its parts: Melody in spoken English*. London: Edward Arnold.

Borràs-Comes, Joan, Rafèu Sichel-Bazin & Pilar Prieto. 2015. Vocative intonation preferences are sensitive to politeness factors. *Language and Speech* 58(1). 68–83.

Boula de Mareüil, Philippe, Philippe Célérier & Jacques Toen. 2002. Generation of emotions by a morphing technique in English, French and Spanish. In Bernard Bel & Isabelle Marlien (eds.), *Proceedings of the 1st International Conference on Speech Prosody*. Aix-en-Provence: Laboratoire Parole et Langage.

Brown, Penelope & Stephen C. Levinson. 1987. *Politeness: Some Universals in Language Usage* (Studies in Interactional Sociolinguistics). Cambridge: Cambridge University Press.

Cresti, Emanuela. 2005. Per una nuova classificazione dell'illocuzione a partire da un corpus di parlato (LABLITA). In Elisabeth Burr (ed.), *Tradizione e innovazione. Atti del VI Convegno Internazionale della SILFI*, 233–246. Firenze: Franco Cesati editore.

Culpeper, Jonathan, Derek Bousfield & Anne Wichmann. 2003. Impoliteness revisited: with special reference to dynamic and prosodic aspects. *Journal of pragmatics* 35(10-11). 1545–1579.

d'Alessandro, Christophe & Piet Mertens. 1995. Automatic pitch contour stylization using a model of tonal perception. *Computer Speech & Language* 9(3). 257–288.

D'Imperio, Mariapaola, Barbara Gili Fivela & Oliver Niebuhr. 2010. Alignment perception of high intonational plateaux in Italian and German. In Mark Hasegawa-Johnson et al. (ed.), *Proceedings of the 5th International Conference on Speech Prosody*, 1–4. Chicago, IL.

Daneš, František. 1994. Involvement with language and in language. *Journal of pragmatics* 22(3-4). 251–264.

Émond, Caroline. 2013. *Les corrélats prosodiques et fonctionnels de la parole perçue souriante en français québécois spontané*. Thèse de doctorat en Linguistique, Université du Québec à Montréal dissertation.

Face, Timothy L. & Pilar Prieto. 2007. Rising Accents in Castilian Spanish: A Revision of Sp_ToBI. *Journal of Portuguese Linguistics* 6(1). 117–146.

Falé, Isabel & Isabel Hub Faria. 2007. Imperatives, orders and requests in European portuguese intonation. In *Proceedings of the 16th International Congress of Phonetic Sciences, Saarbrücken, Germany*, 1041–1044.

Fónagy, Ivan & Eva Bérard. 1972. «Il est huit heures»: contribution à l'analyse sémantique de la vive voix. *Phonetica* 26(3). 157–192.

Fontaney, Louise. 1991. A la lumière de l'intonation. In Catherine Kerbrat - Orecchioni (ed.), *La question*, 113–161. Lyon: Presses universitaires de Lyon.

Frota, Sónia. 2014. *Prosody and focus in European Portuguese: Phonological phrasing and intonation*. Routledge.

Frota, Sónia, Marisa Cruz, Flaviane Fernandes-Svartman, Gisela Collischonn, Aline Fonseca, Carolina Serra, Pedro Oliveira & Marina Vigário. 2015. Intonational variation in Portuguese: European and Brazilian varieties. In Sónia Frota & Pilar Prieto (eds.), *Intonation in Romance*, 235–283. Oxford: Oxford University Press.

Frota, Sónia & João Antônio Moraes. 2016. Intonation in European and Brazilian Portuguese. In Leo Wetzels & Sergio Menuzzi (eds.), *The Handbook of Portuguese Linguistics*, 141–166. New York: John Wiley & Sons.

Frota, Sónia & Pilar Prieto. 2015. Intonation in Romance: Systemic similarities and differences. In Sónia Frota & Pilar Prieto (eds.), *Intonation in Romance*, 392–418. Oxford: Oxford University Press.

González-Fuente, Santiago, Victoria Escandell-Vidal & Pilar Prieto. 2015. Gestural codas pave the way to the understanding of verbal irony. *Journal of Pragmatics* 90. 26–47.

Goudbeek, Martijn & Klaus Scherer. 2010. Beyond arousal: Valence and potency control cues in the vocal expression of emotion. *The Journal of the Acoustical Society of America* 128(3). 1322–1336.

Gussenhoven, Carlos. 2004. *The phonology of tone and intonation*. Cambridge: Cambridge University Press.

Gussenhoven, Carlos & Aoju Chen. 2000. Universal and language-specific effects in the perception of question intonation. In *6th International Conference on Spoken Language Processing (ICSLP 2000)*, 91–94.

Hirst, Daniel & Robert Espesser. 1993. Automatic modelling of fundamental frequency using a quadratic spline function. *Travaux de l'Institut de Phonétique d'Aix* (15). 71–85.

House, David. 2005. Phrase-final rises as a prosodic feature in wh-questions in Swedish human–machine dialogue. *Speech Communication* 46(3). 268–283.

Kochanski, Greg, Esther Grabe, John Coleman & Burton Rosner. 2005. Loudness predicts prominence: Fundamental frequency lends little. *The Journal of the Acoustical Society of America* 118(2). 1038–1054.

Kohler, Klaus. 2004. Pragmatic and attitudinal meanings of pitch patterns in German syntactically marked questions. In Gunnar Fant, Hiroya Fujisaki, J Cao & Yi Xu (eds.), *From Traditional Phonology to Modern Speech Processing: Festschrift for Professor Wu Zongji's 95th Birthday*, 205–214. Beijing: Foreign Language Teaching & Research Press.

Ladd, D. Robert. 2008. *Intonational phonology*. 2nd edition. Cambridge: Cambridge University Press.

Liénard, Jean-Sylvain & Claude Barras. 2013. Fine-Grain Voice Strength Estimation from Vowel Spectral Cues. In *Proceedings of the 14th Annual Conference of the International Speech Communication Association 2013 (INTERSPEECH 2013)*, 128–132. Lyon, France: Curran Associates, Inc.

Liénard, Jean-Sylvain & Maria-Gabriella Di Benedetto. 1999. Effect of vocal effort on spectral properties of vowels. *The Journal of the Acoustical Society of America* 106(1). 411–422.

Mahadin, Radwan & Abdulazeez Jaradat. 2011. The pragmatic function of intonation in Irbid dialect: Acoustic analysis of some speech acts. *International Journal of Humanities and Social Science* 1(9). 243–251.

Mertens, Piet. 2004. Un outil pour la transcription de la prosodie dans les corpus oraux. *Traitement Automatique des Langues* 45(2). 109–130.

Moneglia, Massimo. 2011. Spoken corpora and pragmatics. *Revista Brasileira de Linguística Aplicada* 11(2). 479–519.

Moraes, João Antônio. 2008. The Pitch Accents in Brazilian Portuguese: analysis by synthesis. In P. A. Barbosa, S. Madureira & C. Reis (eds.), *Proceedings of the 4th International Conference on Speech Prosody*, 389–397. Campinas, Brazil.

Moraes, João Antônio. 2012. Illocution and Intonation. In Heliana Mello, Massimo Pettorino & Tommaso Raso (eds.), *Proceedings of the VIIth GSCP International Conference. Speech and Corpora*, 43–50. Firenze University Press.

Moraes, João Antônio & Albert Rilliard. 2014. Illocution, attitudes and prosody: A multimodal analysis. In Tommaso Raso & Heliana Mello (eds.), *Spoken Corpora and Linguistic Studies*, 233–270. Amsterdam: John Benjamins.

Nadeu, Marianna & Pilar Prieto. 2011. Pitch range, gestural information, and perceived politeness in Catalan. *Journal of Pragmatics* 43(3). 841–854.

Ohala, John J. 1983. Cross-language use of pitch: an ethological view. *Phonetica* 40(1). 1–18.

Ohala, John J. 1994. The frequency codes underlies the sound symbolic use of voice pitch. In Leanne Hinton, Johanna Nichols & John J. Ohala (eds.), *Sound symbolism*, 325–347. Cambridge: Cambridge University Press.

Pešková, Andrea. 2018. Intonation of pronominal subjects in Porteño Spanish: Analysis of spontaneous speech. In Ingo Feldhausen, Jan Fliessbach & Maria del Mar Vanrell (eds.), *Methods in prosody: A Romance language perspective* (Studies in Laboratory Phonology), 45–79. Berlin: Language Science Press.

Portes, Cristel, Claire Beyssade, Amandine Michelas, Jean-Marie Marandin & Maud Champagne-Lavau. 2014. The dialogical dimension of intonational meaning: evidence from French. *Journal of Pragmatics* 74. 15–29.

Queiroz, Horácio dos Santos. 2011. *A contribuição da prosódia e da qualidade de voz na expressão de atitudes do locutor em atos de fala diretivos.* Tese de Doutorado em Estudos Linguísticos, Universidade Federal de Minas Gerais dissertation.

R Core Team. 2016. *R: A Language and Environment for Statistical Computing.* R Foundation for Statistical Computing. Vienna, Austria. https://www.R-project.org/.

Raso, Tommaso. 2012. O C-ORAL-BRASIL e a Teoria da Língua em Ato. In Tommaso Raso & Heliana Mello (eds.), *C-ORAL-BRASIL I. Corpus de referência do português brasileiro falado informal,* 91–124. Belo Horizonte: Editora UFMG.

Rilliard, Albert, Donna Erickson, João Antônio Moraes & Takaaki Shochi. 2016. On the varying reception of speakers expressivity across gender and cultures, and inference in their personalities. In Sandra Madureira (ed.), *Sonoridades – Sonorities,* 149–163. Lyon: Edição da Pontifícia Universidade Católica de São Paulo.

Rocha, Bruno. 2013. Metodologia empírica para o estudo de ilocuções do português brasileiro. *Domínios de linguagem* 7. 109–148.

Rocha, Bruno. 2016. *Uma metodologia empírica para a identificação e descrição de ilocuções e a sua aplicação para o estudo da ordem em PB e Italiano.* Tese de Doutorado em Estudos Linguísticos, Universidade Federal de Minas Gerais dissertation.

Searle, John R. 1969. *Speech Acts: An Essay in the Philosophy of Language.* Cambridge: Cambridge University Press.

Searle, John R. 1979. A Taxonomy of Illocutionary Acts. In John R. Searle (ed.), *Expression and Meaning,* 1–29. Cambridge, Mass.: Cambridge University Press.

Spencer-Oatey, Helen. 1996. Reconsidering power and distance. *Journal of Pragmatics* 26. 1–24.

Tamoto, Masafumi & Takeshi Kawabata. 1998. A schema for illocutionary act identification with prosodic features. In *5th International Conference on Spoken Languagen Processing (ICSLP'98).*

Tartter, Vivien C. 1980. Happy talk: Perceptual and acoustic effects of smiling on speech. *Attention, Perception, & Psychophysics* 27(1). 24–27.

Titze, Ingo R. & Johan Sundberg. 1992. Vocal intensity in speakers and singers. *The Journal of the Acoustical Society of America* 91(5). 2936–2946.

Traunmüller, Hartmut & Anders Eriksson. 1995. The perceptual evaluation of F0 excursions in speech as evidenced in liveliness estimations. *The Journal of the Acoustical Society of America* 97(3). 1905–1915.

Traunmüller, Hartmut & Anders Eriksson. 2000. Acoustic effects of variation in vocal effort by men, women, and children. *The Journal of the Acoustical Society of America* 107(6). 3438–3451.

Uldall, Elizabeth. 1960. Attitudinal meanings conveyed by intonation contours. *Language and Speech* 3(4). 223–234.

Vanderveken, Daniel. 1990. *Meaning and Speech Acts: Principles of Language Use.* Vol. 1. Cambridge University Press.

Vanrell, Maria del Mar, Ignasi Mascaró, Francesc Torres-Tamarit & Pilar Prieto. 2013. Intonation as an encoder of speaker certainty: Information and confirmation yes-no questions in Catalan. *Language and Speech* 56(2). 163–190.

Véliz, Mauricio. 2004. Intonational devices used in the distinction of speech acts. *Literatura y lingüística.* 211–220.

Wagner, Petra, Jürgen Trouvain & Frank Zimmerer. 2015. In defense of stylistic diversity in speech research. *Journal of Phonetics* 48. 1–12.

Xu, Yi. 2010. In defense of lab speech. *Journal of Phonetics* 38. 329–336.

Name index

Language index

Subject index

www.ingramcontent.com/pod-product-compliance
Lightning Source LLC
Chambersburg PA
CBHW080916100426
42812CB00007B/2293